OPENING EYES

OPENING EYES

HUGH R TAYLOR
Preventor of Blindness

KERR
Melbourne, Victoria

First published 2025
Kerr Publishing Pty Ltd
Melbourne, Victoria
ABN 64 124 219 638

Copyright © Hugh R Taylor 2025

This book is copyright. Unless stated otherwise, all images are included in the above copyright. Apart from fair dealing for the purpose of private study, research, criticism or review, or under the Copyright Agency Ltd rules of recording, no part may be reproduced by any means.

The moral right of the author has been asserted.

ISBN 978-1-875703-62-3
ISBN 978-1-875703-63-0 (eBook)

Cover and book design: Paul Taylder, Xigrafix Media & Design
Type set in Palatino 11/15
Cover painting: Prof. Hugh Taylor AC, oil on linen, 92 x 122cm 2012 © Evert Ploeg
Ringland Anderson Room at CERA — Centre for Eye Research Australia
Thanks to Evert Ploeg for permission to use his portrait on the cover. Evert has written:
Obviously, this portrait needed to reflect what Prof Taylor and CERA represent. What really came to the fore was Hugh's passion for the 'Eye' with particular attention to trachoma disease and how to eradicate it from the indigenous community. Trachoma still affects 84 million children in 56 countries, blinding 1.5 million adults a year. Hugh's book on trachoma, with a wonderful piece of art on the cover illustrating the eye in an indigenous dot painting, was inspiring. When Hugh showed me a selection of photographs on his computer, some with him working alongside the notable Fred Hollows in remote communities, one sprung out: it was of an Australian Aboriginal woman with the world's best eyesight, reading a tumbling 'E' vision chart some 12 meters away and she could read the second bottom line at 6/1.4. The E chart caught my fancy. I hadn't seen anything like it before. Universal in its language and use, it had the perfect abstract shapes but in a very scientific way. If I could marry up these elements, particularly in the background, it would form my narrative. The collaboration continued with sittings in my studio.

National Library of Australia Pre-publication Data Service:

 A catalogue record for this book is available from the National Library of Australia

To Liz Dax, without whose help and support I would have achieved little, and to our children Kate, Bart, Ned and Phoebe who not only tolerated my frequent absences but also helped and supported me and my work

Foreword

Hugh Taylor is the only Australian ophthalmologist with an international—even inter-galactic—reputation. His mentor, Fred Hollows, in the same league, was a New Zealander.

He was President of the International Council of Ophthalmology 2014–18 and has been a frequent consultant with WHO.

Hugh has won international awards from the US, UK, Canada, China, India, Japan, Pakistan and became an AC, Australia's highest honour, in 2001.

He was a professor at the Wilmer Institute, Johns Hopkins University, Baltimore 1977–90, Ringland Anderson Chair of Ophthalmology, University of Melbourne 1990–2007 and Harold Mitchell Chair of Indigenous Eye Health, University of Melbourne 2007–22.

The Wilmer Institute is one of the world's preeminent centres for eye research—but Melbourne, in large part due to Hugh's leadership, is now in the top four or five.

Hugh is part of an ophthalmological dynasty, grandson of the pioneer ophthalmic surgeon Joseph Ringland Anderson (1894–1961).

He studied in Melbourne with Gerard Crock.

He worked overseas with the inspirational Fred Hollows, and adopted his great drive and passion.

He worked on onchocerciasis (river blindness), discovered the link between ultraviolet radiation exposure and cataracts, and made an enormous contribution to the pathogenesis and control of trachoma.

Hugh has published 820 papers.

I first met Hugh Taylor in July 2000, surprisingly late, through my wife Rachel Faggetter who had been Vice-Master at Ormond College when Davis McCaughey was Master. Since then, I have been a collaborator, henchman, accomplice, co-conspirator, confidant, occasional front man.

An immediate bonus was meeting the wonderful Liz Dax, with whom I have worked very closely, but independently, in a number of policy areas, especially with the Accountability Round Table (ART).

Elizabeth Dax and Hugh Taylor married when they were both 21. Liz has completed three doctoral degrees as well as giving birth to four children. She holds the degrees of MBBS, PhD and MD. She was the director of the National Serology [blood serum] Reference Laboratory for 19 years. She was director of many not-for-profit organisations including the Dax Centre, named for her father Eric Cunningham Dax, a pioneer psychiatrist. The Centre is a museum and houses the Cunningham Dax Collection and aims to promote mental health through art.

It is difficult to think of Hugh's outstanding achievement in isolation: he and Liz are an exceptional partnership.

Hugh has been a wonderful husband, father and grandfather. He has an exceptionally broad cultural sweep—music, theatre, visual arts, literature, concern for the environment, heritage, and sport.

Hugh soon recruited me as a board member of the Centre for Eye Research Australia 2000–11 and Chair of Vision 2020 Australia 2000–14.

I have also been Hugh's travelling companion to conferences in Dubai, Buenos Aires and Hyderabad, and in activities throughout Australia.

Hugh has travelled more than any other human except, perhaps, for David Attenborough.

In August 2008 Hugh and I cornered Prime Minister Kevin

Foreword

Rudd at the Port Arthur Historic Site, which I then chaired, and extracted $58,000,000 from him for a campaign for the elimination of trachoma.

I launched Hugh's remarkable book on *Trachoma* in 2008. It is outstanding in its range—not just epidemiological, but with a fine historical and broad cultural grasp.

I tease him occasionally by reminding him that Taylor has been a famous name in the history of ophthalmology, not always successfully. John Taylor, an English pioneer in the 17th century, was notorious for failing with both Georg Frideric Händel and Johann Sebastian Bach—an impressive double bill.

He and Liz are powerful forces for good—movers and shakers.

Long may they flourish!

Barry Jones

Contents

	Foreword	vii
	Prologue	1
1	Preparing the Mind	5
2	Postera Crescam Laude	21
3	Fred	45
4	Out of Baltimore	79
5	Did the Children have Clean Faces?	111
6	Oncho, River Blindness	147
7	Ivermectin: Breakthrough Drug	171
8	Chesapeake Bay and the Watermen	203
9	MUDO and CERA	217
10	The Melbourne Vision Impairment Project	245
11	Going Global	269
12	Closing the Gap for Vision	303
13	Diabetes	339
14	Attacking Australia's Sandy Blight	351
15	Today	383
	Epilogue	393
	Acknowledgements	399
	Index	401

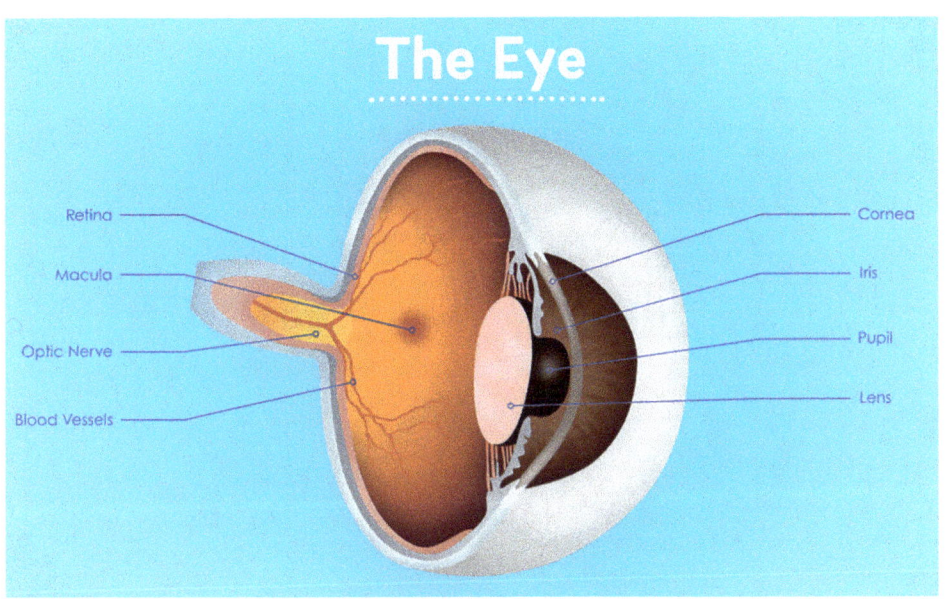

Prologue

> One sows a seed, there is a time lag during which some mysterious invisible process takes place, and then the plant pops up and can be harvested.
> Richard Gombirch, *What the Buddha Thought*, 2009

In December 1980 I found myself in Pakistan. The World Health Organisation, WHO, asked me to look at eye services in Pakistan and make recommendations as to how they could be improved and expanded. WHO considered the time I'd spent in remote places in Australia with Fred Hollows and my new position at Johns Hopkins fitted me to do it.

Soviet forces had invaded Afghanistan 12 months before. About 1.5 million Afghanis had taken refuge in Pakistan.

I went to well set-up refugee camps and examined the eyes of around 500 young children. I found many had active trachoma, a potentially blinding eye infection long term. But far more alarming, many had vitamin A deficiency, a condition called xerophthalmia, which rapidly leads to blindness and often death. I had no warning, no expectation, of these findings; xerophthalmia was a totally unwelcome surprise.

The WHO country representative and I went to the office of the United Nations High Commission for Refugees in Islamabad and told them what the children needed. The UNHCR people pulled out the United Nations Children's Fund's books of supplies. These two UNICEF volumes were big as the telephone directories of old. Small print.

We ordered tetracycline ointment to treat *all* the refugees. We ordered a vitamin A suspension for *all* the children, to be repeated every six months.

Wow!

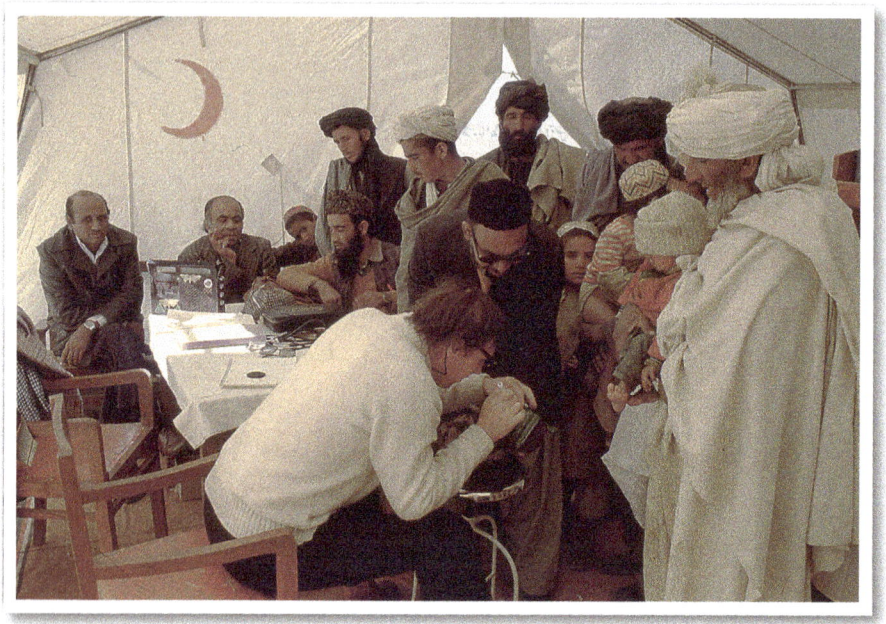

Examining Afghan refugee children in a Red Crescent tent in Pakistan, 1980

I reflected that there was no way I could influence the eye health of more than a million people by sitting in a room testing patients' vision saying with lenses, 'Which is better? One… or two?' Or sitting in an operating theatre doing three or four cataract surgeries in a morning. With a public health approach to eye care, one could improve eye health for whole communities.

A die was cast.

The Afghani children's immediate peril under control, I returned to the task I had been set, the survey of eye care in Pakistan. The key findings in a nutshell were:

The estimated prevalence of blindness in the country is about 2 percent.

Prologue

Cataract and trachoma were the most common causes of blindness.

There is gross mismatch of human resources for eye care across the country.

A total of 45 out of 64 districts are without an ophthalmologist.

Most of the ophthalmologists are urban based, whereas most of the blindness occurs in rural areas.

However, when I presented my report on eye services to the Pakistani Minister of Health, a paediatrician by training, the response was disheartening. He listened quietly while I presented my findings. The WHO country representative gave me his full support. Once I was finished, the minister said, 'Thank you, but I am really more concerned with maternal and child health.'

And that, it seemed, was that.

Opening Eyes

1
Preparing the Mind

Chance favours the prepared mind
Louis Pasteur, 1854

My ancestors came from England, Scotland and Ireland. The first arrived in Australia in 1838, although most came during the gold rushes in the 1850s. Some settled and worked in the Bendigo district in Central Victoria, a big mining centre. Some were pastoralists in the Western District of Victoria. Some were Melbourne businessmen. The last of my ancestors to come to Australia, my maternal grandfather, J R Anderson, arrived in 1880 who became a Presbyterian minister. I am a sixth generation Australian.

My father, Neil Taylor, was born and raised in Bendigo.

Neil's paternal grandfather was a saddler with a shop opposite Bendigo's grand Shamrock Hotel. A young migrant who went door to door selling merchandise stored his handcart each night in my great grandfather's shed. Later, he moved to Melbourne and started the store that still carries his name, The Myer Emporium or Myer's. Neil's parents, Cyril and May came from Bendigo families. Cyril ran a hardware shop. They had four children, Elva, Neil, Phillis who died aged two years, and Norma.

After finishing school, Neil went to Melbourne as an electrical engineering apprentice. He shared a house in Hawthorn with his sister Elva and a family friend Hugh Rogers, both of whom were studying at Melbourne University. Once a year they would raise money for the Student Christian Movement. The elderly man across the road would give a generous donation. Years later they would discover that that man would be one of my maternal great grandfathers, Robert McComas, who had established and ran a very successful wool trading company.

When Neil completed his apprenticeship, he was transferred to Manchester in England. He was there during the start of World War 2 and his factory was bombed over Christmas 1941. While in Manchester he become friends with a fellow Melbournian Tom Balfour. He was brought back to Australia as an essential worker the next year.

Sometime after his return to Melbourne Tom's sister, Beverly Balfour, asked Neil if he would join her and some friends to play tennis. My father did not know that the Balfour family were good friends of the Andersons. This is how, by chance, my parents met. They were married in 1944.

My mother, Mary Nairne Anderson, but always called 'Nairne', was the elder daughter of Joseph and Isabel Mary Anderson, known as 'Mary'. Mary was Robert McComas's daughter. Joe, or my 'Grandfather', had been named after his father. Joe was an ophthalmologist with an international reputation. He served with distinction as a medical officer in World War 1 and was awarded the Military Cross. He then trained in ophthalmology in the UK, practiced in Melbourne, wrote some leading books on retinal detachment and strabismus, and commenced the training of orthoptists in Australia. His second daughter, Elisabeth, always 'Auntie Lib', was a physiotherapist. My mother had a Bachelor of Science degree. However, while we were growing up, she was a full-time mother and wife. We lived in an upper-middle class neighbourhood.

I am the second of five children, Janet, Hugh, Elizabeth always called 'Libby', and the two 'Little Boys' Ian McComas and James. There was a 14-year age difference between Janet and James.

When I was born, we lived in a Victorian, single-storeyed house in Armadale. The back garden's tall liquid amber tree shaded the sandpit we played in. At the end of the garden was an old shed which my father used as a workshop and where I often watched him cleverly making and repairing things. He had worked in his father's hardware shop repairing things and, as an electrical engineer by training, he was always working on something. One time I watched as he fixed an old coffee can to a piece of wood. I had no idea what he was doing. A little later I was presented with my fourth birthday present, a wooden

Me aged 1 playing on the sandpit with Janet

train labelled 'HT 4', the can forming the main part of the steam engine. This model was treasured but disappeared during some construction work many years later before our newborn son could inherit it.

One day I found my mother sitting on a chair in the kitchen, newspaper in her lap and tears in her eyes. The king had died.

This did not mean a lot to me but it did mean that the eagerly awaited visit by Princess Elizabeth, the new Queen Elizabeth, would not happen. Her visit was something we were looking forward to. I had been given a wooden model of the Royal Yacht on which she was to have travelled.

Our early childhood was quiet and settled. We would often visit my grandparents either at home or when they were in Olinda. We would also spend some time at the beach in Frankston and in the Dandenong Ranges. Janet caught rheumatic fever on a visit to Aunty Lib and her husband Stuart Morson in Sydney, I sensed and shared the family's fear. Rheumatic fever was the leading cause of death of 5-to-12 year olds. She was treated with the still new-ish penicillin, but even so still needed months of bed rest. Janet spent a long time in hospital in Sydney, then recovering with the Morsons, before returning to Melbourne. Fortunately, she made a full recovery.

Late in 1952 we moved to a larger house in Hopetoun Road, Toorak. The children moved out as they grew up. My father died in 1984. My mother lived there until her death 13 years later. It had a big garden, an old chicken house used to store firewood, some fruit trees and a good vegetable patch. I had a bedroom of my own tucked under the staircase. When my brothers were born, my bed was moved upstairs into a renovated porch. We had space to have a dog, and 'Smokey', so-called because of his colour, joined us. Janet had a white rabbit that was kept in a cage in the back garden. We lived within an easy walk of my mother's parents' house with its very large garden, swimming pool and two tennis courts, and we used these frequently. My grandparents and parents loved playing tennis.

As children we would often play tennis there and, of course, swim in the summer months. Their garden had been designed by Edna Walling, a famous Australian garden designer. It was a lovely big garden to run around in and play hide and seek. It had a fish pond—as well as fish in the swimming pool. We went

Preparing the Mind

Above: My grandfather with Helen Keller, and Patty Thompson feeding a Cape Barren goose at the Royal Botanic Gardens, Melbourne, with the director and his daughter in 1948. The photo has a barely decipherable dedication to my grandfather written in pencil by Helen.

Left: At Olinda with my Anderson grandparents and the son of visiting Japanese parents

to the local Toorak Presbyterian Church for Sunday School and would often drop into my grandparents' house on the way back. One met all sorts of interesting people who visited my grandparents. Over time these included leading ophthalmologists like Dame Ida Mann and Sir Stuart Duke-Elder but also Billy Graham when he visited Melbourne. I also briefly met Helen Keller but I was too young to remember. However, I treasure the photograph of her with my grandfather in the Royal Botanic Gardens.

My grandparents had a weekend house at Olinda outside of Melbourne. It had a garden that Edna Walling had collaborated with my grandparents to lay out. There was a swimming pool, which was always cold. Sheep grazed the two small paddocks. My parents were also gardeners and so from early childhood it must have brushed off on me.

Sometimes our family drove 150 kilometres north to visit my father's parents and other relatives in Bendigo. My grandparents had an early Victorian house, with an underground cellar, big barns and a wonderful workshop full of tools. There were tools to repair wagons and cars, ordinary carpentry tools, a whole lot of tools for electrical repairs and, of course, everything one would need for work in the garden.

During the summer holidays we usually stayed at the family's old beach house on the beach at Frankston, an hour's drive from home. We could swim, go fishing with dad, row our kayak, sail a little dingy, fly kites and we always got sunburnt. Years later we bore the consequences. Sunblock had not yet been invented! We took horse-riding lessons. Summer provided a wonderful and relaxed way for children to grow up and punctuate the time between school years.

Sometimes we would fly up to Sydney to spend a week or so with Aunty Lib and Uncle Stuart. Stuart would take us sailing on that magnificent harbour on their small yacht, the *Tern*. We could sail, stop to swim, try to catch fish. The *Tern* was moored in Middle Harbour so we rarely went out into the main harbour.

My father, although trained as an electric engineer, moved into sales and marketing. My parents enjoyed the arts, music, film and ballet. Year after year, in early spring, he would attend the Melbourne Film Festival, often with my mother. The Festival was run by a friend of his, Erwin Rado. He would go off in the morning with a fresh daphne flower from our garden in his buttonhole.

They were avid readers so before their proposed trips they always delved into all they could find out about places and activities. After his retirement my father became interested in archaeology, both in Australia and in the Middle East, and went on a few expeditions as an amateur assistant. Through his reading he became well informed. As her children left home, my mother became involved in the ecumenical movement, and especially in supporting Turkish migrant families. My parents explored some ancient sites in the Middle East and Turkey. To help with her work with migrant families, my mother learned to speak Turkish. She ended up teaching the language in a Deakin University building, the old Stonnington Mansion, that had served as the Victorian Governor's residence from 1901 to 1938. It was situated at the end of our street across Glenferrie Road and on the 69 Tram route.

I spent a year at a local kindergarten in Armadale, an easy walk from home, before we moved to Toorak. Once another boy and I got into some trouble for fighting. I don't remember what it was about, but we were chastised which I do remember.

I spent my first year of school at a small private co-educational school, Little St Margaret's, again not far from home. It was just on the other side of Glenferrie Road.

In 1954, at the age of six, I started at Scotch College, a private boy's school where my grandfather had been a student. My brothers would also go there and later our two sons. My mother drove me the first day, but thereafter I walked down to the end our street opposite Stonnington to catch the Number 69 tram

In school uniform, 1956

along Glenferrie Road. The 69 tram carried a lot of students from different schools back and forth. A lot of friendships and some romances started on that tram. Tram conductors tried to maintain order, a challenge with so many students, school bags and on Thursdays the Scotch boys in cadet uniforms with their .303 rifles. So many guns in the hands of so many young people!

I was a moderately successful student, not always the best behaved and I only once won a prize and that was in Junior School. If we were naughty we would be punished with a spanking with an old sandshoe. This happened to me several times for one thing or another. In fifth grade, Tommy Stokes and I were punished for talking or something, we had to write out 'I must be better behaved' 100 times. For a long-lost reason we decided to write that on the backboard in the classroom. Our teacher, Miss Goodenough, went ballistic when she saw this, and we both got the sandshoe. There was a big cypress hedge along the street outside the classrooms. It had been pruned and there were big branches lying on the ground at lunch time, so some of us jousted with these lances for a while. That earned us the cane, 'six of the best'; even worse than the sandshoe!

In fourth grade we all started to learn the recorder. After a year or so I was told that I did not need to continue. Not very musical? We all sang together, particularly in the senior school. I really enjoyed group and choir singing, but my wife later told me to desist as I could not hit a single note. Her efforts to teach me were in vain. Ah well!

In Junior School we played cricket and football and participated in athletics. I swam moderately well, made the swim team in some inter-school and state competitions. With the encouragement of my father who was a keen fencer, I took up fencing for a few years, although not with great distinction.

We were rounded up once a year and taken to the gym in the Senior School. There we would be weighed, our height measured and be checked over medically. In mid-1956 my class was the first from the Junior School taken to the gym, asked to roll up our sleeves, and be injected with the new polio vaccine. When we saw our photo in *The Age* newspaper the following day, we realised that we were the first kids in Australia to be immunised against polio. No parental consent was necessary!

Polio was still a big deal then. The boy next door at Frankston, who I often played with during the summer holidays, disappeared one night, taken to hospital with polio. Victims lost muscle control of breathing, and spent their days and nights in cylinders, sealed in them from the neck down. Air pressure in the cylinders, dubbed 'iron lungs', varied to facilitate inhaling and exhaling, a dreaded prospect in the 1950s. (In 1990, when Liz started work at the Fairfield Hospital, there were still a few polio sufferers living in their iron lungs.)

In 1954 the 27-year-old Queen Elizabeth made it to Australia, and, except for itinerary adjustments made to isolate her from an outbreak of polio in Western Australia, the eight-week visit went smoothly. In the Melbourne leg, nearly 1 million of the city's 1.5 million people lined her route from Essendon Airport to Government House. I had a box seat in my grandfather's consulting rooms. It was a thrill to watch her, driven in an open car through the city, the police horses and motorcycles, bunting welcomes on banks and offices, the cheering crowds; a thrill remembered as if from another world.

In 1956 Melbourne held the Olympic games. I ended up going to an Olympic event each day, except for one when I

Opening Eyes

Christmas 1956 sitting around the diving board at my grandparents' home. Standing; my grandfather, mother, Uncle Stuart, father holding baby Ian. Sitting; Janet, Aunty Lib, (Dougal the dog), Libby, my grandmother, and me.

stayed home to net the white butterflies that seemed to be infesting our garden. My grandfather had arranged tickets for the Opening and Closing Ceremonies which were mightily impressive for a young fellow. Through the games we saw athletics, swimming, basketball, gymnastics and fencing. My father enjoyed the fencing. He knew some of the Australian team, VIPs in his son's eyes.

1956 was also the year television broadcasts started. One of my school friends, Robert Strang, lived at the bottom of our street on the corner of Glenferrie Road, adjacent to my tram stop. We usually went to and returned from school together. He was the one in the middle of 11 children and the Strang's were the first family I knew to get a TV set. I would stop there and watch TV after school with Rob and his younger sisters.

Preparing the Mind

My brother Ian McComas was born in 1956 and James was born two years later.

During junior school my friend Rob Buchanan moved to Canberra. His father, a former naval captain, was transferred there by the defence department. Rob and I often spent a week together during a school holiday. In Canberra they lived close to the Australian War Memorial's museum. As two somewhat naughty boys we often walked in and explored. If no one was around, we looked inside the tanks and clambered around the big guns. Rob and I are still good friends.

In senior school as a summer sport, I swapped swimming for rowing, a sport I came to love. I only ended up in the Third Eight, but it was fun. The Head of the River, the inter-school rowing races, were held on the Barwon River in Geelong. In 1964 I was rowing in the second seat of the Third Eight and my friend Ray Lacey was in the bow seat. While we were setting the boat up, a young woman, Ray's wanna-be girlfriend at the time, came down to see him row. A very attractive young woman wearing a cream twinset and a checkered skirt, and with an infective smile and ready laugh arrived at the boat. That was how I met Elizabeth Dax.

I later learned that when she arrived home that evening, she told her mother, 'Today I met the man I am going to marry.' It seems I never stood a chance, nor have I ever regretted that meeting.

After leaving school, I went back and coached some Scotch crews for three years. In the last year I coached the winning Fifth

A young Boy Scout in 1960

crew. Later, in Ormond College I stroked two winning university college Second Crews.

In Junior School we all played Australian Rules football in the winters. I was not particularly good at it. In Senior School some of my friends started playing rugby and I joined them. After a couple of years, I switched to basketball as I had grown a bit taller. I finished up playing in the school's first basketball team.

At school I thought I might become an architect, a TV show hosted by Australian architect Robin Boyd, a spur. I crammed in some additional art classes in Year 11. However, this proved hard to fit in around the other classes I had to do, so after a term I gave up. Maybe I was not going to be an architect?

Starting in second form we had to study French and Latin. This continued into third form but in the fourth form we could drop Latin and I did, but continued with one more year of French. Later, this would help with multiple trips to different countries and of course with medical terminology.

At about this age I started to make plastic models. The first was a birthday present of the *Golden Hind*. Over time I had a large navy of different warships and an airforce of planes, also a few cars. With time I became adept and handling the smallest pieces and painting them all. It was a hobby that took a lot of time and I filled a glass case with them all. I guess it gave me some practice at handling small things carefully that later would help an eye surgeon.

In senior school everyone had to join the Cadets or the Boy Scouts, and get together after school every Thursday. I joined the Scouts,

Skiing for the first time at Smiggins Holes, 1958

learned how to tie knots, identify trees and birds, collect stamps, do first aid as the various badges dictated. I got more and more badges to sew on the arms of the uniform. I ended up as a Queen's Scout, going to Government House to receive the award. Scouting was fun, especially the camps, hiking in the bush, and climbing mountains. Hikes often lasted several days. We carried our food, sleeping gear and tents, and cooked over open fires. Scouting gave me a range of skills that were to prove useful in my work in the Outback and other places.

I went to a scout jamboree in Dunedin, New Zealand in early 1964 with thousands of scouts from all over the place. I missed a few days when I caught tonsillitis and was hospitalised. Later that year, my last at school, I also participated in the Gang Show, a large musical evening with acts put on by scouts from many different troops and backgrounds. We performed in the Palais Theatre in St Kilda which could hold 3000 people. Recently, there has been talk about sexual harassment within the Scouts. The only time within scouting I was aware of anything possibly suggesting inappropriate behaviour between participants was during the Gang Show, but it did not involve me. Along the way I also gained a Bronze Medallion from the Royal Life Saving Society. I first got interested in first aid while I was a scout. Scouting certainly influenced me to enter medicine but it also gave me lots of other skills and the experience of working with others and living in the bush. The old Scout motto, 'Be Prepared', has accompanied me my whole life.

Waiting for the 69 Tram along Glenferrie Road going to and from school, I would see across the road a tall Melbourne Grammar boy of about my age waiting for a tram going in the opposite direction. Scotch and Grammar were long-term rivals. In 1962 both of us went off to dancing class, the 69 Tram taking both of us there and back. We met girls! There were boys and girls from a wide variety of schools. This Melbourne Grammar boy was Ross Webster and he and his family lived the other side

My family in the late 1960s: Libby, Ian McComas, mother, James, father, me and Janet

of Glenferrie Road. We became, and still are, very good friends. We were each other's Best Man.

Through my school years the family would spend winter holidays skiing at Falls Creek. I joined the Old Scotch ski club at Mt Buller, Koomerang Ski Club. As a family we did a lot of skiing. My mother was delighted when she turned 75 and got free lift tickets! I did a little competitive racing, but poorly, and for one year I joined the Ski Rescue Service. My wife Liz says she always admired my skiing, calling me a 'beautiful skier'. I am not sure what she was after with that over-generous compliment.

On a school trip to Papua New Guinea in the middle of 1962, we spent a few days in Port Moresby, saw the Australian War Cemetery at the start of the Kokoda Track, and travelled to Lae and to Rabaul, where the volcano and the size of its caldera fascinated me. The trip introduced me to how those in less well-developed countries lived; unsettling for a young man from a comfortable background.

In my final school year, I passed the subjects required for

entry into medicine: English, physics, chemistry and maths. However, my best subject by a long way was ancient Greek history, taught by Colin 'Chesty' Bond who really sparked our interest and attention. Chesty could be quite a gruff person but he was a very engaging teacher.

I did sufficiently well in the final exams to qualify for a Commonwealth Scholarship. Building on my first aid experience as a Boy Scout and trying to do something useful, I entered Melbourne University Medical School, a traditional school established in 1862. I clearly had had a privileged upbringing.

Opening Eyes

2

Postera Crescam Laude

> We grow in the esteem of
> future generations.
> Motto of the University of Melbourne

Starting my first year of medicine, 1965, my mind was opened to many questions by our young physics lecturer, Tony Kline. He showed us that everything had not yet been discovered; that there was still much which was unknown and still to be learned. At school we had been taught the accepted knowledge or received wisdom. That was that. All you needed to know. Suddenly, one could see how much there was *still* to engage with or to discover.

During that year I lived at home. A little before I obtained my driver's licence, Ross Webster and I jointly bought a 1928 Singer Senior touring car. My large jar of threepences pretty much paid for my share. The car was named 'Nellie' after Dame Nellie Melba, the famous Australian diva, as she was a Singer too. The big old open tourer took a lot of work and maintenance. So I learned a bit of automotive engineering on the way.

During a break from studying on the Saturday before the first-year exams started on the Monday, I attempted a triple-knee barani on our trampoline. I failed to rotate sufficiently. One knee landed on the steel edge, tearing my anterior cruciate ligament. I sat the exams with a heavily bandaged knee and in pain, but passed well enough.

After starting at university, I started to smoke. Almost

Nellie with me and Ross Webster, 1965

everyone seemed to smoke then. Neither of my parents smoked but they had always had a cigarette box accessible for visitors. I had had the occasional cigarette as a child, but it got me into trouble. At university I became a smoker. Later I ditched cigarettes for the pipe, a bad habit I continued for many years.

Having Nellie to drive around gave me a lot more freedom. In addition to joining the family at the beach at Frankston, I could go with friends and stay on the other side of Port Phillip Bay such as at Port Landsdale or even Torquay. It also made possible somewhat naughty weekends in Olinda. One could get out at night, go to music events and jazz clubs. I heard Louis Armstrong and Thelonius Monk as well as the Seekers, when they were getting started. At the start of my second year I moved into Ormond College, one of the older residential colleges at Melbourne University. During my first year I had attended tutorials there. It was great to join the college as a resident. They

Ormond College: the Upper Tower study was behind the three windows below the clock (*Photo: University of Melbourne*)

had some old buildings out the back that were to be demolished, but until then I could park Nellie there. Later I parked her by the front door of the college's glorious neo-gothic sandstone building.

At Ormond there were various things 'freshers' were made do to. For us, these inductions in Orientation Week were much milder than for those in previous times. The worst I can remember was putting detergent into a city fountain so it became full of bubbles. Through the year there were other activities. One was to do either the 'pass' or 'honours' course. This entailed walking down Royal Parade and Elizabeth Street to Flinders Street and then back along Swanston Street having a beer in each of the 21 hotels. The pass course was a 7-ounce glass, the honours a 10-ounce glass in each. One had to have had lunch in Hall before starting and return in time for dinner in Hall that evening. On the 21st of October 1966 I walked the course.

Opening Eyes

The road outside last pub was full of noisy students protesting the visit of President Lyndon B Johnson and the Vietnam War. Some of the 750 000 people lined the roads to protest as LBJ arrived to spend two days in Melbourne. Only decades later did I learn that my elder sister, Janet, was in the crowd too. To avoid this disruptive crowd the police diverted his motorcade. The protesters twigged and streamed down Swanston Street to catch up with him. I followed along. I picked up a placard that read 'Stop Bombing Undefended Villages' and ran down the road too until I was stopped by police and turned around. I eventually made it back to Hall in time for dinner and so I am now somewhat ashamed to say that I had completed the over-6-litre honours course.

During that year Elizabeth Dax, 'Liz', and I stated to go out together seriously. We had seen each other on and off over the previous year or so and had many friends in common. As was quite common at that time, Liz had done a second Year 12 at Methodist Ladies' College and was house captain and a prefect in both years. I had shared my enthusiasm for ancient Greek history with her. She studied Greek history in her second year and did very well. Although she is six months older than me, having done a second Year 12 meant Liz started medical school a year behind me. Liz became a resident in the college next door to Ormond, St Hilda's College. At that time all the colleges were single sex. Ormond for men, Hilda's for women. That changed in 1973. However, when we were in college all women had to leave Ormond before 10 pm. We were seeing a lot of each other, so this was a bit of a challenge.

Liz's father was Eric Cunningham Dax AO, a British-born psychiatrist who came to Melbourne in 1951 to be the Director of Mental Health Services in Victoria. Her mother, Kathleen, Katie, was a trained midwife, who ran a large and busy household as the mother of Judith, Richard, Liz and Susannah. Liz's brother

Liz Dax on the right with her parents, Katie and Eric, and her younger sister Sue

Richard at that time managed a large catering company and often needed part-time drink waiters to help at events. Sometimes the events were held in private homes, but often in business or government buildings, and occasionally at Government House. I worked at a reception for Queen Elizabeth and Prince Philip. I tried to serve her a gin and tonic. Not a bad part-time occupation, and a great way to earn a bit of money while studying. This money helped keep Nellie singing on the road.

In my last few school holidays, I visited and later worked on a family friend's farm at Henty in southern New South Wales. I would milk cows, collect eggs, move cattle and sheep, cart and stack hay, help harvest wheat and so on. Working out in the hot Australian summers, I also learnt to drink my tea black; kept in the heat, milk very quickly turned sour. Also the joy of washing a hot and sweaty face under a tap with cold running water, something I still do in Olinda. Great fun, working outside, learning lots.

Later during a university break, Liz and our friend Ross Webster drove up to see me in Ross's mother's car. Ross's mother was away at that time. Together we had a lovely day at the Hume Weir. On his return Ross scrupulously cleaned out the car and even turned the odometer back. All seemed well until Mrs Webster asked, 'How did this New South Wales artefact get into the boot of my car?' displaying a bag marked 'Albury Ice Works'.

At the end of second year my old school friends, John Pilkington, Geoff Ford and David James, and I aimed to drive around Australia over the holidays. Three of us had been Scouts at school. Geoff's father had organised a short wheelbase Land Rover for us, a tight squeeze for all our camping gear and luggage.

Our exhaust pipe fell off on the Nullarbor Plain. We arrived in Perth on Christmas Eve, a Saturday morning. We had to find the Land Rover repair shop to have the exhaust reattached. We had a street number in Hay Street, but did not realise the numbers changed as you left Perth City and started all over again. We very noisily drove around in circles trying to find the place. This included doing a U-turn over the median strip of a highway heading out of town; we had to use low-ratio 4-wheel drive to get un-bogged. We were finally guided to the right place by two long-suffering and frustrated policemen.

After Christmas we headed north and hit Wittenoom on New Year's Eve. The big blue asbestos mine closed that day. The locals who were still there had a roaringly good celebration in the pub that night. We woke late in the morning sleeping beside the water in the gorge.

We then headed along the magnificent Eighty Mile Beach with its myriads of beautiful shells to arrive eventually in Broome. By Broome, we needed to have some serious repairs to the Land Rover's front end. While we waited for the parts to come from Perth, we worked on the local pearling luggers, an amazing way to spend a few weeks. The boats were 'all out of the water' for the 'wet season'. We worked on a large supply boat. The tide in Broome can go up and down 10 metres. At high tide the boat floated, and we worked on board cleaning and repainting. At low tide we waded through the mud to clean the barnacles off the hull. In between times we had the occasional beer in the classic old hotel across the road, the 'Roey,' the Roebuck Bay.

By the time our vehicle was repaired the Wet Season had begun in earnest. A cyclone had flooded the rivers and roads, including the Fitzroy River. The way to Darwin was impassable.

We went south, to Kalgoorlie, and intended to make our way up and across to Alice Springs. We were caught in a storm in the Petermann Ranges near the West Australian and Northern Territory border, where we remained bogged for over a week. We had some food with us and were able to shoot some rabbits. After four days a light plane flew over. When it saw us, it circled lower and dropped a message on paper wrapped around a stone. 'If you need help, make signs.' We took a roll of toilet paper and wrote 'FOOD' in large letters. Next day they dropped two drums of food which crashed to the ground. It was great to have the supplies but some of the boxes inside the drums had split—tea leaves in the cornflakes, sugar mixed with flour.

Our Land Rover bogged in the Petermann Ranges in Central Australia, January 1966

The surface water slowly drained and the road dried. We made it to Alice, then back to Melbourne. Our mouldy sleeping bags had to be discarded. We returned home just in time for the start of the university year. We had not driven around Australia, but we had seen a lot of country, learned a lot about the bush, survival and something about the Aboriginal people we passed on the road and the communities we had driven past. Coming into Warburton Mission in Ngannyatjarra Country in the Gibson Desert we saw families living by the side of road outside of the mission village like those in Nene Gare's 1961 novel *The Fringe Dwellers*. Later a Bruce Beresford film of the same name was applauded overseas, although the response in Australia was tepid.

I spent three wonderful years at Ormond. Many of my life-long friendships were made there.

In my third year I shared a study with fourth-year medical student, Roger McLennan, whose five-year residency at Ormond

Roger McLennan in our study in the Upper Tower, Ormond College, 1968

gave him a bit of pull and priority, and thus be allocated the Upper Tower study, five stories up in the bell tower with magnificent views in all directions from its large windows. Above us was the clock and the bell that rang on the hour all day but stopped after 10 pm, the time women were meant to be off the premises.

One night after 10 pm we were sharing a few drinks with our neighbours in one of the two Lower Tower studies. Looking down we saw a very tall shadow and short shadow emerging from the front door. Clearly a gentleman and his female visitor leaving after hours. A bucket of water was tipped down. A few minutes later a very breathless colleague climbed the stairs and announced, 'I don't know who, but someone has just water bagged the Master and the Vice Master!' Oh dear, that was me! The Vice Master mentioned it in his retirement speech. The college chairman also reminded me of it.

Roger was from rural Victoria. When he finished his medical training he studied in England to avoid his Vietnam war draft. He returned to Australia and became a leading oncologist. He moved to Geelong. This gave him easy access to the water in his sailing boat, a great love of his. He is daughter Kate's godfather and we still see him often.

In college we spent time sitting and talking, sometimes in great detail about the state of the world and other affairs, and sometimes with a drink in hand. During one of these conversations someone said, 'Hey, why don't we start a ski club?' The rest of us agreed it was a good idea.

So the work started. This led to the formation of the Ormond Ski Club the following year. However, we became more ambitious and felt that the club should have a lodge. A site was secured at Mt Hotham.

We ran two fund-raising events at our old family property in the Dandenong hills. Ormond Ski Club Wine Bottlings became legendary big barbeques around some large barrels of good red wine obtained from friends at the Morris Winery in north-eastern Victoria. Armed with a plastic tube and a plentiful supply of empty wine bottles, corks and mallets, people filled their cellars. Of course, some wine did not make it into the bottles! Most people got home safely after the event, but some had some hairy stories to recount. In those days there were no booze buses, and we must admit to some foolish behaviour. The money raised at these bottlings helped build the lodge. (Many years later we uncovered a surviving full bottle and were very pleased with its quality.)

For several summers we joined others to spend a week or more building the ski lodge. A few years later we enjoyed many days skiing and convivial nights, and we have fond memories of some great skiing and fine meals. Our later travels took Liz and me away from Australia, so I resigned from the club. We still have friends who are active members.

The second and third years of the medical course were lectures and laboratory sessions in anatomy, biochemistry and physiology. In Anatomy Dissection Room, it felt as though there were a hundred bodies set out on tabletops. The worst of it was the foul smell and acrid catch in the throat caused by the preservative, formalin. Many of us had never seen a dead body, and none of us had cut open someone's arm or leg before. It was challenging. In second year, groups of three worked on either side of the body dissecting the arms and then the legs. In third year, the groups dissected the rest of a body so in total there were 12 of us working on each body. After spending this time together, often in ardent conversation and sharing our experiences in this unusual setting, our dissecting companions became friends.

At the end of third year, we were to start our clinical training. The Austin Hospital was about to become a teaching hospital and receive its first students. Peter 'Porky' Sinclair and I went out to have a look at the possibility of becoming students there. Peter drove what for students those days, was a fancy car, a white Ford Cortina. He was a talented footballer playing as ruck/rover for the Melbourne Football Club in the Victorian Football League.

We were struck by the energy and enthusiasm we encountered at the Austin, and the welcome we were given felt warm. So, we became the first of the students to sign up for their first year of clinical teaching at the Austin.

Being at the Austin was a game changer. Really interesting! So much to learn! The teaching staff and the ward staff were excited to have medical students as there had not been any there before. One of our very enthusiastic lecturers, microbiologist Joan Schiavone, stressed the need to spend an extra hour each night working over our lecture notes and textbooks. This was a very different approach to 'studying' for me, who had enjoyed more than my share of evenings off. Joan was exciting and engaging and she enjoyed teaching and challenging us.

After the fourth-year examinations, to my surprise, I found I had done very well. So well, in fact, that I was offered the opportunity to spend a year doing research work with Peter Morris to gain a Bachelor of Medical Science degree. This seemed like a great opportunity; doing research might be interesting to learn about, and research might be something I wanted to explore further. It meant that Liz would do her fourth year while I spent the year doing research. As we planned to get married at the end of that year, Liz and I would end up doing the last two years of our medicine training together. This would make life much more straightforward because we had long live-in rotations in those last two years.

Liz and I married at the end of 1968. We had both turned 21 that year. Our parents thought we were way too young but as we were now both 21, what could they do?

The wedding plan was that I would drive to the Chapel at Scotch in Nellie. My friend John Spence would drive Liz and

Our wedding in 1968 standing beside Nellie.

her father there in his open 1922 Rolls Royce. After the ceremony Liz and I were to leave in Nellie for the reception at my grandparents' home.

The week before the wedding Nellie broke down and needed her driveshaft repaired. The repairs were delayed and Nellie sat on blocks in my parents' garage waiting to be fixed. The parts arrived on the morning of the wedding. My father, Ross Webster—our Best Man, and I worked hard to get Nellie back together again. At noon, my father told me, 'You have to stop right now. Go inside, shower, make sure you scrub your nails clean and get dressed ready for the wedding. Ross and I will finish this off.'

And they did. Nellie sang to every request made of her.

We were married by the Reverend Davis McCaughey. He was the Master at Ormond College. When he and his family had arrived from Northern Ireland they had been taken under the wings of my two maiden great aunts. So we got to know Davis and his family well.

After the wedding Liz and I headed off in Nellie for our honeymoon at a hamlet called Seaspray in Ninety Mile Beach on Victoria's south-eastern coast.

I had just finished fourth year, Liz third year. With an inheritance from my grandparents, we bought a small old terrace house in Carlton, an easy walk to the university. Liz had to drive Nellie the 16 kilometres to the Austin for her fourth-year studies, while

Skin-grafting rats: me, T S Tiong, unknown, and Peter Morris, 1968

I spent 1969 working with Peter Morris in the renal transplantation and immunology laboratory in the Department of Surgery at the Royal Melbourne Hospital. The hospital was within walking distance too.

Peter Morris was the Reader in the Department. He had returned to Melbourne the year before, having spent time in the UK and US, researching renal transplantation and the immunology of graft rejection. He had identified the importance of Human Leukocyte Antigens, HLAs, in stimulating graft rejections and the role cytotoxic antibodies played in these rejections. If the donor and recipient HLAs matched, the tissue was not likely to be rejected. (Later Peter would move to Oxford to be the Nuffield Professor of Surgery and a world-leading transplantation surgeon. He became President of the Royal College of Surgeons of England and Sir Peter Morris AC. A great teacher and mentor, he became a friend.)

My project was to try to develop immune tolerance to skin transplants using a rat model. We learned how to do skin grafts in rats, how to inject them with various antigen preparations to stimulate their immune system and how to monitor their responses. One of the key outcomes was how long the skin graft remained before rejection.

As student researchers we were also put to work in the laboratory, spending a lot of time typing tissue for patients waiting for kidney transplants and for potential kidney donors. Wendy Law did all the data analysis on the outcomes of the kidney transplants. Each week she prepared a box full of computer cards in the right order. Then she would cross Royal Parade, a busy road, and take the cards to the mainframe computer in the University. One morning she tripped as she crossed. All the cards fell everywhere—there went that week's statistical analysis. Fortunately for me, I did my data analysis on a hand-operated adding machine, the only device that was available to a student at that time. Pocket calculators came later.

Although based in the Department of Surgery, we used the animal facilities in the adjacent Walter and Eliza Hall Institute. The Nobel Prize winning Sir Frank Macfarlane Burnet had been the director of the 'Walter and Eliza'. To celebrate his 70th birthday a Festschrift was to be held. I was excited to learn Sir Peter Medawar was scheduled to attend. He had shared the Nobel with Burnet and I had read many of his papers. But Medawar was unwell and could not make it. Macfarlane Burnet spoke. I found his words very disturbing. He said that essentially everything in immunology had been more of less mapped out by late 1969. There might be a few details left, similar to adding some small rivers or creeks to a geographic map of the continents of the world, but really all the important immunology work had been done. This was deflating for a young aspiring researcher but with the confidence of youth, I just knew he had to be wrong. Of course, he was.

We had a small black and white television set at our terrace home so many of the staff of the laboratory walked with me to our house to watch the moon landing. It was a very exciting time to watch and sort of be part of the history, but it also reflected how well the laboratory team were bound together. Research was fun. I published my first paper, and a second paper as well. I gave my first research presentations. I found I really *wanted* to go to the library to search for and read papers and reports to learn what others had discovered. This was much more interesting and exciting than studying textbooks to pass an exam.

Peter Morris' laboratory provided me with a foundation in research methodology that was invaluable. The work on transplantation immunology opened up future work and opportunities. A year's research had not been in my original plan but it was a wonderful experience and certainly changed my professional trajectory.

Having taken a year out of the medical course to do research meant that Liz and I could do the last two clinical years and the live-in clinical placements together. In fifth year we had to spend 10 weeks living at the Royal Women's Hospital for our obstetrics and gynaecology term, and we were in the same clinical group in our other rotations that year. However, having spent all day together in the same group, there was not a lot for us to talk about and share in the evenings, so in final year we purposely moved into two different clinical groups.

This worked well.

To add a level of complication to our lives, our first daughter, Kathryn, 'Kate', was born in 1971, in the middle of our final year. We all had to complete another two weeks in obstetrics and gynaecology training in the final year. When Liz did this and showed up for yet another delivery, the patient nearly fainted. The woman in labour was about to be delivered by a medical student who was almost ready to be delivered herself. Our daughter was safely delivered a couple of weeks later at the Royal Women's Hospital.

Being married as a medical student was very unusual but having a child was essentially unheard of. Just before Kate was born, dear Nellie broke down. Liz insisted I replace it with something more reliable, arguing that having a baby in a more or less open old car in winter was not a good idea. We bought a second-hand VW beetle. We took Kate with us and back each day, and took her to tutorials, lectures and the wards. People at the Austin Hospital got used to the three of us.

One evening my parents were having a few friends for a dinner that included the professor of paediatrics. He announced 'You cannot believe what the medical students are doing these days. Today I gave a lecture to the final-year students and one of them brought a baby in bassinette in with them. It's unbelievable!'

'That was my granddaughter,' my proud mother replied.

At the end of the year with a bit of effort and some luck, we both did well and passed our final medical exams. I was the top student in the small group at the Austin and third in the year overall. To my surprise I also got the Obstetrics and Gynaecology, and the Psychiatry prizes. New mum Liz, really did an amazing job, passing very well and with an honour in surgery.

While at medical school I became involved in student politics. I am not now sure how this happened but in third year, I became the treasurer of the University's Medical Students Society. I went to conventions organised by the Australian Medical Students' Association, AMSA. Liz came too and we not only had a lot of good times but we also got to meet students from the other universities. I ended up joining the AMSA board and was president in my final year.

In 1968 I was the Australian representative to the Asian Medical Students Congress held in Hong Kong. I had to raise the money for my airfare, and I was given the name of a 'wealthy person' who lived in Toorak who might be able to help. I contacted Sir Charles Spry and we met in his home. He gave me the money for my airfare and asked for some sort of report on my return. I had attended the meeting in Hong Kong. We flew over Vietnam: the war was raging then but we did not see much out of the window of the plane. I had a cheap flight that involved a stop in Djakarta. One of the Indonesian students invited me to spend a night at his home in Djakarta and so I extended my trip by a day. I later learned, to my surprise, Sir Charles was the Director of ASIO, the Australian Security and Intelligence Organisation. I am not sure what secret information he might have expected me to bring back. I told him about the meeting and my travels. I doubt he got any useful information or value for his money, but to me it was an eye-opening trip. I learned about our Asian neighbours and their medical students.

After Liz and I graduated, we were both accepted as first-year interns at the Austin Hospital. In those times interns had to live in full-time. We arrived with six-months-old Kate and presented the house staff a previously unknown challenge. We were shown our allocated rooms.

'What about the baby?' said Liz.

'What baby?'

The residency was in the old nurses' home, not set up for families in any way. In the end we given two rooms on either side of a shared female bathroom and it worked out OK. Through the day Kate was able to go to the child-care that had been set up to care for the nursing staff's children. Usually only one of us was rostered on at night, but occasionally we both were. We would have to call the residents' lounge at night and ask someone to stop watching TV for a minute and to listen to check that Kate was not crying. When we were rostered on for the weekend my mother looked after Kate for us. Despite the less than conventional methods of upbringing, Kate was a very good baby and thriving.

One of the surgical rotations I did was orthopaedics. John Grant, the head orthopaedic surgeon, had started to do a new operation repairing torn anterior cruciate ligaments for footballers. At the end of one of his clinics, I showed him the wobbly knee I had wrecked on the trampoline six years before. Soon I was put on the surgical list and spent about a week as an inpatient. The ward nurses were pleased to have me there, as I could rewrite expiring treatment orders so they did not have to track down the resident concerned. I was mildly reprimanded when I ordered a pre-dinner beer for patient Hugh Taylor, but otherwise I was found useful round the clock. My leg was in a full plaster for six weeks, very differently from how things are done now.

The surgery was just before Liz, Kate and I were to do our three-month country rotation in Echuca on Victoria's northern border. In Echuca we stayed in a hospital house. I hobbled around until my plaster came off. It was fun being in a country town and we were well looked after. Liz was newly pregnant with our second child, Bart. Liz asked if she could sit during a surgical operation as she was pregnant, adding that she didn't want that to be known at that time. The next day in the butcher's shop she was greeted, 'G'day Doc. Hear you are up the duff again!'

Through my early years as a medical student, I had thought that I would like to be a surgeon, someone who could cut things out and fix things up right away. My uncle, Stuart Morson, was a neurosurgeon in Sydney. We would often stay with him and Auntie Lib. As a medical student, I once spent the day with him in the operating theatre and watched him operate. Fascinating. I thought a career in neurosurgery would be perfect for me. Uncle Stuart suggested that I read some neurology textbooks by David Cogan.

However, what really caught my attention was Cogan's book on the various nerves associated with the eye. My grandfather had been a leading eye doctor. He worked to establish the chair of ophthalmology and it was named after him. At the end of my fifth year of medical school, 1970, I had the opportunity to spend a few weeks working in the Melbourne University Department of Ophthalmology, MUDO, and watching Professor Gerrard Crock, the inaugural Ringland Anderson Professor of Ophthalmology, at work at the Royal Victorian Eye and Ear Hospital, the 'Eye and Ear'.

As I contemplated what to do once I had finished my internship, then called a 'first year residency', or 'residency', I became less enamoured with neurosurgery and more and more attracted to ophthalmology. It seemed to combine some of the best of both medicine and surgery, and it was the first and leading discipline to use operating microscopes for microsurgery and to perform laser surgery.

During my intern year I decided I would try to become an ophthalmologist. I spoke to my grandmother about this shortly before she died. This was a comfort to her, but she was more thrilled to be a great-grandmother with the recent birth of Kate.

At the end of my first year as an intern I had, rather precociously, sat the First Part exam for the Royal Australasian College of Surgeons. At this time, the Australian College of Ophthalmologists was still getting established and setting up its own examination and accreditation processes. To become a registered specialist ophthalmologist, one needed to be a fellow of either the College of Ophthalmologists or of Surgeons. Of course, one could be a fellow of both colleges once the appropriate exams had been passed. One had to pass the College of Surgeons First Part exam to be able to sit the joint Fellowship exam in ophthalmology that was run by both colleges.

I stayed for a second year at the Austin as a surgical resident.

Liz started her PhD at the Austin, but then she moved with her supervisor, Colin Johnston, to the Monash University Department of Medicine at Prince Henry's Hospital. She studied neurophysins, the small carrier proteins that drive the synthesis of the tiny hormones oxytocin and vasopressin in the posterior pituitary body of the pituitary gland at the base of the brain behind the bridge of the nose.

While she was doing all this in 1973, she also had our second child, Bartholomew, always called Bart, at the Royal Women's Hospital. A day after the caesarean section delivery, Liz was allowed out of bed. The professor of obstetrics took her, in a dressing gown, on ward rounds, suggesting this was a good way to recover and keep up with her studies.

Bart spent some of his early life in a baby's bassinet under a research laboratory bench. Liz was working hard, studying, running her laboratory, doing clinical work and participating in the weekly teaching rounds, in addition to looking after our two children and me. Over the years we had a variety of day-care, home help and kindergarten arrangements that Liz oversaw and managed.

Postera Crescam Laude

At the end of my second year as a resident at the Austin I applied to start the ophthalmology training programme at the Eye and Ear. I was accepted as a first-year ophthalmology registrar and started in 1974. Liz continued the work on her PhD at Prince Henry's. There were six first-year ophthalmology registrars and we were kept busy with clinics, surgery, the emergency room and night duty. There were also lectures, tutorials and teaching clinics. We worked closely with the second—and third-year registrars. Consultants and staff were helpful and supportive. We learned a great deal, at a great pace.

During my second year as an ophthalmology registrar, I sat and passed the Diploma of Ophthalmology awarded by Melbourne University. This had been an important degree before the colleges set up their fellowships, but soon after became obsolete.

At the end of my second year as an ophthalmology registrar a family friend and my father's tennis buddy, Grecia Sklovsky,

At the French Antarctic base at Dumont d'Urville, 1975

who had once called me the naughtiest little boy he had ever known, asked me if I would like to go to the Antarctic. Grecia had been born in Serbia, completed a PhD in chemistry in France, fought with the Czech Army in World War 2 and emigrated to Australia in 1947. He married an old friend of my family, Celia Weigall, who had trained as an orthoptist with my grandfather and then worked with him. We saw a lot of Grecia and Celia. Their daughter, Janey, babysat for us from time to time while she was a medical student and later became our general practitioner. Grecia had close connections with the French Expéditions Polaires Françaises and had visited their Antarctic base at Dumont d'Urville several times. A supply ship, MV *Thala Dan*, was sent to Dumont d'Urville each year at the start of the summer and again at the end of the summer. Their medical officers were changed on the first trip, and they needed a doctor on board for the second trip: an extraordinary opportunity for me. Again, Liz supported what was to be a further six-week absence from my family duties.

The trip down was uneventful and included a stop at the Australian base on Macquarie Island to unload supplies. At Dumont d'Urville the French army pilots transported the supplies by helicopter. I had plenty of time to explore the ice and the breeding sites for the penguins and seals. They also took me by helicopter for a thrilling, quick sightseeing tour. Glacier walls viewed from inside a crevasse make more shades of blue and white and black than imagination can offer. Antarctic scenery and the colours in the ice are spectacular on the ground or from the water, but even more so from the air.

The trip home was rough; the experienced Danish captain maintained that it was the worst storm he had ever experienced. The hammering the *Thala Dan* took was relentless. Hippocrates around 400 BCE wrote 'sailing at sea proves that motion disorders the body'; damn right: nausea, dizziness, headaches, cold sweats... Australians usually take medicine as pills, Americans prefer capsules, others injections, but the French prefer rectal suppositories. Many of the returning staff had severe sea-sickness. I spent hours hanging on for dear life as I went from one pale face to the next, providing suppositories.

Meanwhile in Hobart, Liz and our two small children were waiting, waiting, waiting for us. I had been away for a long time. They knew about the storm, but they had received no word from us or about us. Much to Liz's relief, we made it back safely, days late.

As an eye registrar I also spent some time under the guidance of Professor Crock studying trabeculectomy, a new surgical procedure for managing glaucoma that seemed to offer many advantages over the then existing methods of treatment. Glaucoma is the blinding eye disease associated with high pressure in the eye. One way to reduce the pressure was to use an eye drop multiple times a day. Another way might be to make a drain, called a trabeculectomy to allow the fluid inside the eye to drain. We studied surgical trabeculectomy specimens with scanning electron microscopy and did experimental surgery in monkeys.

Professor Peter Watson, based in Cambridge, UK was a leading advocate of trabeculectomy. In 1976 he came as an invited speaker to the Australian College of Ophthalmologists' meeting. He had read my recently published paper on trabeculectomy and seemed to be very pleased to meet me and to talk about it. As a young ophthalmologist-to-be it was exciting, very gratifying and amazing to have this world-leading ophthalmologist interested in what I'd done and interested in such a friendly and approachable way. Peter became a friend and colleague over time. Another amazing and fortuitous meeting for my career and future.

During training I became more and more interested in corneal surgery. Halfway through second year I thought that once I had finished my three years of training at the Eye and

Ear it would be worth my while to spend a year or so overseas doing a corneal fellowship. With help and advice from Professor Crock, in mid 1975 I arranged a series of visits to some of the leading centres in the US and the UK. Rather ignorantly, I would ask leading people in these centres why I should come to do a fellowship with them, rather than explaining to them why they should offer me a fellowship. Later I learned that this approach was not how most fellowship applicants approached their interviews.

One of the centres I visited was The Wilmer Institute at Johns Hopkins University in Baltimore, Maryland. Dr Walter Stark was the head of the Corneal Service and was particularly interested in corneal transplantation and HLA matching. He was interested in the research on transplantation immunity I'd done with Peter Morris. The Wilmer was one of the top eye institutes in the world and had excellent research facilities that included laboratories where studies in non-human primates were conducted. When offered a corneal fellowship at the Wilmer to start in July 1977, it was too good an opportunity to pass up. I jumped at it.

At the start of my third year as a registrar, 1976, I sat and passed the conjoint fellowship exams for the College of Surgeons and the College of Ophthalmologists. Dick Galbraith, the head of ophthalmology at the Royal Melbourne, would spend about two weeks each year doing eye surgery in the Solomon Islands, and each year took an ophthalmology registrar along with him as part of his team. I had hoped to be invited to do the next trip with him but he asked another registrar. I was disappointed. However, another serendipitous meeting followed shortly after.

I bumped into Fred Hollows at the annual Australian College of Ophthalmology Congress. My life was about to change. Forever.

3

Fred

> I was led astray by Fred Hollows
> at a tender age,
> and I have been a stray ever since.
>
> My stock answer when asked,
> How come you got involved in this?

I first met Fred Hollows when I was a second-year registrar at the Royal Victorian Eye and Ear Hospital in Melbourne in 1975. Fred held a weekend ophthalmology course in Sydney to which he invited Australian eye registrars. It was free; all one had to do was get there. Eight of us, and two orthoptists, from Melbourne jumped on train to Sydney, *The Spirit of Progress*. I knew Fred was the associate professor of ophthalmology at the University of New South Wales and the Prince of Wales Hospital, and that he'd done some interesting work on glaucoma in the UK. But I knew no more than that.

We spent Saturday in his clinic at the hospital. He led a couple of tutorials and then we saw some of his patients whom he had asked to come in that day so we could examine them. One of them was Patrick White, recent winner of the Nobel Prize for Literature. We learned some of his other patients couldn't be there that day as they were serving time, as usual, in Long Bay, one of the city's prisons.

That evening we all had dinner at Fred's home, Farnham House, a place a former girlfriend and now a good friend of ours, had selected for him. This wonderful old sandstone house, formerly a convent and then a school, was one I came to know very well. On this occasion, as always, there was plenty of food and plenty to drink. There was a bowl of marijuana on the table for those who were so inclined. Although I smoked a pipe, I was not so inclined. On the train home on Sunday, we had a lot to talk about.

By chance, I met Fred again at the Australian College of Ophthalmologists meeting early in the next year. (Later, 'the College' would become the Royal Australian and New Zealand College of Ophthalmologists, RANZCO.) Fred would travel to Bourke in western New South Wales two or three times a year for a 'long weekend' providing eye care and eye surgery for the Aboriginal people and anybody else who lived there and showed up to his clinic. While examining the children he found lots with trachoma and many of the adults with the in-turned trachomatous eye lashes that can go on to cause blindness.

Fred was aware of the work done on trachoma by Father Frank Flynn and by Dame Ida Mann. Flynn, an ophthalmologist, served as a chaplain with the Australian army in the Northern Territory when Darwin was being bombed by the Japanese in 1942 and redeployed to Alice. Later he became an Outback Missionary du Sacré Coeur, a medico-priest. He was the first to recognise 'sandy blight' was trachoma and was rife in the Idigenous people. Post-war, an Englishwoman, Professor Mann came to Australia's dry climate for her husband's health and worked in Perth. After his death she travelled widely and reported on eye health, especially trachoma, among Aboriginal, Torres Strait Island, Papua-New Guinean and other Pacific peoples. She was linked with the new World Health Organisation and its trachoma activities. She was a close friend of my grandfather, and they often corresponded. Growing up I met her once or twice at my grandparents' house. Fred was to become the unlikely next torch bearer in the fight against trachoma.

As part of my ophthalmology training in Melbourne I spent a few months working with Dick Galbraith who ran the eye clinic at the Royal Melbourne Hospital. As he had not asked me to go with him to the Solomon Islands that year, I thought it might be an interesting alternative to spend a long weekend with Fred in Bourke.

'Fred, could I join you on your next trip to Bourke?'

'I will see, and I'll get back to you.'

I did not know at that time that he and the College were in discussion with the Commonwealth Government to set up and fund the National Trachoma and Eye Health Programme, NTEHP. A month or so later Fred rang.

'Taylor, I want you to be in Port Augusta, 19 May.' That was only weeks away. 'I want you to spend two weeks working with me as we start up on this new national programme on Indigenous eye health.'

I learned a lot from Fred, and a lot about him too. He was gruff and used the full range of the English language. He was once described to me by a surgical-supply company executive, as a 'foul-mouthed misogynist'. He was very well read. Frequently he would quote from the Bible or Karl Marx or poets or philosophers or medical writers. Fred was profoundly concerned about equity and the injustice of the desperate state of so many Aboriginal people and their communities. He would often talk of 'disequity' and quote Paulo Freire's book *The Pedagogy of the Oppressed*. Freire had done work with the Indian tribes in the Amazonian jungle and emphasised the importance of education in reducing oppression of cultural groups. Often when the trachoma team was staying in a town, Fred would go to the pub to talk to local people, especially any Aboriginal people who were there. He would listen and was always deeply concerned.

Fred was born in New Zealand into a Christian socialist family who did not smoke or drink. After leaving school, he started out as a theological student. During summer jobs, first working in a mental hospital and then in forestry, he developed a strong liking for alcohol and learned to smoke a pipe. He found he was no longer interested in divinity and so, after two years, he applied and was accepted into the medical school at the University of Otago in Dunedin. For a while he was also a member of the New Zealand Communist Party and he had the New Zealand Security and Intelligence Service tracking him, and for different reasons, the Australian equivalent, ASIO. After finishing his medical studies, he went to Moorfields Hospital in London to do his ophthalmology training. Fred then spent a year working with the epidemiologist Archie Cochrane in the mining valleys of Wales. There with Archie, Fred did a landmark study of glaucoma in the coal miners. Fred's paper on the normal distribution of intra-ocular pressure in the miners defined a pressure above 21mm Hg to be abnormal. This set the standard definition of glaucoma for decades.

His reputation among the profession was rather different from the other ophthalmic academics, but at this stage I did not know much more about him than that. With the author and advocate Frank Hardy, Fred had made visits to the Gurindji people in the Northern Territory after the Wave Hill walk off and had done other ophthalmic work with Aboriginal people. In 1971 he had been arrested for joining the anti-apartheid demonstrations during the South African rugby tour. However, he was a serious academic ophthalmologist and known to be a good teacher. Overall, he was rather an enigma.

Fred was always very supportive to me, a true mentor and teacher. He opened my eyes to the appalling state of Aboriginal health. He showed me what one could do by using a public health approach, by thinking about a community, rather than only individual patients, one at a time. He taught me about the practical aspects of epidemiology and public health. He changed my life. It was the beginning of the rest of my professional life.

Skipping forward, I spent the two weeks with him in May 1976. Then another two weeks a bit later. Then, in August, I was back again 'full-time' and, with a Christmas break, wound up in June 1977 to go to Baltimore. In May 1978 I flew back from Baltimore to Queensland and worked for a further two months.

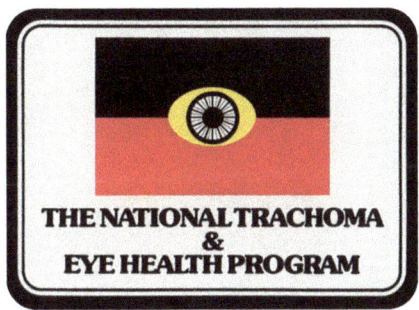

The National Trachoma and Eye Health Programme Logo

On 19 May 1976, I turned up at Port Augusta to start work. I was to miss Liz's 29th birthday, the first of many birthdays and family events I would miss over time. The NTEHP team was led by Fred. Gabi O'Sullivan was the team's orthoptist. Fred and Gabi were a number, there was no question about that. However, that did not stop Fred from being quite harsh and sometimes even derogatory with her. Gabi let the insults and reprimands slide over her, like water off a duck's back, always unfazed. This surprised us co-workers, but we could see they were strong and united. Later, Fred and Gabi would marry and have five children. In 1984, Gabi and Liz were both pregnant around the same time. Fred called Liz and gloated that they would win the kids' race because Gabi was expecting twins.

The field team became a closely knitted group.

Trevor (Buzza) Buzzacott was the Aboriginal community liaison person. Buzza is an Arabunna man who went on to do a lot of good for his people working in state and federal government departments. He was a keen footballer and later, a golfer. He played country and western music on his guitar and chess

Me and Fred Hollows in the field

with Fred in the evening. Buzza and I remain good friends and keep in contact.

Marjorie Baldwin, as she was then known, was an Aboriginal woman from the Kimberley and a member of the Stolen Generation. She grew up with foster parents in northern Queensland and only met her mother during our work in the Kimberley. Later, she married John Thompson, a pulmonary physician, and reverted to her traditional name, Jilpia Nappaljari Jones. She was the first triple-certificated Indigenous nurse, having trained in general nursing, midwifery and then ophthalmic nursing. She was one of the first nurses to work at the Redfern Aboriginal Medical Service in Sydney, which she helped establish in 1971. Fred and Gordon Briscoe also were heavily involved in setting up that medical service, the first in Australia. Later Jilpia worked on Indigenous issues at the Australian National University where she gained a bachelor's degree in political science. Much later, both Jilpia and Buzza joined our Advisory Board at the Indigenous Eye Health Unit that I set up at the University of Melbourne.

Reg and Rose Murray were a wonderful Aboriginal couple who came from the Yorta lands. They were always full of joy and there was much banter about the superiority of Reg's Land-Cruiser compared with the Land Rovers or Range Rovers. Rosie and Reg did a range of jobs helping organising the examination sites and so forth. Reg was also our chief mechanic. He would change wheels and repair flat tyres of our Land Rovers, station wagon and a small truck supplied by the Health Department as well as Fred's Range Rover.

Other more permanent members of the NTEHP field teams included David Moran who worked as the team's epidemiologist and helped in co-ordination and in all sorts of other things. David had recently finished medical school and after the NTEHP he trained as an ophthalmologist with Fred.

Rosie Denholm, who had worked with Fred previously, provided managerial support.

Above: A group of children waiting for their examination in a community with a high prevalence of trachoma. Many show nasal discharge and dirty faces.

Below: A makeshift wiltja or home in the APY Lands

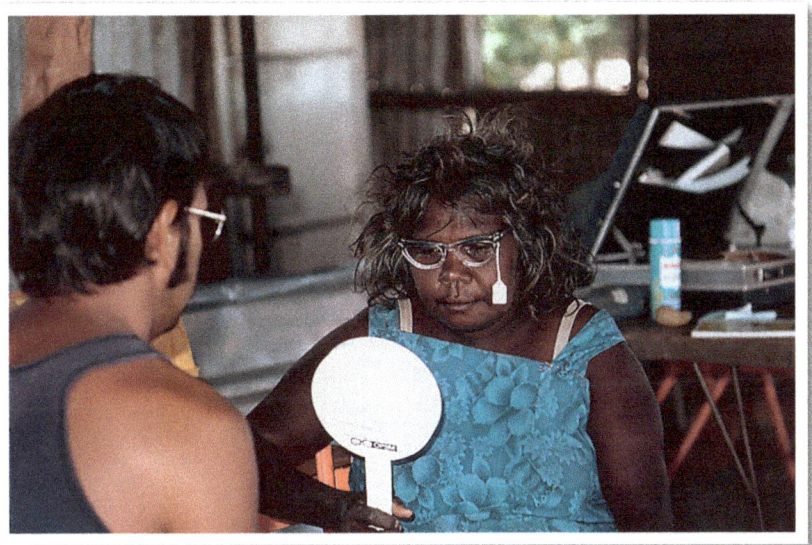

Reg Murray measuring a patient up for spectacles

Just after I left, Patricia (Trish) O'Shaunessy, who worked with us as a field secretary, died after a truck she was driving rolled off the road in the Kimberley. This awful accident upset the whole team; I was advised by letter in the US.

Although there were some other more permanent members of the field teams, there were also many who would come and help the team for shorter periods, usually about two weeks. In all, over 80 ophthalmologists helped with the more detailed eye exams.

The work in a community would start with Buzza as the liaison officer contacting the community to let them know that we were to arrive and what the program was about. He would also sort out where the clinic might be situated. We would arrive and set up the examination area, sometimes in a clinic building, or under a shelter, or in an old army tent that we carried. People would be registered, have their distance vision checked, and then be graded for trachoma. If their vision was poor or if other issues were noted, they would be seen by the ophthalmologist. For the first two weeks, that was me.

We had refracting, trial lenses to measure for glasses, a slit lamp to examine the front of the eye, a tonometer to check the pressure in the eye for glaucoma, dilating drops to dilate the pupil and an ophthalmoscope to examine the back of the eye. We could prescribe lenses and measure up and fit the spectacle frames. Then the prescription was sent to OPSM, an optical company, which would deliver the glasses at no cost to the local clinic a few weeks later; OPSM met all our needs. Sometimes we had an optometrist working with us, but often Reg would do the job as the optical dispenser and measure up the spectacle frames. If patients were found to need further treatment or surgery, we would try to arrange that for them.

A group of children waiting for their examination in a community with a high prevalence of trachoma. Many show nasal discharge and dirty faces.

Having examined all the Aboriginal people in Port Augusta and the adjacent community at Davenport we then worked our way up through the communities into the Flinders Ranges. Here I found a girl with very abnormal findings that looked like a rare congenital condition. At that point I had to fly back to the Eye and Ear in Melbourne; to my 'day job'. However, a few weeks later I was allowed to go back to the Flinders Ranges and followed up on this child and her family. I worked out that she had Hurler Syndrome, a rare type of mucopolysaccharidosis. It is a form of gargoylism that includes changes in the eye. It seemed that the young girl might have inherited it from her great grandfather, who had been an Afghani cameleer. On this return visit I also spent time with the team in the communities in the Anangu Pitjantjatjara Yankunytjatjara (APY) Lands, in northern South Australia, just south of the Northern Territory border.

After returning to the Eye and Ear for a few weeks later in August 1976, Fred called me up again, this time to join the team on a fulltime basis. I was to lead a second team to speed up the work of the programme. Fred had pulled strings with Ken Howsam, the medical director of the Eye and Ear, and with the college to allow me to have the time with Fred and the NTEHP approved to complete my ophthalmic training. This was only possible because I already had passed my final ophthalmology exams earlier in the year.

I was to be the Assistant Director of the NTEHP. The Associate Director was Gordon (Biggo) Briscoe. Biggo had been born in Alice Springs but grew up as part of the stolen generation in an institution in Adelaide with Charlie Perkins and others who had been sent there from Alice. He played soccer for a while in the UK, then studied at Australian National University in Canberra. Later, he became the ANU's first Indigenous PhD graduate. In 1974 he started as a Senior Liaison Officer in the Commonwealth Department of Health. Biggo was really our inside man, based in the department but always ready to help whenever he could. He had worked with Fred and Jilpia in setting up the Redfern Aboriginal Medical Service too and often worked with Buzza. Even though we did not see him often in the field, he was always smiling and full of fun when he joined us.

During his call to me Fred said that I was expected to be in Alice Springs in a few weeks. I had to get a 4-wheel drive vehicle, camping and ophthalmic equipment, supplies and so forth. Liz was in the third year of her PhD and looking after our two children aged 3 and 5. It was going to be tough for Liz, but, as she always did, she gave me her full backing.

The 4WD purchase wasn't easy. Fred had a Range Rover, so I went to Lance Dixon, the Land Rover agents in Melbourne, and they said that it would be a six or 12 month wait. I pressed them. I said, 'This is for important government-funded work with Aboriginal communities in outback Australia.' Eventually they 'bought' the story and found one for me. I had to get bull bars, a roof rack, and a car fridge for medicines and food fitted. I packed the supplies, sleeping gear and equipment, and set off. Liz reminds me that at that time I had not fully considered the impact all this would have on our family and our resources. Liz managed!

I was asked to take Ronald Lowe with me to Alice Springs. Ron was going to help Fred for a couple of weeks. Ron was in many ways Australia's leading ophthalmologist, a recently retired president of the College as well as a past president of the Asia Pacific Academy of Ophthalmology. He was the world expert on a particular type of glaucoma, angle closure glaucoma, and revered at the Eye and Ear. Who was I to drive him around? On the first night we unfurled our swags and slept beside the road. We arrived in Alice the next day. Ron adapted without trouble to our outdoor living and camping. When we arrived, Fred went on about how 'Taylor had arrived in his new Range Rover and was carrying a dozen bottles of whisky and a carton of pipe tobacco.' Fred's blue Range Rover was called the 'Blue Berry' so my red one became the 'Red Cherry'.

By the time I arrived in Alice the NTEHP team had taken over one of the old hospital houses in Hartley Street as a base. It was immediately christened 'Trachoma House'. With my arrival

Setting up a clinic tent in a remote community with the 'Red Cherry' and the 'Blue Berry'

we now worked as two teams. Each team would go out and work in communities for two weeks or so before returning to rest briefly and restock. On the return it was great to have a shower, clean clothes, sleep on a bed and catch up with the members of the other team, go out and have a pub meal and a beer. The Outback Cafe had great big steaks, so Buzza always went there.

Except when we were in a town we almost always slept out in the open in swags and sleeping bags. We would make a fire to cook our meals and then we usually sat around and talked, sung, or watched Buzza beat Fred at chess. Given the rugged roads and the long periods we were on them, we could not take beer or wine to drink nor glasses to drink from. The solution was to pass a bottle of whisky around. One would remove the bottle cap, fill the cap with whisky, drink the cap-full, replace the cap and pass the bottle on. Fred used to smoke Erinmore Flake from a square tin, I smoked Erinmore Mixture from a round tin. (At that time it was common to smoke, anti-smoking messages were a long way in the future. Many fell under the spell of the tobacco companies' advertising or their handing out small packages of free cigarettes and quickly became addicted.) It took me until the mid-1980s and a lot of encouragement from Liz, to finally give up and to 'stop smelling of tobacco smoke'!

Fred and Trevor Buzzacott playing chess late at night

My team visited the communities south of Alice Springs and worked through the APY Lands to the Western Australian border. I paid a short visit to the Petermann Ranges where the four of us as university students had been bogged for a week in 1966. The area looked exactly the same. While we worked south of Alice Springs, Fred and his team worked around Alice and further north.

Membership of the teams changed often. Fred or I would do the trachoma grading and the visiting ophthalmologist or an ophthalmology registrar with each team would do the follow-up eye exams as required. We had an orthoptist with us who would perform the vision screening. We usually had an optometrist or optical dispenser with us and, at times, a microbiologist. We always had an Aboriginal person who undertook the community liaison and there was usually another one or two to help with the work. In each community several community members would be recruited to help us.

Fred was a great exerciser. He would run regularly. When in New Zealand he would climb mountains. For a while, when we were working in the field, we carried a stationary exercise bike on the roof of the Range Rover. It was tricky to run around communities at night and we worked sunup to sundown. With the exercise bike we could at least get some exercise in the evenings.

Archie Cochrane with one of the community members in the APY Lands

While we were working in Central Australia, Archie Cochrane came to visit and see what we were up to. An exciting visitor: Archie was one of the world's leading epidemiologists, a medical giant. He had led the landmark studies of the coal miners in the Rhondda Fach in Wales. Fred had worked with him there for a year. Archie had shown the link between exposure to coal dust and lung disease. This was ground-breaking work, changed how the miners worked, and defined modern epidemiology. (Later, the Cochrane Collaboration was established in his memory. The Collaboration is a global network of leading epidemiologic researchers who distil research findings to guide health policy and medical practice.)

I flew back to Adelaide with Archie. On the plane Archie asked me if I had been involved in student politics.

'Oh yes. While a med student I'd been president of the Australian Medical Students Society. What about you?'

'Well, I left my medical studies to go and fight with the Internationals in the Spanish Civil War.'

I felt a bit insignificant at that point. Nevertheless, we had a very friendly and interactive conversation. To have time with someone of his expertise and experience was inspiring.

A bit later Fred and I had a week's trip back to Melbourne to participate in the Royal Australasian College of Surgeons meeting. It was so good to see Liz and our two children again, even though it was a busy time with all the meetings. Liz was still working hard on her PhD plus managing the children who were growing up fast. Our tiny house filled with people—again Liz managed with equanimity. During this brief visit there was a total eclipse of the sun that was fully realised in Melbourne. It occurred in the middle of the day and the whole area went quiet, the birds stopped singing and it was very dark. The visit seemed so brief. I missed them at least as much as they missed me. It was hard to go back to the field.

As we worked through the communities, we saw many people in need of surgery. Some were blind from cataract. Others had trichiasis from trachoma where the in-turned lashes had scarred the cornea, the front of the eye, and eventually blinded them. Others had pterygium, a fleshy growth over the front of the eye. With help from Gordon Briscoe, the Department of Health, and the Army, Fred had organised for the Australian Army Field Hospital to be set up in Amata in the APY Lands.

The soldiers, of course, knew exactly what they had to do to set things up, but I was meant to organise the ophthalmology side of this. Dick Galbraith came as the senior surgeon. Dick had plenty of experience from his trips to the Solomon Islands of operating in unusual circumstances. He was an excellent surgeon, a very good teacher, fun to be with, and we got along very well. He had previously worked with Gerry Crock at the Eye and Ear and there was a certain degree of competition between the Eye and Ear and the Royal Melbourne Hospital. Dick brought his team from the Royal Melbourne which included his wife,

Penny, who was the theatre nurse. Donald Ferguson, a local Pitjantjatjara man who was working with us, coordinated the patients and the community.

The Army group was led by Brigadier William ('Digger') James, the then Director of Army Medical Services. He was an expert on field hospitals. After stepping on a land mine in the Korean War in horrifying but heroic circumstances, he was patched up in a US MASH unit and hospitalised in Japan and Melbourne. He lost his left foot, was awarded the Military Cross, quit the army, trained as a doctor, and re-joined the army as a medic, commanded the 8th Field Ambulance during the Battle of Nui Dat in Vietnam, and then worked for St John's Ambulance in the aftermath of the Biafran Civil War in Nigeria. He was a very nice man to talk with, but he also knew exactly how things needed to be done in true army style. Everything ran smoothly under his command. (Later, as an ex-Major-General, he would become the president of the Returned Services League.)

The Army Field Hospital in Amata SA, November 1976

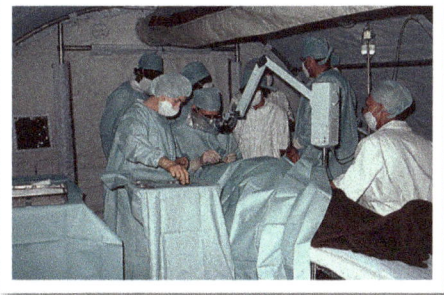
Operating in the Operating Tent in Amata SA

The Army brought their gear and troops in by truck and plane. They set up large tents for the patients and the patients all had camp stretcher beds and army blankets. The operating theatre was a smaller inflatable white tent set up inside a much bigger tent. The operating theatre tent was filled with sterile air pumped in under pressure. This meant that we had a safe and sterile environment in which to operate. We felt like we were in scenes from the TV series *M*A*S*H*. With all the Army's support, the superb staff, and the support for the patients, the many surgeries went well and we did a lot of surgeries!

The day after surgery the cataract patients would have their eye pads removed and would be given a pair of the heavy cataract glasses that were used at that time. The patients' responses to seeing again was emotional and moving. To see the reactions of those who had been blind for years as, suddenly, they realised that they could see again, was heart stopping. Their hands would go up in the air and their faces would break into huge grins. There was cheering and applause, and clapping and singing. The soldiers and others would gather around to watch this and to share the feelings of joy and satisfaction. The soldiers were excited to be doing some real medical work. Since they had been withdrawn from Vietnam they had only been on exercises, putting a bandage on one leg, then taking it off and putting it on the other leg. However, here they were treating and looking after real patients and restoring sight to the blind. It was almost biblical.

The first dressing after surgery: Dick Galbraith and David Kaufman standing behind the patients

Fred

The Army pilots would fly those from more distant communities into Amata and fly them home after they had recovered. They flew in a Pilatus Porter, a plane used extensively as a spotter in the Vietnam War. When all the patients had left, I got a lift back to Alice Springs in it; the most extraordinary flight of my life. Maybe not as beautifully stunning as the helicopter ride in the Antarctic but very exciting. We flew at about 10 metres above the ground, going up and down over sand dunes, trees and other low-level obstacles. We were running a bit late, and the pilots were worried they would not arrive in time to pick up supplies for the evening. They repeatedly tried to call through to their base in Alice, but there was no answer. Then, out of the blue, came an American voice saying, 'Army, can I help you?' The speaker was in some sort of US surveillance outfit that had picked up our pilot's calls; he offered to pass the message on to Alice. This was an eye opener for me. I knew we were not that far away from Pine Gap, the highly secretive US intelligence and tracking base outside Alice, but this sort of surveillance, well understood by my pilots, was totally new to me.

For about two weeks we had one of the largest eye hospitals in the Southern Hemisphere. It was terrific that we did such a lot of good there, but then, almost in the blink of an eye, it was gone.

The trachoma teams were due to head back to Sydney for a break over Christmas. We headed off to one or two more communities, then, after having examined the community at Fink in the south-east of the Northern Territory, we headed home in the Red Cherry and a Land Rover along a very questionable 'track' that, more or less, ran alongside the rail line between Alice and Port Augusta. The track was so bad that, for a short while, we drove over the railway tracks themselves, bumping over the sleepers.

It was hot. Even the butter in the car fridge melted. The thermometer we had topped out at its maximum, 52^0 C. We arrived in Oodnadatta exhausted. By chance, *The Ghan*, the train that ran along that railway line from Alice to Adelaide, was heading south and was due to stop in Oodnadatta a little while after we arrived. With a fair bit of hard talking, we got our vehicles on board and joined the passenger car to Port Augusta. What a relief! Instead of nearly expiring in the heat and bouncing like the pea in a referee's whistle, we were able to relax in 'luxury' on the train for long hours.

We were off-loaded in Port Augusta and drove through to Broken Hill in New South Wales. Then on to Menindee and Wilcannia where we examined the people in these communities. We finally arrived in Sydney on Christmas Eve. Liz, Kate and Bart had flown up from Melbourne and were waiting for me there.

We all stayed with my Aunty Lib and Uncle Stuart in Sydney. Liz was so exhausted she slept for two days and only got up for water and the toilet. We had a lovely Christmas Day together with our Sydney relatives and then as a family drove back to Melbourne on Boxing Day, a long drive, but, for me, to get home, to our own house, and to be able to spend all day with my wife and our two children was nirvana.

We were back on the road in mid-January. We started in Kalgoorlie in Western Australia. At this time Dr (Para) Pararajasegaram joined us. Para was a Sri Lankan ophthalmologist who had trained with Fred in London. A gentler, more caring man you would not meet anywhere; his empathy and wonderful sense of humour was a tonic to patients and co-workers alike. Among the many volunteers who helped with the work for each team, usually ophthalmologists and optometrists, but also others who came for a few weeks to help in one way or another, was my father who drove with me across the Nullarbor Plain to Kalgoorlie. We had done about half that trip together when I was about 14. The vehicles were better, but the roads were still the same very wide dirt roads with lots of potholes and ruts hidden by dust. Nowadays, of course, all are sealed. My dad stayed on

Fred

Sorting gear in Kalgoorlie: Dr Pararajasegaram, my father, Fred (with his back to us), Gabi, Brian Brown and Reg Murray

to help with the field work in Fred's team for the next few weeks.

My team visited communities in the Goldfields region and the communities along the highway towards Perth. Then I went to Cunderdin, a small community 160 km east of Perth. Other epidemiologic studies had been done there so I had some help in recruiting non-Indigenous study subjects. Because I was to spend the next nine months working with Fred, it seemed a good idea to collect data on Aboriginal eye health and possibly write it up as a Doctor of Medicine thesis, the equivalent of a medical PhD at the time. As part of

Measuring refractive error with a retinoscope

my research thesis, I had started collecting data on the eye health of Aboriginal people. One study was to compare the visual acuity and refraction of Aboriginal adults with that of non-Indigenous Australians. I was also looking at the causes and distribution of blindness and their relation to exposure environmental factors.

In Cunderdin I examined all the non-Indigenous adults aged between 20 and 30 years. I took 20 to 30, rather than 20 to 29 (as is usual in epidemiological studies) to try to avoid confusion when I was recruiting Aboriginal subjects whose exact age was uncertain. I measured each person's vision on a special 'Illiterate E log-MAR Chart', a vision test chart that starts with large letters and went down to very small letters, the size of the letters in each row following a logarithmic progression. The 'E' was used rather than other letters as people with limited literacy could easily point in the direction the E was oriented. To keep the chart well-lit but out of the shade or shadows I had a small music stand with a white umbrella on top; this gave good illumination. I also

The Illiterate E chart used for testing vision, mounted under an umbrella to provide even illumination

Fred

measured everyone's refraction with retinoscopy after dilating their pupils with drops. This was the most objective method then available. I did similar measurements on all Aboriginal adults in the communities that I visited over the next six months.

My data confirmed that healthy Aboriginal people had much better vision than non-Indigenous Australians, and better, in fact, than any other group in the world. We call 'normal vision' 6/6, or in the old terminology using feet, 20/20. This means that at 6 metres the person could read the letters a so-called 'normal' person can read at 6 metres. Poorer vision might be 6/12, when at 6 metres a person could only read the letters the 'normal' person could read at 12 metres. Fifty percent of Aboriginal adults could see 6/2.4: at 6 metres they could read what so-called 'normal' people would only be able to read from 2.4 metres away. Only 20 percent of non-Indigenous adults could see as well as this. More amazing was finding that some Aboriginal people could read 6/1.5, that is reading the letters at 6 metres that the

The woman who could read the second bottom line of letters when the chart was 12 metres away with each eye alone and both

'normal' person would only see at a distance of 1.5 metres. Some Indigenous adults could see 6/1.5 with both eyes open, but one woman could do this with each eye on its own. She could see four times better than defined 'normal vision'.

Much later I sent this information off to *The Guinness Book of Records*, but they did not take it up. Very much later, I was contacted by some astronomers who were examining the Aboriginal descriptions of the stars and constellations recorded in the mid-nineteenth century. Stars described were invisible to the astronomers when they looked up into the night sky. After discussions about my findings, they went back with binoculars and could easily fill in all the missing stars that the Aboriginal people had described and could see with their naked eyes.

I also showed that Aboriginal people had almost no myopia or short-sightedness. While myopia can be an advantage in industrialised societies for reading, writing, counting money and many other societal-related things, it is a real disadvantage for hunter-gatherers who need excellent distant vision to spot game or plant food and to navigate, rather than good near

The need for reading glasses for near work

vision. Although myopia is, in part, genetically determined, later studies have also shown the importance of childhood time spent outdoors to prevent myopia. Aboriginal children have plenty of time outdoors. In many Asian countries rapidly increasing rates of myopia had become a very significant public health issue (See page 255).

Although they didn't have myopia, Indigenous Australians all would develop presbyopia—difficulty seeing things up close—with age, so reading glasses are still needed.

In March 1977, after Cunderdin, we drove back to Kalgoorlie and then on to Alice, examining people in the communities as we went. On the way we again passed through Docker River and the Petermann Ranges where I and three other university students had been bogged. Still no change.

On a long open and barren stretch of road we saw a cloud of dust approaching. We stopped and waited for the oncoming vehicle to reach us. It also stopped and an elderly man stepped out.

Measuring glasses for a patient who had had cataract surgery who we met on the road

'Hello, how are you going? It is hot out here. My name's Hugh Taylor.'

'Yes, it is hot. My name's Nugget Coombs.'

He wanted to know what we were doing out there. I explained the work we were doing. I knew who he was but was amazed to see him in the middle of the outback. He had recently retired as the first governor of the Reserve Bank and then chair of the Office of Aboriginal Affairs. He was out and about visiting remote communities. You never know who you might meet.

On the way we saw some of the people we had operated on in Amata, some of whom needed an examination on the road and their glasses checked.

Once Fred and I reached Alice, we prepared for the distribution of antibiotic treatment for trachoma for all the communities around the town and in Central Australia. We recruited Aboriginal people from each community and medical students to help with the distribution of co-trimoxazole, a sulphonamide trimethoprim combination antibiotic. It had to be taken by everyone, in each community, twice a day, for 21 days. This was an amazing and unheard-of undertaking.

There were very few Aboriginal health workers then and most of the community volunteers were senior elders, like Shorty Lungkata Tjungurrayi, a senior Pintupi man. Shorty and his family were among the last to come into settlements from the Western Desert in the late 1960s and only then started painting on board and bark with modern paints. His paintings now hang in galleries around the world. His 1972 'Women's Dreaming (two Women)' regarded as a classic is in the Art Gallery of NSW. He was a senior *ngangkari* (traditional healer). I was amazed to walk past him and a group of other Aboriginal elders and hear Shorty, a very traditional man whose whole life had been spent in a small family group in the desert until a handful of years before, arguing the case that LandCruisers were much better than Land Rovers. A knowledgeable motoring critic!

Fred

How we found all the medical students to help, I really don't know. Most were from Australia, but some were from overseas. Fred's staff had got the word out one way or another. Each community member was assisted and supported by a student. We spent a week training in Alice with everyone going over what needed to be done, especially in culturally sensitive ways.

Because we were to be in Alice for a while, Liz and our children had come to visit. Kate was 5 and Bart 3. It was lovely for me to have them and let them see the work that we were doing. During the training sessions Kate went on stage with Fred to

Right: Fred with Kate teaching health workers and medical students how to follow the antibiotic with a mouthful of orange juice.

Below: Liz with Kate and Bart having lunch on the road with a liaison worker as we go to check how antibiotic treatment is going in a remote community.

show how the medicine should be given to young children and to wash it down with a drink of orange juice. Fred was aware of the work done on vitamin C deficiency in Aboriginal children by Archivides (Archie) Kalorkerinos, a Greek Australian doctor who had worked for years in the small community of Collarenebri in western New South Wales. He made strong claims for the need for vitamin C for Aboriginal children. Given the often grossly deficient western diets they were fed, we used orange juice to wash the medicine down rather than just water. Liz, Kate and Bart came with me as I went to some of the communities to see how the treatment was progressing. I was proud and pleased to have my family with me, to spend time together, and they enjoyed it too.

At that time, we treated nearly 11 000 people in Central Australia and with three subsequent treatment programs in other regions the NTEHP treated another 15 000 people.

We left the Alice and drove back to Western Australia to continue the field work. The other team had covered a lot of communities there while I was in and around Alice. I caught up with the team in communities around Shark Bay and Useless Loop. At first, I was tricked by the name 'Useless Loop', last in a long list of communities we had in a computer printout. I thought it was some computer jargon for odd data or left-over data! It was actually a real town, a closed company town producing tons of salt in huge saline crystallisation ponds. After that we moved on to Carnarvon, Port Hedland and into the desert and on to Jigalong. The Ophthalmia Range is in this region, named by the explorer Ernest Giles; he caught trachoma, or Sandy Blight, there and temporally lost his vision in 1876.

Then it was time for me to go back to Alice to set up the second army field hospital exercise at Utopia, over 250 km north. Here, Alyawarre people speaking Alyawarre, the landowners of 3500 square km under the Territory's Land Rights Act of 1976, were our hosts.

Fred

This time Dick Galbraith and his team included another ophthalmologist, David Kaufmann. David and I had gone to school and trained in ophthalmology at the Eye and Ear together. Again, this surgical exercise went well. We did a range of operations, mainly cataract and correcting the in-turned eye lashes from trachoma. Again, the first post-operative dressing and the removal of the eye pads was a time of excitement and joy. The astonishing and exciting lesson was that one could assemble resources in such a remote area so that world-class eye surgery services could be provided. When it was all over the Army folded everything up and left. It would be years before any real eye services returned to this region, let alone regular ongoing eye care. As successful as it had been, temporary army hospitals were not a long-term, sustainable solution for providing eye care in outback Australia.

Fred and I then went to the College of Ophthalmology congress in Melbourne. It was a flying visit, but I had a little time to see Liz and the children and to catch up a bit. Liz was working flat out finishing her PhD thesis. It was particularly hard to leave her and the children that time.

Fred and I then flew to Broome in Western Australia and examined people in multiple communities in the Kimberly region including Fitzroy Crossing. Barrie Jones, a leading expert in trachoma and the Professor of Ophthalmology at the University of London, joined us for a few days. Originally from New Zealand, Barrie was the first professor of ophthalmology appointed in the UK and had done highly significant work on trachoma, particularly in Iran. Some years later, when I was at Johns Hopkins, Barrie tried to recruit me to London.

A little later, in mid-June 1977, I flew from Derby to Melbourne. Two more children's birthdays missed, as well as another of Liz's; not good.

We had to pack our house and our things so Liz and me and our two children who now had just turned 4 and 6, could fly to Baltimore, Maryland. I was to start a Corneal Fellowship at the Wilmer Eye Institute at the Johns Hopkins Hospital there and Liz, who had just submitted her PhD, was hoping to find a postdoctoral fellowship at the National Institute of Health, though this was not yet confirmed.

After I had left for Baltimore, the NTEHP teams continued their work across Northern Australia until they reached Far North Queensland, where political problems arose. Joh Bjelke-Petersen was the very conservative premier of Queensland, and he had a state election coming up. Some of the community liaison officers working with the NTEHP were accused of encouraging local community members to register to vote. This outraged the premier. He insisted that the prime minister stop this work and pull the NTEHP out of Queensland. Fred had no option. The work in Queensland stopped. The teams moved on to New South Wales and Victoria.

Six months later in April 1978 the way was open for the work to resume in Queensland. I was a busy corneal fellow in Baltimore when Fred called me.

'Taylor, I want you in Brisbane on the first of May to lead a team up the Queensland Coast.'

I explained I had a presentation to give at the annual meeting of the Association for Research in Vision and Ophthalmology, ARVO. My presentation was scheduled for the day before.

'Even if I could travel on the Concord, I could not get there at that time, not to mention the time changes involved with crossing the International Dateline.' The Concord of course did not fly to Australia; I was just trying to make the point.

I arrived in Brisbane a day or so later than the impossible date Fred had suggested. Thereafter Fred would say, 'Bloody Taylor, he expects to fly on the bloody Concord.'

However, all was good. I led a team that worked up the Queensland coast from Brisbane to Cairns. It was great fun to be back doing this work again, catching up with colleagues, and seeing some wonderful people and the spectacularly beautiful Queensland Coast that I had not seen before. The communities along the coast were mainly in towns and so quite different from those in the remote communities in the outback. Meanwhile, Fred led a team up through the outback communities in central Queensland. We joined up for a while at Charters Towers and then I went back to the coast and up to Cairns where I finished. I left 'examining the Cape' to Fred and his team.

I left Cairns to travel to Alice Springs and then on to one of the remote communities. There I examined the children a year after they had received their antibiotic treatment. Before treatment about one third of children had well-established trachoma. One year later that had dropped to only 5 percent and most of those children had only minor signs of trachoma. At that time, a single dose of treatment was thought to be all that was needed. That understanding would change over time as trachoma would gradually return.

My trip back to Baltimore was not direct. Fred had been invited to attend the inaugural General Assembly that launched the International Agency of the Prevention of Blindness, IAPB, in Oxford, UK. Fred was obviously busy with the NTEHP field work and so could not go. He suggested I should return to Baltimore via the UK and attend this meeting. It was an extraordinary chance to meet the world's leaders in eye care and so establish many contacts and associations that developed further over time.

This was a historical moment in the global work to address blindness and vision loss. The International *Association* for the Prevention of Blindness had been formed in 1929, just as the Wall Street Crash occurred and the Great Depression followed. The Association did not achieve much and disappeared during the Second World War. In 1975 a new International *Agency* for the Prevention of Blindness was started by John Wilson of the Royal Commonwealth Society for the Blind and Edward Maumenee, the president of the International Council of Ophthalmology. This followed the WHO World Health Day that year which focussed on Blindness. IAPB brought together all the non-government organisations working on eye care and linked them with WHO. WHO changed its Trachoma program to become the Prevention of Blindness program in 1978. Together IAPB and WHO started to work in a concerted partnership to address global eye care.

After the IAPB, it was back to Baltimore. My trachoma days seemed over.

After all the field work finished there remained the massive task of putting it all together and writing a report. After winding up in a community, the community was always given a copy of the findings. All 62 116 Aboriginal and 38 616 non-Indigenous

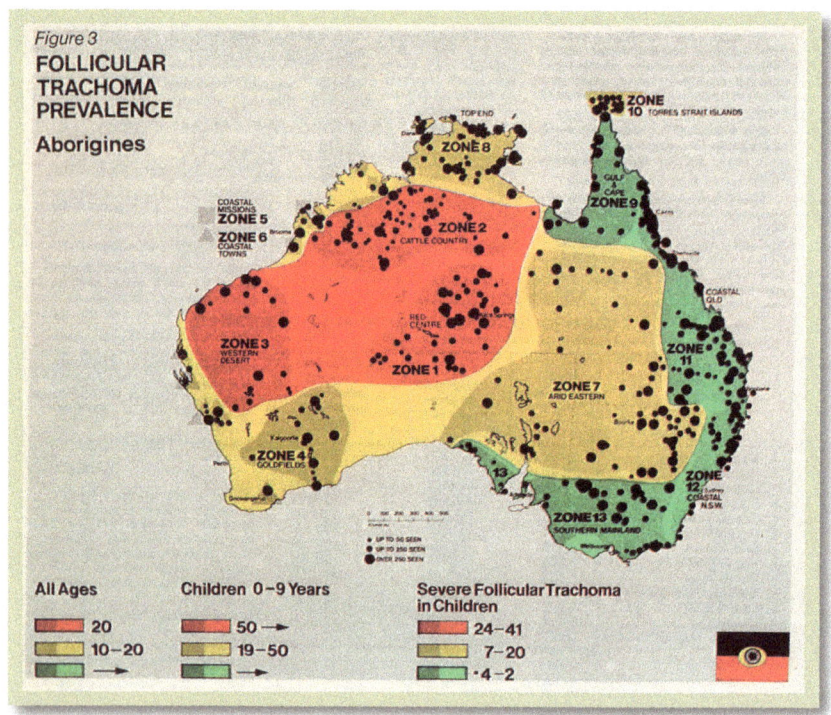

The distribution of trachoma across Australia found by the NTEHP
(*Source: The NTEHP Report*)

people had been examined. Aboriginal people had 10 times more blindness. Trachoma was widespread, affecting 11 percent of Aboriginal children overall, and over 40 percent in some regions. The proportion of Aboriginal people of all ages with active trachoma or scarring was over 30 percent; for non-Aboriginals it was less than 1 percent.

In 1977 I still thought I would become a corneal surgeon, working primarily in private practice and doing some public work. I had not had time to work through all that I had seen or the meaning of the experiences I'd had while working with Fred. We had been so busy doctoring and on the road, there had been little time for reflection. I had signed up for the corneal fellowship at the Wilmer, and it was going well. However, a seed had been sown. More and more I found that I was reflecting deeply on what I had learned and what I had seen and heard in remote Australia.

Opening Eyes

4

Out of Baltimore

*There is a saying in Baltimore that
crabs may be prepared in fifty ways
and that all of them are good.*

H L Mencken

I started my corneal fellowship with Walter Stark, Head of the Corneal Service at the Wilmer Institute and the Johns Hopkins Hospital in Baltimore, Maryland, in Jimmy Carter's first year as president, July 1977.

The year before, Walter had phoned me. 'Would you like to start your corneal fellowship more or less straightaway? An opportunity has come up?'

'Thank you, but no. I'm very sorry, but I simply can't. I have to finish my ophthalmology training here and I still have six months to go.' (The call came before Fred Hollows gained approval for the NTEHP work to count as the end of my training.)

Later, chatting in the registrars' quarters, Lawrie Hirst, who was a year ahead of me, said he was looking for a corneal fellowship. The position in the UK he had hoped to start had fallen through. I suggested Laurie contact Walter. He did, took up the offer and took off.

In 1977 there were no direct flights across the Pacific, so travelling with young children was difficult. We flew from Melbourne to Fiji and spent two nights in a hotel near the airport.

Opening Eyes

Above: Me, Bart and Kate flying across the Pacific, my pipe totally unacceptable today!
Below: The children swimming at the apartments in Mt Washington, 1977

We had left in the middle of Australia's winter, but it was hot in Fiji. We asked the hotel staff if we could buy bathers for the children so they could swim in the pool and we were told not to worry about bathers for the children. The kids loved that pool. Next stop was Hawaii, where we discovered that Americans did not approve of children swimming nude even on a fairly remote beach, but we were able to buy bather pants and that was fine. In San Francisco we spent a night with one of Liz's colleagues. Then onto Los Angeles for a day at Disneyland. Bart grizzled a bit and that night his ear drum burst which explained his not feeling well. Once in Baltimore we had to buy new bathers for the children, bathers of a type that met local acceptance.

Liz, our two young children and I arrived in Baltimore in summertime. We moved into the condominium Lawrie and his family had rented during the previous year. They moved into a more suburban Baltimore house because Laurie was going to spend more time at Wilmer. He did a neuro-ophthalmological fellowship with Neil Miller and then joined the corneal service at Wilmer. (Later, he was appointed head of the ophthalmology department in St Louis, before returning to Brisbane as the University of Queensland's professor of ophthalmology.)

The condominium was in Mt Washington, a leafy, green suburb where many Hopkins staff lived. The block was large and included a community swimming pool.

While at the pool in our apartment complex Liz met Theo Greene, the wife of another doctor at Hopkins, Bruce Greene. Bruce was the Chief Resident in Medicine and who was interested in tropical diseases. They had three boys, the elder two who roughly correlated in age with our two. Theo was a godsend. She became Liz's support person. When we arrived, Liz was without family support or friends, and she still had to find a post-doctoral job. She had submitted her PhD thesis but had come without a confirmed post-doctoral position. There simply had not been time enough to apply for one. Shortly after we'd arrived, a school friend of Liz's, Wendy Breitner, moved into the neighbourhood with her family. Her husband was a psychiatrist who had joined the Johns Hopkins medical faculty and worked on dementia. Suddenly, Liz had two supporting 'sisters'.

To be a corneal fellow at the Wilmer Institute at Johns Hopkins, one of the world's leading eye research institutes, was a privilege for me. I had intended to stay for a year, or maybe two, then return to Melbourne, presumably to go into private practice.

It took us a while to sort things out domestically. We had to get two cars so we were each mobile. Liz thought she might get a position with an endocrinologist she had met earlier. He was based in the National Institute of Health, NIH, in Bethesda, 40 miles or a 50-minute drive away. However, after receiving stern advice from this notable NIH chief that travelling to Bethesda daily from Baltimore would not be a good option, she was referred to the National Institute on Aging, NIA, located in East Baltimore. Her work there followed on from her PhD in some ways, particularly using micro-assays to measure small levels of hormone molecules. Liz was able to get Kate into the local city school and Bart into a suitable nursery.

I had some money from the McComas Fellowship from Melbourne University. When it was set up in the 1960s to support young trainees my family had no idea that later I might be an awardee. I also had another small fellowship from Melbourne, but our funds were tight. We had not really understood how to manage our money in the US. For example, we had paid for our two second-hand cars in full and that took up a good deal of our available cash on hand. One evening I invited a senior visiting Australian ophthalmologist to join us for dinner. Liz had only one sausage, brown rice and not much else in the fridge, but as an amazing cook, she managed to make a very acceptable meal. In the new year financial constraints eased a bit. Liz had a job and Walter Stark was able to find some money from the Wilmer.

Walter was kind, generous and full of information. There was a lot to learn from him about corneal disease and cataract surgery, and he had an almost endless stream of interesting patients to see. One thing that did surprise me was seeing Walter in the middle of a consultation, light up a cigarette and smoke it in front of a patient, something I had never seen in Australia. He was ophthalmologist to the Baltimore Colts, screening players to see if they had eye problems, and attend football games in case someone was injured. A player for a team out of New York, the Buffalo Bills, had heard good things about Walter's clinic and came to have his eyes checked. He gave me a portrait photo of himself inscribed 'To Kate and Bart, love from O J'. O J Simpson was controversially acquitted of the murders of his former wife and her friend 18 years later.

With some other residents, I was taken to a Baltimore Orioles home game. I was a veteran spectator of many cricket matches and Aussie football games, but baseball was all new. The games were exciting, crowds noisy, and the Orioles often won; our family became dedicated O's supporters. That first game was my introduction to crab cakes, which became dear to my taste buds.

The other corneal fellow was Claude Cowan, an African-American ophthalmologist who had been through medical school at the African-American Howard University in Washington DC. Established two years after the Civil War, it has the world's largest and most comprehensive libraries of black studies, not only of America but of Africa and beyond. Much of what I learned about American history and racial issues came out of talking with Claude. The details of the events that saw US Army troops with fixed bayonets on the streets of Baltimore nine years earlier, following the murder of the Rev Martin Luther King and protest, was part of his peoples' story, a revelation to me.

As fellows, Claude and I could examine patients and assist Walter at surgeries, but we did not get to operate as such. Walter was an early adopter of the intra-ocular lens, IOL. As registrars in Melbourne we were taught intracapsular cataract surgery where the patient's whole lens, the cataract included, was removed and patients given heavy cataract or aphakic glasses. The first IOLs were used in such patients' eyes. Extracapsular cataract surgery was a new surgical method where the lens matter is sucked out and removed leaving the lens capsule or 'bag' intact. The newer intra-ocular lenses could be put into the bag so people could see without needing glasses. Later phacoemulsification was developed: it used ultrasound to remove the old lens material. Walter was a leader in the new surgeries so Claude and I learned by assisting him. Later, when I joined the faculty, I taught other senior ophthalmologists at Wilmer how to do this new surgery.

Walter was particularly interested in corneal graft rejection and the role of the HLA—Human Leukocyte Antigens—and immunocompatibility. He supervised a small laboratory run by immunologist Seth Wolf (who was married to Charity Fox!) and later by Elaine Young. My lab task was to establish cultures of corneal epithelial cells, the cells on the *surface* of the cornea, in small plastic petri dishes. Another fellow, Monte DelMonte, was to grow corneal endothelial cells, the cells on the *inside* layer of the cornea. We had, more or less, one or two half days each week in the lab. We tried all sorts of things to establish reliable methods. The late 1970s were very early days in the development of cell culture, now a standard procedure, routine even. But then, no-one had been able to establish culture lines for these particular cells. We had some success and found the cells grew much better using a supportive layer of fibrocytes, fibre-generating cells. (Johns Hopkins is famous for establishing the first ongoing human cell culture, the HeLa cells, a line cultured from the cervical cells taken from a cancer patient, *Henrietta Lacks*, in 1951. The first immortal human cell line, HeLa cells have been dividing and growing indefinitely ever since.)

I had taken my collected data on the vision and the refraction of Australian Indigenous and non-Indigenous adults with me to the Wilmer. I had also collected data on the presence of cataract and corneal changes in Aboriginal people across a wide geographic area. So I started to work through these data in my 'spare time' over the next year or so.

Technical people at Wilmer helped me transfer my data from sheets of paper to their small mainframe computer. This was a vast improvement on the data analyses I used for my research as a medical student eight years previously! Others provided further help with the analysis, including Frederich (Rick) Ferris, then a Wilmer resident. (In Australia young doctors doing their ophthalmology training are called 'registrars', in the US 'residents'.) Rick was always ready to help and share a laugh, a great friend. (When he completed his ophthalmic training Rick moved to the National Eye Institute in Bethesda. He became one of the most famous of ophthalmic epidemiologists and ran huge long-term clinical trials that transformed eye care. He and Emily Chew became close collaborators and enduring dear friends.)

Once analysed, my data showed the low prevalence of myopia and refractive error, and the vastly superior visual acuity of Aboriginal people.

The later got attention from an unexpected quarter, when I presented the visual acuity data to Wilmer insiders.

Rick was fascinated by the E-chart I had used to measure vision. The letters followed the LogMAR principles and had smaller letters than most charts, so that I could test finer vision (see page 67-68). The LogMAR design made charts much more useful for measuring small changes in vision. Rick was then about to help set up a large clinical trial on the treatment of diabetes changes in the eye, the Early Treatment of Diabetic Retinopathy Study, ETDRS. Having seen my presentation he took the LogMAR principles and designed the ETDRS vision chart that immediately became the standard for future clinical trials in eye care.

One of my fellow students at Ormond College, Ian Barton, was working at Commonwealth Scientific and Industry Research Organisation, CSIRO, Australia's national science agency. He had just published the first maps of UV-B radiation—the part of the sun's rays that cause sunburn, skin darkening and thickening, melanoma and eye problems—across Australia.

I combined his maps with my data on the locations of the people I had seen with eye disease. This showed, for the first time, the strong correlation of UV-B exposure with the development of cataract, pterygium and climatic droplet keratopathy, a clouding of the cornea.

I put the correlations together as a thesis called 'Vision of Australian Aborigines' and submitted for a Doctor of Medicine degree at the University of Melbourne.

Somehow, Archie Cochrane, whom I had met while working with Fred, was asked to be one of the reviewers. He wrote: 'This is the best MD thesis I have ever read—and I have read many.'

What a huge honour and an inspiration for a young person embarking on a career of public health ophthalmology!

At the end of my first year at Wilmer, I went to a Christmas party put on by the Immunology Laboratory people. Arthur (Art) Silverstein, head of the lab, chatted with me, asked about what I was doing, and what I had done before coming to Wilmer. Art was one of the first immunologists to work full-time on eye issues, an unremarkable move now. He was interested in the work I had done with Fred and the NTEHP. He asked, 'How easy is it to get trachoma?'

'Oh, it's so easy. All you have to do is be reinfected often.'

'Would you like to set up an animal model of trachoma to prove that?'

'Why not? It would be easy.'

That easily made agreement profoundly changed my work trajectory, my way ahead, my life. Happy Christmas!

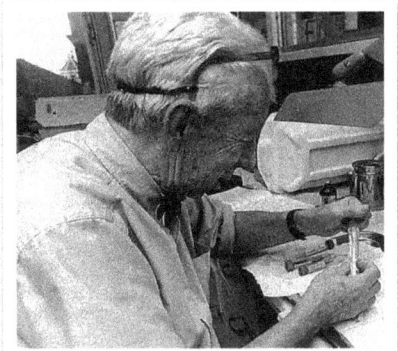

Arthur Silverstein in lab, 1983   Bob Prendergast

Experiments on monkeys are a challenge.

We knew that monkey models obviously and closely approximate the responses seen in human primates. Early trachoma studies had been done in monkeys. One can examine their largish eyes with standard medical ophthalmological instruments and their immune responses closely follow those of humans. Some work on chlamydial infection had been done on guinea pigs, but today most of the chlamydial research is done in mice. Although mice are small and an easy animal to study, their immune responses do differ in many ways from the immune responses of primates: human or monkey. Furthermore, their eyes are tiny and hard to examine and test.

Art arranged for us to receive a small grant to get things started. We went to Fort Douglas, the US Biological Research Center, to explore how we could borrow Physical Containment Level 3 cages, called P3s, in which to keep the infected monkeys. These cages were sophisticated, with pressure-controlled airlocks, special vents and filters, and more, to stop the infection spreading. At that time the US had banned all offensive biological weapons. When we were at Fort Douglas, we were told with some pride that 'To have a good defence, you have to know about a good offence.' It was unclear what *they* were working on…

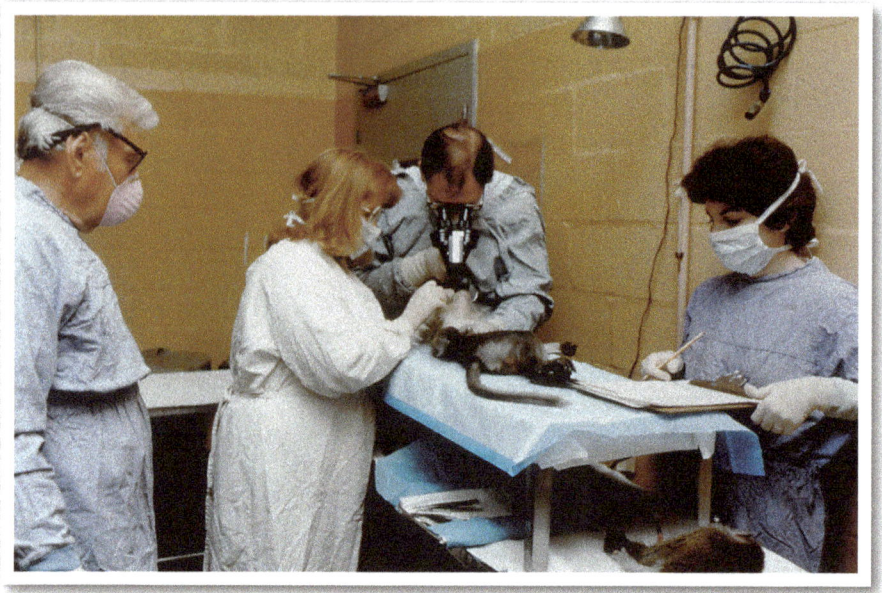

Examining an anesthetised monkey with a hand-help slit lamp. The animal handler and Laurie DeJong holding the eye open on the left, Vivian Velez recording the findings on the right.

We got cages, and then some cynomolgus monkeys. We talked with Chan Dawson, a leader in trachoma at the Proctor Institute in San Francisco, and his colleague Julie Schachter, one of the leading chlamydiologists there. They provided vials of live chlamydia. I set up a small lab led by Shirley Johnson to do the testing we needed. This initially included isolation cultures for chlamydia in chicken eggs and then tissue culture when it became available. Shirley was a microbiological assistant. She had worked in the US Army in Okinawa before joining Art and his group at Wilmer. She ran a ship-shape lab.

Originally, I had said to Art that we should infect the animals daily as I assumed that was what was happening in the Aboriginal communities. However, we couldn't anaesthetise the monkeys so frequently, so we settled on weekly examination and inoculation. Sure enough, the monkeys developed a chronic follicular conjunctivitis indistinguishable from active trachoma.

This continued for as long as we reinfected them. When the reinoculations were stopped the inflammation slowly waned. We followed their clinical responses, culture results, and antibody responses in serum and in tears.

Another group were just given a single inoculum of chlamydia, and they developed the classical chlamydial inclusion conjunctivitis that settled spontaneously over two to three months. When rechallenged, these monkeys showed some minimal protective immunity or slight resistance to infection but still developed inclusion conjunctivitis again, though of a slightly shorter duration.

Art was amazed! After chlamydia were first cultured a number of people, including Art, had tried but failed to produce an animal model of trachoma. I had not known that Art had had an NIH grant to do this, but after a few years, he'd given it up. He had used a single inoculation that failed to produce trachoma. We had shown that *repeated* reinfection was the key to the chronic and ultimately blinding disease.

Meanwhile, we continued to inoculate monkeys every week and over time they developed trachomatous scarring. If we stopped the repeated infections, the clinical signs of inflammation would slowly resolve but the scarring remained.

Other monkeys were challenged with bacterial secondary infections which did not seem to exacerbate their clinical disease significantly. Bob Prendergast was enormously helpful with all these studies and did histology and immuno-histo-chemical studies with us. Bob was a senior ocular immunologist in his own right and worked closely with Art. Bob was very friendly and down to earth. I learned a great deal about immunopathology from Bob.

We studied the cellular immune response with Elaine Young and Judy Whittam Hudson. Judy at that time was a young postdoc and was a highly accomplished laboratory worker. She had previously worked in the chlamydia laboratory in Boston, so came with very relevant experience. (She took charge of the Wilmer immunology laboratory later.)

We experimented immunising the monkeys with various vaccine antigens and different methods of administration. We particularly wanted to stimulate mucosal immunity to protect against infection occurring in the eye as trachoma and other chlamydial infections occur in the body's mucosal surfaces. Some of these studies were done with Nate Pearce. Nate was a leading expert on cholera vaccines in the Hopkins School of Hygiene and Public Health. We included cholera toxin as an adjuvant to specifically stimulate the mucosal immune response. Monkeys that had recovered from a single infection had weak partial protection to a subsequent challenge infection, but they still developed classical trachoma if reinfected frequently. As mentioned, the primary infection only gave partial protection. The vaccine trials showed that we could induce strong local mucosal or systemic antibody responses but these gave little more protection than recovery for a single episode of infection. Similarly, we could induce chlamydia-specific T-cell responses both in the body systemically as a whole and in the conjunctiva, but again they gave no better protection than recovery from an initial infection either. Work has continued for decades to try to find and develop a chlamydial vaccine but to date without luck; none is any better than having an initial infection. Our findings suggest that the discovery of an effective chlamydial vaccine will be tricky.

Tom Quinn arrived in Baltimore in 1981 having studied sexually transmitted and gastrointestinal infections in homosexual men in Seattle with King K Holmes. King was a world expert on sexually-transmitted diseases, particularly HIV/AIDs. Tom's studies had included work on chlamydial rectal infections. He gained an appointment at NIH and a joint appointment in the School of Medicine at Hopkins. To finally get to meet him I had to travel to the international chlamydial meeting in Lund,

Sweden in 1982. Once we met, we became good friends and collaborators. Tom is a very energetic and engaging man, who was perfectly placed at NIH and Hopkins to work on the newly emerging disease that became known as AIDS. Tom had worked on AIDS in Haiti and African countries and became an international AIDS expert.

Starting in 1983 Tom would join us to examine monkeys in our various experiments, looking at different strains of chlamydia and routes of infection. Each week Tom would bring the latest buzz and news from NIH about the big topic of the day, AIDS. It might be fungal; no, it's not fungal; it might be viral, and then it was viral—a new virus—HTLVIII, later named HIV. These hot-topic revelations made the weekly monkey examinations very lively.

We did other studies with Harlan Caldwell, a leading scientist working on chlamydia in the Rocky Mountain Laboratories in Montana. He purified a number of chlamydial antigens. We tested the responses of the monkeys to these new, exciting pure antigens, both as a protective vaccine and as an ocular challenge; and to see if the purified antigens would stimulate a response in animals that had recovered from infection.

Our studies seemed to show that the immune response in the eye was driven by a specific chlamydial heat shock protein, HSP60. Within a day or two, a drop of HSP60 into a monkey's eye induced a marked immune reaction in those that had recovered from a previous chlamydial eye infection and so were sensitised.

Dorothy Patton was working on a monkey model of genital tract infection. Dorothy too worked in Seattle with King Holmes. While we could easily observe the reaction in the eye and collect repeated specimens, similar observation in the female genital tract was far more difficult. Dorothy came up with the great idea to use subcutaneous pockets that held a segment of the monkey's fallopian tube. She could infect multiple pockets, then sample them one at a time. Working in collaboration with us, she found that her studies and findings were surprisingly similar to ours. It suggested that, in this experimental model at least, chlamydial genital tract infection closely follows our findings in the eye.

In 1978–79 academic year I was a busy second-year corneal fellow working in the clinic, writing clinical papers on corneal graft rejection, doing the monkey experiments, and completing my doctoral thesis analysing the NTEHP data I'd collected. Then we started work on onchocerciasis

Dr A Edward Maumenee and Dr Arnall Patz (*Photo: Wilmer Institute*)

Towards the end of that year Edward Maumenee, the director of the Wilmer, was getting ready to retire and Arnall Patz was to take over. They together approached me and invited me to join the faculty as an assistant professor. I had to be the last faculty member appointed by Ed and the first by Arnall. They hoped I would continue the work on trachoma and onchocerciasis as well as my corneal clinical work. Big challenge, but a great offer.

Al Sommer was expected to return to Wilmer in about a year and set up an international public health ophthalmology unit or group. Until then, I should get things started. I had known of Al's leading work on xerophthalmia—a blinding eye change caused by vitamin A deficiency—and I had been looking forward to meeting him when I started at Wilmer. However, Al's residency ended as my corneal fellowship started and he had left for Indonesia before I arrived. I did meet him when he came back briefly to give a lecture on xerophthalmia, but that was it. Then he was in London writing up the results of the ground-breaking studies he had been doing on Vitamin A deficiency, xerophthalmia and its ocular complications. He later won a Lasker Award for this work.

As we were going to stay longer in Baltimore than we intended, we started to look for a house to move into. We looked around the Mt Washington area in which we already lived. One day Liz came back and said, 'I've found the perfect house, and I've already made an offer!' This was before I had even seen it. Neither of us had been inside!

It *was* a great house. Three storeys of timber, or in the US 'frame', on an exposed stone foundation as its basement. It had been built in 1853 as a summer house. In summer it was fine, despite Baltimore's days of 90 degrees, 90 percent humidity and a 90 percent chance of a thunderstorm. In winter we were warm and cosy, the oil-fired boiler's thermostat keeping it that way.

Our house in Mt Washington

Once, when we arrived back after a Christmas in Australia, we found the pipe from the outside oil tank to the inside boiler had frozen. Everything in the house was frozen too, including the first 10 inches or so of the children's aquarium. The poor fish were surviving in the bottom inch or so of very cold water and swimming very slowly. We had to replace the toilets, dishwasher, washing machine and refrigerator.

However, the house was perfect for raising two, then three and finally four young people. We were sorry to leave it when we did.

To keep the family and house together, Liz arranged to have help, either live-in or living close by. This was essential with the amount of travel we did, particularly my extended field-work absences. The household ran well.

We started to see the excellent local theatre, and hear the Baltimore Symphony Orchestra play in the Meyerhoff, the city's superb concert hall. Sergiu Comissiona was the conductor for some time and then David Zinman, who was Australian. Cellist Yo Yo Ma played with the BSO many times.

With a house we could call home, we could have a dog, and a miniature schnauzer, Emily, joined us. She often ran around the garden. One day we were expecting Bob Murphy and a friend to come for lunch. Emily ran out to 'welcome' our guests. She was barking and carrying on. 'Emily! Shut up. Sit! Sit Down. Behave yourself!' Then I caught sight of a bewildered, diminutive Asian woman wide-eyed and frozen in the act of alighting from a car in the driveway. After many embarrassed apologies, that's how we first met Dr Emily Y Chew.

She was a fellow at the Wilmer, and she and Bob married a bit later. Emily moved to the National Eye Institute and worked with Rick Ferris and then independently. She co-ordinated several huge clinical trials that transformed eye care, especially new treatments for diabetic eye disease and age-related macular degeneration, a major cause of blindness in older people. (She is now the director of Division of Epidemiology and Clinical Applications at the NEI. Bob and Emily had three daughters. I am godfather to their second, Emma, an obstetrician and gynaecologist in New York, and Bob is godfather to our younger daughter Phoebe.)

While we lived in Baltimore we often had friends and sometimes relatives stay with us as they travelled through the US. My parents came over for Christmas in 1983, in a very cold winter for Baltimore. Very different to Christmas on the beach in Melbourne! That was the last time I saw my father. He died eight months later. One regular visitor was John Funder. Liz had worked with him while she was doing her PhD at Prince Henry's Hospital. 'Funder', as he is always called, is an endocrinologist and often participated in meetings in the US. He always brought a frozen Australian leg of lamb for us. American lamb just does not taste as good as the grass-fed Australian lamb.

In August 1979 Ed Maumenee asked me to go to Sitapur in north India.

For many years Wilmer residents had gone to Shiraz in Iran for several months to work under Ali Khodadoust. Ali had spent some years working at Wilmer and with Art Silverstein before he returned to Iran. Working with Art, Ali had completed some ground-breaking studies on corneal graft rejection. The Khodadoust Line is still the hallmark of cornael graft rejection. With the expulsion of the Shah and the invasion of the US Embassy in Tehran that year, a rotation to Shiraz was no longer feasible. As the nascent head of a yet-to-be-formed unit, it was my responsibility to see if Sitapur might be an appropriate replacement for residents to rotate there thenceforth.

It was my first trip to India. I flew to New Delhi and after a night in a hotel in Delhi I took the train to Lucknow. Walking the footpaths around the hotel I was amazed to have to tread around the piles of human waste that were deposited there. Nor did I understand the challenge of Indian trains, the crowds, the noise, the bustle, and myriad of the daily goings on. I stayed in Lucknow and then was driven to Sitapur for a few days. I was given the full exposure to rural India, both its strengths and weaknesses.

I saw, and was most impressed by, the very successful, high level service delivery eye hospital in action. Cataract operations were done in a matter of three or four minutes with one surgeon and his assistants working on three operating tables . Hundreds of operations were performed in a morning. Given that after surgery people were given standard +10 D aphakic cataract glasses, the results were very good. The return train to Delhi again went past Agra, but I needed to get back to Baltimore and I still have not seen the Taj Mahal. The rotation in Sitapur did not work out, but later, residents would travel to the Aravind Centre in Madurai, south India.

Back in Baltimore, I became even more interested in the factors that would lead to the ongoing *transmission* of trachoma—there were plenty of contenders to consider—and I wanted to explore this in the field. At the International Agency for the Prevention of Blindness, IAPB, meeting in Oxford I spoke with people about this interest.

It was suggested that it might be possible to do such a trachoma trial in Kenya, where one could combine co-trimoxazole antibiotic treatment with fly control. The best spray for the control of flies was a relatively new compound, pyrethrum, manufactured by Glaxo in Kenya. Glaxo also made the co-trimoxazole I proposed to use. When I spoke with people from Glaxo they were interested in my proposed study, and helped fund my trip to Kenya early in 1980 to explore setting up the study.

In Kenya I talked further with local groups, found co-investigators, and identified a potential study area. This all seemed to go well. However, after this initial enthusiasm, everything ground to a halt. Opthamology professor Barrie Jones (not the Australian politician), who had spent a few days with the NTEHP team in the Kimberley, from London, and Sir John Wilson, the head of the Royal Commonwealth Society for the Blind (later renamed as SightSavers) and the founding president of the IAPB, had both visited Nairobi. Reportedly, high-level conversations had taken place there and it was agreed that it should be someone from London doing these studies in Kenya, and not some Australian based in the US. Oh goodness, gracious me! Our plans were scuppered! The 'British' study never happened.

In 1976 the WHO's World Health Day focussed on the prevention of blindness, slogan:

"Foresight to prevent blindness"

The WHO Trachoma program had started 28 years before, and in 1978 was transformed into the Prevention of Blindness Program, PBL. Mario Tarizzo had led the trachoma program and became the PBL's program director. At the end of the that year, WHO held a meeting at Asilomar on the Monterey Peninsula, on the central coast of northern California, famously beautiful country and coastline. The meeting was to draw up the WHO 'Guidelines for Programmes for the Prevention of Blindness Program'. This landmark document was to become the guidebook for all the work around the world supported and sponsored by WHO and the NGO members of IAPB. It changed the course of the activities aimed at preventing avoidable blindness.

It was flattering to this 31-year-old ophthalmologist to be invited; I had the unprecedented opportunity to meet many of the world leaders who wanted all the world to see, or get as close to that as possible.

The facilities at Asilomar belonged to the University of California San Francisco. We were allocated two-bedroom apartments. The first night I was on my own. The next night another person arrived. I introduced myself. He said his name was 'Dick'. Well, that was all good and Dick and I got on swell. Next day it became clear Dick was the apartment owner's professor of ophthalmology, G Richard O'Connor, Director of the Proctor Institute Foundation who was running the meeting and very much my senior. The meeting itself was not only very successful, it was interesting and fun, and it developed the first handbook for WHO on prevention of blindness and primary eye care.

I also met world leaders including a very tall young Swede, ophthalmologist, Björn Thylefors, who was working with the Onchocerciasis Control Program based in Ougadougou, Burkina Faso. Fred Hollows was also at the meeting and after the meeting he and I went to visit the spectacular Yosemite National Park. We did not do any rock climbing, however.

By the beach during the meeting in Asilomar, CA: *from left*: Pararajasegaram, Barrie Jones, Fred Hollows, Björn Thylefors, Pauline Jones and Gabi Hollows, 1979

Following the contacts I had made at the Asilomar meeting I was asked to spend some time as a WHO Consultant for PBL. First, I was asked to go to Pakistan to make recommendations about eye care services there.

I spent six weeks there at the end of 1980. My first priority was to look at the existing eye services and make recommendations for change. I visited Norwell Christie and his magnificent missionary eye hospital in the city of Taxila. He was providing really top-class eye services in an isolated area. I visited the eye services in all four provinces. Services were limited, badly underfunded and understaffed. There was little or no outreach services for eye care.

The high of that visit—WHO-UNHCR's provision of millions of blindness-preventing vitamin A capsules to Afghan refugee children—and the low—my findings and recommendations landing on the Minister of Health's desk like a stopover on the way to his wastepaper basket—are described in the first pages of this book, to be continued in the last.

Shortly after leaving Islamabad, I was again asked by WHO to travel, to Egypt and Tunisia to assess whether the eye centres there would be appropriate to be designated as WHO Collaborating Centres for the Prevention of Blindness. Indeed, they both were so designated.

This provided me with a wonderful opportunity to visit these two countries for the first time. I had time to explore the historic sites in Cairo, Alexandria and Carthage. In Cairo I stayed in a small hotel near the Egyptian Museum, which opened about 8.30 in the morning, but the crowds of tourists didn't really flood in until 9.30 or 10. Most mornings I would go there when it opened and had time to do one section all by myself before it got too busy and I had to go and work. Such access to such an iconic museum, in the true sense of the word, was bliss.

Al Sommer returned to Wilmer in 1980. I had been appointed acting director of the International Center for Epidemiologic and Preventive Ophthalmology, ICEPO, in the interim before his return. He and I set it up together.

Born in New York City, Al gained his MD from Harvard and then, in 1969, undertook obligatory public service as an epidemic intelligence officer at the Centers for Disease Control. He was sent with his wife, Jill, and their young son, Charles, to Dhaka in East Pakistan, now Bangladesh, for two years to work on cholera. He also helped manage the impacts of a massive cyclone. He was also caught up in the turmoil of the bloody war of independence when Bangladesh separated from Pakistan. After the war he worked to control the subsequent smallpox epidemic. Then he returned to the US.

Al had trained in ophthalmology at Wilmer and had a Masters of Health Science from Hopkins. While an ophthalmology resident at Wilmer, he did studies on xerophthalmia and Vitamin A deficiency in El Salvador, which was extraordinary for someone in the middle of their ophthalmology training. When Al finished his residency, he had gone to Indonesia for three years to undertake a massive series of observational and interventional trials into Vitamin A deficiency and ways to prevent and treat it. He then spent a year in London working through the data they had collected and writing it up. This was when I started at ICEPO

In 1980 Al had a Eureka Moment. Analysing his data from Indonesia he noticed that many of the children they had seen with signs of Vitamin A deficiency did not turn up for their next set of examinations. They had died. His analysis showed, for the first time, the significant increase in mortality rates of children with Vitamin A deficiency.

Publication of this led to a major international effort by UNICEF and WHO to address Vitamin A deficiency around the world. Al's subsequent work showed that a taking capsule of Vitamin A once every six months would reverse this risk. Of course, Al received many accolades and awards for this great work, including the 1997 Lasker Award, often called 'America's Nobel' as many have won both, for 'Vitamin A therapy for preventing infections and blindness'.

Al has been supported in all he does by his wonderful wife Jill and their two children, Charles and Marni. Charles got a law degree and worked in investment and business management. He has retrained several times and now is a psychologist. Marni studied nursing and got a PhD after working on the health of adolescent girls in Tanzania. She continues this work as a professor at Columbia University.

The focus for Al's research was clearly on xerophthalmia, but also on glaucoma. I was working on trachoma, onchocerciasis and cataract risk factors. This worked well, as between us we covered The Big Five, the major global causes of blindness. Al and I worked together most productively. We became, and still are, good friends.

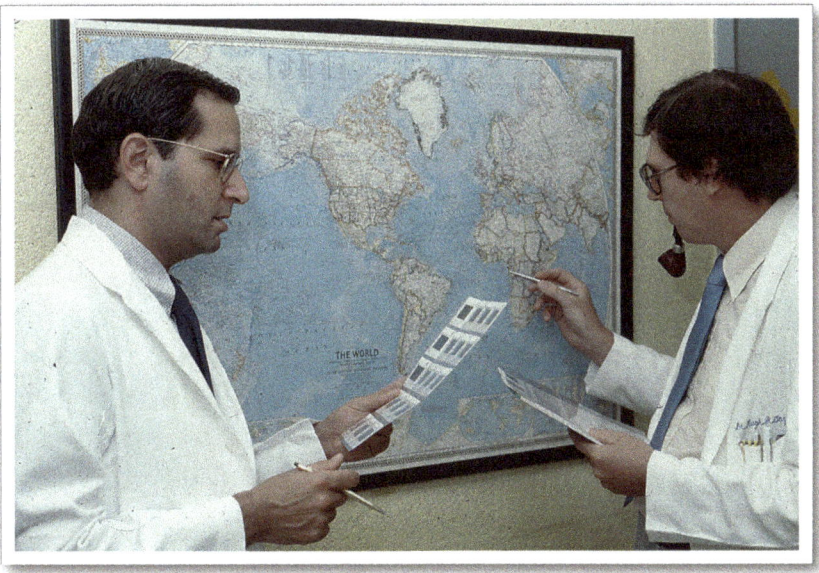

Al Sommer and me in the hallway at Wilmer planning work in Africa

I did some field work on Al's vitamin A deficiency projects. One trip took me to Haiti. I spent most of my time in Port au Prince and worked in the hospital. We examined the young children there who were malnourished. I found cases of xerophthalmia and taught the staff how to recognise and treat it. I visited some regional towns and again worked in the clinics. I did not see any children with trachoma but there were more children with xerophthalmia. I am not sure if Haiti has ever been stable but at that time, with Papa Doc firmly in control, there was no obvious political unrest. Things were disorganised with outbreaks of acute haemorrhagic conjunctivitis caused by an enterovirus called Apollo 11 conjunctivitis as it had first appeared in Ghana in 1969 at the time of the first moon landing. People were using all sorts of damaging long-standing traditional treatments which only made things worse. There was little one could do about this on such a short trip.

I stayed in the Hotel Oloffson, a classic old building in central Port au Prince. It was built as a private home in the late nineteenth century but was seized by US marines in 1915 and used as a military hospital until 1935, when it became a hotel. Graham Greene stayed there in 1965 and a year later published the novel *The Comedians* that was based there. One character was a local journalist who drank at the veranda bar each afternoon. He was *still* there. The rooms were named after famous visitors such as Greene and Mick Jagger.

Another trip looking at xerophthalmia and trachoma took me to Bolivia. You fly into their international airport at 4060 metres then descend to the city of La Paz at 3600 metres (13 000 and 12 000 feet respectively). Coming from Baltimore, sea level, I found that if I sat quietly, I could breathe quite well, but as soon as I stood up or took a few steps I immediately became short of breath. The next day I had to give lectures on xerophthalmia and trachoma. My Spanish was only fair and I occasionally substituted a French word for a term I was unsure of, but it seemed that, for the most part, my message got through. Al's work on vitamin A was mostly funded by USAID, so I made contact with the US Embassy. They invited me to join them the next day on a trip to Charquini Glacier at about 5000 metres (17 000 feet). Of course, I said 'Yes' and, of course, it was magnificent, but walking around was very hard. However, when I returned to the 'low altitude' of La Paz, I found breathing easy!

I visited villages in the high country around La Paz and one or two down on the edge of the Amazon rainforest. These small villages reminded me of those in Mexico but this time there was no trachoma. I saw Lake Titicaca and its boats made of bundles of reeds tied together; a sidelight but a highlight.

We also did a study on the eye health of the Inuit in far northern Alaska. We had to start this in early January. If we had waited until summertime, most people would be out hunting and fishing. In some ways, the isolation of the communities and difficulties of connecting with the outside world reminded me of

In Alaska unloading examination gear from the ski-plane to a snowmobile trailer, January 1986

Opening Eyes

working in remote communities in outback Australia. However, the temperature was *minus* 40° Centigrade instead of *plus* 40°! When we started in the first week of January it was only light for about an hour. But the days have to go from 24 hours of darkness to 24 hours of daylight from midwinter to midsummer; days seemed to lengthen by about 20 minutes each day. It was very disconcerting as one day it was pitch black at 11.15 and the next day sunlight.

Baltimore and Odessa, USSR, established a sister-city relationship in the 1970s. In 1985 Wilmer was approached to see if, under this program, Wilmer might start a relationship with Odessa's Filatov Institute of Eye Diseases. The Filatov Institute was a large and leading eye hospital and training centre with a strong research program. Odessa was established on the site of an early Greek and Ottoman settlement on the Black Sea. It was rebuilt by Catherine the Great starting in the late eighteenth century and was modelled on French and Mediterranean cities. It was an important port for Russia and then the USSR. It became famous for the 'Potemkin Steps' after an uprising and massacre there in 1905 as a prelude to the Russian Revolution.

When I was asked if I would go and see what could be arranged, how could I decline? Would Liz agree to yet another absence? She agreed!

After transiting through Moscow, I was warmly welcomed at the airport. My hosts had booked me into a splendid old hotel with the largest and most lavishly furnished hotel room I think I have ever stayed in, and I have stayed in a few. I spent two days visiting the Institute, which was very impressive. Built in the late 1930s it was large, busy, the patients well-cared for and, to my surprise, nearly all the doctors were women. A young male ophthalmologist who was Ukrainian, as were about two thirds of the staff, was my guide. Everyone had to speak Russian, and one had to be careful not to have blue and yellow colours together, as in the Ukrainian flag. Mikhail Gorbachev had started as the new leader of the Soviet Union earlier that year, but I was not aware of any major changes in policies.

I returned through Moscow and had a day to explore. I wandered around Red Square, St Basil's Cathedral and the Kremlin, and also inspected Lenin's Tomb. Then I walked around the block that housed the KGB, the secret police. Being undisturbed I chose one of the radial roads that led from Red Square and walked in as straight a line as far as I could for an hour or so seeing shops and offices, apartment blocks and lots of people on the street, some standing in lines at shops but most walking around and looking well-dressed. I reached a ring road and walked until I found another main road back to Red Square and my hotel. As far as I knew, I was not followed. I was not accosted. The only video monitors I saw were those outside the US Embassy. Interesting.

I flew back via London to San Francisco to attend the American Academy of Ophthalmology congress. Heathrow airport was closed for a while by fog and the only place that would allow our Soviet Aeroflot plane to land and wait for the fog to clear was Luxembourg; I do not know what politics were going on there. I only just made my connection in London but arrived in San Francisco safely. The next morning, as I walked from my hotel down Union Square to the convention center, I was accosted about every 20 or 30 yards by someone begging, often by men with a little sign saying they were a returned Vietnam veteran. Not long before, Ronald Reagan had called the USSR 'an evil empire'! I felt confronted. What 'freedoms' are important or should rank one over another? Freedom of speech, freedom from hunger, freedom to work, freedom to eat, freedom to sleep in a house? The contrast was challenging and made me think deeply about these fundamental issues.

After this visit ophthalmology residents from Wilmer went to the Filatov and some of the Filatov's young ophthalmologists came to Wilmer. I have lost track of how long this exchange lasted.

Opening Eyes

In 1980 Liz and I welcomed the safe arrival of our second son, Edward, usually called Ned. But once again Daddy was off travelling, this time back to Liberia, and Mummy was not only literally left holding the baby, but also continuing her research and clinical studies at the NIA.

Just before Ned was born the Rev Davis McCaughey, who'd married us, and his wife Jean, stayed a night or two with us on their way to spend a sabbatical in Princeton University, New Jersey. He had recently retired as Master of Ormond College and was the head of the newly formed Uniting Church in Australia. He offered to baptise Ned. When Ned was 12 days old we all went to Princeton to have Ned christened. We toured the university and the flowering cherry blossoms as Liz worked to protect her recent caesarean wound. A few years later Davis would be governor of Victoria.

Kate was now nearly 9 and Bart nearly 7. In 1985 Phoebe was born. Again, Daddy was travelling: a Pan American Health Organisation, PAHO, meeting on blindness in Lima, Peru. Liz did an amazing job looking after our children and running her lab, by 1985 at the National Institute on Drug Abuse, NIDA, while the AIDS epidemic was raging.

I wore regular ties at work, but I found them a nuisance when I was examining patients' eyes, tucking them into my shirt to keep them out of the way. If you spilt soup or toothpaste on a lovely Italian silk tie, too bad. Many at Wilmer wore bow-ties, so I tried. I figured that if I did not wear one every day, I would forget how to tie it, so I wore one every day. If I spill something, only the shirt needs washing.

Liz was by then working as a Lab Chief at the NIDA. With her laboratory experience she had become very skilful at running sensitive assays for small molecules. She had set up the drug testing for the clinical studies being conducted by NIDA. Suddenly, she also landed in the middle of HIV work. The idea that HIV/AIDS was just a 'gay disease' had emerged. In order to conduct a national survey of HIV prevalence in injection drug users, NIDA had her set up a laboratory to test the collected blood samples. As soon as testing for HIV became available, she was given the responsibility at NIDA to do all the HIV testing. Her lab group was among the first to describe HIV infection and its relevance among injection drug users; it assessed the efficiency and quality of the performance of different HIV tests. Her proficiency in HIV testing also led to her gaining clinical experience with HIV-affected patients as she continued her other clinical endocrinology work.

Her clinical work at NIDA involved drug users who were injecting. She studied their hormonal changes as surrogate for possible drug-induced immunological changes. The TV series *The Wire* portrayed people like many of those who were enrolled in her studies. The series portrayed Baltimore inner-city life in the 2000s, which had not changed much since the 1980s and early 1990s. Watching it was both fascinating and saddening. Baltimore certainly has a very rough and different face for many people. We lived 'among the woods', as Omar and Slim from *The Wire* would say. They lived 'Way Down in the Hole' as the theme song—as sung by The Blind Boys of Alabama in one series—puts it.

Liz and I were busy and happy in Baltimore. In 1989 Kate had decided that she would like to return to Melbourne for university and to enter medical school there, so she returned to do Year 12. We started weighing up whether we were to remain in the US or return to Australia. We knew that we could always return to Australia for a holiday and take our children with us so they could meet and catch up with members of the extended family. When we wanted to retire, we could also return and live in Australia. Hmm, but if we did that where would the children and hopefully grandchildren be living? If we waited that long, would they all be living somewhere in America? Would we want to live in Australia then?

I was invited to look at several positions in the US and

Canada and one in Brisbane but none of them seemed right. Australian jobs in ophthalmology were scarce, so we waited to see how things progressed. We heard that Gerry Crock, the professor of ophthalmology in Melbourne, had announced he was to retire. Unfortunately for me, another Australian had applied for and been offered the position. Too bad. But then, in late 1989, he turned down the job so he could remain in the US where his children had grown up, worked and lived. His situation was as we feared ours could have became, but we were younger, in our early forties still. I was approached. I said, 'Yes, please.'

We arranged for Bart to begin Year 11 in Melbourne at the start of 1990. Liz, Ned, Phoebe and I returned to Melbourne in August 1990. Although when we arrived in Baltimore we had intended to make it our home for a year, maybe two, it was home for over 13.

Within a month of my leaving Wilmer in 1990, Al also left the Center and became Dean of the Johns Hopkins School of

Our last Christmas in Baltimore, 1989: Bart, Kate, Liz with Phoebe, Ned and me

Hygiene and Public Health, a graduate teaching and research school, the world's largest public health school. Shortly before we left, we had a very heavy evening with Al discussing the various options. It was a great opportunity for him and he was tremendously successful there and essentially rebuilt the school over the next few years. The school received donations of US$1.8 billion in 2016 and $1 billion eight years later from Michael Bloomberg, co-founder of the finance, data and media company and Hopkins graduate from the class of '64. Al's school has been renamed, now the Johns Hopkins Bloomberg School of Public Health. There is an auditorium, a scholarship and professorship named in Al's honour.

Whenever I am planning a visit to Baltimore, Al always reminds me that there is a bed made up and waiting for me; and it is a grand Indonesian wedding bed too.

Al and I started ICEPO up in 1980 with a small group of researchers which grew. We worked hard and productively on an array of projects and activities. ICEPO was as a joint initiative with Wilmer as part of the Hopkins School of Medicine and the Hopkins School of Hygiene and Public Health. Al and I held joint appointments in both schools, although we were physically based in the Wilmer. In 1982 we moved into the almost luxurious old offices on the ground floor of the original Wilmer building. The Center became a designated WHO Collaborating Center for the Prevention of Blindness and later Onchocerciasis was added to the designation. This further strengthened our links with WHO and their global network. In 1984, after a very generous donation from the Dana Foundation, ICEPO was renamed the Dana Center for Preventive Ophthalmology. We also started a Master of Public Ophthalmology degree with the School of Hygiene and Public Health.

I'd left the ICEPO in good shape and in good hands and it has continued to do extensive work preventing blindness world-wide.

Opening Eyes

5

Did the Children have Clean Faces?

Clean faces, strong eyes
Public health slogan,
Katherine West community NT, 2010s

I was sitting quietly at a slit lamp in the dark counting microfilaria in the eye of a farm worker in the city of San Cristobal de las Casas, in Chiapas, the southernmost state of Mexico, just the two of us. Then, the voice of a third party, in English:

'Is there someone here who knows something about trachoma?'

What could I say?

'Yes. That'd be me.'

The head of public health in Chiapas, Francisco Milan Velasco, had arrived in my life.

Thwarted in studying trachoma in Kenya, I was going ahead with studies on onchocerciasis. Between scheduled eye and skin examinations for that onchocerciasis study, we went to a community in the highlands near San Cristobal and examined the whole community for trachoma. One third of the younger children had active trachoma and about 12 percent of those over 40 had trichiasis, the in-turned lashes that rub on the front of the eye and lead to scuffing and blindness. A serious problem that needed to be addressed.

I thought here was an opportunity to do the big study on

Opening Eyes

An elderly Mexican woman, blind from trachoma, feeling her way up a path

fly-control and trachoma antibiotic treatment. Mexico was not a Commonwealth country like Kenya, so, I thought we might get a clear go here.

I talked with the people at GlaxoSmithKline, who were happy to proceed with a trial in Mexico. That was very encouraging. We started with flies. What were the densities of them? I went to Chiapas with Milan Tripis, the head of entomology at Johns Hopkins. I told people later that he spent the whole week catching butterflies because there were no flies to be found. That put an end to the thought of controlling flies to eliminate trachoma, at least in Chiapas.

Although flies were not an issue, the availability of water for washing was. Even in the mountainous areas of Mexico—San Cristobal sits in a valley at 2200 metres, Kosciuszko's height, surrounded by mountains—water still flows downhill, so villagers had to carry water up to their villages perched along the

Did the Children have Clean Faces?

Mexican women carrying water on their backs up the road to their village

top of the ridges. I talked further with Glaxo and we decided to go ahead with a randomised controlled trial with co-trimoxazole or placebo. Half the communities would get the antibiotic; half, the placebo. We had a considerable wait for the placebo to be made, the drugs to be shipped, customs cleared and to work through the ethical clearances.

Once this was accomplished we got underway, working closely with Francisco. Francisco Milan was trained in medicine and in public health. He lived in San Cristobal, not Tuxtla, the capital, but was responsible for public health for the state. He came from a long line of established local families. On one trip we boated in and stayed a night in one of his family's old haciendas. It was a large old single-storey house with many beautifully furnished rooms and wide verandas in a place by a river with steep mountains on either side. We were fed delicious traditional Mexican meals, were well looked after and discovered what life could be like for some in the 'old days'.

Opening Eyes

To get the study underway we recruited our field teams and spent a week training them in the field. The last day of training, Friday, 29 March 1982, was spent working in one of the communities. These were small traditional villages of the predominantly subsistence-farming families of Tzeltal Indians. They spoke Tzeltal, the Mayan tongue of their ancestors, and wore the distinctive traditional home-weaved clothing specific to their village.

As we returned to San Cristobal on that Friday evening there was a magnificent sunset. A huge cloud in the sky and a beautiful but unusual light.

In town, we learned that a volcano thought dormant, El Chichón, about 100 miles away, had erupted. Next morning San Cristobal's trees, rooftops and roads was covered with inches of grey volcanic ash and the air smelled of sulfur. It looked a bit as though there had been a heavy snowstorm, except it was not cold and the smell and the dust were everywhere. People

With a driver, left, and Francisco Milan, right, in San Christobal the morning after the volcanic eruption with everything covered in ash

Did the Children have Clean Faces?

walked with scarves tied over their mouths to keep the dust out. Shops were shut, food was hard to find. That eruption was the mountain's first since the 1350s. It spewed forth again on 3 April and yet again the next day. Nine villages were obliterated, 2000 people dead, 20 000 displaced from their homes. One of the consequences of the eruption was the ash it threw into the planet's atmosphere. It reportedly caused torrential rain in Hong Kong.

Slowly, people began to clear the streets and footpaths. All our newly trained field staff were called away as emergency workers for the relief program in the affected villages. Our study did not grind to a halt—it was blown the day before it was to begin. Eventually, the drug made its way back to the UK. The placebo was disposed of as it was no longer of any use. Bounced out of Kenya. Blown out of Mexico. Another trachoma trial had bit the dust (read ash!).

The monkey studies showed the need for repeated episodes of reinfection for the inflammation in trachoma to be sustained to lead to the scarring that causes blindness. Repeated infections were so important in the monkeys, they surely had to be important in humans too. Therefore, I thought we should look in more detail at the factors that affected transmission in afflicted communities. Though I didn't anticipate it then, this started a whole new avenue of work.

Despite the debacle of our volcanic explosion, I still thought Mexico would be a good place to look at the issues around transmission. Clearly, in southern Mexico at least, flies were not important transmitters. I discussed this with Al Sommer: what else might we do to see what contributed to repeated episodes of reinfection? Al and I concluded we should look at hygiene issues such as, 'did children have clean faces?' This turned out to be a breakthrough moment for us and what led us to the whole new line of work that ended up showing the critical role of facial cleanliness.

Opening Eyes

Al joined Francisco Milan and me in a detailed study in two small, very isolated communities in the mountains of Oxchuc, again in Chiapas.

With a small field team and translators, we went house to house asking questions about family size and structure, personal and family hygiene practices, water availability and use, and we examined everyone's eyes for trachoma. I was lucky to have daughter Kate join us on one visit. It was a great chance to show her what her dad was actually doing when he was away so often and she was a great help in the field. From a sample of people, we took photos of their eyes for later grading of trachoma and took conjunctival smears to look for chlamydia infection.

We found no correlation between children having trachoma and a range of the family and household features. These included distance to water, use of water, house construction, crowding, faecal or garbage disposal. Again, very few flies were seen.

The main finding was the strong and significant association

Kate helping examine people in a village in Mexico

between trachoma and the frequency with which a child's face was reported to have been washed. In children whose faces were washed infrequently, the risk of trachoma was high and even higher if clothes—lapels, sleeves or mum's skirt—were used to dry their faces after they were washed, or if clothes were used to blow their noses. These factors were not relevant in those who washed their faces frequently. There was no relationship with the use of soap, nor with allowing the face to air-dry or using a towel. These findings were exciting. (However, in retrospect, we had not measured what was the most important factor, the outcome measure: whether the child's face was actually clean or dirty. Years would pass before that penny dropped.) The risk of a child having trachoma was significantly higher if another child in that house had trachoma.

We again went back to Chiapas, this time with Martha Wilson. Martha was a medical student from Louisville, Kentucky, who volunteered to join us. We examined children in another four villages. This time the frequency of face washing was less significant, but the higher rate of trachoma in girls stood out. After she completed her training as an ophthalmologist Martha moved to practice in Texas. However, she continued to visit Chiapas and to provide eye care there. Her earlier visit with us had encouraged that career trajectory.

During this time a new method for detecting chlamydial infections became available: direct micro-immunofluorescence cytology, DFA. This used fluorescein-labelled antibodies designed to stick to the chlamydial elementary bodies in a sample that then could be observed using a microscope. DFA proved to be more sensitive than previous Giemsa dye staining and had many advantages over trying to grow chlamydia in the laboratory. We did studies using DFA in the monkey model. We also studied infection using DFA in the Mexican study with Martha Wilson. We found DFA had a fairly low sensitivity—that is, it missed many cases of clinical trachoma. But it was highly specific—that is, if DFA were positive the person did have clinical trachoma. We found that only a third of those with trachoma were DFA positive. But almost everyone who was DFA positive did have clinical trachoma.

With Peter Rapoza and Tom Quinn, I did a study on ophthalmia neonatorum; conjunctivitis in new-born babies. Peter was an enthusiastic ophthalmology resident at Wilmer and later became a well-known corneal specialist in Boston. We found nearly half the cases of conjunctivitis in newborns seen at Johns Hopkins were due to chlamydial infection that had come from the mother's infected genital tract. Later, we did a similar study in people with acute conjunctivitis who had only had symptoms for less than a week and who presented to the Emergency Department at Hopkins. We found no cases of chlamydial infection in these acute cases. However, in a subsequent study of people with chronic conjunctivitis, that is people who had had symptoms for weeks, we found 19 percent were caused by chlamydia. (A similar study on those with acute conjunctivitis that I did with Suzanne Garland in Melbourne in the early 1990s found that only 2 percent of cases were positive for chlamydia.)

In 1984, Joseph Cook, the medical director of the Edna McConnell Clark Foundation, reached out to people because the Foundation was exploring potential new areas it might support. Joe had done work on schistosomiasis—a tropical disease where parasitic flatworms from freshwater snails invade the body—work that the Foundation had supported. I had made suggestions to Joe about work on trachoma and onchocerciasis that might be of interest. Joe asked me to convene a workshop on each disease. For each meeting, a dozen or so international experts came together for a three-day workshop held in Coolfont, West Virginia. The trachoma workshop focussed on the scope of trachoma, its pathogenesis and immunology, its epidemiology and control, and laboratory studies. The oncho workshop also was broad based.

Following these workshops, the Clark Foundation set up a trachoma group that I led. Another group, led by Bruce Greene, looked at oncho. The Foundation developed its strategic plan and, over time, provided very significant funds for studies in each of these areas, but particularly for trachoma. In 1998 Pfizer committed to donate azithromycin for the treatment of trachoma in developing countries. Joe Cook established the International Trachoma Initiative, ITI, to oversee this donation program.

The WHO system for grading trachoma was first set out in 1952. Over the years it had grown increasingly complicated: it included 20 signs to be graded using a slit lamp. In the early 1970s WHO revised their grading, which improved it somewhat, but it remained complex. For our work in the NTEHP, Fred Hollows had come up with a more usable grading scheme, one that was more or less consistent with the revised scheme that WHO had developed. WHO then published this in their 1981 manual.

In 1983 Al and I worked on a large epidemiological study looking at both xerophthalmia and trachoma in people living in the Lower Shire Valley in Malawi. Field work was led by Keith West, a nutritionist, and Jim Tielsch, an epidemiologist, both from ICEPO. In preparation for this study, we tried out the recently revised WHO trachoma grading with four experienced ophthalmologists as graders. Agreement between them was poor to very poor.

Clearly, something better was needed. We then used our own simplified version of the WHO grading scheme. It worked well: there was good agreement between each of the graders.

The Malawi study found that in children under six a greater distance to water, not having a latrine, and having brothers or sisters with trachoma were each significant risk factors for trachoma. Crowding as such was not a risk factor. The frequency of face washing was highly significant on its own, but not in the multivariant analysis when all the other risk factors were

Examining people for trachoma in Malawi: Gordon Johnston, left, and Moses Chirambo, right

included. (Again, in retrospect, we had missed the target, the real end point: was the face actually clean or not? If it is clean, it does not *need* washing.)

At an infectious diseases meeting in Calgary, Canada, we took the opportunity to hold a small side meeting to talk about trachoma. After it, we had a day off between meetings. Some of us went to Banff for a walk in the Rockies. On this walk I got talking with Björn Thylefors, who was now the program manager for the WHO Prevention of Blindness Program, PBL. We discussed our Malawi findings and the problems with the current WHO trachoma grading system.

Following our conversation Björn called together a group of trachoma experts—Chan Dawson from San Francisco, Barrie Jones from London and me—to discuss a new Simplified Trachoma Grading Scheme at WHO in Geneva.

In April 1983 the same core group went to Tunisia to test the new scheme with Professor M T Daghfous, the professor of ophthalmology in Tunis. Overall, the grading system worked well but we found we needed to refine the definition for active trachoma with severe inflammation: Trachomatous Intense Inflammation, TI. A year later the same core group tried the revised scheme in Burma, now Myanmar. Dr S Lwin from Rangoon and Dr Pararajasegaram joined us. Sheila West from ICEPO came too and helped with statistical analysis. This time the revised definitions worked appropriately and the new WHO Simplified Grading Scheme became the standard for nearly every trachoma study since then. See overleaf.

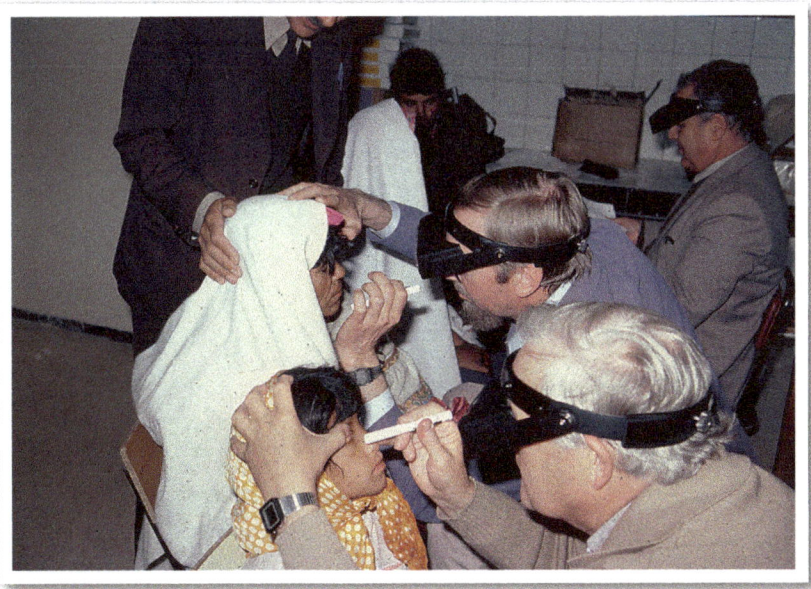

Björn Thylefors and Barrie Jones testing the WHO simplified grading for trachoma in Tunisia, Professor Daghfous in the background

Opening Eyes

TRACHOMA GRADING CARD

- Each eye must be examined and assessed separately.
- Use binocular loupes (x2.5) and adequate lighting (either daylight or a torch).
- Signs must be clearly seen in order to be considered present.

Normal Healthy Eye

The eyelids and cornea are observed first for inturned eyelashes and any corneal opacity. The upper eyelid is then turned over (everted) to examine the conjunctiva over the stiffer part of the upper lid (tarsal conjunctiva).

The normal conjunctiva is pink, smooth, thin and transparent. Over the whole area of the tarsal conjunctiva there are normally large deep-lying blood vessels that run vertically.

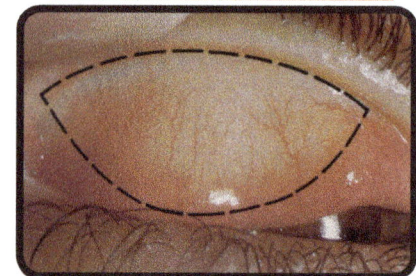

Normal tarsal conjunctiva (x2 magnification). The dotted line shows the area to be examined.

Trachomatous Follicular (TF)

TRACHOMATOUS INFLAMMATION - FOLLICULAR (TF): *The presence of five or more follicles in the upper tarsal conjunctiva.*

Follicles are round swellings that arepaler than the surrounding conjunctiva, appearing white, grey or yellow. Follicles must be at least 0.5mm in diameter, i.e., at least as large at the dots shown, to be considered.

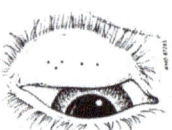

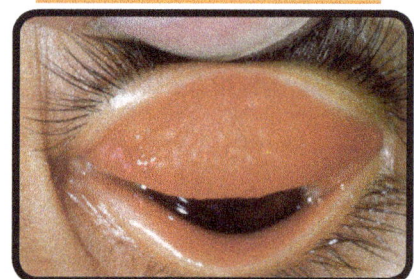

Trachomatous inflammation- follicular (TF)

Trachomatous Intense (TI)

TRACHOMATOUS INFLAMMATION - INTENSE (TI): *Pronounced inflammatory thickening of the tarsal conjunctiva that obscures more than half of the normal deep tarsal vessels.*

The tarsal conjunctiva appears red, rough and thickened. There are usually numerous follicles, which may be partially or totally covered by the thickened conjunctiva.

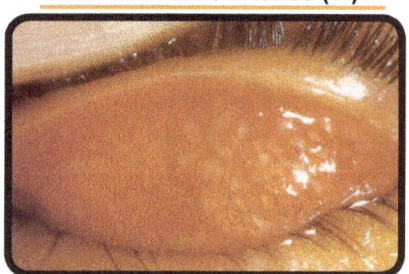

Trachomatous inflammation- follicular and intense (TF + TI)

 Adapted from:
**WORLD HEALTH ORGANIZATION
PREVENTION OF BLINDNESS AND DEAFNESS**

Support from the partners of the WHO Alliance for the Global Elimination of Trachoma is acknowledged.

Did the Children have Clean Faces?

TRACHOMA GRADING CARD

- Each eye must be examined and assessed separately.
- Use binocular loupes (x2.5) and adequate lighting (either daylight or a torch).
- Signs mus be clearly seen in order to be considered present.

TRACHOMATOUS SCARRING (TS):
The presence of scarring in the tarsal conjunctiva

Scars are easily visible as white lines, bands, or sheets in the tarsal conjunctiva. They are glistening and fibrous in appearance. Scarring, especially diffuse fibrosis, may obscure the tarsal blood vessels.

Trachomatous Scarring (TS)

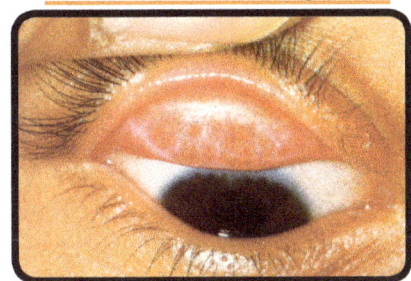

TRACHOMATOUS TRICHIASIS (TT):
At least one eyelash rubs on the eyeball.

Evidence of recent removal of inturned eyelashes should also be graded as trichiasis.

Trachomatous Trichiasis (TT)

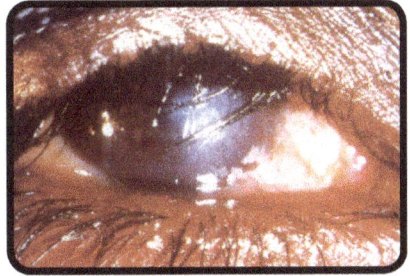

CORNEAL OPACITY (CO):
Easily visible corneal opacity over the pupil.

The pupil margin is blurred viewed through the opacity. Such corneal opacities cause significant visual impairment (less than 6/18 or 0.3 vision), and therefore visual acuity should be measured if possible.

Corneal Opacity (CO)

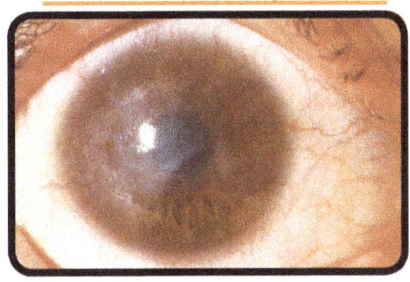

TF and or TI: Treat all household members with azithromycin according to CDNA guidelines
TT: Refer to ophthalmologist for trichiasis surgery

Adapted from:
WORLD HEALTH ORGANIZATION
PREVENTION OF BLINDNESS AND DEAFNESS

Support from the partners of the WHO Alliance for the Global Elimination of Trachoma is acknowledged.

The grading was designed for health workers in developing countries so that teams could find the prevalence rates of trachoma and assess the risk of blinding trachoma as being present; it was not designed to give specific individual diagnoses and did not include milder early signs of trachoma. From a public health perspective, it did what it was meant to do. Children who had less inflammation than TF were unlikely to develop sufficient scarring to cause trichiasis and blindness. It set the benchmark for WHO for the elimination of 'blinding trachoma'.

However, for later in-depth studies and especially those combining very sensitive laboratory testing such as PCR or serology, the Simplified grading does not include the milder early cases of active trachoma. Many of these children are likely to be PCR or serology test positive. This gave rise to a lot of confusion and controversy in research studies where researchers tried to use PCR or serology to assess the prevalence of trachoma without having to rely on clinical examinations and grading.

In 1986 I visited Bebedouro, an inland city in São Paulo State, southern Brazil. I worked there with Norma Medina, a Brazilian ophthalmologist who had recently completed a Master of Public Health Ophthalmology with us at the Dana Center. Together we examined 3000 people of all ages. Of the boys aged 1 to 10 years, 8 percent had active trachoma; the girls had 5 percent. This was unusual. Typically, girls have higher trachoma rates than boys, attributed to the child-caring role given to girls, even at an early age. We were examining children who attended school and we didn't know if girls from less well-off families might not be attending school. Other family factors that increased the rates of trachoma were the number of children in the family and the number of children sharing a bed, as was the lack of garbage collection. Access to water was also a risk factor, but in Bebedouro it was a question of whether the piped water went into a house or was drawn from an outside tap. This was a very different picture from what we saw in Africa where women

Did the Children have Clean Faces?

A Mexican girl with her sister

might have to walk an hour or more to get water. However, the findings in Brazil probably pointed to the relatively easy access to their water supply and its greater utilisation.

In 1998 Norma and I returned to Brazil, to Recife on the Atlantic coast. We examined people in the small, isolated villages in the rainforest areas inland from Recife and on the coast. Here we found significant pockets of trachoma with trichiasis in older people. This study was to see if trachoma existed in this area; it was not a risk-factor study, as such. Norma subsequently helped lead teams to follow-up with treatment strategies both here and around São Paulo. Since then, much work towards eradication has been done on trachoma in Brazil.

In 1985 Al Sommer was exploring places in Africa to work on the interaction between vitamin A deficiency and measles. Dr Joseph Taylor, an experienced missionary ophthalmologist, suggested that we visit the mission hospital at Mvumi in central Tanzania.

So we did. Mvumi is about 30 miles from Dodoma which subsequently became the new capital of Tanzania. At that time Dodoma was a small but important railway hub and Mvumi a small town on the open savannah. There we met the young missionary doctor Allen Foster. Later, Allen went back to London, did his ophthalmic training, and returned to Tanzania for a while. Then he went back to the UK to lead the International Centre for Eye Health, ICEH, at the London School of Tropical Medicine and Hygiene. He became the director of the very large non-government organisation, Chrisoffel Blinden Mission, CBM. In Mvumi we talked with Allen about a study to look at the interaction between xerophthalmia and measles, then I raised the possibility of a study on trachoma. Allen introduced us to Dr B B O Mmbaga, a top Tanzanian assistant medical officer in ophthalmology, an ophthalmologist equivalent, who was based in Dodoma. With Mmbaga's help and with funding from the Clark Foundation, Sheila West and I set out to do a more detailed study of trachoma, looking especially at the outcome of all those hygiene parameters but this time including facial cleanliness.

Sheila West organising subject data at the examination site

Did the Children have Clean Faces?

Our study in Kongwa in central Tanzania started in 1986. Kongwa, about 60 miles east of Dodoma, is a small town at the foot of some hills and faced north over a huge plain. Most of the country is used for subsistence farming and herding cattle, but driving along one would often see antelope and the occasional giraffe or even an elephant. After World War 2 the British had tried setting up large peanut farms to make oil for margarine. The soil was so hard it wrecked the army tanks that were converted to work as tractors for ploughing, and, after local protests and drought, the project was scrapped. This trachoma study was a massive undertaking with a large team. From Wilmer, Shirley Johnson ran the laboratory studies and organised cylinders of liquid nitrogen to ship the chlamydial swabs back to the laboratory in Baltimore. Also from Wilmer, Peter Rapoza and Matt Lynch joined the team. They did field work and recruited patients. Sydney Katala, a Tanzanian ophthalmic nurse, became the chief trachoma grader. We took photos of each eye for later grading; Sydney's clinical gradings stood up well. Allen Foster helped us with the training and getting things set up. We also trained a local team to help with recruitment, interviewing and examination process.

Except for those who already lived in Kongwa, we stayed in an old guest house there, Rahmatullah's, and went out to the villages each day. We usually returned exhausted after a long day's work. We ate a variety of meals, but ugali, the traditional Tanzanian dish made of maize meal, seemed to be standard for every meal. The ugali porridge was usually accompanied by some meat and vegetables.

We worked in 20 villages and examined children in a cluster sample of houses in each. We visited each sampled household to collect household data on water, sanitation and hygiene. During this home visit we graded the children's facial cleanliness as the presence or absence of eye or nose secretions and dirt on their cheeks or foreheads.

We also assessed household fly density with a simple method I developed that used 'Mirinda boards'. These were sheets of composite board moistened with the PepsiCo soft drink, Mirinda. We placed moistened Mirinda boards on either side of the entrance of a house and counted how many flies got stuck on them. After this, the mothers and children came to a central site where they were examined for trachoma, ocular and nasal discharge, and scabies as another marker of general hygiene. The men in the communities were also examined.

Almost all the houses were of rammed red-mud bricks. They had flat roofs, most of them made of wood. Ceilings were low—I had to duck down low to go inside! There were usually a few rooms with some sort of bedding around the edges. Cooking was done over an open fire in the main room. Water was stored in buckets or gourds. People often had to walk 2 hours or so from dilapidated old pumps or deep wells to get water to carry home. Often there was a yard adjacent to the house to keep the families' cattle in overnight. There were no bathrooms and almost no toilets. The only latrines were in little huts over a big open pit. Most of these were not used. Many men had multiple wives and each wife had her own 'house' that was built around an open area. When they worked at home most women spent a lot of time sitting outside their houses on their traditional low three-legged wooden stools.

We ended up examining 98 percent of the 3916 eligible children aged 1 to 7, of whom 60 percent had active trachoma, TF, and 10 percent had intense trachoma, TI. Beatriz Muñoz, the gifted biostatistician in the Dana Center who did all our data analyses, found that the most significant risk factor for trachoma was having an unclean face. At last, I felt we had hit the jackpot!

We also found significant risk factors for trachoma in the children whose households followed traditional beliefs, had high Mirinda-board fly scores, and were without a latrine. The risk of trachoma was lower in houses that had tin roofs, a marker of higher socio-economic status. Although scabies was common, we found no link between having scabies and trachoma. Families that lived further than 30 minutes from their water source had a higher rate of trachoma, although there was no relationship between the quantity of water the household used and trachoma. As usual, girls had higher rates of trachoma than boys and they had it for longer.

From a subsample we also collected specimens for chlamydial culture and for DFA cytology. We found that 33 percent of those with active trachoma (TF) were culture positive and 49 percent were DFA positive. For those with more intense trachoma (TI) 51 percent had a positive culture and 71 percent were DFA positive.

We were interested in trying to identify the type of chlamydia that was causing trachoma here. Chlamydia is typed into different groups called 'serotypes' based on the antigens on their surface. Serotypes A, B, Ba and C are associated with trachoma, serotypes D through to K with genital tract infections, and serotypes L1, L2 and L3 with lymphogranuloma venereum—a nasty spreading ulcer from a genital infection. We cultured sufficient elementary bodies for serotyping from 29 specimens: 18 were serovar A, 10 B and 1 Ba.

We found 8 percent of those over 55 years had trichiasis, TT, and women were four times more likely to have trichiasis than men. Further analysis showed a clustering of trachoma both between villages and within villages. This was not related to access to water, but to the overall traditional hygiene practices. Later, Ginny Turner undertook a case-control study with us on why women had so much higher rates of trichiasis. She studied women in the Kongwa area for her PhD. She recruited 205 women with trichiasis and two matched controls for each. Poor living conditions during their child-bearing age were significant risk factors. Those included living in traditional mud housing, having cooking fires and sleeping areas in the same space, lack of education, having had multiple children die, being unmarried,

Opening Eyes

Above: The household fly density being assessed with Mirinda Boards in Tanzania
Below: Family and household data being collected at a home by one of our field staff

Did the Children have Clean Faces?

Above: Sheila West organising subject data at the examination site

Below: Trachoma screening exams at the examination site. Allen Foster with the examination loupes on his head and a blue shirt is bending down and talking to participants.

Opening Eyes

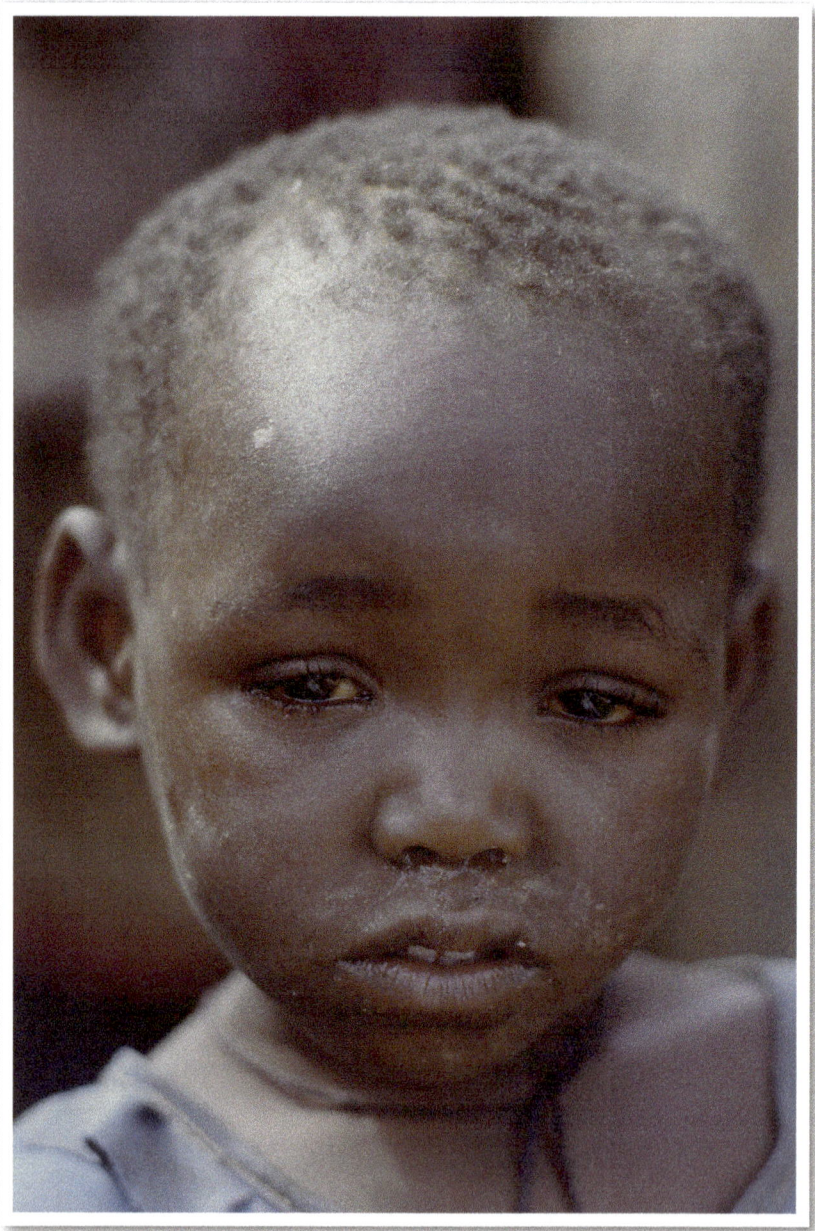

A Tanzanian child with trachoma and an unclean face

Did the Children have Clean Faces?

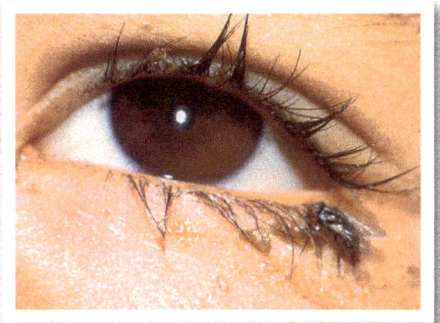

Left: A child's dirty eye with adherent dried secretions and an eye-seeking fly

Below: Children playing at the village's water pump

and having had a mother who also had trichiasis. All indicators related to being from less well-off families.

The consequence of TT is the development of corneal opacities or scarring, CO, and the resultant loss of vision or blindness. Peter Rapoza examined our data for people of all ages. He showed that bilateral opacities occurred in 1.2 percent of adults and were twice as common in women. Half of the bilateral corneal opacities were due to trachoma, the rest followed trauma or other conditions. Unilateral opacities occurred in 2.1 percent of people and a quarter of these were caused by trachoma. Of the eyes with opacities, 73 percent of them were blind.

With Jon Siler from the Dana Center, we undertook a longitudinal study of nine families in a community near Kongwa. Henry Mkocha, who worked in that area with Mmbaga, joined our team. This study included 100 family members who were examined once every three months for one year. Their eyes were graded and photographed for trachoma, and had specimens collected for DFA and for tear antibody levels. Almost 90 percent of the children had trachoma at baseline. Children with trachoma were given tetracycline ointment, but on the follow up three months later, the ointment seemed to have had little discernible effect. The highest rates of trachoma were, as always, in those children under 6. Half the children under 15 years had clean faces, and about half of all the children would have two or more flies on their face when examined. Half the children who started with TF continued to have TF throughout the study: they tended to be younger, male and were heavy shedders of chlamydia. Over the year some children recovered from trachoma and others acquired it. Those who had recovered—that is, they no longer had TF—had been laboratory test negative for three to six months before this. This suggested that the inflammatory changes of trachoma would resolve in three to six months after reinfection stops. This was very similar to what we had seen in the monkeys. Serotyping of tear antibodies showed antibodies to serovars A and B. The serology was usually consistent within all family members, although a few houses had someone, usually an adult, with antibodies to the other serovar. This, again, indicated that most transmission occurs within the family.

Interestingly, from a subset of children we took paired conjunctival samples for DFA to detect the presence of chlamydia. The two samples were taken five minutes apart and showed a 10 percent discordance, that is the first one was positive and the second one was negative. This was despite each specimen having a more than adequate number of cells confirming the discordance and was not because of poor specimen collection. For specimens collected two to eight days apart, the discordance was even larger, 22 percent. Although some of these specimens came from children with low elementary body, EB, loads—that is less than 20 EB in a sample—about half the children had much higher loads. Later, we used Alan Hudson's 'home-brew' RNA probe to test some of those samples from children who had TF but who were negative on DFA testing. Alan was one of the first to develop nucleic-acid probes to detect chlamydia. In the small number of DFA negative samples, one third were positive with his new, more sensitive RNA probe. Once it was fully developed, Polymerase Chain Reaction testing, PCR, became the standard test for detecting chlamydial nucleic acid and the presence of chlamydia, and became widely used.

This longitudinal study with 12 months of follow-up showed young children with active trachoma could shed chlamydia persistently, and once children cleared the infection, the clinical signs would slowly resolve. It might have been more powerful if the follow-up intervals had been shorter. A subsequent study done in The Gambia by Robin Bailey from London re-examined families at monthly intervals. However, I wondered if weekly examinations might not provide even more information about chlamydial transmission between children that might even happen on a daily basis.

Having shown lack of facial cleanliness was the biggest risk factor for trachoma and an obvious method of transmission of infection, the key was to prove this within a clinical trial or study to show that promoting facial cleanliness would reduce the levels of trachoma. Again, this was to be no small undertaking. Sheila West returned to Kongwa and led this study. Our team included Matthew Lynch, Beatriz Muñoz and of course Mmbaga and Mkocha. Sheila reassembled a local team to help with recruitment, health promotion and education, examinations and treatment. Six villages were randomly assigned to receive either: (1) mass treatment with tetracycline ointment, the standard treatment for trachoma at the time; or (2) tetracycline ointment and the promotion of face-washing and facial cleanliness. All children aged 1 to 7 in these villages were assessed for trachoma and facial cleanliness at baseline and then at 2, 6 and 12 months.

The health promotion program to improve facial cleanliness was community-based with locally-led neighbourhood meetings to build consensus. Reinforcing activities included school plays, seminars, work with the traditional healers, and meetings with other village groups. The mass treatment was tetracycline ointment to the eyes once a day for 30 days. At baseline 66 percent of children had trachoma and only 19 percent had clean faces. Pre-schoolers had the highest rates of trachoma and of dirty faces.

The intervention did have, albeit modest, impact on improving facial cleanliness. At the trial's one-year mark, 35 percent of children in the three intervention villages had sustained clean faces and the children in these villages were 60 percent more likely to have clean faces. In those villages the risk of active trachoma, TF, was reduced by 19 percent but this did not quite reach statistical significance. However, the risk of severe active trachoma, TI, was significantly reduced, by 42 percent, there. In those with a sustained clean face the impact was even greater, the risk of active trachoma was reduced by 42 percent and for severe trachoma by 65 percent. Data analysis showed there was less re-emergence of trachoma in previously affected children who had sustained clean faces. This clearly showed a decrease in chlamydial transmission associated with clean faces. Hooray!

Further analysis showed that sustained severe trachoma, TI, was twice as common in girls, and it was also twice as common for those children who lived in a family with other children who had trachoma. This again showed the importance of reinfection

Did the Children have Clean Faces?

Above: A health promotion and education session for the men in a village
Below: School children performing a song and dance prompting facial cleanliness

within the family. The idea that a caring role for village girls at very young ages renders them more liable than boys to be reinfected, seemed proven.

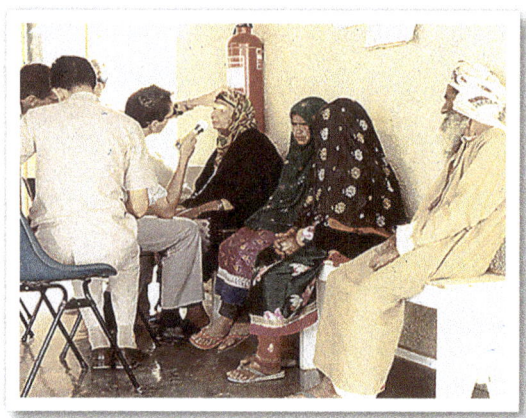

Mark Reacher in Oman examining women with trichiasis prior to surgery

Some dismissed this study because there was not a strong, statistically significant drop in trachoma, TF, in the three intervention villages. This criticism overlooks some key issues. The one-year study was still a short-term intervention that tried to make a massive change in culture and behaviour. It did lead to a significant increase in facial cleanliness, and this was associated with decreases in trachoma, especially the severe TI inflammation. It used the only available antibiotic treatment, tetracycline ointment. (Tetracycline ointment is less effective than azithromycin, but azithromycin did not become available until years later.) Further, the study did not address the environmental factors directly relating to water availability and usage. It should be noted that the intervention did not have as much impact in one intervention village as it had in the other two, and this has a strong effect on the outcomes. However, to my mind, the study clearly demonstrated the importance of clean faces. Certainly enough to influence the trachoma interventions for the years to come.

During this time, Mark Reacher, a recently qualified ophthalmologist from the UK, came to study with us at the Dana Center. He had worked in the Sultanate of Oman and had a Master of Public Health degree. Mark reviewed the literature and found about

60 papers that described 30 different methods for operating on the upper eye lid to correct the in-turned eye lashes that rub on the eye, trachomatous entropion and trichiasis. The wide range of possible surgical techniques made things very confusing for would-be surgeons. This was reflected in the poor results many had with surgery, results that led to further changes in the surgical techniques.

I went with Mark to Oman to set up a large, randomised trial of trichiasis surgery. In this study we looked at three different ways to deal with minor trichiasis, two surgical procedures for major trichiasis, and two surgical procedures for trichiasis with defective lid closure. For major trichiasis, one procedure was called 'bilamellar tarsal rotation' that cut through the whole eyelid. Another was 'tarsal rotation advance' that cut some of the eyelid but left the skin intact. The bilamellar tarsal rotation performed significantly better for both major and minor trichiasis. For those cases with a lid-closure defect the 'tarsal advance and buccal mucosal graft' performed a bit better. Consequently bilamellar tarsal rotation became the standard surgical procedure for trichiasis and was recommended in the WHO manual. This was widely used and taught to ophthalmic medical assistants and ophthalmic nurses around the world. In the last few years Emily Gower and Shanna Merbs have done a lot of work to further refine the surgical techniques and now many prefer the further modifications to the 'posterior lamellar rotation procedure'.

In October 1989 we organised an Edna McConnell Clark Foundation meeting for those working on trachoma. At the meeting we reviewed what had been learned and what still needed to be done. The meeting was held at Oxford on the eastern shore of Chesapeake Bay, Maryland. We ate crabs and oysters, the classic Chesapeake eating experience, and spent one late afternoon out on a skipjack, the classic Chesapeake Bay working sailboat. The meeting outcomes reinforced the need for more and better

Time off on a skipjack on the Bay

surgery to correct trichiasis, reinforcing the importance of Mark Reacher's Oman project, then underway. There was a need for better antibiotic treatment for the chlamydial infection—tetracycline ointment was not well tolerated and its effect was only marginal. We had shown the need for easy access to safe water supplies. There was a push, particularly from me, to focus on how we could improve facial cleanliness.

Starting in 1990 Joanne Katz and Keith West from the Dana Center began a major study on the impact of vitamin A supplementation on child survival in the Terai of Nepal, the southern lowlands bordering India. Al led the study. I helped too. Al's previous work in Indonesia had shown the association between vitamin A deficiency and increased childhood mortality but a prospective randomised trial was needed to confirm this.

As part of this big vitamin A study, we also examined nearly 900 children aged between 2 and 6 years for trachoma. They were randomly selected from 20 Nepalese local government wards: 24 percent had trachoma and nearly 50 percent of those aged 2 years old were infected. This time, there was no significant difference in trachoma rates between girls and boys. Trachoma rates varied greatly between wards. Wards with tube wells had lower rates. At the household level, trachoma rates were lower in houses of those better-off: those that had servants, less than five people in a room, owned a bicycle, had a thatched roof, or owned land that could be irrigated. These were all measures of socioeconomic advantage, presumably associated with better living conditions and hygiene. Some other factors of interest that were not significantly related to trachoma included maternal literacy and ownership of watches or radios.

In 1990 Al, Sheila and I went to Saudi Arabia in the middle of the holy fasting month of Ramadan when Muslims abstain from food, drink, smoking, gossip and sexual relations from sunrise to sunset. The latter two were no real impediment to us, but in

July, mid-summer, it was boiling hot. Fortunately, as visitors, we were given some leeway and allowed water and some snacks.

The visit was arranged by Akef al Magrabi, a leading Saudi ophthalmologist, and Prince Abdulaziz Ahmead Abdulazia Al Saud. We knew Akef well: he was a member of the International Council of Ophthalmology. The prince was closely linked to the IAPB, and was the regional chair for the Eastern Mediterranean. Blind himself, he proved warm, supportive and generous.

After a day or two in Riyadh, we flew in the prince's comfortable private jet to a regional capital and spent the day examining people for trachoma. We returned to the regional governor's palace in the evening to break the fast and stay the night. While everyone prayed after sundown, we walked in the beautiful cool palace gardens. After, we sat at a big square table in a huge hall with many diners and ate amazing Saudi food. All the while the prince and the governor held a conversation in a loud voice and in Arabic that we, the audience, were somehow meant to follow. After dinner we went to our rooms where our bags were waiting for us. The next morning our bags would be collected, we would have a police escort through town to the airport tarmac to board the plane and fly to the next region. This was field work of a new and different type, an amazing adventure. An air-conditioned jet is a top way to travel!

We found trachoma in about 20 percent of the Bedouin children whose families lived out in the desert in tents and with their camels. Every two weeks or so they packed up their tents, loaded their camels into their Mercedes trucks and moved to another desert site. Many Bedouin had moved into new homes and apartments in towns, where the rate of trachoma had fallen to about 2 percent. Some other Bedouin had moved to towns but still lived in their tents in large compounds where they had good access to water, electricity and facilities. Periodically, they would reposition their tents in their compound.

However, their rate of trachoma was 10 percent, indicating

Did the Children have Clean Faces?

Above: Prince Abdul Aziz and Akef Al Magrabi on the prince's plane flying over Saudi Arabia

Below: Examining eyes of Bedouin children in the Saudi Arabian desert

that for facial cleanliness, it is the software that is important, not necessarily the hardware.

After visiting Saudi Arabia, I took up my new position at the University of Melbourne. Although I was busy as the professor of ophthalmology and director of eye services at the Royal Victorian Eye and Ear Hospital, the work on trachoma continued around the world, and I could not let it go altogether.

In the following year the first reports of the use of a new tetracycline-related drug, azithromycin, for treating chlamydial genital infections were published. In 1993 Robin Baily reported a small trial of azithromycin to treat trachoma in The Gambia. In 1997 Chan Dawson and Julie Schachter published the results of a large, controlled trial in Egypt that they had started five years before, comparing the use of azithromycin pills with tetracycline eye ointment: they found a single oral dose of azithromycin was as effective as six weeks of tetracycline.

In early 1995 we had started an open study of a single dose of azithromycin treatment with Andrew Lamming in Central Australia (see page 352) Without any other interventions, at 12 months the prevalence for trachoma had bounced back. We had not included any emphasis on facial cleanliness in this study, but it showed that even this exciting new one-off oral antibiotic on its own was not sufficient to achieve the ultimate goal: the elimination of trachoma.

Azithromycin clearly greatly reduces infection: detailed studies of genital infection indicate that without reinfection a single dose of azithromycin can clear about 95 percent of infections. So, while on its own it is not a perfect cure for trachoma, it does reduce infection and therefore would reduce transmission at least in the short term. Although transmission is reduced quickly, some transmission continues and increases over time, so trachoma rates will still increase. Thus, for the sustained elimination of trachoma, transmission has to be stopped; to stop transmission children have to have clean faces; and whatever else is required to achieve this needs to be done.

Subsequent studies from Africa and around the world, have time and time again confirmed that single dose or even repeated annual doses of azithromycin on their own will not eliminate trachoma.

In 1993 WHO, with support from the Clark Foundation, published a report 'Achieving Community Support for Trachoma Control'. This report was written by Victoria Francis and Ginny Turner. Ginny had completed her PhD at Hopkins and was then working with Helen Keller International. This was the first real step to address trachoma in a more comprehensive way, setting out the SAFE Strategy.

SAFE is an acronym: S for trichiasis Surgery, A for Antibiotic treatment, F for facial cleanliness, and E for Environmental improvement. From a public health perspective, the four components are in the wrong order, and it should be EFAS but that does not work as well as an acronym. In French the acronym becomes by chance CHANCE.

The first WHO Global Scientific Meeting on trachoma control was held in Geneva in June 1996. After much discussion and with the SAFE Strategy endorsed, a goal for a global program was set: 'To eliminate blinding trachoma as a public health problem by 2020'. Aware of the American Academy of Ophthalmology's program to end vision loss from diabetes by 2000, which they had called 'Diabetes 2000', I suggested the trachoma program be called 'GET2020', the 'Global Elimination of Trachoma by 2020'. This was adopted and confirmed by the World Health Assembly in 1998. GET continues to be used as the program name, even though the 2020 target date has been dropped and the end-goal extended to 2030.

In 2000 I worked with Sheila West and Dominique Negrel from WHO to write a WHO manual called, 'Guidelines for the

Rapid Assessment for Blinding Trachoma'. As the program activities expanded, country managers needed a reproducible, simple and effective way to ascertain the distribution and magnitude of trachoma in their countries at a district level. 'The Guidelines…' were to make sure that data were collected in a consistent manner over time and from various areas.

Lead by Joe Cook in 1998, the Clark Foundation and the pharmaceutical company Pfizer established the International Trachoma Initiative, ITI, to oversee trachoma control activities and manage the donation of azithromycin. Initially, the donations went to five countries. Joe Cook was the first director. In time ITI took the responsibility for all donations of azithromycin. Between 1999 and 2024 over 1 billion azithromycin treatments had been donated. The number of people with trachoma fell from 1.5 billion in 2002 to 103.2 million in 2024. By 2024, 20 countries had been certified by WHO as having eliminated blinding trachoma as a public health problem and eight more were waiting for WHO confirmation.

I attended each of the three subsequent WHO Global Scientific Meetings to review and refine the activities and goals of the GET program. After each meeting a report was published by WHO to set out the way ahead.

I also attended most of the annual GET meetings. At the annual GET meetings the country representatives, the various non-government organisations and researchers review the progress that had been made, country by country. These meetings have usually been in WHO Headquarters in Geneva but also in Regional WHO offices and some have been held in endemic countries.

6

Oncho, River Blindness

> On average, a person infected with river blindness is blind by age 30. Years are lost that otherwise would be prime time for providing for one's livelihood, supporting a family, and contributing to the community.
>
> James Wolfensohn, World Bank president 1995–2005

Professor Maurice Langham wound up his lunchtime talk on the state of onchocerciasis control and treatment in 1978. 'Are there any questions?'

'Why,' I asked, somewhat arrogantly, 'had you not done a proper controlled clinical trial to see if this DEC lotion really works? Why have a treatment group and not have a placebo or control group?'

'Why don't you help me do that? Let's do it together.'

At the Wilmer Institute senior faculty members gave these occasional talks about their current work. Although I was just a corneal fellow at the time, it was always interesting to hear about the work that others were doing. His response stunned me. By pure chance a major new path in my life was about to open up.

Maurice Langham was an English pharmacologist who had been at Wilmer for a few years as head of a small group working on ophthalmic pharmacology. He had done the leading work on developing the oral diuretic acetazolamide—Diamox—which became a leading treatment for glaucoma and blinding eye disease related to high pressure in the eye that leads to optic nerve damage.

In 1978 I went along to his talk thinking I would learn something more about glaucoma—a major misconception. He talked about onchocerciasis, (*say* ong-koh-sur-kai-ah-sis). Those working on it usually call it 'oncho' (*say* on-koh). I knew next to nothing about it. It was all quite strange information to me and the rest of his audience. He talked about a small trial, mixing a drug he called 'DEC' (Diethylcarbamazine) into Nivea body lotion and rubbing it on the skin of a small number of people with what to us was an obscure infection. In trials, big is good; small is not good: this led to my question, and the snap of the teeth of a spring trap that was laid for this young sucker!

Onchocerciasis is a blinding parasitic disease caused by the filarial worm *Onchocerca volvulus*, a nematode. It is transmitted by species of biting black flies, the commonest one in Africa appropriately called *Simulium damnosum*. Like mosquitos, the female black fly bites a human to get blood before she can lay her eggs. If she bites someone with onchocerciasis, she may well pick up tiny microfilariae from under their skin. Black flies breed in the well-oxygenated white water around rapids in fast flowing rivers and streams, so people living along or near such rivers are those most affected. This led Sir John Wilson to call onchocerciasis 'river blindness' after he visited affected communities in Zambia in the 1950s. This name has stuck but those working on it still use the term 'oncho'. Once ingested by the black fly, the small microfilariae migrate and transform through three larval stages—first, second and third stage larvae—over about seven days. The next time the female black fly bites another human, the third stage larvae are ready to migrate into the subcutaneous tissue and so infect that person.

Oncho, River Blindness

Rapids and white water provide a place for washing and form a breeding site for blackflies on this river in the Firestone plantation

Once in the human body, the larvae undergo two more moults to become either a female or male adult worm. It takes six to 12 months for them to mature into adult worms and they form nodules where they reproduce. Nodules typically have two or three female worms that can be up to 50 cm long and one male about 4 to 5 cm long. The worms are tightly coiled and wrapped together and become encapsulated by fibrous tissue. Each nodule develops to a couple of centimetres in diameter, but

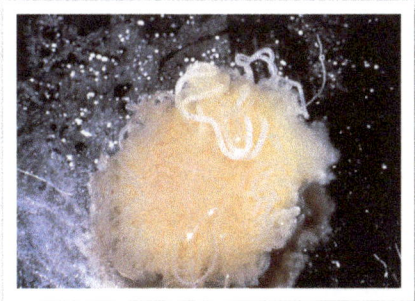

A partially dissected excised nodule that contained two adult female worms still in a tight ball, and one smaller male worm at about 2 o'clock

several nodules may be located together to form a larger cluster. The nodules are typically under the skin and often attached to underlying bone. Adult female worms can live for up to 15 years.

The female releases a thousand or so microfilariae every day, so over time a heavily infected person may have billions of microfilariae in their body. A microfilaria is 200 to 300 microns long and, unless taken up by a black fly, they live for about 18 months. Most microfilariae are found in the skin, but they can migrate throughout the body. A skin snip from a heavily infected person may have up to 500 or so microfilariae per milligram of skin. Although the microfilariae escape detection by the immune system while they are alive, the dead and dying microfilariae cause small explosions of local inflammation.

The edge of a skin snip (lower right corner) examined under a microscope. Many microfilaria that have emerged from the skin snip can be seen swimming.

The skin manifestations of onchocerciasis include severe itching, rashes, lumps or papules, and pustules. Sometimes there is marked swelling of the face—*erisipela de la costa*, hyperpigmentation—and *mal morando*. Although uncommon, it can cause dramatic swelling, darkening and thickening of the skin of one leg—*sowda*. More common is the atrophy of the skin, often with extensive depigmentation and characteristic spotting of the legs aptly named 'leopard skin'. These skin changes can be very disabling. In West Africa collectively they were called '*craw-craw*'. It was in 1875 that a British naval surgeon, John O'Neil, found and described the microfilariae that causes these changes.

When microfilariae migrate into the eyes they can be seen in

Oncho, River Blindness

the cornea, the front surface of the eye, or swimming in the front chamber of the eye, the anterior chamber. Sometimes hundreds of them can be counted in an infected person's eye. When the microfilaria die in the cornea, they cause small punctate opacities and later scarring. Much more seriously, they initiate extensive scarring in the retina, at the back of the eye, and sometimes damage the optic nerve. This all leads to profound blindness, for which there is no treatment. In endemic areas blindness typically occurred in those aged between 20 and 40 years, often parents and farmers. In hyperendemic communities oncho blinds up to half the adults. It is devastating to see the blind sitting forlornly in the villages, unable to do anything to look after themselves or help their families.

A man blinded by onchocerciasis being led on a stick by his son in the centre of Ougadougou

Blind fathers were led on a stick by one of their children so that they could go out to their fields and farm. Sometimes I saw a single farmer on the end of a stick being led out to his field by his son. At other times I saw lines of four or five blind men being led out by one boy, each man joined by holding a stick between one and the next. In the middle of town in Ouagadougou, the capital of Burkina Faso, I once saw a blind man being led on a stick by his son. Onchocerciasis devastates families and communities.

Up until the 1970s onchocerciasis was endemic in most of the sub-Saharan countries in Africa. The slave trade brought onchocerciasis to Latin American countries where there were local black fly species capable of transmitting and spreading the infection through local populations.

In the 1980s, globally some 123 million people were at risk, 18 million were infected and some 268 000 were known to be blind.

During World War 2 American troops fighting in the Pacific became infected with elephantiasis, or lymphatic filariasis. This infection was common in the Pacific Islands and in most other tropical Asian and Sub-Saharan African regions. Elephantiasis is caused by *Wucheria bancrofti*, a filarial parasite related to *O. volvulus*, but which is transmitted by mosquitos, not black flies. In lymphatic filariasis, the adult worms locate themselves in the lymphatic system, particularly in the groin. The lymphatic drainage system becomes blocked. Lymphatic fluid accumulates that causes the swelling of the leg, lymphoedema, and in men very large and swollen scrotums. The impact of lymphatic filariasis on the American troops led to the research and development of the drug, diethylcarbamazine, DEC. DEC was quite effective for treating lymphatic filariasis.

In 1948 a Mexican doctor, Dr L Mazzotti, thought to use DEC for some of his patients with onchocerciasis. He reported that they had strong reactions to DEC treatment that included severe pain, fever, rashes, swellings and oedema, arthritis, and cardiovascular changes. This reaction to DEC occurred in nearly everyone with onchocerciasis and became known around the world as the 'Mazzotti Reaction'. DEC killed all the microfilariae, but the dead microfilariae stimulated the severe immune response that caused the reaction. However, DEC had no effect on the adult worms.

The only other treatment for onchocerciasis at that time was an intravenous injection of suramin, a drug developed to treat sleeping sickness.

Sleeping sickness is another African infection, trypanosomiasis, transmitted by tsetse fly bites. It is usually fatal so the 1 or 2 percent mortality associated with suramin treatment was not a major barrier for its use for trypanosomiasis. Suramin was the only drug known to kill the onchercal adult worms. Six weekly injections were required to kill them. However, the significant mortality rate effectively precluded Suramin's use for onchocerciasis.

Another approach to control onchocerciasis was to spray the black fly breeding sites to reduce black fly populations and stop transmission. The Onchocerciasis Control Program, OCP, was a mammoth effort run by the World Health Organisation, the World Bank and the UN Food and Agriculture Organization, FAO. The OCP started in 1974 and was based in Ouagadougou in Burkina Faso. It had a fleet of aircraft and helicopters that were used to spray the breeding sites each week in 11 countries. It was effective in controlling the black flies and reducing transmission in savannahs. However, because of the tree canopy in the rainforests, planes and helicopters could not fly close enough to get the insecticidal spray to the breeding sites in the rivers. Therefore spraying was not an option for controlling onchocerciasis in rainforest areas.

This is where things stood when Professor Maurice Langham started to think of ways to eliminate the microfilariae without initiating the Mazzotti Reaction's systemic side effects. His idea was to have the DEC lotion kill the microfilariae in the skin and so avoid the systemic reactions.

Chance played yet another role. After we arrived in Baltimore, we had spent the first two years living in a condominium. Liz met Theo Greene and her husband Bruce (see page 81). Bruce Greene was a big man but gentle with patients and very serious, but with a wry smile. He was the chief medical resident at Hopkins and worked on infectious diseases, including schistosomiasis, snail fever. Free-swimming flatworm larvae released from freshwater snail hosts enter the human body and the adult worm lodges in the liver. It is a killer. (It still affected over 236 million people in 2019.) As we sat around and talked, I said, 'Maurice Langham at Wilmer has invited me to do a proper trial with DEC lotion in oncho. Would you be interested in joining us on that, Bruce?'

Bruce jumped at the idea. So started a strong collaboration and an even stronger friendship. In February 1979, working with contacts of Maurice Langham, we started the first of two double-masked, or double-blind, clinical trials of DEC lotion. 'Double-blind' is the term used for randomised controlled trials when neither the investigators nor the patients know which treatment—here, DEC or placebo—they are giving or receiving; that is, they are 'masked'. For studies of eye disease, for obvious reasons, ophthalmologists refer to these as 'double-masked' studies rather than double blind.

The following studies we did were all properly conducted, randomised controlled trials, each with the appropriate ethical clearances and informed consent. Those participants who received placebo may not have received much benefit other than attention to other medical issues they might have. Those who received active treatment had a significant reduction in their onchocerciasis. The ultimate goal of this work was to find a safe and effective treatment for all those infected and end river blindness.

The first study was in Guatemala with help from Langham's Guatemalan ophthalmic colleagues. We worked in a somewhat isolated coffee farm or *finca* in the mountains with surrounding volcanos. Bruce could not join us for this trial, but Liz could and helped me for the initial week of the study. All the work was done on the *finca*, where we set up an examination site and stayed. Our food was all prepared by a local woman who cooked hand-made traditional tortillas and delicious meals, but with little variation. Our only disappointment was with the coffee, and it was a very big disappointment. Here was a place growing world-class premium coffee beans; not a single bean was roasted there. The only coffee available for us was Nescafe instant; decaffeinated to boot.

We screened over 300 workers from adjacent *fincas* and enrolled 187 with onchocerciasis into the study. Half were treated with the Nivea lotion with DEC, the other half received just Nivea. (One small problem for a study on river blindness in Guatemala was using a lotion whose name 'Nivea' almost meant 'no see' in Spanish). Patients applied the lotion daily for a week and then weekly for seven weeks. We examined them daily for side effects, including an eye exam. They were examined again at three and eight weeks.

Liz testing subjects' vision during the DEC study in Guatemala

Subjects applying lotion in the DEC trial in Guatemala

One third of those treated with the DEC lotion had moderate to severe side effects compared with 2 percent in the placebo group, so despite using the lotion instead of a tablet, a significant number still developed a Mazzotti Reaction. However, the microfilaria counts in both the skin and the eye dropped in the treatment group.

Liz and I had arranged to have a college student stay in our house to look after Kate and Bart while we were away. As we flew back to Baltimore a huge snowstorm moved in. At 10.30 pm on Sunday night our plane was the last to land before the airport was closed. The snow was already inches deep. A lot of persuasion and a very substantial tip eventually persuaded a reluctant taxi driver take us, shivering in our Guatemalan clothes and sandals, home. By the next morning nearly 3 feet of snow had fallen and our poor long-suffering babysitter was stuck with us for another three days.

Oncho, River Blindness

Starting in March 1979 Bruce and I undertook a more detailed study of DEC lotion in Liberia. Liberia sounded hard to get to, but Pan Am had regular flights that stopped at the Robertsfield Airport in Liberia on their way to Accra in Ghana and Nairobi in Kenya. We worked on the Firestone Rubber Plantation and recruited the rubber tappers who worked there. Their day job was to go from tree to tree to collect the liquid latex sap that exuded after the bark of the tree had been cut. They then carried their large and heavy buckets to a weighing station where the latex was collected in big trucks and sent off to the factory to be processed. As the area was a rainforest area and the plantation was full of rubber trees, aerial spraying for oncho vector control was not an option.

The Firestone Rubber Plantation in Liberia was set up in 1926. Nearly 200 000 acres, over 800 square kilometres, it displaced

Rubber tapper in the Firestone plantation collecting liquid latex, sap, into a small bowl after recutting the bark of the rubber tree. Dried latex is collected as crepe rubber.

many communities. In 1941 the airstrip at Robertsfield was built as a stopping point for US Army transport planes on their way to the fighting in North Africa. The planation employed a lot of workers who lived with their families in small clusters of company compounds. The expatriate staff lived in comfortable 1950s buildings. Over the years there have been disputes about wages, child labour, daily latex-collection and production targets, work and housing conditions, and so forth. However, when we arrived all seemed to be working smoothly. Much of the latex was shipped as crepe rubber—crinkled sheets, packed for further processing—but Firestone was said to produce 90 percent of the world's liquid latex that was used to make things like surgical rubber gloves and condoms.

We were based at the Firestone Medical Center where we recruited 20 male employees with onchocerciasis who were hospitalised for the first two weeks. This time we compared DEC lotion with a DEC tablet. Again, it was a double-masked trial: half the patients received DEC lotion and a placebo tablet; the other half received a DEC tablet and placebo Nivea lotion. For the first week the tablets were given three times a day and the lotion was applied daily. Starting in the second week the tablets and lotion were given once a week and were continued for six months. All medication was given under supervision, a huge task for the devoted nurse from the medical center. The patients were examined before and during the week-long treatment and at two weeks, and then when we returned two months and six months later.

We did detailed physical examinations and took skin snips for microfilarial counts. The ocular examinations included vision tests, slit-lamp examination and retinal photography.

Bruce and I stayed in the comfortable visitors' quarters on the plantation and were well looked after. We had the use of a small car to go back and forth to the hospital and to Robertsfield. At Robertsfield, besides the airport and its nearby hotel, was the

Oncho, River Blindness

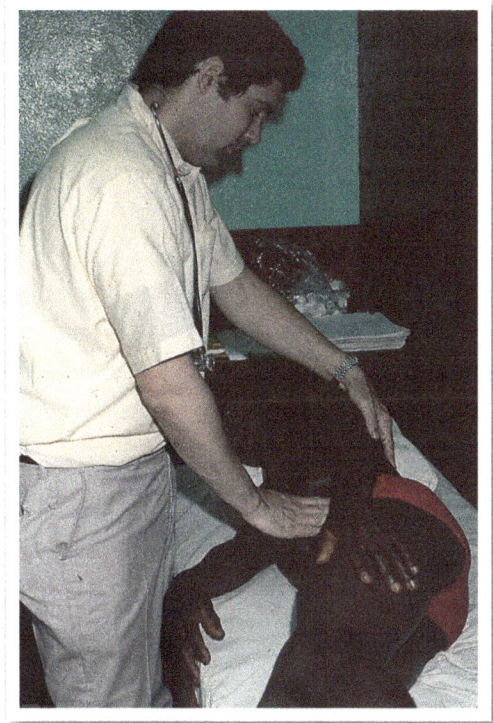

Left: Bruce Greene examining a subject for nodules

Below: Performing an eye exam in Liberia

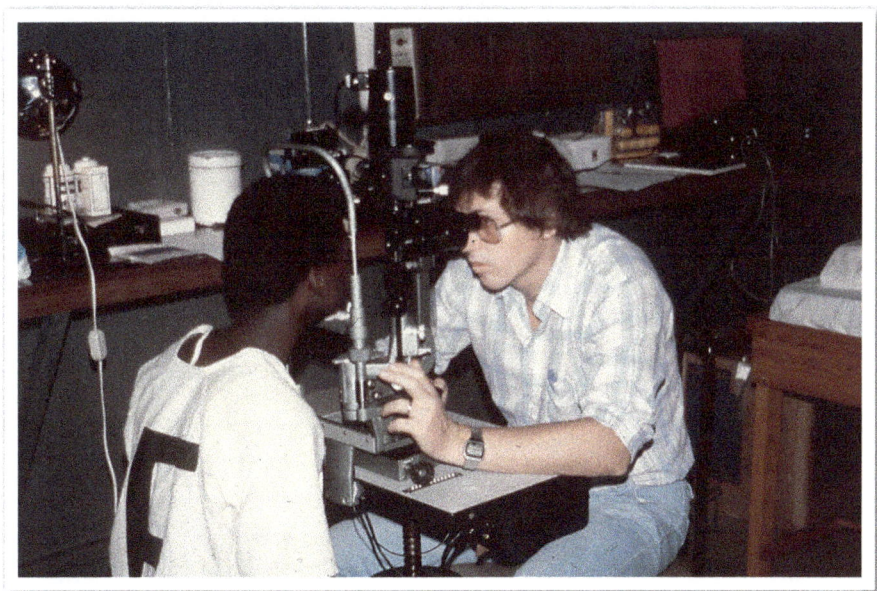

base of the Liberian Institute of Biomedical Research, LIBR. Initially established with funding from the Rockefeller Foundation, it was then led by Alfred Prince and Betsy Brotman from the New York Blood Center.

LIBR were doing the foundational studies on viral hepatitis B and maintained a large colony of chimpanzees for them. The chimps were usually brought to LIBR as abandoned babies that had been found on their own in the wild. However, it was unclear if their parents had been illegally hunted down for bushmeat or not. We became good friends with Betsy and her team and later did some other collaborative work together.

With time we also got to know some of the Pan Am hostesses who stayed in the hotel in Robertsfield. They would fly from New York to Robertsfield then spend 24 hours there while their plane flew on to Nairobi. When it returned, they would fly back to New York. The crew from Nairobi would spend time in Robertsfield also, and fly back and forth. We learned from them that the meals on the flights were always 'leather or feather', beef or chicken. Ah, well… With these studies and all our trips, we got to know Pan Am quite well. It was only some years later that the various frequent flier programs started, otherwise we would surely have been platinum members!

Our study showed that with treatment, all the patients developed at least some degree of the Mazzotti Reaction with swellings and rash. Most also had ocular changes. Some developed kidney problems indicated by protein in their urine, a complication that had not been previously described with DEC treatment. The reactions were usually worse in those using the DEC lotion. However, the decrease in microfilarial skin snip counts was dramatically different, significantly lower in those who had received DEC tablets. The palpable nodules were removed from each patient at six months and examined by Hartwig Schulz-Key. Hartwig was a parasitologist from Heidelberg, Germany studying onchocerciasis at the Bong Mine in

Eastern Liberia. He found no difference in the numbers of viable worms in the nodules from each group. Our study showed that oral DEC was more effective in reducing microfilarial levels in the skin and the eye, and actually had less side effects than the lotion.

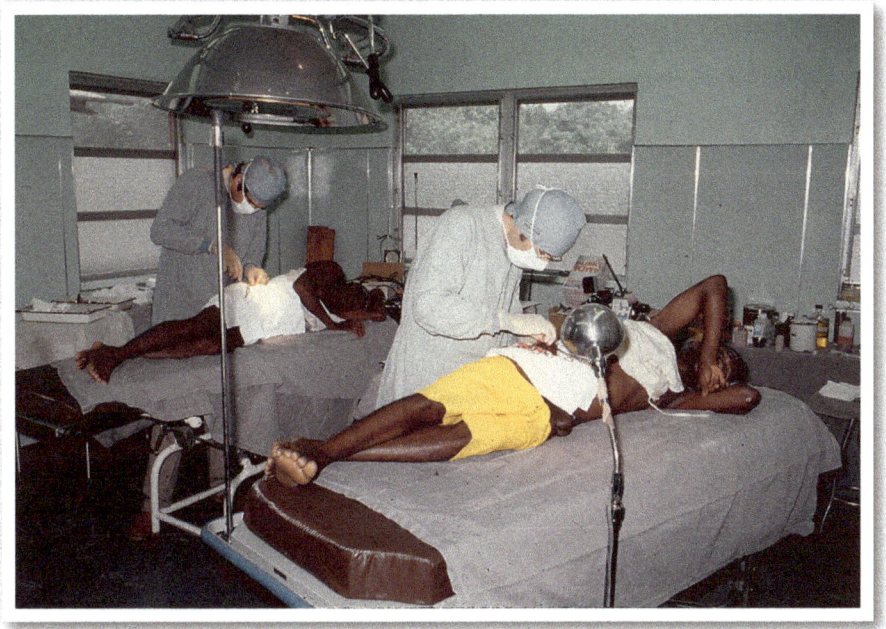

Bruce Greene and Monte DelMonte performing nodulectomies

In a later study, Henry Newland, an Australian ophthalmologist working with us at the Dana Center, showed that DEC lotion could be used as a diagnostic test for the presence of onchocerciasis. A small amount of cream is smeared on the buttocks. Next day, the patient is examined to see if they developed a reaction demonstrating that they had onchocerciasis. This simple test is sometimes still used.

Bruce also did some laboratory studies looking at the immunologic reactions following DEC treatment. He showed a strong correlation between the presence of circulating immune complexes—an antibody with its antigen circulating in the blood—and the occurrence of the more severe systemic and ocular side effects and complications. He also looked at how serum antibodies and immune cells might kill microfilariae. This was of interest because living microfilariae would migrate through the body essentially unimpeded by the immune system but when killed by DEC, the dead microfilaria initiated a marked response. However, in the laboratory, immune cells could easily kill the microfilariae, with or without serum antibodies. We were unable to explain the difference between what happens in life and in the laboratory.

On the way back from one of the trips to Liberia, we travelled through Ougadougou and visited the OCP to find out about the work they were doing with the spraying and vector control and the other research that was going on there.

I met up with Björn Thylefors, the Swedish ophthalmologist with the OCP who I had first met at the WHO meeting in Asilomar. (In 1982 Björn succeeded Mario Tarizzo as the director of PBL at WHO in Geneva. He and I continued to work together for many years, a connection that led to a solid friendship. I would sometimes stay with Björn and his wife Bente when I was in Geneva for a WHO meeting. Once Liz and I and our children spent a few days with Björn and his family at their beachside house south of Gothenburg in Halmstad, Sweden. We had some lovely days on the beach with them, but I broke my toe in the surf. Just not careful enough with an unexpected wave. Broken toes get very painful while sitting on long plane trips.)

On another trip back from Liberia to Baltimore I stopped in Geneva to visit the WHO PBL to talk about trachoma. They suggested that I should meet Dr Brian Duke, head of the WHO program on filariasis that included onchocerciasis and lymphatic filariasis. Brian had worked on onchocerciasis in the Republic of Cameroon for many years before he moved to the WHO. I had read many of Brian's papers; he was clearly the world's expert on onchocerciasis. He was a delight to meet in person.

Brian Duke and his wife Diane, and daughters Lotti and Molly outside Lancaster Castle, 1998

Over time, we too became strong friends. He later married his former administrative assistant at WHO, Diane. When Brian retired from WHO he moved for a few years to the Armed Forces Institute of Pathology, AFIP, in Bethesda, Maryland, just down the road from Baltimore, so our families were able to get together. They came with their elder daughter Lottie, and soon after Molly arrived. I am Lottie's godfather and when Lottie was married some years after Brian died, she gave me the honour of walking her down the aisle.

When Brian and I first met in Geneva we discussed our recent DEC trials. What on earth could be the next step forward? Professors Alan Bird and Barrie Jones (not politician Barry Jones), both ophthalmologists based in London, were working on onchocerciasis and of course Björn Thylefors was still with the OCP. However, there seemed to be very few ophthalmologists working on oncho, and so without being aware of it, one would quickly become one of the 'leading' oncho ophthalmologists.

A new benzimidazole drug, mebendazole, had emerged from clinical trials for treating threadworms and other soil-derived worms. Could mebendazole be useful against the onchocerciasis one?

In 1980 a military coup in Liberia overthrew the government of William Tolbert and installed Samuel Doe, the blood of deposed MPs soon flowing on Monrovia beach. Liberia had become too dangerous for further studies for a while, although somehow the Firestone plantation was able to keep working.

Through various contacts, including those of Bruce Greene, we started a new trial in Mexico in May 1980. By then Bruce had left Johns Hopkins and had moved to a faculty position at Case Western Reserve in Cleveland.

Our study was based at the Centro de Investigaciones Ecologicas del Sureste, CIES, in San Cristobal de las Casas, Chiapas in the highlands of southern Mexico, that wonderful old colonial city that dated back to 1528. We worked mainly with medical researchers Roberto Rivas-Alcala and Alfredo Dominguez-Vazquez and their team at CIES. (Roberto continued in academia and Alfredo became a member of Onchocerciasis Elimination Program for the Americas that finally eliminated onchocerciasis from Mexico in 2015.)

We stayed in an old colonial hotel in the centre of San Cristobal. We walked in town, seeing many people still wearing the traditional locally-specific patterned hand-woven clothing again. We learned a lot about true Mexican food and ate plenty of it: tamales, tortillas, frijoles-refried black beans, mole and huevos a la Chiapaneca-Chiapas-style eggs, and drank a tequila or a margarita or two from time to time. CIES was a short car ride outside of the town.

For this study we recruited 40 local Mayan men with onchocerciasis from a community in the Sierra Madre. They had no

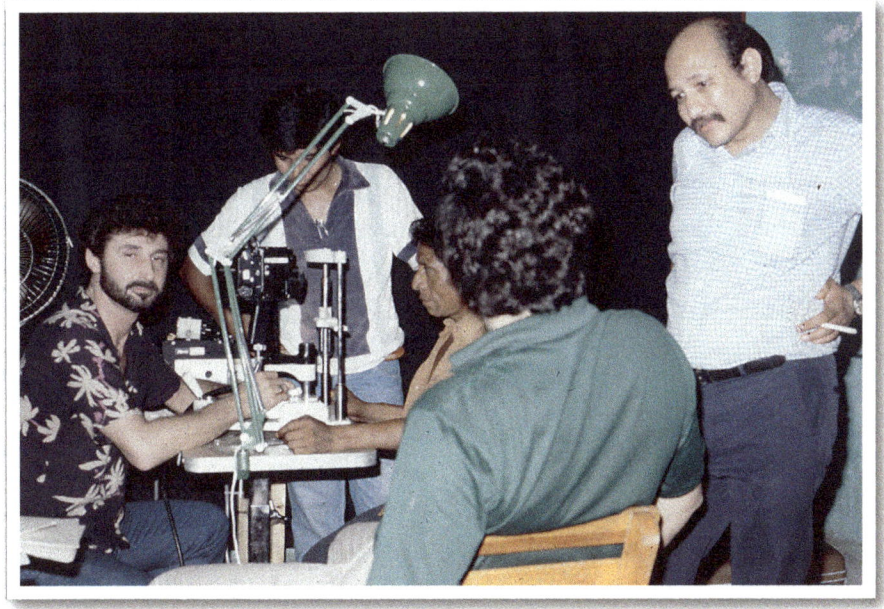

Richard Belt (from Wilmer) taking retinal photos in the mebendazole study in Mexico with Bruce Green (with his back to us) and Roberto Rivas, right

English and we had to learn some Spanish on the run, 'look up… look down… open your eyes' and with time we became more fluent. The patients were a delight to work with.

For this study we had four treatment groups: one received mebendazole, another levamisole, another both mebendazole and levamisole, and the fourth DEC. Those who received DEC were also given dexamethasone for the first four days to dampen the Mazzotti Reactions. Again, this was a double-masked trial and the appropriate placebos were used.

All patients had extensive clinical work ups, laboratory testing and skin snips as well as even more detailed ocular exams that included fluorescein angiography. This entails the injection of a fluorescent dye into a vein and then a series of photographs are taken as the dye passes through the blood vessels in the back of the eye. We were very fortunate to again have Terry George, head of photography at the Wilmer, helping. Terry would spend hours obtaining the best retinal photographs of the changes caused by onchocerciasis.

DEC produced the more rapid fall in microfilarial skin snip counts, but by six months the counts were only moderately reduced and the DEC and mebendazole groups were comparable. After six months the counts had started to rise in the DEC group. Side effects were more severe and more frequent in those who had received DEC. Adding levamisole made no difference in either of the groups who used it. Nodules were removed and studied by Charles McKenzie after eight weeks of treatment. Charles was an Australian parasitologist based in London who studied onchocerciasis. The number of developing embryos and microfilaria in the female worms were reduced in the mebendazole groups and the numbers of developing microfilariae were 40 times lower. However, overall adult viability was not different from untreated controls. This study showed that mebendazole was relatively safe and may have had a moderate effect on microfilarial loads and probably some effect of inhibiting embryogenesis in fertile female worms—but it did not kill the worms.

In 1981, while we were wrapping up the mebendazole study results, information became available about another benzimidazole drug, flubendazole. In other filarial worms flubendazole was shown to be more effective in stopping embryogenesis and possibly killing the adult worms. Would it do the same for the onchocerciasis ones?

Bruce and I started a new study with the team at CIES. We again had Terry George handling retinal photography and fluorescein angiography to study better any retinal changes.

Because of the retinal changes we found in the previous study, I was delighted to have a retinal specialist from Wilmer, Bob Murphy, join us on this study. Bob and I were good friends and when not working at Wilmer, or working on onchocerciasis studies, we co-owned a 23-foot trailer-sailer and often sailed together on Chesapeake Bay. Bob married Emily Chew (see page 85 and 94).

In the Mexican study we had two groups of patients. The 'treatment' group of 10 men received the contender drug flubendazole by intramuscular injection once a week for five weeks. They also received placebo tablets. The control group of nine men received DEC tablets and intramuscular injections of saline. We followed a detailed clinical, laboratory and ocular examination protocol including fluorescein angiography similar to that used in our previous study. Patients were followed at two, three, six, nine and 12 months. Palpable nodules were excised at two months.

The skin snip counts fell quickly with DEC but had almost returned to pre-treatment levels by 12 months. Flubendazole counts dropped slowly but were almost zero after nine months. The systemic and ocular Mazzotti Reactions were again prominent in the DEC group, but they did not occur in anyone in the flubendazole group. However, the flubendazole injections were extremely painful and patients found them very hard to bear. Findings from the examination of the nodules were unclear about whether flubendazole killed the adult worms or not, but it had a dramatic effect on stopping embryogenesis.

The flubendazole injections could not be tolerated as a standard of care, and the search would need to go on for a better and safer drug or combination of drugs. Nevertheless, these findings were close to show-stopping. They strongly suggested that if flubendazole could be delivered safely, it might be possible to stop the production and release of microfilariae because the worms would be infertile until they died. This would not only stop the disease, it would eliminate its ongoing transmission, fulfilling our aim to make onchocerciasis a footnote in history.

In that same year, I worked with Kwablah Awadzi in Tamale, northern Ghana. Kwablah had set up the Onchocerciasis Chemotherapy Research Centre for clinical trials on the top floor of the hospital, a big, tall building built in the early 1970s. To reach Tamale, Terry and I had to fly with our retinal camera and all our other bulky equipment to Ouagadougou Aéroport in Burkina Faso and then drive for 7 hours south into Ghana and into Tamale. We were lodged in a little guest facility on the roof of the hospital. As our visits progressed, one of the two lifts stopped working. On our last visit neither lift was working. It felt like a long way up to the ward on Floor 7 and to our apartment on the roof.

We were there to add ophthalmic examinations, including fluorescein angiography, to a study Kwablah was conducting to assess combined treatment of mebendazole and levamisole compared with placebo treatment. We had 10 men in each group and examined them before and during treatment and we returned for the two-, six—and 12-month examinations. This meant multiple trips to Tamale.

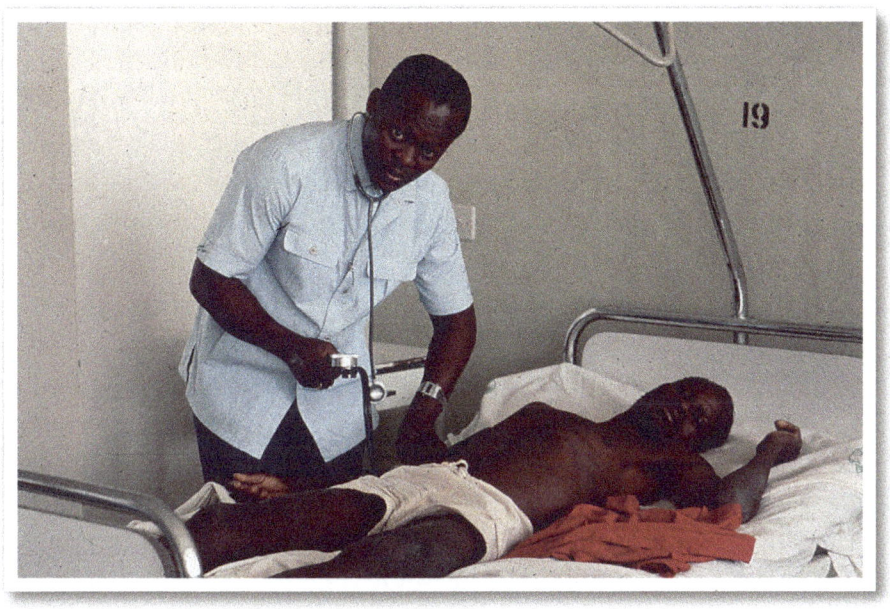

Above: Kwablah Awadzi examining a subject in Tamale, Ghana

Left: Terry George after a hard day's work enjoying a meal in our roof top residence in Tamale

Basically, we found no significant difference between the two groups, showing mebendazole had little or no effect on the microfilariae and caused no significant clinical or ocular reactions. However, we built stronger relationships with Kwablah that became important for subsequent studies. We also had the opportunity to visit and meet with members of the Onchocerciasis Control Program in 'Ouga' (Ougadougou) as we flew in and out and learned more about the work they were carrying out.

With these various studies we had shown that none of the currently available drug treatments for onchocerciasis were satisfactory. Bruce and I had established ourselves as competent researchers in this field, but what were we to do next? We felt like detectives who had checked out and confirmed the alibis of all the suspects on the list, but had no idea who the murderer was. Vector control with fly spraying was working well in the savannah areas but in the rainforest transmission persisted unchecked. There was still a pressing need for a good, safe and effective drug to end river blindness.

7

Ivermectin: Breakthrough Drug

> The importance of Ivermectin for improving the health and wellbeing of millions of individuals with River Blindness and Lymphatic Filariasis, primarily in the poorest regions of the world, is immeasurable.
>
> William Campbell, Nobel Laureate 2015

In Baltimore we had settled into Mt Washington, a neighbourhood on the northern edge of the city. There were many older houses, some dating back to the 1860s. The streets were tree-lined.

On a Saturday morning in July 1982, I was out on a walk around our friendly neighbourhood when I bumped into a friend and colleague from the Wilmer, Stuart Fine. 'I read an article this morning in the *New York Times* about some new drug Merck had developed. Have you seen it yet?'

'No, we get the *Baltimore Sun* and not the *Times*.'

'You really should follow it up. It looks very interesting.'

Saturday morning walks can have amazing consequences.

Merck and Co are one of the world's largest pharmaceutical companies; outside the US they are known as Merck Sharp and Dohme, MSD. The article was about a paper that had been just published in *The Lancet*. The paper was written by Mohammed Aziz, an infectious disease doctor with Merck, who did the source study with his colleagues in Senegal. Aziz was originally from Bangladesh and had spent time working in Africa before moving to Merck and Co in New Jersey.

Merck had identified an astonishingly effective anti-parasitic drug, ivermectin. Ivermectin was to become their largest selling drug, after being developed for use against a wide range of veterinary parasites in the 1980s. A round of golf can have amazing consequences too. Biochemist Dr Satoshi Ōmura had isolated ivermectin from a fungus he had found growing beside the fifth fairway of a golf course in Japan. As part of Merck's search for new antibiotics Dr Bill Campbell from Merck studied ivermectin. They were looking for new antibiotics but also tested the different compounds against other organisms, including some parasites. Bill Campbell found that although ivermectin was not a very powerful antibiotic, it was magnificently effective against a range of parasites. (In 2015 Ōmura and Campbell received the Nobel Prize in Physiology or Medicine for this discovery.)

Aziz had pushed Merck to let him try ivermectin against onchocerciasis. He was finally given permission and set up a Phase 1 study in Senegal with 32 men who had oncho. They started with very low doses: 5 μg/kg (5 micrograms of drug per kilogram of body weight) and 10 μg/kg. These doses had no effect on number of microfilariae seen in skin snips. However, doses of 30 μg/kg and 50 μg/kg dramatically reduced and, in some cases, eliminated the skin microfilariae. To Aziz's amazement all doses were without any significant or detectable side effects. This seemed potentially revolutionary for onchocerciasis treatment. Clearly, more studies were needed.

Aziz and co-workers undertook studies in Paris on African migrants who had oncho. They tested doses of 75 μg/kg and 100 μg/kg and found minimal side effects; mostly mild pruritus, itchiness. The microfilarial counts fell and were negative at two months. In later studies they also assessed the safety and efficacy of higher doses, 150 μg/kg and 200 μg/kg in a similar way.

Ivermectin: Breakthrough Drug

On a trip back to Australia in 1982 I visited Bruce Copeman and his colleagues at the James Cook University in Townsville, Queensland. They were doing studies on the related filarial parasite, *Onchocerca gibsoni*, one that infects cattle. They showed ivermectin was effective against *O. gibsoni* and reduced the levels of microfilaria. This suggested that it might work as a chemoprophylactic, a chemical barrier to infection.

Next year, on my way back from Tamale in Ghana, I went to Burkina Faso and met with Aziz, Bruce Greene, Kwablah Awadzi from Ghana, Michel Lariviere from France, Samba Diallo from Senegal, and Hartwig Schulz-Key from Germany in Ougadougou. We discussed and designed multiple Phase 2 clinical trials of ivermectin. Bruce and I were to do one study in Liberia, Awadzi another in Tamale, and Lariviere and Diallo a third in Senegal. The three groups were all to follow the same protocol with a double-masked controlled trial. One group of patients was to receive 100 µg/kg of ivermectin, another the standard dose of DEC and the third a placebo.

Meeting in Ougadougou to plan the ivermectin studies. From left to right: Hartwig Shultz-Keys, Samba Diallo, Michel Lariviere, me, Mohammed Aziz, Bruce Greene and Kwablah Awadzi.

Opening Eyes

The upheavals in Liberia that followed the 1980 coup by Samuel Doe had more or less settled down. However, this time we worked in the hospital at the rubber plantation of the Liberian Agricultural Company, LAC, in Buchanan. It was a bit further away but quite safe and quiet. We started our study there in March 1984 with 10 men in each of the three groups. Patients were examined during treatment, then at two and six months. Albert White, a Liberian doctor who had trained with Bruce Greene, joined our team. Bob Murphy joined us again as the retinal expert and Sam D'Anna from Wilmer came to take his superb retinal photos. Bob and Sam were able to observe and photograph microfilaria in the retina, a new finding. Mohammed Aziz came for the initial assessments and treatment. We all stayed in guest quarters not far from the hospital but also not far from a beautiful, wide sandy beach. We ate in a staff canteen where there was plenty of food, including seven different meals of local lobsters. One could select a different lobster dish each day of the week, and that's what I did. We could sit in the shade on the sand and watch the local fishermen come and go. The hospital and the guest quarters were on their own and isolated from the working areas of the plantation. Life could have been quite peaceful if we had not worked so hard on this critical study.

We carefully examined the 30 patients each day for the first week and tended to any other issues they had. We left after two weeks and returned to repeat the examinations at three and six months. During the field work, both Mohammed Aziz and Brian Duke came at different times to visit us and assess how things were going.

In the first two weeks those who received ivermectin had minimal clinical reactions while those receiving DEC were often quite unwell. Again, significant ocular reactions were seen with DEC, but they were far fewer with ivermectin. Both ivermectin and DEC lowered the skin counts quickly. However, the ivermectin counts remained low at six months whereas those for

Ivermectin: Breakthrough Drug

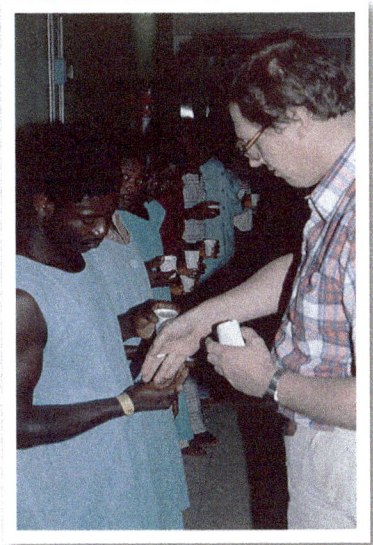
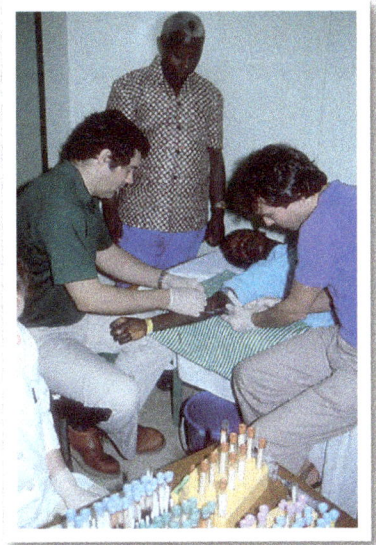
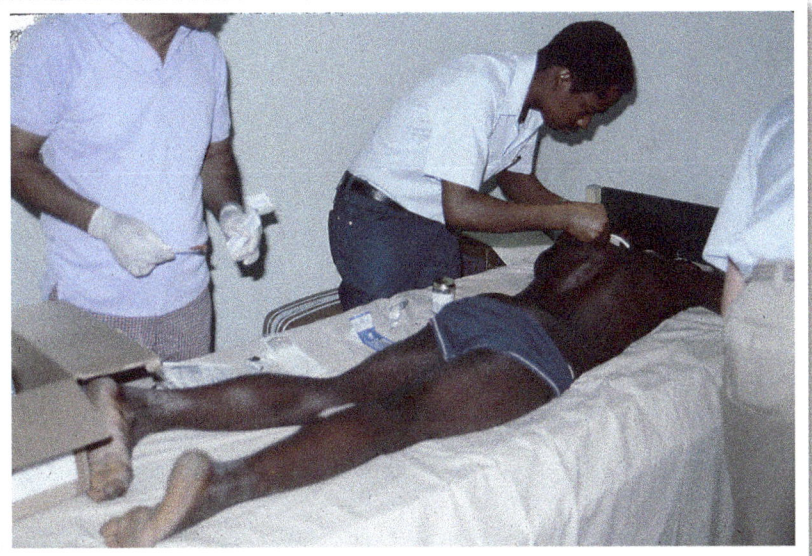

Above left: Distributing the first treatment in the ivermectin study in Liberia
Above right: Bruce Greene collecting blood samples
Below: Albert White taking skin snips to assess the microfilarial load

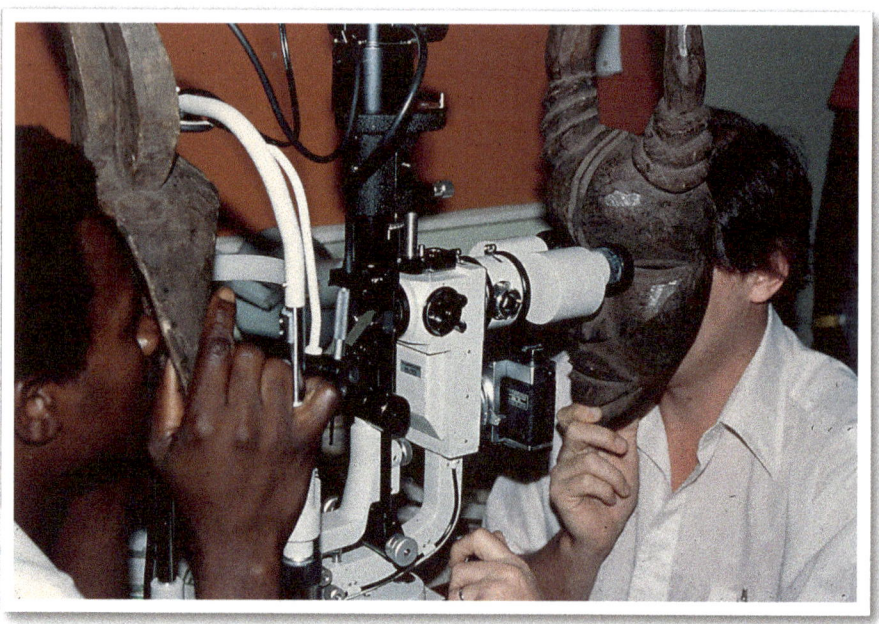

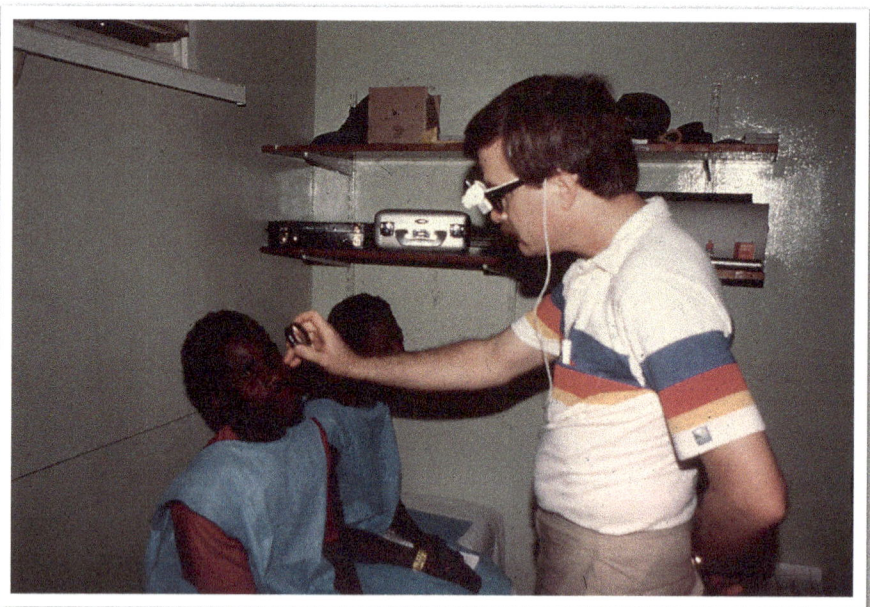

Above: Thinking I was doing an eye exam. Because it was a 'double-masked study' we needed to use African masks!
Below: Bob Murphy examining the retina

Above: Mohammed Aziz talking with a patient
Below left: Sam D'Anna enjoying some time off on the beach
Below right: The beach at Buchanan, Liberia

DEC were rising again, as had been seen in other studies. At six months we examined the excised nodules. There was no effect from either drug on embryogenesis or adult worm viability.

Given Bruce Greene's notable background and expertise in laboratory studies on immune responses, naturally we embarked on studies to understand better the pathogenesis, the disease processes, and the reactions to the drugs.

Bruce's laboratory studies showed serum antibodies did not protect from infection and that infection inhibited cell-mediated immunity to some *O. volvulus* antigens. This immunosuppression may reduce the immune response to live microfilaria, but not the response unleashed by the many microfilariae killed at the same time by DEC treatment. Although ivermectin also seemed to 'kill' microfilariae as quickly as DEC, that is the skin snip counts dropped in parallel with DEC, there had to be a different mechanism of action.

Ivermectin is a GABA agonist and binds to GABA chemical receptors on the surface of cells including microfilaria; this immobilises the microfilariae. These immobile microfilariae were carried by the lymphatic system to the draining lymph nodes and died there. (Later studies done by Peter Soboslay, who was working with Bruce, showed significantly reduced motility of microfilariae emerging from skin snips in those treated with ivermectin, supporting this concept.)

At six months after treatment, Ed Cupp, an entomologist from Cornell University in New York joined us. He looked at the uptake of microfilariae by the biting blackflies. He let flies feed on some of the study patients. The number of microfilariae taken up by flies from those who had received either ivermectin or DEC was very much lower than those who had received the placebo and those who received ivermectin were even lower than from those who received DEC.

This reduction in uptake by the flies and the consequential potential reduction of transmission was an exciting finding. It followed that an interruption of transmission or even a partial reduction in transmission, could break the life cycle of *O. volvulus*, and therefore have a tremendous impact on the levels of onchocerciasis infection and consequent blindness, especially in rainforest communities.

The staff at the Liberian Institute for Biomedical Research, LIBR, were doing world-leading research on hepatitis vaccines

Ivermectin: Breakthrough Drug

and had a large colony of chimpanzees. Betsy Brotman at LIBR, Ed Cupp and Milan Tripis, the head of Entomology at Johns Hopkins, raised blackfly L3 larvae—the infecting third-stage form—and grew them in the laboratory. They then let the adult flies feed on infected volunteers.

The flies grew in the laboratory for three days and were then dissected to separate the larvae that had developed from the microfilariae. These larvae were then injected into three groups of six chimps.

Some of the chimps at the Liberian Institute for Biologic Research

One group was given ivermectin on the day of inoculation to see if the drug would kill the L3 infective larvae and prevent infection.

Another group was treated with ivermectin at 28 days to see if ivermectin would kill the next and last stage, the L4 infective larvae that develops into the adult worms.

The third group was untreated control chimps.

Skin snips were taken monthly for the next 30 months and we also examined their eyes. Only one of the six chimps treated on the day of inoculation became skin snip positive whereas four of the delayed treatment and four of the control animals did. This suggested that ivermectin may have some impact on the infective, L3 larvae but unless taken very frequently would not be of value as a prophylactic drug for onchocerciasis.

Bruce Greene and his team undertook further immunological studies with the infected chimps, looking at their antibody and cellular immunity responses with results similar to those in humans.

We normally flew Pan Am from New York to Robertsfield in Liberia, but sometimes, depending on flights and other commitments, we flew back to the US via Europe. Bruce was keen to get a source of live microfilariae that he could use in his laboratory in Cleveland, Ohio. He injected live L3 larvae into a white rabbit he had brought from Cleveland so that the larvae would develop into adult worms and release microfilariae. We were due to fly out of Liberia back to New York on Pan Am, take-off at around 11 pm. We were all packed up and ready at the airport, the rabbit in its portable carrying box. Then we heard the Pan Am flight from Nairobi fly over the top of us. It was refusing to land. The explanation involved perhaps not paying landing taxes or some other unclear problem. However, it left us stranded with the precious white rabbit.

Plan B was to fly the next day to Accra, then to Ouagadougou and then to Paris where we could catch a flight to New York. The rabbit reached Accra, still in good health despite flying with a fierce, caged, barking dog in the hold. When we arrived in Paris it had been a long time since the rabbit had had anything to eat or drink, and Bruce was quite anxious and clearly wanted to check on the precious animal. The Air France ground crew were all very polite and helpful but could not understand why we would want to see the rabbit. They asked several times 'Is it a Special Rabbit?' We did not know at the time the French double entendre of a 'special rabbit' (read sex-worker). Anyway, it was eventually sorted out and the rabbit was all right.

Finally, we arrived safely in New York. Bruce and the rabbit flew on to Cleveland. On his way home from the airport, Bruce stopped at a McDonalds and bought a Big Mac. He gave the lettuce to the rabbit. Bruce and the rabbit got back safely to his laboratory. Many experiments followed.

Our work on the immunology of onchocerciasis stimulated

interest from some of our colleagues at Wilmer. John Donnelly, who later moved to the Scheie Eye Institute in Philadelphia, and Richard Semba, a Wilmer resident, set up a guinea-pig model to study a related parasite of cattle, *O. lienalis*. Richard would later work with us in Liberia. Because we did not have ready access to human tissue for these experiments we thought a guinea-pig model could be helpful.

John and Richard showed the importance of IgE antibodies, the 'allergy antibodies', in amplifying the immune and clinical responses in the cornea following DEC treatment. Their later studies in monkeys showed limited reactions to microfilariae injected in the cornea of sensitized animals. However, they found marked reactions when microfilariae were injected into the vitreous cavity of sensitized animals with retinal changes that resembled those seen in humans. The eyes and immune responses of monkeys usually match those of humans, whereas at times those in mice and guinea pigs can be quite different. The poor correlation with markers of the immune response suggested the importance of other inflammatory mediators, at least in this model.

Bruce Greene and I were asked to join Brian Duke and some others from WHO to meet with Roy Vagelos, the CEO of Merck; Mohammed Aziz; and some other senior Merck staff in their headquarters in Rahway, New Jersey. We discussed the study findings we had at that time and possible future studies. There was obviously great interest in the potential for ivermectin to have a considerable impact on onchocerciasis. Were we going to end river blindness?

In September 1984 Joseph Cook, the medical director of the Edna McConnell Clark Foundation, asked me to host a meeting to discuss the future directions for research in onchocerciasis in a similar way we had done for trachoma. Twelve researchers from the US, UK and Switzerland came together for five days to discuss and review what was already known about onchocerciasis and map the anticipated research challenges. The challenges that were deemed the most pressing included better methods to diagnose the infection, understanding its pathogenesis, the potential role for vaccines, and of course its treatment. Following this meeting Bruce Greene was asked to head up an Onchocerciasis group for the Foundation in the same way that I would lead the Trachoma group.

The results of our Phase 2 study in Liberia were very exciting. We published them in the top medico-scientific weekly, the *New England Journal of Medicine*. Our results were mirrored by the other two studies from Ghana and Sierra Leone when they were published subsequently. Together, they showed that ivermectin was at least as effective as DEC if not better at reducing microfilariae and again very much safer. The three studies had used a low dose of 100 µg/kg of ivermectin. There was a lot of interest to see how a higher dose might affect the adult worms. No adults, no larvae, no infection, eradication on the table.

In November 1985 Bruce and I started an ivermectin dose-ranging Phase 3 study at LAC in Liberia to explore the efficacy of higher doses. We selected 200 infected adults who were randomised into four groups each of which would receive a single dose of ivermectin of 100 µg/kg, 150 µg/kg, 200 µg/kg, or a placebo tablet. Subjects were examined before and during treatment and again at three, six and 12 months after treatment. Albert White and Henry Newland led this much larger study. Richard Semba helped with the patient examinations and Sam D'Anna again photographed their retinas.

Although the adverse reactions at Day 3 were more common in the two higher doses than the lowest dose or placebo, there was no difference from Day 4. There were no significant ocular changes seen with treatment in any group. Skin snip counts fell dramatically with each ivermectin group but the lowest and most prolonged drop was in the patients who had received the highest dose, 200 µg/kg. Although our study ended in 1986, our study results were finally published in September 1987.

At 12 months, the patients in each ivermectin treatment group were randomised again to receive either a second dose of their initial ivermectin dose or a placebo. Those who had been in the original placebo group now were treated with ivermectin 150 µg/kg at six monthly intervals. This meant that we could compare 150 µg/kg given six monthly or 12 monthly, as well as the effect at two years after the different single doses. In each group there was a significant reduction in the microfilariae in the eye. There was no real advantage of six-monthly treatment over annual treatment. And two years after treatment the skin counts had increased somewhat.

Annual treatment with 150 µg/kg clearly seemed the way to go.

Over this time we had collected serial retinal photographs on a number of patients, in some over periods of up to three years. Richard Semba and Bob Murphy studied the progression of the changes in the retina in detail. In some cases, the retinal scarring was so advanced that it progressed even though the treatment had more or less eliminated the microfilariae.

We also undertook further laboratory studies of the immune response in those with oncho. Michaela Gallin, who worked with Bruce, showed that the suppression of the cellular immune response to onchoceral antigens varied in individuals with different clinical manifestations. She also looked for antigens that could be used as a screening test for disease. Later, in collaborative studies with Edgar Lobos and Tom Nutman with colleagues from the National Institutes of Health and others, an onchoceral antigen, OV-16, was characterised and cloned. Having antibodies to this antigen proved to be a very good indicator of infection in both chimpanzees and humans. These serology tests—blood serum analysis of the body's antibody response to introduced antigens, here larval worms—continue to be used.

We also helped in studies conducted by Eberhard Albiez from the Bernhard-Nocht Institute in Hamburg, Germany. Maurice Langham had reported that higher doses of DEC might affect the adult worms. Eberhard undertook a study in up-country Liberia to assess this with groups receiving normal doses of DEC, higher DEC doses, DEC lotion, or ivermectin. The higher doses of DEC caused severe Mazzotti reactions. In those who received DEC the skin snip counts fell initially but rose progressively at two and 10 months after treatment. Nodules were removed and examined at two and 10 months. DEC showed short term disruption of embryogenesis at two months but there was no effect on the viability of the adult worms and embryogenesis had returned to normal by 10 months. Ivermectin did not affect the viability of the adult worms but at two months almost all the intrauterine microfilariae were degenerated. Embryogenesis had recovered somewhat at 10 months.

In a later study at LAC with Brian Duke we tried giving 100 µg/kg of ivermectin once every two weeks for 12 weeks. Even with this high total dose there was only a moderate effect on the viability of adult female worms.

On one of our trips to Liberia, Bruce took his son Jim and I took my son Bart. We flew New York-Nairobi. We spent a week going to game parks and enjoyed the wonders of Kenya with its animals. The boys had a great time and we did too. We visited several game parks and saw elephants, wildebeest, impala, the occasional lion, and lots of other animals. We spent a night at Treetops which was where Princess Elizabeth was staying in 1952 the night she became Queen. The boys (and their fathers) were thrilled in the evening to watch from the roof top as the elephants, rhinos, waterbuck and buffalos came to the waterhole to drink. We ended our trip at Mombasa down on the coast.

At Bruce's insistence he and I had always been extra careful about food poisoning. Starting in San Cristobal in Mexico, when we were travelling, we always took a dose of doxycycline with the last cup of coffee at breakfast each morning. This was to reduce any chance of the effects of inadvertent food contamination. However, travelling with our sons and because we were staying in resort hotels, I was a bit less vigilant. I had an ice cream at our hotel in Mombasa after Bart and I had been swimming in the hotel pool. The next day the worst attack of diarrhoea I'd known overtook me on the plane as we flew back from Nairobi to Liberia. Fortunately, the boys remained healthy. Anyway, we arrived safely in Liberia and Bart and Jim worked hard helping with our examinations during that visit.

Here's another dreadful gastro story. During another visit to Ougadougou, Bruce and I were caught up within a nation-wide general strike. All flights out of Ougadougou were cancelled. Our hotel essentially shut down with no food or electricity. Somehow, we were able to get tickets on a train to Abidjan in the Ivory Coast. We boarded and sat in the only seats we could find at the end of the train. It was a 24-hour trip and as we stopped

Bart in red shirt and Jim Greene, right, helping subject registration

at stations along the way passengers would jump off and buy food, including live chickens. At a subsequent stop, when a chicken was dead, plucked and ready to cook, they bought live coals and cooked the chicken on the train. I developed diarrhoea, probably from something I ate at the hotel before we left; we had not eaten on the train. During all our field work this was only the second time I came down with diarrhoea. So for the most part doxycycline really did work. The train had the rather primitive latrines that discharged straight onto the track below. We learned that there was a dining car at the front of the train and we worked our way forward to it. There we remained until we reached Abidjan and a hotel. What a relief!

Although the results from these clinical trials were exciting, in 1986 we had no idea how the community-based distribution of ivermectin would work in practice. There were important questions to be addressed: was it going to be safe, what about its use in pregnancy, would it really reduce transmission et cetera?

So, in December 1986 we went back to Liberia to try to answer these questions in a Phase 4, community-based trial. This study started almost a year before the registration of ivermectin or the start of the donation program. This time our team was led by Michele Pacque, a Belgian public health doctor who had joined us at the Dana Center. We returned to LAC's plantation and aimed to distribute annual treatment to the whole population and to maintain surveillance for any side-effects. The population was about 14 000 and they lived in 72 camps or settlements. We did a door-to-door census. We excluded from treatment children under the age of 5 years, women known to be pregnant or who were breast-feeding children under the age of 3 months, or those with illnesses or neurological disorders. In the sample of adults who had skin snips taken: more that 80 percent were positive for onchocerciasis.

We used the 150 µg/kg dose of ivermectin, deemed to

Ivermectin: Breakthrough Drug

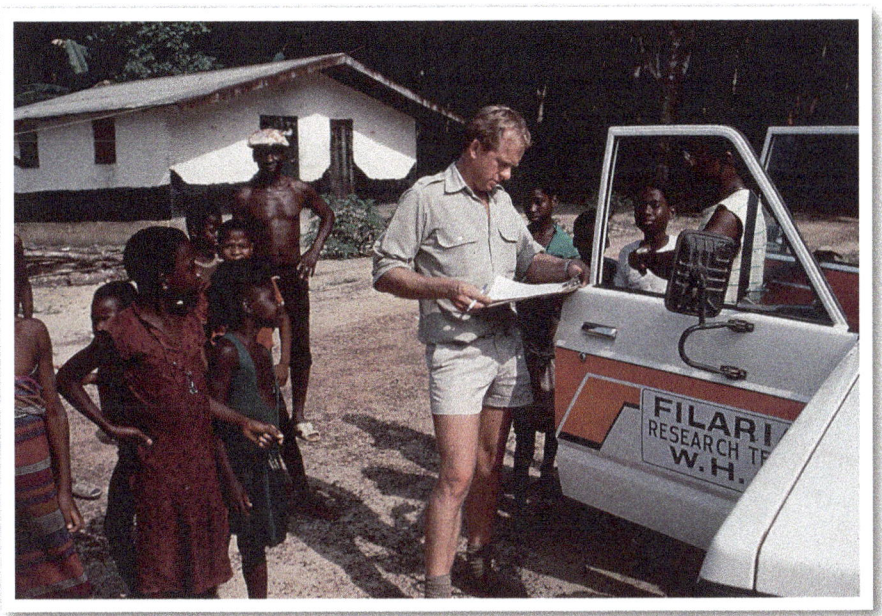
Henry Newland in a community checking on missing subjects for the Phase 3 study

Michele Pacque coordinating the Phase 4 community wide study

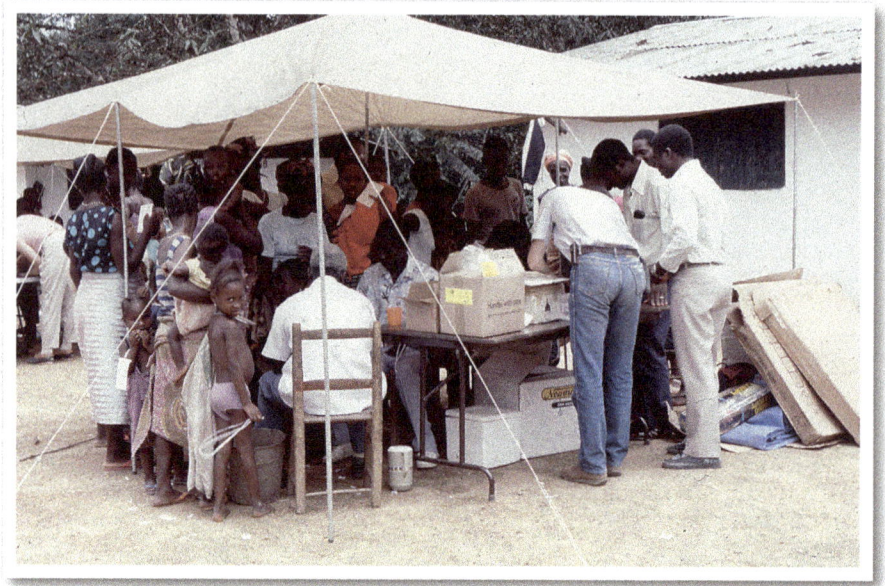
Community examination site in the Phase 4 study

John Barchua working house by house on the monthly checking of births and deaths

become the standard dose. Ivermectin was distributed house by house, weighing everyone eligible. Overall, 98 percent of them accepted treatment. Household residents were checked on Day 3 for adverse reactions. That initial round of treatment showed about 1 percent reported some side-effects, but after the second and third annual treatments only 0.1 percent reported reactions.

Microfilarial counts in the skin snips dropped by 84 percent at 2 years, but not to zero. Interestingly, and importantly, the rate of new infection in children was reduced by over a third; a clear demonstration of a reduction in transmission.

Gretchen Poetscke examining children who were born after their mother had taken ivermectin, looking for any abnormalities

Every month after treatment, one of our Liberian team members went to every house to check whether there had been any births or deaths. When someone had died, a verbal autopsy was undertaken. We also checked on any people presenting to the plantation hospital with possible reactions to ivermectin. We had a subgroup of people who had had severe onchoceral skin disease but within three months of treatment their skin disease had resolved. In addition, at the annual follow-up examinations, Jeanne Foose, a neonatal paediatrician from Case Western, did a full paediatric examination for all babies born to women who had received ivermectin the previous year and a control group of children. These mothers had either not known that they were pregnant when they were treated or had become pregnant soon after receiving treatment. Only one third of women who were in their first trimester were aware that they were pregnant at the time of treatment. We identified 203 children who were born to women who were treated when pregnant. There was no difference in the frequency of birth defects or developmental status of the babies born to treated women compared with other babies. Administration of ivermectin in pregnancy appeared to be safe. This was an important finding because it meant that pregnancy testing was not necessary for treating every woman who was not obviously pregnant.

Transmission studies were done by Milan Tripis, who had also helped us with the initial trachoma study in Mexico. He compared the pre-treatment rates of infection in flies with those after the second round of treatment. The number of infected flies had decreased by 95 percent and the monthly transmission potential had been reduced by 75 percent.

In late 1989 we completed our third annual distribution of treatment and follow up. We had intended to continue for one more year. However, in December 1989 Charles Taylor started an armed uprising and a brutal civil war broke out. President Samuel Doe was brutally tortured and executed in 1990, but his government fought on. Any further work in Liberia was too dangerous, completely out of the question. Some of our local field staff disappeared. Our vehicles were commandeered. Our equipment disappeared. The carnage was terrible, a sudden, unexpected and heart-rending end to our extraordinary series of studies.

Unlike in 1980, the Firestone and LAC plantations were not spared this time. Rebels occupied it. The US Army helped evacuate the expatriate staff to Firestone's headquarters in Akron, Ohio. Taylor received visitors in the grandest of the company's homes and offices, including the Visitors Center where we had spent our nights. His fighters, some just armed-up children, roamed all over. Liberian staff and their families were terrorised, robbed, beaten, raped, evicted and driven away. Many were killed. The rubber trees were unattended and many were overgrown or tapped so much that they died from lack of sap. Firestone was taken over by the Japanese conglomerate, Bridgestone. A deal was made in 1992 with Taylor's de facto government. Bridgestone re-occupied and re-established the area. The war ended when Taylor was elected president in 1997, after 200 000 Liberians were killed. Two years later, a second rebel invasion and four-year civil war killed 50 000 more.

In 1989 the Firestone plantation produced something like 90 percent of the world's high-quality liquid latex, raw material used for things like surgical gloves and condoms. The demand for latex products had gone through the roof with the need for protective latex products brought on by the HIV/AIDS epidemic. To stop transmission, many people, from nurses and dentists to chefs and food servers, were wearing latex gloves. Condoms were heavily promoted as well. With the closure of Firestone, the world turned to Malaysia for liquid latex. But the Malaysian latex had about 30 times more latex allergens that the purer Liberian latex had. This led to many people becoming severely allergic to latex products. Our daughter Kate was one. She had to stop her training as an ophthalmologist and leave medicine altogether. Contact with latex would cause her anaphylaxis, a very severe reaction needing medical resuscitation. Her highly successful career took many twists and turns after that.

Few ophthalmologists were working on onchocerciasis in the 1980s. In 1982 I had been invited to join the Scientific Working Group on Filariasis, part of the Tropical Disease Research program (TDR) at WHO. At these meetings I learned a lot about other types of filariasis, including lymphatic filariasis and sleeping sickness—much more than the average ophthalmologist might ever encounter.

Opening Eyes

In 1983, with the increasing interest in the treatment of onchocerciasis, I was asked to join a new group, the Scientific Working Group on Onchocerciasis Chemotherapy. I chaired it for several years. I also served as a member of the WHO Expert Committee on Onchocerciasis in 1986. For some years I was a member of the Expert Advisory Committee to the Onchocerciasis Control Program that met in Ougadougou.

It was a privilege to go to these meetings and learn so much about developments in these various diseases and programs and, of course, meeting so many of the world's leaders in these fields. In Geneva we usually stayed in hotels that had been booked by WHO, usually near the central station. We always met in the WHO building and most took the Number 8 Bus to get there. Each evening the committee members had to go somewhere for dinner. That was no hardship in Geneva where there was not only lots of great options for dinner, but the dinners also provided a wonderful opportunity to catch up with other committee members and form strong friendships. Fondue at least once on every visit was an imperative as was some perch from Lake Geneva accompanied by the local gewürztraminer.

One way or another, I was back and forth to WHO in Geneva several times a year, and sometimes found time in March to get in a day or two skiing in the Alps. In March when two different groups were to meet, I worked hard to have WHO arrange the meetings with a free weekend in between. That gave an incidental weekend for skiing; not a bad lurk. Much later, after she had left medicine, our daughter Kate worked for the World Economic Forum in Geneva. It was wonderful to spend a couple of nights sleeping on her couch and then spend a weekend with her on the slopes.

By early 1987 it was clear that ivermectin was the game changer for onchocerciasis.

Here was a drug that with a single oral dose would

dramatically reduce the microfilarial load in the skin and the eye, and reduce symptoms without inducing significant reactions to treatment. Early results indicated that it might also have a significant role in reducing rates of transmission by reducing the numbers of microfilariae in the skin. Because it did not kill the adult worms, it would have to be given for a long time, until the adult worms died which could be up to 15 years.

The big question then was: 'Who could afford this drug?' Already used widely in veterinary medicine, it cost about US$20 a dose. What country could afford to treat millions of people year after year at that cost? Many African countries had an annual health budget per person of that amount or less to cover everything.

This problem was raised by Brian Duke in a magazine interview. Maybe, he suggested, Merck could provide the drug for free?

Within a few days, he was summoned to the WHO's director general's office. Apparently, Merck had complained to WHO about Brian's suggestion.

However, in October 1987, Roy Vagelos, the CEO of Merck, announced that Merck would indeed provide ivermectin free to treat people with onchocerciasis anywhere in the world and provide 'as much as needed, for as long as needed'. This was an extraordinary commitment and clearly broke new ground in terms of public-private partnerships. No other pharmaceutical company had done such a thing before. Until then drugs for what become known as the 'Neglected Tropical Diseases', such as malaria, sleeping sickness, lymphatic filariasis or schistosomiasis, were always on the commercial market, so treatments were unaffordable for most people or governments of developing countries.

Merck's most generous donation set a precedent that other companies would follow later with the provision of subsidised or donated drugs for widespread infections in developing countries. This led to programs such as the Global Fund that oversaw the distribution of treatment for HIV/AIDS and TB, and Roll Back Malaria. Many years later, in the 2000s, our daughter Kate, while working with GSK (formerly GlaxoSmithKline) spent some time on the board of Roll Back Malaria.

Mectizan became the new trade name used for ivermectin. Merck then established the Mectizan Donation Program with the Task Force for Global Health that was part of the Carter Center in Atlanta, Georgia. The donation program would receive requests from countries for ivermectin. These countries were expected to report back on their progress and outline future needs. The program was strongly supported by former President Jimmy Carter and led by Willian Foege, a former director of the Centers for Disease Control.

I served on the Mectizan Expert Committee from 1991 to 1993. By that time, I was back in Melbourne so I made the long flights each way for one-day meetings in Atlanta, but well worth it, a privilege. We met ex-President Jimmy Carter on several occasions. On one occasion we went to a hall that had a magnificent organ, and Dr Ade Lucas, a Nigerian physician who was the head of the WHO/TDR program, gave us a recital. It was surreal to sit next to Jimmy Carter and be transported by that magnificent music. When I retired from the committee, I was presented with a Carter Center plaque signed by Jimmy Carter.

A certificate of appreciation from Jimmy Carter at the Carter Center for serving on the Mectizan Expert Committee

William (Bill) Baldwin, the former dean of Optometry in Houston, had been going to Nigeria once a year as a volunteer to provide eye care. In 1989 he had decided to distribute some ivermectin on his annual visit. John Moores, an American philanthropist, heard about the work Bill was doing from his brother Barry Moores, who was also an optometrist. In his earlier years John worked at IBM as a programmer; he had developed software so that mainframe computers could 'talk' to each other. The story is that the IBM company was not interested in proceeding with this, so John was free to take this work and set up his own company. He established BMC Software and the software became the key to linking automatic teller machines to central computers so the ATMs could function safely all over the world. When he sold that company, he became a generous philanthropist. Hearing about Baldwin, his work with ivermectin and his desire to raise funds to extend this, John Moores and his wife Rebecca (Becky) set up the River Blindness Foundation based in Houston. Aim: help distribute ivermectin.

Bill Baldwin put together an amazing board with some academics, former ambassadors, and heads of large banks. It also included Brian Duke and me. The Moores ended up giving some $25 million to help the foundation fund projects to distribute ivermectin. John was very much involved and participated in all the meetings.

At coffee breaks I would chat with him beside the coffee machine where so many important conversations occur. In 1992 I mentioned to John that I was going back to Melbourne via San Diego, where John and Becky had a home. I was going to attend an ophthalmology meeting that conveniently was to be held at the same time as the America's Cup Races that were being held in San Diego. John immediately offered me the use of his car, a Rolls Royce. When I said I would be at a meeting, that I didn't need a car, he offered his Porsche. Then Becky joined us, and offered me her Bentley as a second choice because her Mercedes was being repaired. I declined all offers.

When I arrived in San Diego, to my surprise, someone was there to meet me and give me the keys to the Rolls. My colleagues were very impressed, of course. They had to have a drive in it. When I returned to the hotel one somewhat jealous Australian colleague asked, 'Hugh, have you hired that Rolls Royce?'

'No.' He immediately assumed I must have bought it.

'Hugh! That's outrageous. How on earth could you have bought it?' The meeting was at the hotel, so I did not have much opportunity to drive the car around, unfortunately.

The hotel staff insisted that I park it out the front, near their entrance. As I paid the bill I learned that this parking spot cost four-times what it cost in the regular carpark!

In 1992, with advocacy from multiple sources, including the River Blindness Foundation, the Onchocerciasis Elimination for the Americas, OEPA, was established by the Pan American Health Organisation and the World Bank. OEPA funded and supported the distribution of ivermectin in the endemic countries in Latin America and started community-based distribution.

This also saw the celebrations in the UN Building in New York to mark the fifth year of the Mectizan donation and the establishment of OEPA. This was an important event and was led by Jimmy Carter, with whom I sat for the elaborate lunch. It made one feel that this was a real contribution.

Sometimes, simple ideas lead to significant outcomes that dramatically improve the ways things are done. In 1993 Brian Duke and I analysed data from different treatment programs in Africa and Latin America. At that stage, everyone still had to be weighed to determine the correct dose. We showed a strong correlation between the dose that a child should get when it was determined by their weight or when determined by their height. It was a much easier thing to mark a measuring stick, or even knots on a string, at the right heights to simply measure the child's height, easier than carrying scales, often over rough country on foot, and the need to weigh everyone. The use of these 'measuring sticks' soon became the standard method for determining the ivermectin dose for children.

In 1995 the African Program for Onchocerciasis Control, APOC, was officially launched. It was one of the first public-private partnerships and included WHO, the World Bank, and non-government organisations. It took over the funding and oversight of the national programs, distributing the ivermectin provided by Merck through the Mectizan Donation Program at the Carter Center. The River Blindness Foundation saw that in many ways its mission was accomplished and so it donated its residual funds via the Carter Center.

In 2015 APOC was restructured and in 2016 WHO started ESPEN, the Expanded Special Project for the Elimination of Neglected Tropical Diseases in Africa. Among its goals was the elimination of onchocerciasis, not just control of it. This work was to be organised and controlled at the national level by the countries involved. The River Blindness Foundation left a lasting legacy. Its logo was a blind man being led by a young boy, the classic picture of the devastating impact of river blindness.

Above: River Blindness Foundation Logo
Right: My River Blindness statue

Opening Eyes

Several small sculptures were made showing the small boy leading the blind man. One sat in the Foundation's office. Some were given to board members: both Brian Duke and I received one when the Foundation closed. Others had seen the impressive small sculptures. Larger than life-size replicas were cast. One was placed in Merck's headquarters in New Jersey; another outside the entrance to WHO; a third in the atrium in the World Bank in Washington, DC; a fourth at the Carter Center; and the fifth at the Onchocerciasis Control Programme in Ougadougou. The sculptures have become significant monuments that welcome all visitors to these places, reinforcing the importance of all the work done for those with onchocerciasis and their treatment: eye doctors counting microfilaria at slit lamps, generous donors, barefoot community health workers trudging through rough tracks, and all the many others.

For our part, the late Brian's sculpture lives in his house in Lancaster UK with his wife Diane. Mine sits in the entrance of our home in Melbourne, Victoria. In 2006 I received the Mectizan Award from Merck, which also sits proudly at home.

Brian Duke beside the River Blindness statue at WHO, Geneva

In 2007 I had thought that my days working on oncho were well and truly over. However, I was contacted by Annette Kuesel at WHO that year.

Annette was interested in trialling moxidectin. Moxidectin is a drug related to ivermectin, but it has a much longer half-life and lasts much longer in the body. In animal models it reduced microfilarial loads more effectively than ivermectin. It was thought it might be able to kill the adult worms. Its patents were held by Wyeth, the pharmaceutical company that made moxidectin. An initial study was carried out with Kwablah Awadzi. Kwablah had moved to Hohoe in Ghana, still stalking *O. volvulus*. A further study was conducted in Liberia. Moxidectin seemed to kill the adult worms. However, Wyeth was not particularly interested in progressing with further work on this.

Belen Pedrique of Drugs for Neglected Diseases took up the challenge to see if moxidectin, as a microfilaricide, could really replace ivermectin and if it would be safe in areas where Loa Loa infection and onchocerciasis coexist. Loa Loa or 'eye worm', or loiasis, is another filarial infection transmitted by biting flies where the much smaller adult worms migrate through the subcutaneous tissues and can at times be seen around the eye. Although usually treated with DEC, people with loiasis can have quite severe reactions if given ivermectin.

Mark Sullivan, founder of Medicines Development for Global Health, based in Melbourne, took the lead in these studies. Together, they obtained a large grant from the Global Health Investment Fund to undertake larger Phase 3 trials between 2009 and 2012 in Ghana, Liberia and the Democratic Republic of the Congo, DRC. Planning for clinical trials has become much more sophisticated than it was back in the 1970s and 1980s, but it was a buzz to be called upon to give some advice and suggestions about the ocular assessments of these studies and participate in several meetings and many email exchanges.

The trials worked well. The drug was approved by the US

Food and Drug Administration as a New Drug with a Priority Review Voucher in June 2018. This was the first not-for-profit company to register a drug through this process. Mark became the Victorian Australian of the Year in 2019 for this work. As an Australian of the Year, he was asked to provide an item that could be shown in the Australian Museum to signify his work. At his request I loaned him my river blindness sculpture. It has been exhibited in museums around Australia.

When I retired from the Mectizan Expert Committee and the River Blindness Foundation Board, my work on onchocerciasis felt as though it had finished. Back in Melbourne, my focus and work centred on Australia's blindness problems rather than those of Africa or Latin America.

Nevertheless, I keep a keen interest in the progress and developments.

By the end of 2023, onchocerciasis had been eliminated from four Latin American countries with the extensive community-based distribution of ivermectin: Colombia, Ecuador, Guatemala and Mexico. The latter two were where we had started work many years ago. Yemen in the Middle East had also eliminated onchocerciasis. Some African countries had eliminated it from many districts and recently Niger eliminated it nationally. In 1998 Merck extended the donation to include lymphatic filariasis. About 400 million doses of ivermectin are distributed each year. Merck has donated more than 4.8 billion tablets in all. What an extraordinary commitment.

In 2020 COVID-19 brought ivermectin back to the attention of the world. The drug was touted as a cure. This was one of the weird suggestions made by many, including the President of the US! His weirdest of the lot was the suggestion of intravenous injections of kitchen bleach. A laboratory study had shown that high concentrations of ivermectin in a petri dish would slow or stop the corona virus from replicating in tissue cultures. However, even at higher doses than used for onchocerciasis, large scale, properly designed, controlled trials ultimately confirmed that ivermectin was not effective against human infection with COVID-19.

In 2012 I was approached to join the board of a new non-government organisation, 'One Disease at a Time'. This had been established by Sam Prince, a young general practitioner who had also set up a chain of Mexican restaurants, Zambrero. He was aware of the problem scabies was in outback Australia and wanted to eliminate it, starting with work in the communities of the Northern Territory. Scabies is a parasitic skin infection. He contacted me for two reasons: scabies persists where personal and communal hygiene is poor and so is closely linked with trachoma; and, because scabies is also sensitive to ivermectin, he wanted my input and experience about the use of the drug. One Disease ran a very successful program for 10 years, and, although it did not eliminate scabies, it led to a dramatic reduction in the frequency of infection, particularly of severe scabies.

Liz coincidently worked on another retrovirus, Human T-cell Lymphotropic Virus. Her team found that Indigenous children infected with HTLV were also most likely to have severe scabies.

Opening Eyes

8
Chesapeake Bay and the Watermen

> There is a widespread hope and expectation…
> to give the world men who can not only
> sail by the old charts, but who can make
> new and better ones for the use of others.
>
> John Shaw Billings (1858–1913), pioneer
> professor at Johns Hopkins

Cataract is a clouding of the lens of the eye that progressively reduces vision. Our later work showed that, on careful examination, by the age of 80, everyone would have some cataract or had already had cataract surgery. Although most of the development of cataract is attributable to ageing, other factors—such as some diseases, exposures, drugs and trauma—can lead to cataract. With my training in Melbourne and Baltimore I became an expert cataract surgeon. With modern surgery people have their vision restored the day after surgery, now an outpatient procedure. The joy people experience when their eye pad is removed reinforces one's commitment to ophthalmology. They can see again!

There are three types of cataracts: nuclear that are in the centre of the lens, cortical that are in the outer layers of the lens, and posterior sub-capsular that are underneath the back lining of the lens.

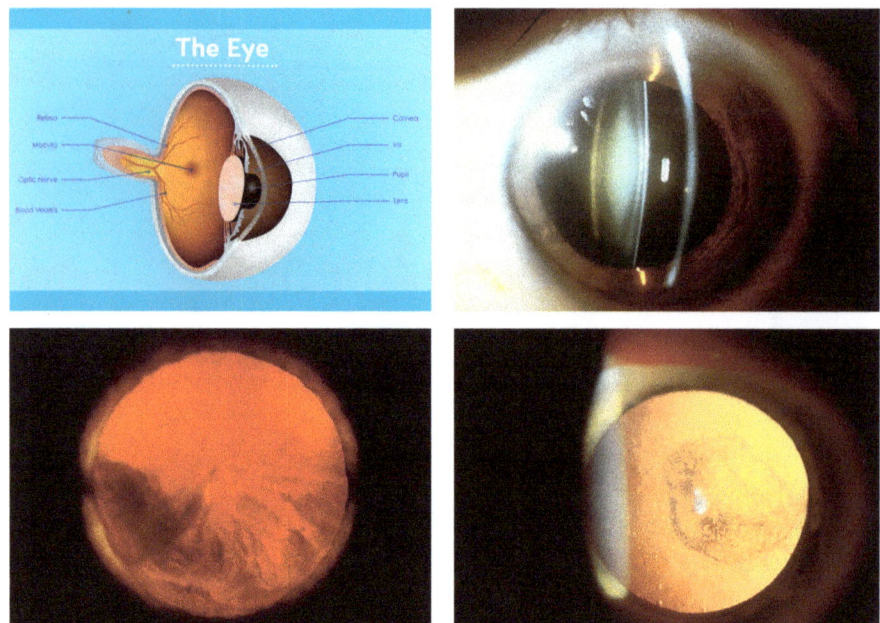

Above left: A diagram of the eye

Above right: Nuclear cataract, shown by the thin beam of light coming from the right, from the slit-lamp

Below left: Cortical cataract, shown by the light reflecting from the retina — retro-illumination

Below right: Posterior subcapsular cataract, also shown by retro-illumination

While working with Fred Hollows and the National Trachoma and Eye Health Programme, we found cataract was the leading cause of blindness. We had to do something to address that without delay, so surgery was arranged.

I also collected data in the Aboriginal people we examined and looked for possible environmental impacts on cataract and blindness. I examined in depth a sample of 350 adults who had vision loss from cataract. At that time cataract was called 'senile cataract' and I did not separate the three different types. Most were mature cataracts, that is very dense, and the person was usually blind. I collected data on occupation, alcohol intake, ocular trauma and of course, trachoma. None of these factors showed any link with the presence of cataract.

However, there was a strong association between the presence of cataract and being closer to the equator. This led me to look at environmental factors such as temperature, rainfall, evaporation and so forth, but none of these was linked to the presence of cataract. There was a significant association with sunlight hours and annual radiation, but a stronger association with Annual UV-B Radiation.

This was the first time an association between exposure to ultraviolet light and cataract had been demonstrated. UV-B is the medium-range wavelengths of sunlight. Most of it is absorbed by the Ozone Layer, but what isn't produces Vitamin D, tans our skin and may well cheer us up; it also causes sunburn, DNA damage including that leading to malignant melanoma and, as we will see, eye damage. There had been some laboratory data to suggest a UV-to-cataract connection was possible, but none of the few epidemiologic studies of cataract that had looked at this had shown it. I had access to the regional UV-B data provided by Ian Barton at CSIRO (see page 86). This meant I could determine the UV-B radiation for the areas where people had lived.

I also found a surprising number of Aboriginal men with psuedoexfoliation of the lens, PXF. When one examines an eye with PXF one finds little flakes that look like dandruff on the surface of the lens and some are distributed in the front of the eye. It was usually associated with glaucoma. PXF had been described in the Nordic countries and was generally thought to be genetic, so it seemed very odd to find it in Aboriginal men. It was found mainly in those men who had worked as stockmen looking after cattle, so were out in the sun all day. It was not associated with UV-B radiation, but with the total levels of Annual Global Radiation. Two other corneal changes were also noted: Climatic Droplet Keratopathy or CDK, and pterygium. These were also related to working in sunshine all day. I could find no definite environmental linkage for CDK, but pterygium was strongly linked to environmental UV-B radiation.

Baltimore is a city with many different historical and geographical aspects. It is an old port and industrial city that has affluent leafy neighbourhoods and wretchedly poor ones. It sits on the Patuxent River that flows into Chesapeake Bay, which has more shoreline, 6000 miles of it, than all the rest of the US (excluding Alaska and Hawaii) put together. Chesapeake Bay is beautiful and the abundant source of delicious crabs, oysters and rockfish. These are collected or caught by 'watermen', an old English term dating back to the fifteenth century. They are not 'fishermen'!

Once we had settled into Baltimore, I purchased a small trailer-sailer with our friend Bob Murphy. This meant that our children could enjoy a day on the Chesapeake, and Liz could have one day at the weekend to herself to do the things she needed to do. It worked well. We fell in love with the Bay.

On our boat enjoying Chesapeake Bay

Above: Waterman out crabbing

Below: Painting of a skipjack by Jack R Schroeder. Hon Lawson gave me this as I left Baltimore

It prompted me to think that it would be a great idea to look at the effects of UV-B exposure on the watermen. They had great outdoor exposure with the added reflection of UV-B from the water. Much of their work was very traditional: they could only dredge for oysters under sail, work would start at dawn and catches needed to be delivered by 1 pm. This meant that their exposure would not have changed much over time, unlike, say, policemen who would have walked the beat years ago but then spent most of their time in a car, or farmers who used to sit on an open tractor but now sat in an air-conditioned cabin. A study of UV-B exposure in the watermen sounded like a great idea. It opened a great opportunity to explore the Eastern Shore with its intriguing little communities, and eat a lot of crabs and oysters.

I thought I needed to find a control group of people who would have a much lower occupational exposure to sunlight and UV-B. I explored the possibility of examining coal miners in Western Virginia. We did a small study with help from Stuart Fine, Oliver Schein and Maureen Maguire. Stuart was the head of the Medial Retina Unit, Oliver an ophthalmology resident and Maureen a young biostatistician, all at Wilmer. However, we found that the miners would work underground in the mines for an eight-hour shift but then most of them ran their own farms, and so had indeterminant amounts of UV-B exposure. So this study went nowhere. To work out the potential impact of UV-B exposure, we had to first work out a way to actually measure people's ocular exposure to UV-B, not rely on a history of occupational exposure alone.

Unperturbed and after three failed attempts we finally received a National Eye Institute grant to carry out the Chesapeake Bay Waterman Study in 1984.

First, we had to work out how to measure how much UV-B reached the eye and then the effect of wearing a hat, glasses, sunglasses and so forth. We did some work with Frank Rosenthal, an environmental physicist in the School of Hygiene and Public Health. We put UV-B dosimeters in the eye sockets and on top of the heads of mannequins. We placed the heads on a turntable on the roof of the school, and measured the amount of UV-B that reached the eye as a proportion of the total ambient UV-B. We then assessed the effect of hats and glasses. UV-B sensitive film was calibrated with the dosimeters, so that in the field the film could be placed on watermen's hats or glasses to measure exposure.

Above: Alexander Bakalain and Frank Rosenthal on the roof of the Johns Hopkins School of Public Health measuring the proportion of UV-B that reaches the eye using rotating mannequin heads

Left: A head with UV-B sensitive film monitors on the cap and UV-B sensors in the eye socket and on top of the cap.

We showed that 80 percent of ambient UV-B reached the eye. Further, this was not greatly altered by surface reflection from the ground or water. A hat halved the ocular exposure. Close-fitting UV-B-absorbing sunglasses reduced it by about 92 percent.

We then fitted the UV-B-sensitive film in cardboard squares with a hole that let the light in while stuck conveniently to the watermen's hats or glasses to assess some real-life exposures as they worked on different activities through the year.

Hon Lawson catching crabs while wearing a UV-B film monitor on his cap

Then we were ready to start examining the eyes of the watermen.

Sheila West, who later did much work on the trachoma studies, had returned to Baltimore from the Philippines and joined me in the Dana Center to work on this study. She and I developed a standardised grading system for each of the three types of cataract—nuclear, cortical and posterior subcapsular—that was used both clinically and with specific photos of the lens. Our grading scheme used a standard photo showing the four degrees of nuclear opacity—essentially the density of the cataract—and used standardised ways to quantify cortical and posterior subcapsular opacities. Leo Chylack, an ophthalmologist at Harvard, was also doing some research on cataract epidemiology at the time. He described a lens opacity grading system he called LOCS 1. Over time this became LOCS 2 then LOC 3, incorporating some of the approaches we used, but still with some differences. Much later, working with Mark Bullimore and Ian Baily at the University of California Berkeley, we developed a scaled method of grading that improved the sensitivity.

Ian Baily was the Melbourne-trained optometrist who developed the LogMAR vision charts as a more accurate method to measure visual acuity and I had followed these design principles to develop the charts to measure vision in the visual acuity studies in Aboriginal Australians (see page 66). These charts had become the gold-standard for measuring vision in clinical trials.

With help from Neil and Susan Bressler and under Stuart Fine's direction, we developed a grading system for age-related macular degeneration using retinal photos. Neil and Susan were young retinal specialists who were working with Stuart (and went on to become leaders in medical retina ophthalmology).

Edward (Ted) Emmet, an Australian dermatologist at Hopkins, worked with us to assess UV-related skin damage. As someone who grew up in Australia, Ted had a very good understanding of sunburn and UV exposure. He was particularly interested in the changes caused by UV-B exposure, such as solar keratosis—rough scaly patches on skin, skin cancers and melanoma. He and his team helped us grade the skin changes that were found in the watermen.

Our team assembled and we went down to the Eastern Shore and got started.

A detailed history was collected for each person in the study, including demographic and background characteristics,

Opening Eyes

Sheila West and the team at an examination site on the Eastern Shore of Chesapeake Bay

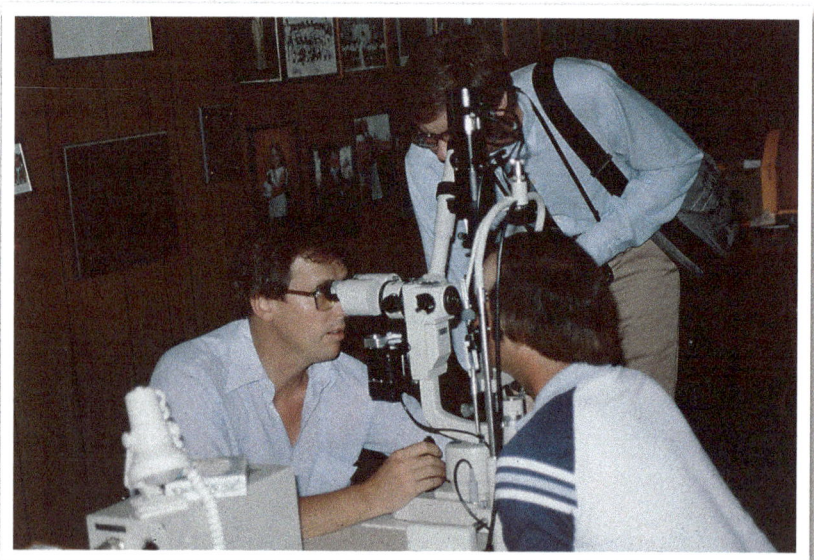

Performing an eye examination

residential history, medical history, medication use and any history of smoking. A specific history was taken of sun-exposure that included a detailed occupational history covering each year of life from the age of 16. Daily work exposure was recorded on a monthly basis, and a similar history was taken for leisure activities. These histories included information about the number of hours spent outside, use of hats, glasses and any history of arc welding, a source of UV-B radiation in itself. The detailed eye exam included vision, dilated slit-lamp and retinal examination and grading, as well as the lens and retinal photography.

A number of staff and other volunteers helped with the field work. Some local watermen helped too. One, Wayne (Hon) Lawson, a waterman from Crisfield—a boom-and-bust town literally half built on a midden of shucked oyster shells, famous for its Atlantic blue crab—kept everything together. Hon's first American ancestor arrived in the Bay in 1609, a decade before the *Mayflower*'s Pilgrims. As mentioned earlier, Henry Newland, an Australian ophthalmologist who came to Wilmer to study public health, joined us and he did a great many of the eye examinations.

We stayed in a local hotel or guest house in each village where we worked. We had a lot of gear that was needed for the various examinations. It was one thing to load it into the back of a car and another to load it on and off boats and then cart it to an examination site.

Of course, we ate a lot of crabs and oysters, depending on the season. You can only collect oysters in the months that have an R in their name; so May to August was the off-season. When we were working on Smith Island in the middle of the Bay, we stayed at Mrs Kitching's Guest House. Frances Kitching, her guest house, her cookbooks and her crab loaf and 10-layer Smith Island cake—Maryland's state cake—were famous. She kept the team in good spirits. They all worked hard, but none lost weight.

We examined 808 watermen.

Above: Lugging our luggage and equipment on Smith Island
Below: Our luggage waiting for a boat to more to the next examination site

When it came to the handling and analysis of these data, Sheila's experience was gold standard but we were fortunate to have the expert help of Helen Abbey, the head of Biostatistics in the School of Hygiene and Public Health and Beatriz Muñoz, a young statistician at the Dana Center.

The editors of the *New England Journal of Medicine* accepted our paper reporting our findings. With a rejection rate of 90 percent of papers submitted to it, and with the *NEJM*'s prestige, we were walking on air. When it was published, ours was the lead article.

Cataract was increasingly common and, of course, occurrence increased with age. However, we had found the strong correlation between UV-B and cortical cataract. This was the first time this specific linkage had been demonstrated. This demonstrated the fundamental need for protection against ocular exposure to UV-B.

There was no association between UV-B and nuclear cataract. We found a weak association between smoking and nuclear cataract. This potential link was also novel but more work was needed to clarify it.

Some watermen had pterygium or climatic droplet keratopathy. This was linked to their exposure to each of three wavelengths of UV exposure—UV-A1, UV-A2 and UV-B. This confirmed my earlier findings in the Aboriginal study.

The paper generated press interest; front page of the *Baltimore Sun*! I got a phone call from Norman Swan, medical reporter for the Australian Broadcasting Corporation, wanting a radio interview. When he heard my accent, he was surprised and asked if I was an Australian. Norman, originally a medical graduate from Scotland, is an outstanding health journalist. (Later, we had conversations and interviews about eye research, particularly about Indigenous eye health and diabetes.)

We undertook further data analysis on Age-related Macular Degeneration. AMD is a potent cause of blindness. The macula, the central retina at the back of the eye, is responsible for fine central vision. It is seen in older people and at that time there was no known cause or treatment. Over the last 40 years things have changed significantly on both counts. It is somewhat ironic that when we did this study cataract was still called 'senile cataract', although senile macular degeneration had been renamed age-related macular degeneration, and not long after, senile cataract also was renamed. We found no relation with AMD and either UV-B or UV-A radiation nor with visible light exposure. AMD was correlated with nuclear cataract, but interestingly, in the light of future findings, we did not see a correlation with smoking in this study.

For non-melanotic skin cancers we found a strong relationship between Squamous Cell Cancers and higher annual average UV-B exposure. We did not see this relationship for either Basal Cell Cancers or Actinic Keratitis, non-malignant skin changes caused by sun exposure. These later findings were consistent with 'dose-saturation' that is seen in those who have higher levels of UV exposure; that is where a low dose of UV-B exposure is enough to trigger the changes and the risk does not increase further with higher doses.

Sheila and I put in for another NEI grant to undertake a five-year follow up study on the watermen. The grant was funded in 1990 just as I was about to return to Melbourne, so Sheila took over as the principal investigator. The follow-up study re-confirmed the importance of smoking as a risk factor for both the incidence and the progression of nuclear cataract.

The Chesapeake Bay Waterman Study had come up with some exciting and important findings. It reinforced the need to be careful in the sun and to avoid unnecessary sun exposure. It also raised a linkage between eye disease, cataract, and cigarette smoking. It also showed the power of collaborating with people with skills and experience in different areas. Furthermore, all those who had joined us had a lot of fun too.

9
MUDO and CERA

> Dull and piffling questions give dull and piffling answers… it matters what the answer is—whether to science generally or to mankind.
>
> Peter Medawar 1977

In August 1990 Liz, Ned, Phoebe and I flew back to Melbourne, and I took up the chair named after my grandfather, the Ringland Anderson Chair. As professor I was the head of the Melbourne University Department of Ophthalmology, called MUDO. I was also the director of Eye Services at the Royal Victorian Eye and Ear Hospital and on their board for some years. I also had clinical and teaching responsibilities as head of the Corneal Clinic.

With my various clinical, teaching and administrative responsibilities I had little time for field research and needed to concentrate my efforts at home and within Australia.

The move was a major challenge for all our family. The job was a big change from what I had been doing in Baltimore, where I had left my projects, friends and colleagues. There was much to do to develop MUDO into the vibrant research centre I wanted it to be.

Liz had obtained a new position, but as we hit the deck her role changed dramatically and expanded enormously. She had been appointed as the associate director of the National HIV Reference Laboratory, later the National Serology Reference Laboratory, NRL, then located at the Fairfield Infectious Diseases

Hospital in Melbourne, a hospital which had specialised in infectious diseases for a century.

Almost as soon as she arrived, Ian Gust, who had established the NRL and was its director, left to take up a role at the Commonwealth Serum Laboratories, then a wholly government-owned enterprise.

Thus, soon after arrival, Liz became the director of the NRL and of the WHO Collaborating Centre for Laboratory Detection of Blood Borne Infections. The NRL oversaw the quality assurance of all the HIV and Hepatitis B testing in Australia. When new quality regulations came in for blood donation services, the NRL became responsible for the quality assurance of the testing for all blood-borne viruses in all the blood services and the state reference laboratories. Her WHO Collaborating Centre role took her to many countries—in Asia, Africa, Europe, North America and the Pacific—to help develop and improve their laboratory management, blood transfusion services and HIV testing procedures, and to advise on national policies.

Kate was 19, Bart 17, Ned 10 and Phoebe 5.

Kate had returned for her final year at school the year before and had started to study medicine at Melbourne University.

Bart had started Year 11 in Melbourne in February 1990, back when we made the decision to return. He made friends with some of the school leaders and fitted in well. He also played in the school's tennis and soccer teams.

Ned and Phoebe had to start in new schools and in a different culture. Ned started mid-year in Year 5. Both Ned and Bart were at Scotch College, my old school. Ned probably had the hardest adjustment. He knew nothing about Australian Rules football teams, and no-one cared about our baseball team, the Baltimore Orioles, which we had followed passionately. However, Ned had seen episodes of *The Simpsons* in the US the year before they were then due to be screened in Australia. Knowing what was to come earned him some status as the go-to *Simpsons* oracle.

Phoebe started preschool at the Methodist Ladies College, Liz's old school.

It was not easy to wrangle places in schools where most children had been registered at birth. Liz persisted relentlessly for the final success. Things were crazy busy for us all.

Pool of our Balwyn home

For the first year or so after our return we lived with my mother in my old family home. I loved being back in Melbourne, catching up with many old friends and activities, like following the football: the old Victorian Football League had metamorphosed in the Australian Football League that year. I had been a mad follower of the Melbourne Football Club since early childhood.

We built our new home in Balwyn, a residential suburb 10 kilometres east of the city centre, and moved in October 1991. This took a great deal of time and effort, particularly from Liz.

While the foundations were being built, our next-door neighbour saw a hole with reinforced walls in the middle of the house.

'Building an indoor swimming pool?'

'No,' I replied. 'That's for a wine cellar.'

Liz and I enjoyed good wine and letting it age. We built up a respectable collection that proved a bit of a problem when we had to downsize. The house gave us space for the four children, studies for Liz and me, and room to entertain as was required of a department head. The block gave us the opportunity to lay out a new garden from unbroken soil, making for busy pleasant weekends. The garden included a swimming pool that was heavily used through the summer months. The location gave good access to the children's schools and was a reasonable commute for Liz and me.

I resumed playing golf, which I had missed in Baltimore. Melbourne offered a wide range of arts and music as had Baltimore, so much so that it was tricky deciding what to go to and what to forego, what to subscribe to and what not. We settled on being becoming regulars at the opera, not possible in Baltimore, because it presented music, singing, acting and sometimes dancing—almost everything all in one show. We quickly became ardent opera fans.

On our return Liz had investigated finding someone who could help with the younger children after school and helping in the household. She interviewed a young woman from Bairnsdale, a rural town in eastern Victoria, and offered her the job. Margie Binse was a godsend and continues to help us more than 30 years later. She helped bring up Ned and Phoebe and is now doing the same for Kate's children. She is an amazing woman who had twin sons and a daughter. These 'children', now grown, are dear to us and in some ways regard us as having grandparent status.

I spent my first day at MUDO sitting in an enormous, half-filled office wondering what I was going to do.

I decided on building walls to make a much smaller office

Above: The Royal Victorian Eye and Ear Hospital
Below: Hector McLean and me at MUDO

for me and make more office space available for all the new research staff I started to plan for. From that small decision, big things came. It was a day well spent.

MUDO and the Eye and Ear were busy, and I was soon to be more than busy too. On Mondays at 8 am we had a clinical meeting and then did a corneal ward round. On other mornings ward rounds started at 8. My office was on the first floor, our first ward was on the fifth so we all walked up the stairs, then up to wards on Floors 7 and 8; good exercise! We held the corneal clinic two half days a week. I also had an operating session and a private clinic once a week, plus teaching sessions one evening a week, hospital meetings, university meetings and so forth.

MUDO had five other staff members in 1990: Associate Professor Hector McLean, the other ophthalmologist; Nan Carrol, electron microscopist; John Scrimgeour, retinal photographer; Lubjo Perocic, ophthalmic engineer; and Bev Vaudrey, administrative officer. Gerrard Crock had retired from the university and the hospital but had a near-by private practice. He would often drop in to see if he could help. He had an identical twin, Harry, a distinguished orthopaedic surgeon. Harry would sometime drop in to try and confuse me.

The Crock twins, Harry left, and Gerrad right, in front of Gerrard's portrait

Hector, a Scot from Dundee, had been recruited by Professor Crock, seduced in the early 1970s by the promise of using MUDO's scanning electron microscope, a rare asset to have in the early 1970s. He had been at MUDO for 17 years and, a gifted teacher, was happy to continue taking the lead in teaching. He ran the professorial general clinics and the Low Vision Clinic. He worked a lot with children, and seemed to have an inexhaustible supply of Smarties, M&Ms and chocolate frogs.

When I was a registrar, Nan and I had done a scanning electron microscopic study of trabeculectomy together. Then, she was nearing retirement. John too had been around MUDO for a long time. He had come to the US to spend some time with us on the Waterman study.

Lubjo had developed a very impressive range of microsurgical instruments with Gerard Crock. These included the vitrectomy instruments that transformed vitreous surgery and instruments for corneal grafting. Later, Lubjo and I worked together on projects with Fred Hollows and then with the Fred Hollows Foundation. We developed angled surgical loupes or magnifying glasses for cataract surgery, low-cost surgical needles, and explored the development of low-cost ophthalmic lasers.

This last project involved a trip to St Petersburg and Moscow in January 1992 to meet with the physicists who were developing portable lasers. It felt very cold coming from Australia's mid-summer, but to walk across St Petersburg's frozen Neva River from the Peter and Paul Cathedral on one side to the Hermitage Museum on the other was unforgettable. In the middle of winter, the upper galleries of the Hermitage were almost deserted. There were still a few tourists on the ground floor but once you got upstairs the only other people in the galleries were the occasional elderly *babushka* keeping an eye on things. I had the full collections of French impressionists all to myself, a once-in-a-lifetime treat. We did obtain a Russian laser to try out, but it was not very successful and the project lapsed.

My ambition, in addition to my day jobs—the clinical work and teaching –Director of Eye Services, Head of the Corneal Clinic, and Professor and Head of the Department of Ophthalmology—was to build a research department. I wanted to bring some of my experience and what I had seen and learned at the Wilmer to transform eye research in Australia. Melbourne was the main hub for medical research in Australia, with world-leading centres like the Walter and Elisa Hall Institute and the Howard Florey Institute. It took me some years, but I came to the realisation that I needed to find a better way to get the growth I wanted while remaining within the University. That ambition would eventually lead me to set up CERA, Centre for Eye Research Australia. However, first we had to do some practical studies of benefit to the Victorian community to build the Department's relevance.

The first step was to identify the main eye problems in the community, then set up programs to address them. This meant I needed to focus on the various eye issues in Australia, rather than spending a lot of time travelling and working overseas. The new focus led to the MVIP, Melbourne Vision Impairment Project (see page 245-267).

First, I had to establish an eye bank. In my job interview I had been told explicitly what my first job was: set up the Lions Eye Bank. Lions Australia was established in Australia in 1947. Lions donate their time and prodigious energies and talents to Lions Club projects, which has included everything from cyclone relief to raising money for the research that led to the development of the bionic ear. In 1925 Helen Keller was invited to speak at the Lions Clubs International Convention in Ohio. She challenged the Lions to become 'knights of the blind in the crusade against darkness'. The Lions contribution to eye health has never faltered and for which it is an international leader. In Australia, Lions have supported many eye care and research

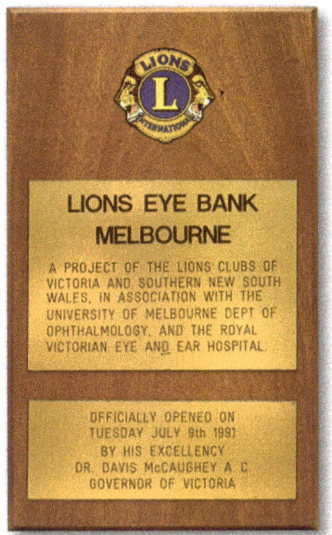 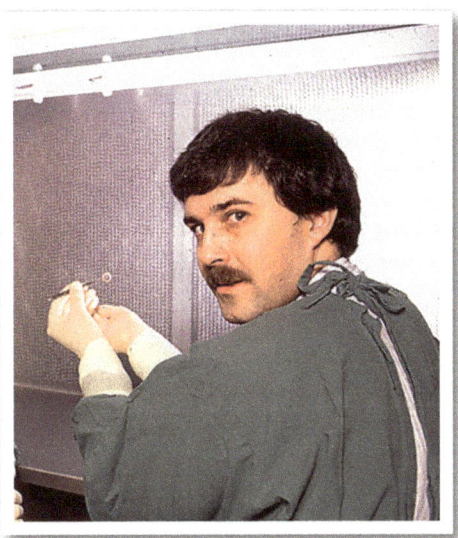

The Lions Eye Bank Plaque and Graeme Pollack soon after the Lions Eye Bank opened

programs, including the Lions Eye Institute in Perth, and later work on diabetes and the Lions Eye Health Program. Before I was appointed, the Lions Clubs in Victoria had raised the money to get the eye bank started, and did not want any further delay in getting it going.

I had spent some time while at Wilmer on the board of the Maryland Eye Bank, one of the largest and most progressive eye banks in the world. With their help and advice, we set up Australia's first. We found some empty space in the hospital and set up the eye bank laboratory. I recruited Graeme Pollock to run the eye bank. He continued to run it for 33 years. The eye bank staff promote the value of eye donation and corneal transplantation to restore sight to those with corneal blindness. They worked with the large hospitals and funeral directors to collect and prepare the tissue for corneal transplantation. (In 2023 they provided tissue for nearly 500 such surgeries, as well nearly 300 sclera surgeries, both sight-restoring or blindness-preventing.)

We also helped set up eye banks in Vietnam, Nepal and elsewhere. As eye banking has grown and expanded, the Lions

Tissue Donation Service, as it is now called, has grown and continues to participate—as a world leader.

In the year I started at MUDO, the first reports came out about the use of excimer laser to treat people who had myopia. Most myopia is benign, easily corrected with lenses, but severe near-sightedness can be sight-threatening, inducing retinal detachments, cataracts and glaucoma. Excimer lasers send a pulse of ultraviolet electrical energy through a high-pressure mixture of a noble and a halogen gas. The resultant laser beam can remove corneal tissue without damaging surrounding tissue as there is no heat generated. This technology generated a lot of interest among corneal surgeons and especially in people in private practice. Because it was all new and not well established, the hospital was not going to embark on this new technology and no individual ophthalmologist could do this on their own.

After a lot of discussion, MUDO decided to set up the Melbourne Excimer Laser Group; 25 ophthalmologists joined us and contributed the funds to buy the laser and pay the staff. After crowding into a small office for months, we found some space in a hospital-owned, beautiful Victorian building adjacent to the Eye and Ear. Two excimer lasers were available. One could

Terry Couper assisting a surgeon using the excimer laser

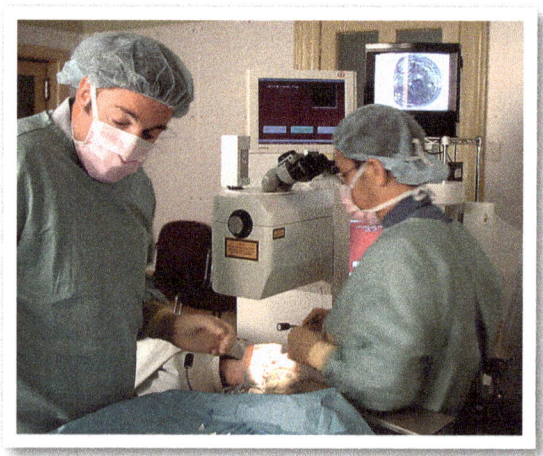

only treat simple myopia and had been ordered by a group in Sydney. We purchased the other type of excimer laser, one that could also treat astigmatism, where the cornea is more steeply curved in one direction than in another.

We performed our first excimer laser surgery in November 1991 and were one of the first groups in the world to report on the effectiveness of the laser to treat astigmatism as well as myopia. We also did some of the first studies on treating higher degrees of more severe myopia. Excimer laser surgery developed further, became widely available and very effective. The Melbourne Excimer Laser Group continues to operate.

Liz had moderate shortsightedness and wore her glasses all the time. When we started doing the excimer surgery, she asked about it but we left it at that. Later, she was in Europe attending a series of meetings. As she checked in for the Paris-to-Berlin train her hand luggage was stolen. Bye-bye passport, favourite sweater and her spare multifocal glasses, reading glasses, prescription sunglasses and multifocal sunglasses.

When she returned, I was preparing a poster presenting our latest results of the excimer surgery. I had the data and graphs spread out on our dining room table. Liz looked at the data with her expert analytic eye. 'This all seems to work very well. You have to fix my eyes or else it will cost you thousands to replace my stolen glasses. You have no excuse now.'

What could I do? Liz was scheduled for the surgery. She was thrilled to see the stars in the sky and the leaves on the trees without glasses.

During a meeting of those working on excimer lasers I met Charles McGhee, then a young professor of ophthalmology in Sutherland in the Highlands of Scotland. We kept in touch and put together one of the first books published about excimer laser surgery. When Liz and I were in the UK in 1998 we visited Charles his wife Jane, by then in Dundee. They took us whisky tasting, which sounded like fun. I tasted the first offering. With a half

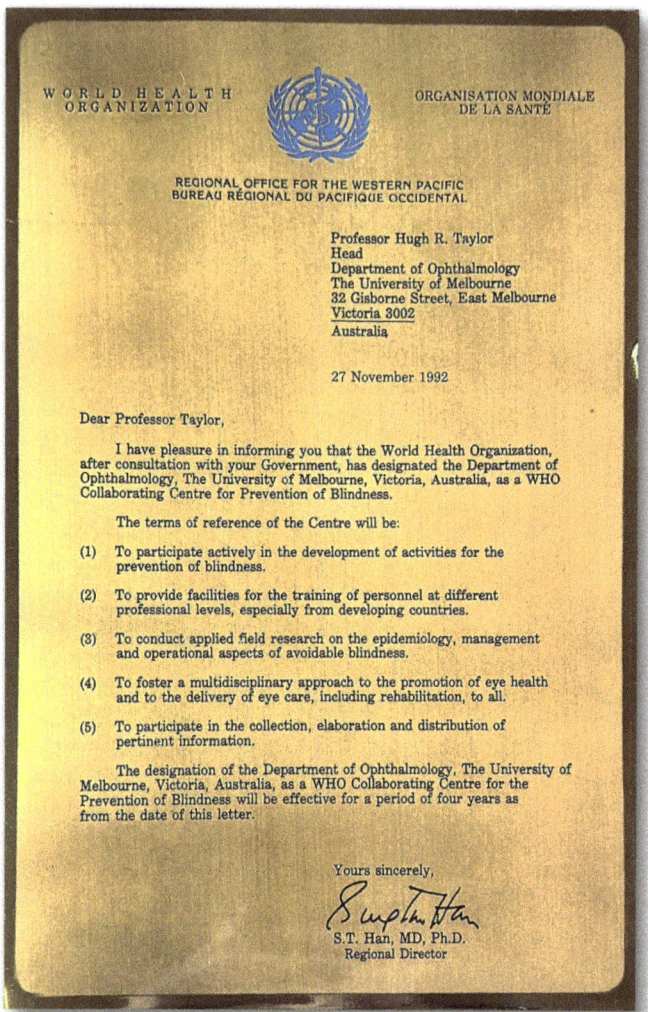

The plaque for the WHO Collaborating Centre

mouth full, I searched for the spittoon. I had done a lot of wine tasting. I was well used to—and recognised the need to—to spit out each taste. There was no spittoon. One had to swallow. Then there was another whisky… After visiting the second distillery, Charles and I were giggling in the back seat of the car, while Jane and Liz wondered what on earth they would do for the rest of the day, one that had just started.

MUDO and CERA

In 1992 MUDO became a WHO Collaborating Centre for the Prevention of Blindness. Liz also ran a WHO Collaborating Centre, her one on Diagnostics for Blood-borne Viruses. At that time there were 19 WHO Collaborating Centres in Australia, but we were the only two directors that met every day for breakfast. Later CERA took over the role as the Collaborating Centre.

I really was keen to get some laboratory work started. There was some recently vacated space in the old building on the floor above the excimer laser unit. It had been vacated when the pathology service was transferred across the road to St Vincent's Hospital. I thought I could recruit some part-time staff if I could find some funds for them. But how to get money and equipment? The family had helped set up the Ringland Anderson chair, that is true. Could they help further? By going back a generation to my great great-grandfather, John Wesley McComas, I could bring in more relatives. The expanded family came to the party and the McComas Family Laboratory was duly opened. A little later Paul Baird joined us, and he continues to do great genetic work in the McComas Laboratory.

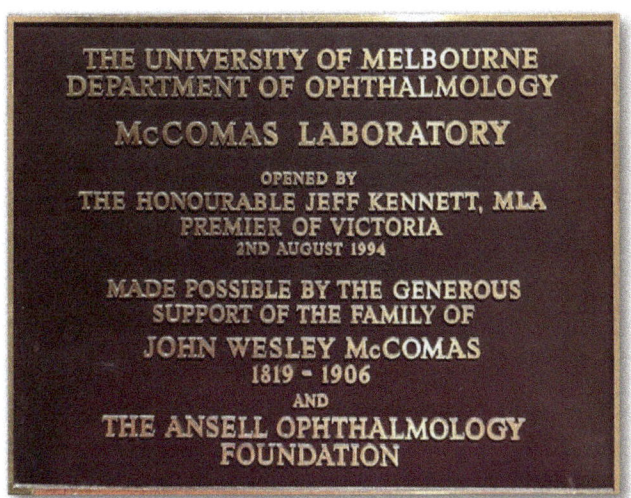

The McComas laboratory plaque

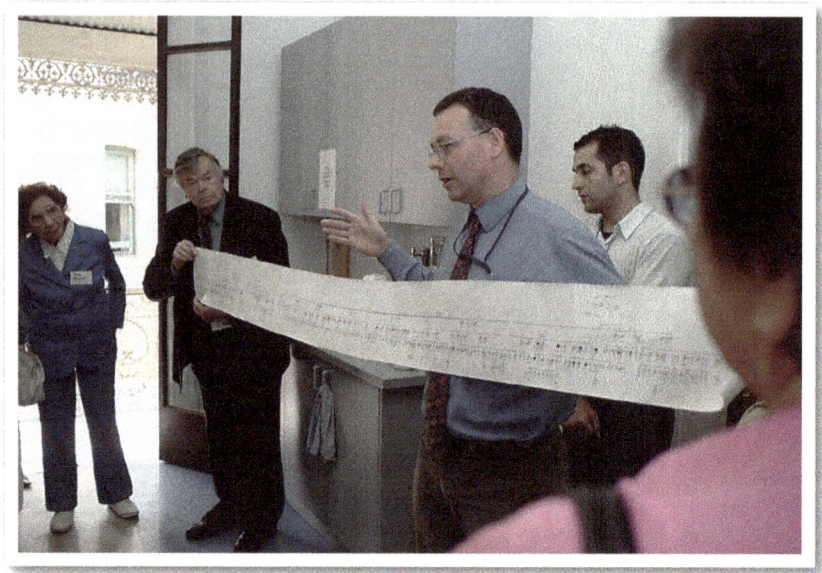

Paul Baird in the McComas laboratory with staff members

Skipping forward a little over two decades later, I was contemplating moving on from MUDO and CERA. I had cause for the satisfaction I felt. When I started, we were half a dozen. I'd worked hard to find research money, recruit staff and take on research students. We'd done well. MUDO had grown along with CERA.

Among the early staff was Jill Keeffe, who had just finished her PhD on Low Vision Services and Education with Hector McLean. As an expert in low vision Jill is still in continuous demand by WHO, Lions International and other bodies. Robyn Guymer was interested in medical retinal diseases and especially AMD, Age-related Macular Degeneration. She is now a world leader in AMD research and the development of new treatments for it. With Graeme Pollack we had set up the Lions Eye Bank. We also had some clinicians as part-time academic staff: Grant Snibson and Mark Daniell (cornea), Julian Rait and Anne Brooks (glaucoma), and Alex Harper (retina). All have gone on to wonderfully productive academic careers.

We were fortunate to receive some funding from the Ansell Foundation. The family of the rubber products company, Kathleen and Lloyd Ansell, patients of my predecessor, Gerry Crock, set up a foundation to support MUDO's eye research, and included me on its board. After discussions with the Ansell board about how to raise more funds and grow our research, it was decided that we should establish a new, independent eye-research institute. This tantalising prospect required investigation.

Graeme Clark, then the professor of otolaryngology, was also located at the Eye and Ear. He and his group had invented the Bionic Ear and established the Bionic Ear Institute. I learned that the independent research institutes in Victoria received funding from the state government. The memorandum and articles of association of the Bionic Ear Institute seemed to be a good place to start. I asked Graeme if I could look at them and he was happy and gracious enough to share them. It was interesting to see that they were based on those of the Walter and Elisa Hall Institute, which started in the 1920s. We adapted them and CERA was registered as Not-For-Profit company.

I needed to bring people together to establish this 'fledging institute'. A 'professor' always stood out; a professor was a target at times for those within their hospital or from the profession. A university department, such as MUDO, was seen to be detached from the 'real' work of the hospital. With waiting lists, who had time for research? Also, a professor was perceived by some practitioners to have an unfair attraction for private patients seeking care. To establish a new institute, I had to have the support of both the University and the Hospital, and ideally my fellow ophthalmologic practitioners too.

The composition of the board was critical for the fledging CERA to be successful. Both the University and the Hospital had to have a representative, as did the Ansell Foundation. I wanted to bring in the ophthalmologists, so a representative of the Royal Australian College of Ophthalmologists (subsequently, the Royal

Australian and New Zealand College of Ophthalmologists, RANZCO) was included. I also brought in the Lions Clubs which supported the Eye Bank, CBM Australia, and the organisations of, and for, the blind, the Royal Victorian Institute for the Blind and the Association for the Blind. (These two institutions had been around for more than 100 years and at times had had some acrimonious legal discussions. After sitting around the table together in board meetings for a few years, these two bodies and the Royal Blind Society of New South Wales amalgamated to become Vision Australia.)

After slowly putting together some structure, we decided we would call the new institute the 'Centre for Eye Research' CER. I thought calling it an 'Institute' would be rather presumptuous; after all we were only small and new, and research institutes in Australia and elsewhere were usually large and prestigious. We were making progress in getting CER up and running, when, during a meeting in Perth, I had a call from our lawyers. They had found that there was already a Centre for Eye Research registered in Queensland and that we would have to come up with another name. I added 'Australia', so the Centre for Eye Research Australia, CERA, was duly founded in 1996.

We applied for state support as a research institute and were delighted—and more than a bit relieved—when we received it.

CERA worked within the University structure and followed all their policies. Most academic staff had joint appointments. Papers listed both the University and CERA. It worked well. CERA grew and grew.

The initial CERA logo

The University Medical School had separate departments of medicine and surgery in each of the teaching hospitals. Similarly, ophthalmology and otolaryngology were also separate and stand-alone departments.

In about 2014 the various small departments were amalgamated. MUDO became part of the new large Department of Surgery. It was called Surgery in Ophthalmology and was no longer MUDO. The head of CERA remained the Professor of Ophthalmology but was now a member of the Department of Surgery. This did not really make any significant difference in the way the Department of Ophthalmology and CERA worked together.

Our first effort to promote eye health and eye examinations was to try to set up a home screening program so that people were encouraged and able to check their own vision. This work was led by Jill Keefe and Cathy McCarthy. In 1994 Jill had developed a Vision Testing Kit to screen for low vision in community and aged-care settings. It had been adopted by WHO and translated and adapted for many cultures. Jill had used the kit and taught others how to use it in the Philippines and the South Pacific, particularly in Fiji. Later, she ran courses on screening for low

Cathy McCarthy and Jill Keefe

vision for WHO in some African and Asian countries.

Jill had adapted the testing kit into the Home Vision Test Kit with a simple vision screening card and instructions for people to test their vision. There was information on what to do if they noticed a problem or changes in their vision. This was particularly designed to detect under-corrected refractive error that the MVIP had shown was the commonest cause of vision loss. Alison Pitt, an experienced orthoptist joined CERA. Jill and Alison ran a pilot test to see how well the Home Vision Test Kit worked.

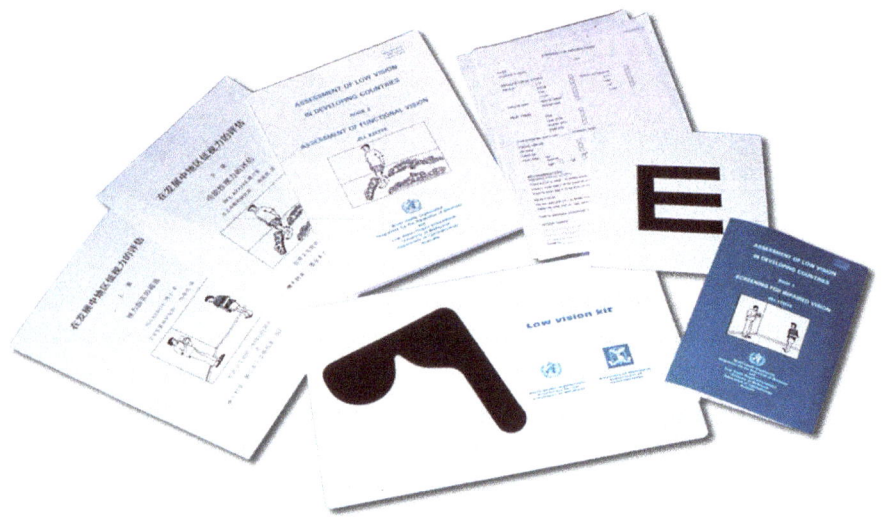

The Low Vision Test Kit

I had worked with Michael Wooldridge, the federal minister for health, on a review of Indigenous eye health in 1996–97. I spoke with him about vision screening, and he suggested that we try the pilot in his electorate of Chisholm in the eastern suburbs of Melbourne. We called the project 'The Vision Initiative' and had kits delivered house by house and we got favourable feedback. Alison and Jill organised tests of people in age-care services. This followed on from MVIP findings of the high rate of vision loss in those in aged care.

With the good results of the pilot tests, we talked further with Michael Wooldridge about how we might expand this project. At his suggestion, we talked with the ACT Health Department where initial interest was shown, but an election led to a change of government, and interest evaporated. Another tack we tried was with the Australian Post Office, but that too went nowhere.

About the same time Jill started a project working with the Lions Clubs called the Lions Eye Health Promotion program, LEHP. This seemed an alternative way to promote the messages about eye exams. Brochures, posters, videos, and other materials were developed that particularly targeted those with glaucoma or diabetes to encourage them to have regular eye exams. We developed small cards with a multiple year calendar that could fit into a wallet so each person could tick off their most recent exam and use it as a reminder for their next. The Lions distributed these materials widely across the country.

Later, Jill and the Lions Clubs developed the Lions Low Vision Initiative that operated in Victoria and Fiji.

With the Lions and with their support we made some significant improvements in eye health, the eye bank and eye health promotions. They also helped raise funds for CERA with the Lions annual bike ride and their support of CERA in the Melbourne Marathon. I would usually run the 5-kilometre segment, and once the half marathon, and waited to congratulate and thank those who were running for us. Liz often did the half marathon, usually with a good bit of walking and once walked the whole marathon. For this collaboration with Lions. I was honoured by the Melbourne Lions with their Melvin Jones Award in 2002.

We kept pushing to expand the promotion of vision screening. We wanted to make it into a fully-fledged campaign, similar to the QUIT campaign to stop smoking. We had finished the five-year follow-up work of the MVIP and decided that rather than just doing further follow-up examinations, we should do something about putting our findings into practice. As well as publishing our results in the scientific literature, in 1999 we assembled the results into a booklet called 'Eye Care for the Community'. It was officially launched in 2000 by Michael Wooldridge at a national meeting of eye-care providers we had organised.

In 2001 we approached John Thwaites, then the new Victorian minister for health, to talk about the ideas we had for eye health promotion. He asked us to develop a proposal for a program in Victoria. He accepted the proposal for The Vision Initiative and offered the money to CERA in the next year.

However, at the same time and as part of the WHO and the International Agency for the Prevention of Blindness program, 'Vision2020: The Right to Sight', Brien Holden and I were setting up an Australian group to be called 'Vision 2020 Australia'. Rather than having the money for The Vision Initiative in Victoria come to CERA, I felt a better solution would be for the program to be within Vision 2020 Australia with the hope that such an initiative could be extended nation-wide. A similar program to The Vision Initiative in Victoria ran in Queensland for a while.

To reinforce the need for vision screening, we went to Victoria's Parliament House and set up a vision testing room for parliamentarians to have their eyes checked. Many members came in and were tested. Vision 2020 Australia has conducted parliamentary vision testing events in Canberra and in Macquarie Street, Sydney since then.

In 2006 the federal health minister, Tony Abbott, funded a national TV campaign about eye care, a campaign somewhat along the lines of the QUIT campaign. It focused on a range of advertisements and TV promotions about 'Which eye is healthy'.

Unfortunately, it did not last past the change in government in 2007. However, Vision 2020 Australia had continued to receive Victorian government funding to maintain the Vision Initiative

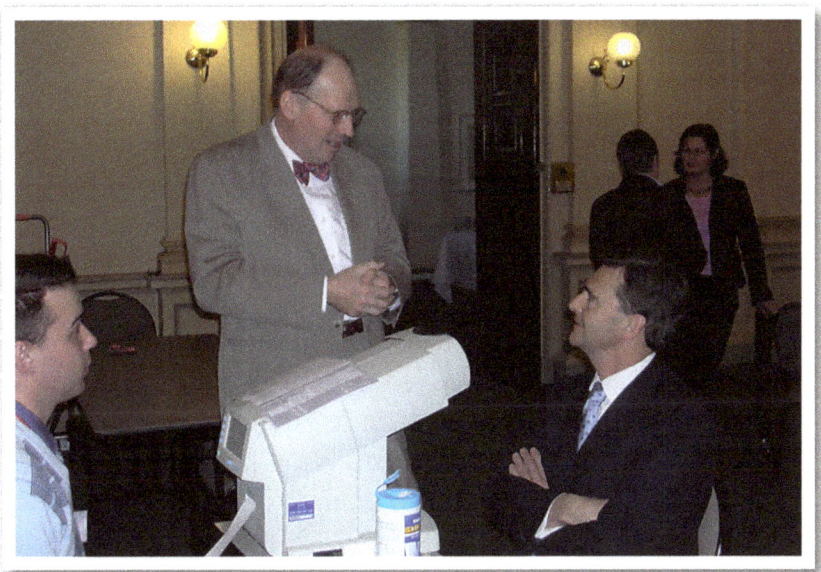

Eye screening in the Victoria's Parliament House with Premier John Brumby

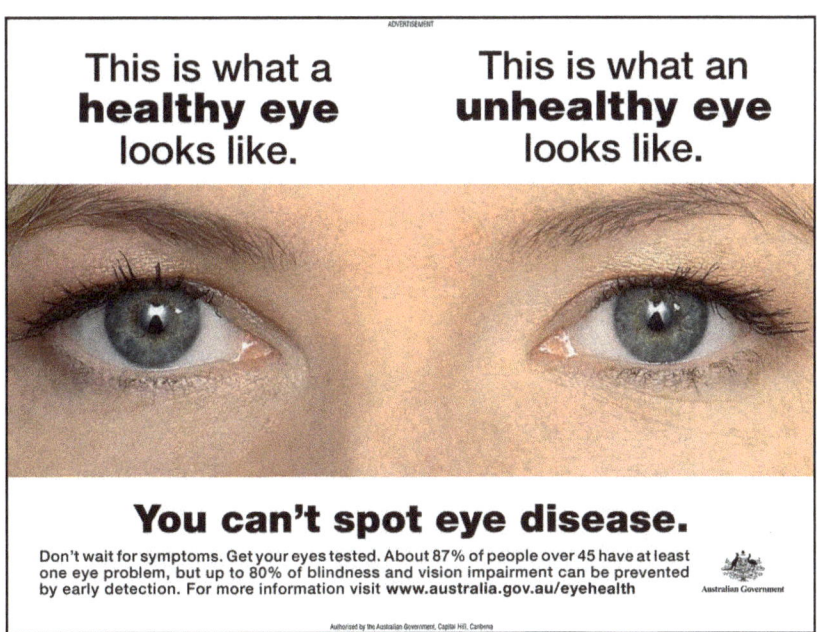

The Commonwealth government's advertisement for 'Healthy Eyes' that ran in 2006

in Victoria in one form or another. All through this work the emphasis had been on the need for regular eye exams and particularly their need in high-risk groups. This took and applied the findings of the MVIP and put them into practice.

Vision 2020 Australia continues to be very effective in advocating for improved eye care and effectively promotes 'The right to sight for all' at both the national and international levels.

Brien Holden was a big man, in every sense. Burly and bearded, he was physically large, had a loud voice he was happy to use, and a great creative mind full of wide-ranging ideas. An optometrist at the University of New South Wales he did extraordinary work developing and improving contact lenses: the 'soft' silicone hydrogel contact lens is his most feted achievement. He led major eye-health education and service-provision programs, earning him the epithet 'the most influential optometrist of our generation'. The income for spin offs funded the work of the Institute for Eye Research. Later, his organisations would become the Brien Holden Vision Institute and the Brien Holden Foundation.

Brien Holden and I at the ARVO meeting 2001, Fort Lauderdale, Florida

Brien received a large 5-year Federal grant in 1991 to set up the Cooperative Research Centre for Eye Research and Technology. He received further funding until 2003. During this time his work had expanded into areas of uncorrected refractive error and the need to include refraction and optometry in the global work on preventing blindness.

In 2002 the previous CRC was due for renewal and Brien wanted to expand the prevention of blindness work, and work on Indigenous eye health. I and CERA were asked to join the new Vision CRC, which was funded in the next year. With international partners it continued to do innovative work on contact lenses and the control of myopia, as well as conduct public health work in Asia and Africa. Brien died very suddenly in 2015 when he was chatting with Serge Resnikoff over dinner. Fortunately, his work is continued by the Brien Holden Vision Institute.

For many years as a British colony and then as part of the British Commonwealth, distinguished Australians would receive various Imperial honours and awards. In 1975 Prime Minister Gough Whitlam introduced a new Australian honours system, the Order of Australia. It has four categories, Companion being the highest, then Officer, Member and a Medal of the Order. Many academics would receive an honour recognising their contributions to Australia and to academia. One day in early 2001, while Liz was away and I was home by myself, a letter came in the mail from the Governor General's office. This was a big surprise. It told me I had been nominated to receive an award. I was amazed and read the letter too quickly to take it all in. I guessed sooner or later my work might be recognised, but not at this relatively early stage. Later I went back and re-read the letter. Companion in the Order of Australia! This had to be kept secret until it was announced on the Queen's Birthday weekend a few months later. When Liz returned there was also a letter for her. She was to be a Member.

Opening Eyes

We arranged for family and a few friends to come and join us for lunch in Olinda to mark the Queen's Birthday public holiday and the completion of our renovations of a new kitchen and family room. The awards were announced in the newspapers that morning. When people arrived, some had seen the announcements, others had not. Kate was very suspicious about the event and had checked the newspaper: she found Liz's award and called very excitedly but she had not looked through the small number of Companion awards. We had a wonderful celebration.

My award was to be presented by the Governor General in Canberra. We decided to drive to Canberra and the children were able to join us. The presentation was on Thursday, 13 September 2001. With the rest of the world, we reeled at the news on Tuesday, the 9–11 attacks. The next day, the airline Ansett Australia, closed down and never again took off. Travel chaos followed. But we were on the road and got to the Governor General's residence in Yarralumla for the ceremony. And spent a wonderful time after it, celebrating with the family.

Family at Yarralumla after the conferring of my Order of Australia: *from left*: Phoebe, Ned, me, Liz, Bart and Kate.

2001 was also the centenary of Australia becoming an independent federation within the British Commonwealth, and there were events to celebrate and mark this. During the year schools and voluntary organisations were invited to participate in a large-scale, community-art installations and to nominate a notable person to be displayed on the lawns around, and on the roof of Parliament House in Canberra. My old school, Scotch College, nominated me. At the end of that year my image stood on top of Parliament House for 10 days!

Phoebe and me at Peoplescape, December 2021

Today, in the mid-2020s, 17 years since I led it, CERA has become one of the top three or four eye research institutions in the world. It has a staff of over 200, with an outstanding reputation for their amazing work. It has moved into a spectacular new space with large, well-designed laboratories and plenty of workspace, and a large, world-class Cerulea clinical trials unit.

In 2015 they started a small company Oculo, led by my daughter Kate, that networked optometrists and ophthalmologist and enabled online data sharing (see page 347-349). In 2022 they also started a company Mirugen to develop gene therapy. All this is the fruit of the work of Tien Wong, Jonathon Crowston and Keith Martin, the subsequent directors, and their leadership of all the staff at CERA along with their multitude of collaborators and supporters.

Among CERA's other outstanding projects are the Bionic Eye; Clinical Genetics; Corneal Biosynthesis; both Macular and Uveitis Research; the Retinal Gene Unit and the Centre for Excellence in Ocular Gene and Cell Therapy; the Visual Neurovascular Unit including glaucoma studies; the Ocular Oncology Unit; and an international neuroscience consortium and company, Enlighten Imaging, to identify people at risk of developing Alzheimer's Disease. CERA continues its epidemiologic research and is a WHO Collaborating Unit for the Prevention of Blindness, one of 11 world-wide.

I started CERA over 30 years ago and left others to run it nearly 20 years ago. As founder, ex-advocate, ex-administrator and ex-co-worker, I feel I can retain some bragging rights, but CERA's position, productivity and prestige today is the fruit of the work of many, medical and non-medical, people, and that was always the case. In the mid-2020s CERA workers publish between 200 and 250 scientific papers a year, and I still read a few. The institute attracts close to $7 million from governments, and a similar amount from philanthropic grants, donations and bequests each year. CERA's activities have, like all medical research organisations, been heavily influenced by the explosion of genetic knowledge and the prospects of bioengineering. In cocktail-party conversation mention of local trials with four blind patients using a second-generation bionic eye garners intense interest; almost everyone I talk to is surprised to learn how far CERA's team has moved, how audacious their goals are.

CERA has become an outstanding success. I am immensely proud of the work and the development that has spawned the extensive outcomes of those who have continued to lead and achieve at CERA.

Opening Eyes

10

The Melbourne Vision Impairment Project

Think globally, act locally
Environmental activists' precept

Pondering over where to start studies on how we could improve eye health in our own community, I considered my previous work on chlamydial eye infections at the Wilmer. Would surveying those eye problems be a good place to start?

As a first up we did a small study in hospital Emergency Rooms to see how common chlamydia infection was in people presenting with conjunctivitis. Working with Anne Malatt, a registrar at the Royal Victorian Eye and Ear, and Suzanne Garland, a medical-school colleague, who was the director of microbiology at the Royal Women's Hospital, we found that only 2 percent of patients presenting with conjunctivitis had chlamydial infection. Most of those with chlamydial conjunctivitis were adults with chlamydial genital tract infections who had transferred their infection to their eyes. However, given the low prevalence of chlamydial conjunctivitis presenting to the Eye and Ear, there was little point in setting up a chlamydia laboratory to continue the type of experiments we had carried out in Baltimore.

I had to re-focus.

To identify clearly the eye problems and issues of a

community, a proper epidemiologic study was needed. To get funding for such a study takes time.

The first step was to write a grant application. These types of studies are expensive and complex. Often a single granting agency will not fund all the work, so we submitted several grant applications to different bodies for different aspects of the work. We received funding from the National Health and Medical Research Council, the Victorian Health Promotion Foundation, the Ophthalmic Research Institute of Australia, and several private trusts and foundations.

Towards the end of 1991 we were ready to get the Melbourne Vision Impairment Project, the MVIP, underway. The aim was to determine the prevalence and causes of vision impairment and blindness in Melbourne. We would survey a sample of Melburnians over the age of 40.

The sample was drawn from randomly selected pairs of Census Collector Districts. Nine pairs were selected to give a projected sample of 3500 people. We went from house to house to identify and recruit all those who were eligible. The team was superbly led by Charles Guest, a public-health doctor. When Charles left to become the head of Public Health in Canberra, Cathy McCarty took over. Cathy was then a young American epidemiologist who had just finished her PhD. She moved to Australia to join the study. Her then husband Dan took up a position working on diabetes epidemiology with Paul Zimmet at the International Diabetes Institute. Dan later joined our group at CERA. Trish Livingston expertly set up the sampling and recruitment models for the MVIP as part of her PhD.

We set up temporary examination sites in each of the nine areas. The first was in a church hall, but other examination sites were in houses, shops or offices. Subjects had a brief interview in their homes and then went through a more comprehensive interview at the local examination site we set up. There they underwent a detailed eye exam with all the tests available: visual acuity, refraction, visual fields, and after dilating their pupils a slit-lamp exam, then lens and retinal photography. A few people with mobility issues were examined in their own homes.

Above: The MVIP team and signage outside a local house used for the examinations

Left: An initial interview conducted at home

After the local letter-box-drop appeal for subjects the examinations were just getting started at the first site in Albert Park, when a confident, good-looking 30-something man walked in.

'Hello. What are you doing?'

That is how I met John Thwaites, the local member of the state parliament, later a long-term minister of health and deputy

Opening Eyes

Above: Trish Livingston interviewing in an examination site
Below: A subject having her vision measured

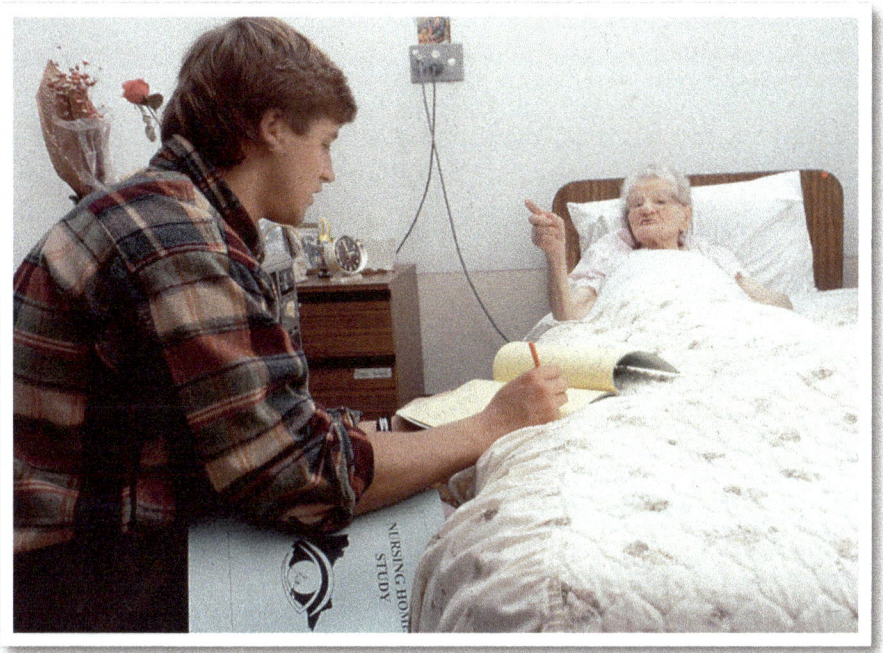

Todd Robin interviewing a subject in a nursing home

premier. (John was to prove to be a great help in developing some of the later eye care programs with Vision 2020 Australia.)

In our initial sample participants were those over 40 years who lived at home, and all within the Melbourne metropolitan area. To get a better representation of older people, we did a follow-on study of aged-care residents, the youngest 46 years old. We studied those in 13 aged-care facilities linked to our previous sample areas.

'What about country residents?' Good question. We randomly selected four regional sites to expand our sample.

Cathy McCarty also did a small study of patients with schizophrenia living in a mental health service community. They had a higher rate of cataract than the MVIP population. It was unclear if this might be directly related to schizophrenia or perhaps to some of the drugs used to treat it.

We collaborated with Paul Mitchell in Sydney who was

conducting a somewhat similar study in the Blue Mountains. Paul had studied under Fred Hollows. I had met him while he was doing his PhD study on diabetic retinopathy in Newcastle. We shared our examination protocols with him, and he graded our retinal photographs. The Blue Mountains Study was also a detailed, community-based epidemiologic study of eye disease but in one regional area.

The MVIP combined the three main study groups, urban, rural and in aged care. Although statistically it now represented the population of Victoria, we continued to call it the Melbourne Visual Impairment Project. The findings of the MVIP were to guide our future work on improving the eye health of Victorians, and then Australians, and then beyond.

What did we find?

In total we had examined 5147 people: 3271 or 83 percent of those eligible in the urban sample, 1473 or 91 percent of the eligible rural sample, and 403 or 91 percent of those eligible in aged care.

In the non-institutionalised people aged 40 years or older, we found good 'presenting vision'. Presenting vision is the vision of people who are tested and who either did not have glasses or who walked in wearing their glasses. After age-standardisation we found that only 4.2 percent had presenting vision worse than 6/12 (see page 67). Presenting vision rates for moderate vision loss (6/18 to 6/60) were 2.6 percent, and for bilateral blindness (worse than 6/60), 0.36 percent. Unsurprisingly, vision loss and blindness were much more common in older people. Blindness was also much more common in the aged-care and nursing home populations where 8 percent were blind. Not much was being done about addressing this disturbing finding.

If people had the appropriate glasses for them, that is they had their 'best corrected vision', the rates of moderate vision loss were reduced by about half. Uncorrected refractive error only caused about 4 percent of blindness. Overall, 60 percent of those with some vision loss improved by at least one line of letters on the vision chart with proper correction. This showed that under-correction of refractive error was a significant problem. Some loss of visual fields was found to be quite common, occurring in about 16 percent of people. Nevertheless, these rates of vision loss were much lower than those reported in studies from the US for example, presumably because Australia has a more equitable and accessible healthcare system.

We found the main cause for vision impairment of less than 6/12 was uncorrected refractive error. This was followed by cataract, AMD and glaucoma. Glaucoma and diabetic retinopathy were more common causes of vision loss in younger people, whereas cataract and AMD were more common causes in the more elderly. Uncorrected refractive error was important across all the age groups. This study confirmed that most of the observed vision loss was unnecessary; it was either preventable or treatable. For blindness the picture was different. Nearly half of blindness was caused by AMD, and refractive error only accounted for 4 percent of blindness. At that time there was no effective treatment for AMD, although glaucoma, cataract and diabetic retinopathy could all be treated and the vision loss they caused prevented. We had to try to have changes made to address and remedy these adverse findings.

One of the major reasons for undertaking these studies was to look further into the epidemiology of cataract in Victoria. Put simply, we found that by the age of 80 everyone will develop at least some cataract and half of those who had developed cataract had already had cataract surgery. Women and people with brown eyes had an increased risk of having either cortical or nuclear cataract, but not posterior subcapsular cataract. In those who had not had cataract surgery, 30 percent of the cataracts were cortical cataracts; 43 percent were nuclear cataracts and 17 percent posterior sub-capsular cataracts, PSC. We found

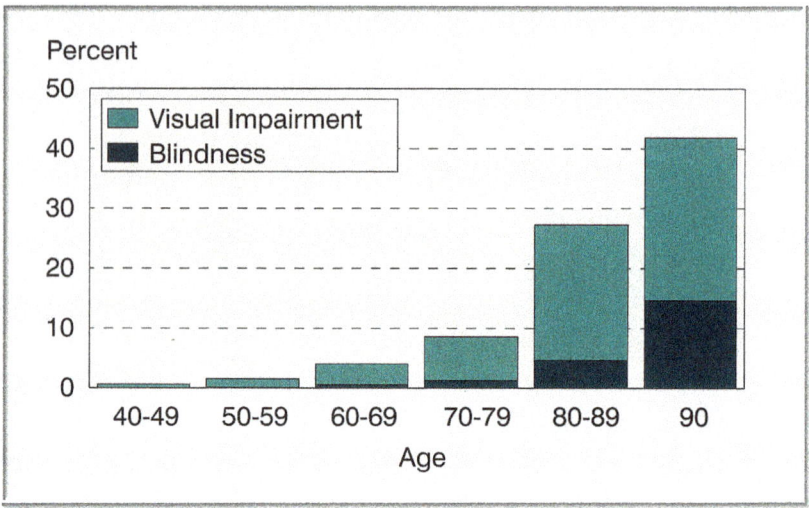

The prevalence of visual impairment and blindness by age, Australia 2004

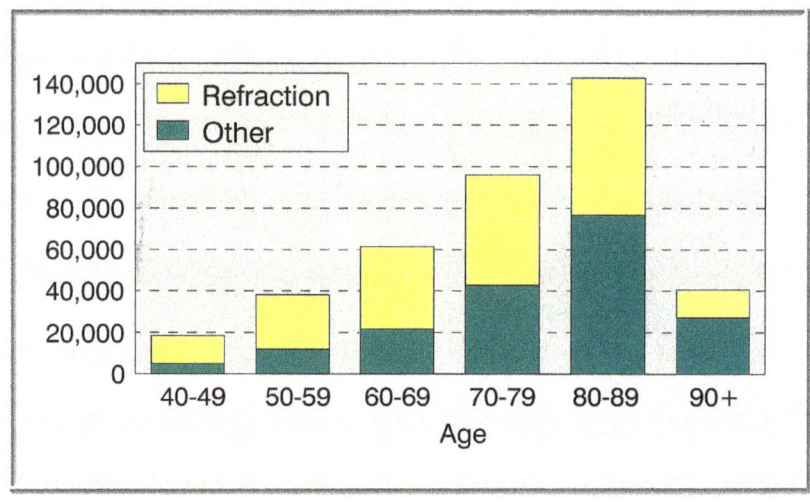

The estimated numbers of people with visual impairment due to uncorrected refractive error by age, Australia 2004

The Melbourne Vision Impairment Project

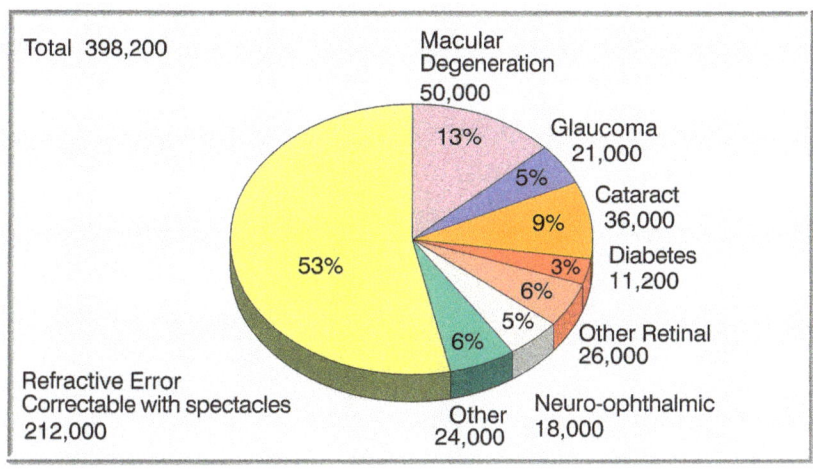

The causes of visual impairment in those over 40 years, Australia, 2004

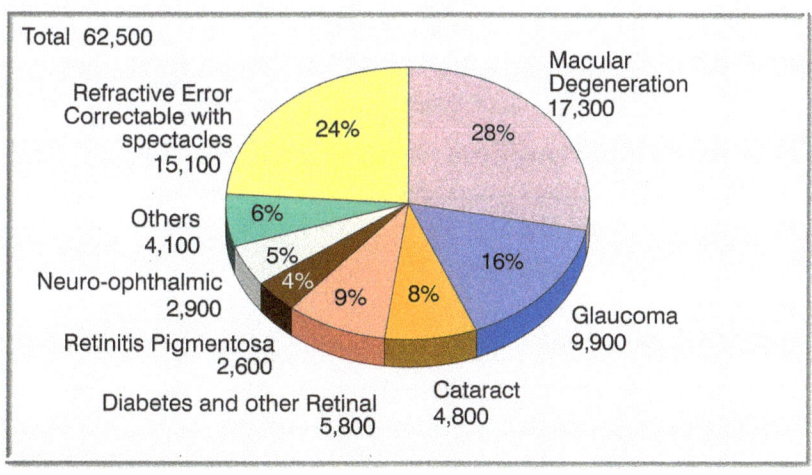

The causes of blindness in those over 40 years, Australia, 2004

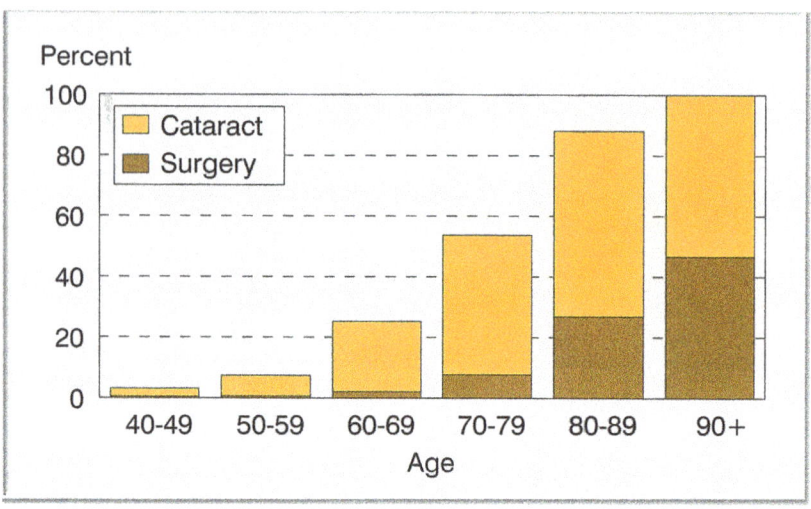

The rates of detectable cataract and those who have had cataract surgery by age, Australia 2004

that 18 percent of people had some measurable cataract in one or both eyes, about two thirds of whom had both eyes affected. Overall, only 3.4 percent of all those in the 1990s survey had had cataract surgery.

Higher UV-B exposure was again shown as a significant risk factor for cortical cataract, again confirming the major finding of the Chesapeake Bay Waterman study. Having diabetes, myopia, arthritis, or gout were also risk factors for having cortical cataract. For nuclear cataract, smoking stood out as the most important risk factor after increasing age. Diabetes and myopia were important risk factors for nuclear cataract, as was the presence of AMD and being a rural resident. Myopia was the most important risk factor for PSC along with rural residence and the use of thiazide diuretics. We used multivariant analyses—a statistical analytic tool used to find patterns and correlations in data where there are many variables. We tested a wide range of possible risk factors, including demographic, occupational, medical, smoking, drinking and diet.

With the MVIP data, we examined the projected needs for cataract surgery. If surgery were to be done on those with any lens opacities or 'cataract', irrespective of their vision, twice as many operations would be needed compared with a threshold of vision loss of 6/12 or more.

We were also able to look at the results of cataract surgery. About 20 percent of those who had cataract surgery did not have intraocular lenses and wore the old-fashioned thick cataract glasses. The rest had had the more modern surgery that used intraocular lenses to restore vision. We found vision was 6/12 or better in 85 percent of those who had had cataract surgery. We looked at age, gender, residence, ethnicity, and if people had health insurance. There were no specific demographic differences between those who had had cataract surgery and those who had not.

When examining the frequency and types of refractive error we found 46 percent with emmetropia—that is, normal refraction with no need for glasses; and 37 percent with hypermetropia or long-sightedness. The rate of any myopia or short-sightedness varied greatly with age, going from about a quarter in those in their 40s, to less than 10 percent in those in their 70s.

Myopia was more common in those of Asian background, university graduates and professional workers. This is consistent with the current understanding that increasing the time young people spend outdoors will protect them from developing myopia as they age. (For many years, there had been confusion with the inverse: that too much spent indoors, reading or looking at screens, caused short-sightedness. As a consequence of our changed understanding of the causes of myopia, children in many countries including China, South Korea, Taiwan and Singapore, are now required to spend at least one hour outdoors during school hours to reduce their risk of developing myopia or having it progress further.)

Overall, 10 percent of the people we examined in the MVIP

had a significant uncorrected refractive error. This meant they either needed to have glasses if they did not have them, or they needed their current glasses replaced. Rates of under-correction increased progressively with age. They were higher in those who did not speak English at home, lived in urban areas or had not had a tertiary education. Those who had not had an eye exam in the preceding four years were more likely to have uncorrected vision loss. Again, these findings indicated the need for health promotion and education to ensure that *all* people receive the regular eye exams that are needed.

Age-related Macular Degeneration increased sharply from the age of 70 to 80, as expected. For those over 90 years 80 percent had at least some AMD changes. Many subjects had signs of early AMD, but the age-standardised prevalence of severe 'wet' neovascular AMD was 0.38 percent and 'dry' atrophic AMD 0.27 percent. There was no gender difference.

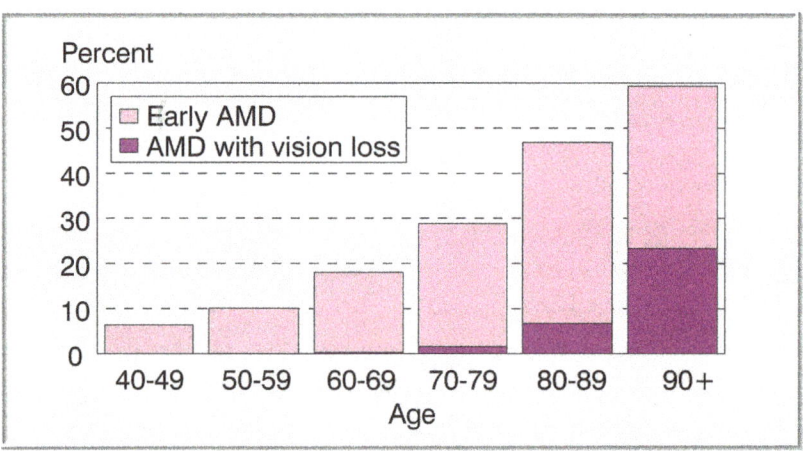

The rates of age-related macular degeneration by age, Australia 2004

AMD was strongly associated with increasing age and with a history of cigarette smoking. It was also related to some medications, including the ACE-inhibitor drugs used to treat high blood pressure, and cholesterol-lowering drugs. Despite looking at the whole range of potential factors for which we collected data, including UV exposure and dietary intake of antioxidants or supplements, we found no other associations for AMD. In this study we did not collect information about any family history of AMD. Later studies by others would show that up to 80 percent of AMD could be attributed to inherited genetic factors.

Since the flurry of articles arising from the MVIP were published in the 1990s, treatments for neovascular AMD were developed. These are mostly given as repeated injections into the eye. More recently, some treatments for atrophic AMD have become available, including laser treatment pioneered by Robyn Guymer at CERA. Part of this work has looked at the very early detection of the changes of AMD using retinal photographs taken with a wide range of different wavelengths of the electromagnetic spectrum not just light, a process called 'hyperspectral imaging'.

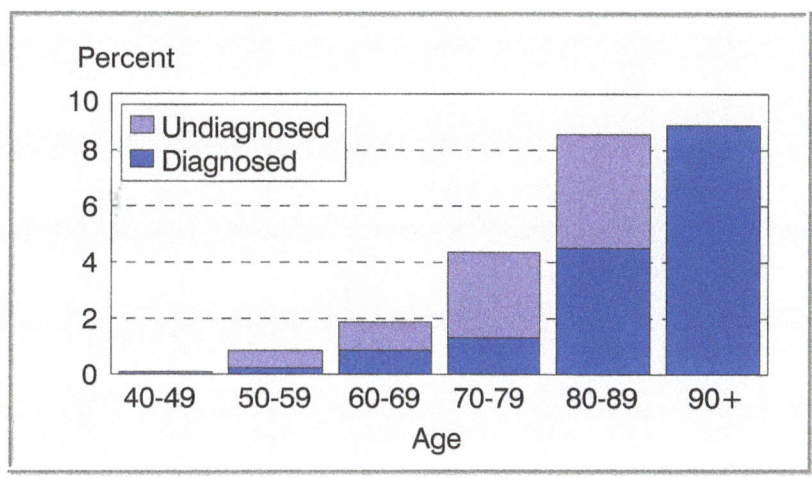

The rates of glaucoma by age, Australia 2004

Glaucoma is an important cause of blindness where high pressures in the eye lead to the death of the nerve fibres in the retina, causing optic disc changes and loss of the visual field. The overall prevalence of glaucoma also increased progressively with age, going from 0.1 percent in those 40 to 49, to 9.7 percent in those aged 80 to 89. There was no gender difference but having a family history of glaucoma was significant, increasing the risk three-fold.

Astoundingly, 60 percent of those found to have glaucoma had not been diagnosed previously. Half of them had had an eye examination in the preceding year, but their glaucoma had been missed. Here was a real need, a cast-iron case, for better education and awareness for both optometrists and ophthalmologists to be more thorough in their examinations to detect glaucoma.

Of people examined in the MVIP 5.1 percent had diabetes, some of it sight threatening.

The MVIP identified other eye problems not necessarily associated with decreased vision. We found dry eyes in 6 percent of people that was more common in older people, in women and in those with arthritis.

A history of eye trauma was reported by 34 percent of men but only 10 percent of women. For men in rural areas, the rate of eye trauma was 42 percent. Most injuries occurred at work, but 24 percent occurred at home. Protective eye wear had not been used in 87 percent of those with injuries and 15 percent of all these injuries resulted in vision of less than 6/18. Injuries were commonly associated with rural work, hammering at nails or other metal, and sport. All these were other areas requiring better public education and health promotion.

The Victorian Health Promotion Foundation had a Sports Safety Committee. It was chaired by Terry Nolan and I was a member for some years. This was when I first met Terry. One of the areas I was able to help change was the use of protective eyewear for those playing squash as well as the more general use of protective eyewear.

We examined the impact of some socioeconomic factors on vision loss. In the MVIP findings none of them was statistically significant, although there was a trend of more vision loss in households with a low household income.

In the MVIP we had used a food-frequency questionnaire to assess dietary antioxidant intake. We found no effect of diet or vitamin supplement intake on the presence of cataract. This was of interest because I had been approached by John McNeil, the Professor of Epidemiology and Preventive Medicine at Monash University who was interested in the possible role of vitamins and aspirin in influencing cataract development.

After several tries to 1998, John and I received NHMRC funding for a prospective randomised controlled trial. After a lot of discussion, we left out aspirin because of the lack of supportive evidence and because the Waterman study had found no protective effect of aspirin. I knew that my friends Rick Ferris and Emily Chew at the National Eye Institute were starting the Age-Related Eye Disease Study, AREDS, in the US. Their study looked at the combination of vitamins A, C and E as well as mineral zinc. A recent study had shown a higher risk of cancer in smokers given vitamin A supplements. Most higher intakes of vitamin C passed straight into the urine. Given this, vitamin A and C supplementation did not seem likely to influence the development of cataract.

Previously, in Baltimore, Susan Vitale, then a young researcher at the Dana Center, Sheila West and I did a study on the participants of the Baltimore Longitudinal Study of Aging. (In Baltimore, Liz first worked with the National Institute on Aging. When she moved to the National Institute on Drug Abuse, she was the longest serving physician on the Baltimore Longitudinal study.) In our study we took lens photographs and used four years of dietary and serum testing data to test for correlations between dietary intake and cataract. The data had shown that higher serum levels of vitamin E were associated with a reduced risk of nuclear cataract and may have some effect on cortical cataract. This study found the intake or levels of vitamin C and vitamin A had no effect on the presence of cataract.

Given all this, vitamin E seemed the most likely to have an impact and we could see little role for the other supplements. So, we started the Vitamin E and Cataract Study, VECAT. We had two groups, one to receive daily vitamin E and the other a placebo. We recruited 1195 participants aged between 55 and 80. Luba Robman, an ophthalmologist from Almaty, which is now in Kazakhstan, joined my department and later worked with John McNeil. She did a great job with the detailed eye examinations and photography.

After four years of taking 500 International Units of vitamin E each day, there was no difference in the incidence or progression of nuclear, cortical or PSC cataracts in those receiving vitamin E or the placebo control. Neither was there any influence on AMD, whether early or later, or neovascular ('wet') or atrophic ('dry').

For my fiftieth birthday, Cathy McCarty presented me with a tall glass bottle full of capsules from the VECAT study labelled 'Elixir of Youth'. I still have the bottle and the capsules, half of which contain vitamin E and half placebo, a nice reminder of what one doesn't know: like which is which.

AREDS was the major American multi-centred clinical trial of the effects of vitamin supplementation on the development of cataract and macular degeneration. Run out of the National Eye Institute, NEI by Rick Ferris and Emily Chew. That study also found no effect of vitamin supplementation on cataract development, nor on AMD as a whole. However, when AMD was categorised and analysed as 'dry' AMD versus neovascular 'wet' AMD, supplements were shown to reduce the progression of neovascular AMD. Therefore, it must have had the reverse effect on dry AMD. This led to a lot of promotion of supplement use for the treatment or prevention of AMD. The NEI was pleased to promote it as a successful study. Vitamin companies were pleased to promote it to increase sales. Ophthalmologists were pleased to promote it as it was something they could offer to their patients at a time when there were no other treatments available for them. Patients were pleased to take the supplements as they offered hope. There are clear lessons here.

Having completed the MVIP field work, analysis and writing up the results, in 1999 we undertook a five-year follow up of the original urban cohort.

Of our original people over 40 years old, 7 percent had died. Death was twice as likely in those who had had some vision loss. Other risk factors for death were, of course, age, but also male gender, a history of smoking, hypertension and arthritis. There were some people who had moved interstate or overseas and some who refused to be studied again. We were able to re-examine 2594 people, or 79 percent of the original sample.

We found that 4.2 percent of those we re-examined had developed some degree of visual impairment. The main cause for this was under-corrected refractive error. Other causes were AMD, cataract, glaucoma, diabetic retinopathy, and neuro-ophthalmic disorders that affect the links between the eye and the brain.

Again, we were surprised to find that approximately half of those who we found to have undiagnosed glaucoma had been seen by an optometrist or ophthalmologist in the preceding 12 months and their glaucoma had not been recognised. They nearly all had visual field defects but often did not have the higher intraocular pressures usually associated with glaucoma. If their visual fields had been tested, their diagnosis certainly would be picked up and they would have been started on treatment, but if only their intraocular pressure were measured, they could have been missed.

We found that 24 percent of those with diabetes had not had an eye exam since we last examined them. Again, this reinforced the need for some real action for health education and the provision of services to provide these exams.

Further analysis of the follow-up data showed that those who had had vision loss at their initial examination had more falls, reduced activities of daily living, and were more likely to be admitted to a nursing home. What makes this worse was that 90 percent of the vision loss was unnecessary because it was preventable or treatable. Vision loss is bad for you and bad for your health!

Any lingering thoughts about a 10-year or 20-year follow-up, often part of public health surveys of populations, were dismissed. We'd taken our snapshots, identified the problems and seen enough of the trends. The time to address the needs we had uncovered had come. The MVIP moved from being a search to being the backing of our argument for action and remedy.

'All right,' we said, 'what are we to do next about all this?'

The MVIP clearly identified the unmet need for access to, and for an increased use of, eye-health services. It demonstrated many preventative measures that needed to be implemented, and identified the services required to provide eye care for those who needed it but who were not getting it.

Trish Livingston assessed the public's knowledge of eye diseases and blindness prevention. Most people understood what a cataract was. Most people had heard of glaucoma but only 18 percent understood what it was and what it meant. Less than 5 percent of people were aware of AMD and even less understood it. Knowledge and understanding were higher in the young, in women, in those born in Australia, and in those who spoke English at home. Having a family member affected or having had a recent eye exam also increased people's understanding.

Health education and health promotion about eye health throughout the community were clear imperatives.

The relationship with UV-B and cataract was well established. Something had to be done about that. There was the relationship we had found with smoking and both nuclear cataract and

AMD, another area to act upon. There was a clear need for health education and promotion about eye diseases, and about the need for regular examinations for those with diabetes. We could not do everything all at once, but there was a pressing need to start advocating for changes and to help develop useful public health messages. Obviously wearing a hat or wearing sunglasses greatly reduced the UV exposure to the eye.

The Victorian Anti-Cancer Council, later renamed the Cancer Council of Victoria, was led by Nigel Gray. He had started the world's first campaign to protect against UV-induced sunburn and the consequent skin cancers, including malignant melanoma: the 'Slip, Slop, Slap' campaign—Slip on a shirt, Slop on the sunburn cream and Slap on a hat. It was hugely successful in raising awareness with advertisements everywhere, on TV, radio and billboards.

A cartoon to show the amount of UV-B that reaches the eye using different degrees of protection. It ranges from 72 percent of total UV-B for those out of doors and unprotected, to 8 percent for those who wear a hat and sunglasses.
(Source: the Waterman study.)

I had been asked by WHO to attend a meeting on the adverse effects of UV exposure that was held by the International Agency for Research on Cancer (IARC) in Lyon, France. I was there because of the previous work I had done on UV-B and cataract, and we had recently helped write a document for WHO Prevention of Blindness Programme on that topic. The meeting had UV experts from all over the world. I met David Hill there. He is a public health physician who worked with Nigel Gray in Melbourne. I talked to him about adding sunglasses to the Slip, Slop, Slap message. Back home we met with Nigel. He agreed to include an eye protection message. 'Slide on some sunnies' was added then, and later 'Seek some shade' was also added. I found it deeply satisfying to be a part of this work.

For years David Hill had arranged for photographs to be taken of the crowds attending the Australian Open as a measure of how many people were wearing hats and sunglasses at the tennis. Several TV infomercials were developed to promote protecting your eyes from UV exposure. We made a health promotion video called 'Don't fry your

Above: Cancer Council ad for sun protection

Left: The Don't Fry Your Eyes advertisement that won the Palme d'Or in Cannes

eyes' with help from Peter Clemenger who ran a large advertising agency. The advertisement showed two eggs in a frying pan and as the heat went up both eggs (eyes) were fried and then burnt. The video went on to win a Palme d'Or at the Cannes Lions Awards!

Jumping forward a bit I took a sabbatical leave in London in 1998. Liz and I lived in a flat in Kentish Town. She was writing up some findings on the quality of HIV testing with British colleagues, and I worked in the Institute of Ophthalmology at Moorfields Eye Hospital. What I really wanted to do was to pull together the work that everyone else had been doing on ophthalmic epidemiology and look at the various risk factors that had been identified. In Melbourne I had kept up with the medical journals every month, but I had not had the time to sit and think about how to integrate the various new findings. I needed the opportunity and quiet to work through the reports methodically and try to pull it together to build a more comprehensive picture. That year both Liz's mother and my mother had died within a day of each other. With the sadness and sense of loss, reflection and meditation came naturally to me at that time.

On sabbatical I had time to search Medline for relevant papers and go down to the basement library to find them. I found it edifying to have to blow the dust off the 1988 *New England Journal of Medicine* to re-read our Waterman paper.

I studied the numerous papers that Ron and Barbara Kline had written about their Beaver Dam studies in the US, Paul Mitchell's papers on the Blue Mountains Eye Study in Australia, Paulus De Jong's on the Rotterdam Eye Study in the Netherlands, and Al Sommer and Jim Tielsch's on the East Baltimore Eye Study. All added grist to the mill.

What really stood out for me reading these papers was that none of these studies contradicted the link between UV-B exposure and cataract. Reassuring. However, the consistency with which the link between cigarette smoking and both cataract and AMD was striking, but not followed up. No studies had been done.

When I returned to Melbourne, I talked with Nigel Gray and David Hill again, about smoking. That summer, with input from Paul Mitchell in Sydney, we developed a health promotion video for TV about smoking and AMD as part of the QUIT Campaign. Nigel had started the campaign in 1984 and it had developed some impressive advertising messages about the harmful effects of smoking and cancer, heart disease and other risks. QUIT was the world's first significant public health campaign against cigarette smoking.

We decided to focus the advertisement on AMD rather than on cataract. The AMD video was brilliant and visually challenging. The camera starts in front of an eye, then zooms in through the pupil to the retina at the back. Suddenly the retina swells, blood vessels rupture and an explosion of blood fills the screen. 'Smoking causes blindness' was the message. I was told that it was the TV video with the highest consumer recall of any of the QUIT campaign messages. QUIT campaigners lobbied the government to pass laws to print one of 13 health warnings on cigarette packets. In 2011 the Minister of Health and Ageing, Nicola Roxon, speaking in support of the Tobacco Plain Packaging Bill, held up a cigarette pack for journalists, the 'Smoking causes blindness' one. The Bill passed and survived a challenge from a tobacco company in the High Court and appeals to international trade organisations. We had identified a major risk factor for blindness and then successfully advocated for health promotion messages about it. We had come a long way. Smoking rates dropped.

To make the MVIP findings more relevant and useful we had to get out some specific public health messages to promote eye health. The MVIP had identified the huge, unmet need for eye care in our community, despite all the health resources available in Victoria. What could we do to remedy this? How could we address the eye care needs of Victorians, both then and in the future?

The Smoking Causes Blindness warning on a packet of cigarettes held by the federal minister for health and ageing, Nicola Roxan, announcing plain packaging and health warnings on all tobacco products, 2010

Opening Eyes

11

Going Global

The pace and demands in any field, be it genetics, nanotechnology or cosmology, can only be met with increased international cooperation and collaborative projects.
Priyamvada Natarajan, astrophysicist, 2016

From the late 1970s I found myself becoming more and more involved with international projects and bodies. That involvement has been a big part of my life for nearly half a century. Three organisations dominated: the International Agency for the Prevention of Blindness, IAPB, the World Health Organisation, WHO, and the International Council of Ophthalmology, ICO.

The IAPB was started by two extraordinary advocates for eye care and care of the blind, Sir John Wilson and Edward Maumenee. The organisation aimed to bring together all the non-government organisations working on eye health, and to act as a forum to work with WHO on its newly redefined program on the Prevention of Blindness, PBL.

John was blinded during a North Yorkshire classroom chemistry experiment at the age of 12. He referred to this affliction as his 'confounded nuisance' thereafter. A trip to West Africa in 1946 led him to establish the British Empire Society for the Blind in 1950, later the Royal Commonwealth Society for the Blind and then today's SightSavers. He was the IAPB's first president.

In the 1980s he led a program called IMPACT, an international initiative set up during the United Nations 'Decade of disabled people' to promote awareness and interventions to prevent avoidable disability. He was always warm and welcoming, an essential asset for a public health advocate.

Ed Maumenee—'Dr Maumenee' as he was always called—was the professor and chairman at the Wilmer Institute at the Johns Hopkins Hospital, a world-renowned ophthalmologist, and my boss when I started there. He held a Monday Morning Conference at 7.30 am at the Wilmer, a clinical meeting when cases were examined, then presented and discussed. All the clinical staff at Wilmer attended, Dr Maumenee chaired it. When he retired and Arnall Patz took over as director, Ed continued to attend those meetings. In nearly every discussion about a patient, he would ask a pertinent question about how some recent paper or finding impacted on the case being discussed. He continued clinical and surgical work into his eighties. I looked after his patients when he retired and hoped my patients would do as well as his. Liz fondly remembers visiting the Maumenees in their superb garden, Ed pushing her on their garden swing. She became firm friends with his wife, Irene, also a faculty member at Wilmer. They played tennis on Thursday mornings whenever they were both in town.

My initiation into international engagements and global eye health was when Fred Hollows asked me to fill in for him at the first General Assembly of the IAPB in Oxford, UK in 1978 (see page 75ff). There, I met many working on eye care from around the world, including those with illustrious names.

This led me to be invited to participate in the first WHO meeting on the prevention of blindness held later that year in Asilomar, California (see page 97). The Asilomar experience was, well, an eye-opener. The aims were audacious, the scope a new way of thinking, and the confidence intoxicating. The prime, stated goal was to draft up a WHO publication on the prevention of blindness and the ways to improve and expand eye care to achieve this. This was the first time that a global health body had seriously considered what was needed to be done to eliminate avoidable blindness. This, with the launch of IAPB three years before, started the process that led to Vision2020 and the global emphasis on eye care. At this meeting I met people who worked at WHO. I was still only part way through training as a corneal fellow, yet when I was asked to do some work for WHO, how could I turn them down?

At Asilomar, my work on trachoma led to close links with Mario Tarizzo. Mario managed the WHO program for trachoma that morphed into the Prevention of Blindness Program, PBL. It was Mario who invited me to travel as a WHO consultant to Pakistan, Egypt and Tunisia. I met Björn Thylefors for the first time. He was a tall Swede with an infectious laugh and a broad understanding of blindness issues and public health. Björn was the ophthalmologist with the Onchocerciasis Control Program in West Africa and would become the head of PBL when Mario retired. Later, my work on oncho linked me with Brian Duke, who ran the WHO Filariasis Program and was known for his ground-breaking studies on onchocerciasis in the Cameroons.

Under Al Sommer's leadership, the International Center for Preventative Ophthalmology, ICEPO, became a WHO Collaborating Center for the Prevention of Blindness. Later, oncho was added to the remit of the Center. Once we were a WHO Collaborating Center Al and I were invited to the annual WHO PBL Program Advisory Group meetings held in Geneva. The IAPB would often take advantage of having most of its board members in Geneva for these PBL meetings to hold its own board meeting. As we were there too, Al and I were invited to attend these IAPB meetings. I attended each of the IAPB General Assemblies that were held every four years. This was another way to keep in touch with many friends and colleagues, make new contacts, and keep up with the work that people were doing around the world. The most memorable General Assembly was the one held in 1986 in New Delhi. Opened by Rajiv Ghandi, Indian's prime minister, it was appropriately elaborate because he was a leader and committed to eye care. He was killed by an assassin in 1991. A charitable trust named after him was established in 2002 and built the Indira Ghandi Eye Hospital and Research Centre in Amethi, Uttar Pradesh: this big, busy, modern and affordable institution is a fitting tribute.

In 1982 I was invited to become a member of the WHO Expert Advisory Panel on Parasitic Diseases (Filarial Infections) and also of the Scientific Working Group on Filariasis that was under the Tropical Diseases Research, TDR, program. In 1983 I joined the Scientific Working Group on Onchocerciasis Chemotherapy as its chair. One way or another I was travelling back and forth to Geneva on a regular basis. I would leave Baltimore in the mid-afternoon, fly via the JFK airport in New York, and arrive in Geneva at around 8.05 am to go straight to WHO for the start of the 9 am meeting. The routine became well established. Attendees usually stayed in the same downtown hotel near the railway station. We went out together for splendid Swiss dinners and conversation. When I got home, I always arrived exhausted, even though I took melatonin to help with the jetlag. This was the same Swiss Air flight that crashed into the sea near Nova Scotia in 1998, killing all on board including some famous Hopkins professors going to a WHO meeting on HIV in Geneva.

Over time I served on other expert advisory boards and committees for the prevention of blindness, trachoma and onchocerciasis. After the Waterman study and our findings on UV radiation and cataract, I also worked with WHO on cataract, and participated in the United Nations Environment Programme working group on UV and the Ozone Layer. All this helped maintain the focus of our work, but it also helped to have our findings translated into action, either through programmatic changes or changes on the ground.

Going Global

Two years after I had returned to Melbourne, the Melbourne University Department of Ophthalmology was designated a WHO Collaborating Centre. We soon after held a meeting for WHO/PBL on the role of intraocular lenses in cataract surgery. Two years later, in 1994, I became a member of the Executive Board of IAPB. One way and another, I became more and more involved in IAPB and WHO.

In 1990 Fred Hollows was named the Australian of the Year. As such, he needed to travel across Australia and speak at events. Mike Lynskey was funded by the Australian of the Year Awards to help support Fred with this. Fred was not well. He'd developed kidney cancer and was constantly involved in various investigations and treatments for it. During this time Fred talked to me about his desire for his work to continue by establishing a foundation. He asked me to join the board of the yet-to-be established Fred Hollows Foundation. Of course, without alternative, I said 'Yes.'

The initial board chair was Ray Martin, a prominent and respected journalist who had worked with Fred over many years. During the National Trachoma and Eye Health Programme in the late 1970s Ray had interviewed Fred several times and had followed his activities since then. It was a real privilege to serve on the board and I met interesting and prominent people who served on the board.

Fred was becoming increasingly unwell. We had planned a trip to the Vietnamese Institute of Ophthalmology in Hanoi that had to be rescheduled when Fred was receiving treatment. When he did get to Hanoi late in 1992, he would spend some time with us in the operating theatres teaching cataract surgery and then retire to his room to rest up for the next few hours.

I last saw him at home in Farnham House, a few days before he died. He was in bed reading the current issue of *The Lancet*.

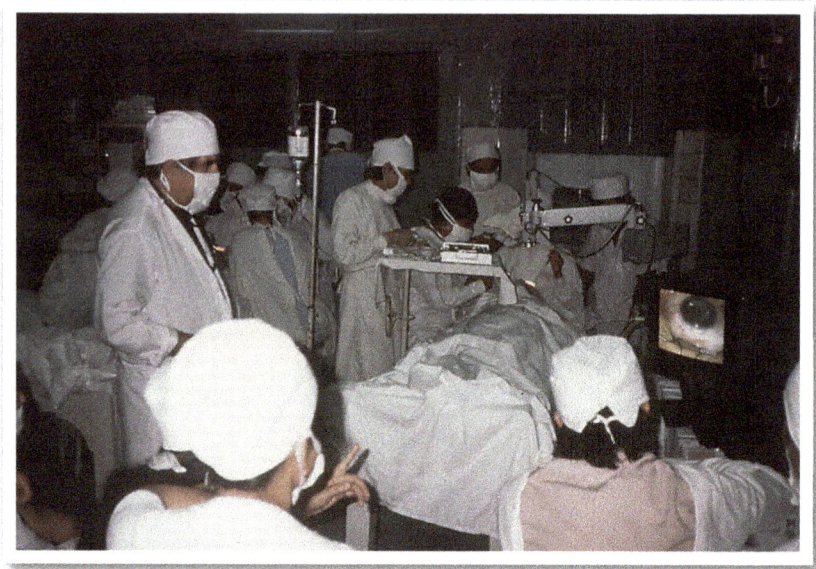

Fred Hollows in the operating theatre in the Vietnamese Institute of Ophthalmology, Hanoi while we taught modern IOL cataract surgery, October 1992

'Taylor, I see you have been pestering *Lancet* again and published another bloody paper there.'

I had recently had an article published there which he'd read.

He died in February 1993.

Under Ray Martin's leadership and with Mike Lynskey at the helm, the Foundation grew and raised the issues concerning the prevention and cure of blindness to a high profile. Factories to manufacture intraocular lenses were built in Asmara, Eritrea and Kathmandu, Nepal. I was able to visit both sites while they were under construction and attend their official openings. Gareth Evans, Australia's minister for foreign affairs attended the opening in Asmara. In 1995, at the opening in Kathmandu, the king of Nepal and the prime minister appeared together in public for the first time since the *coup d'etat* earlier in the year.

In addition to the IOL Laboratory in Kathmandu, the foundation helped establish the Tilganga Eye Institute. It is led by Sanduk Ruit with support from Reeta Gurung. When I was

Above: The official opening of the Hollows IOL factory in Asmara, Eritrea. *From left*: Gareth Evans, President Isaias Afwerki, and Cam and Gabi Hollows, 1994

Below: The official opening of the Hollows IOL factory at the Tilganga Eye Institute in Kathmandu, Nepal. Prime Minister G P Koirala, seated on the left, talking with King Birendra, seated centrally. Australian Ambassador Les Douglas is seated on the right, 1994

at the Eye and Ear Hospital in Melbourne, we would send a registrar to Tilganga to spend weeks working with them there, and on outreach eye camps each year. One year, my corneal fellow at the time, Geoff Tabin, an American ophthalmologist, went instead of a registrar. In his interview Geoff told me he had done some mountain climbing and written a few journal articles. I later learned he was the second person to climb the highest peaks, including Mt Everest, on each of the seven continents and that at least some of his papers had been in *Penthouse* and *Playboy*. He and Ruit got on very well together after a rough start—'hyperactive jumping jack… made me feel giddy; said Ruit; 'stand-offish… made clear he was the professor… and I was the student,' said Tabin—and when Geoff returned to the US they set up the Himalayan Cataract Program. I was on the board for several years and they did extraordinary work training ophthalmologists not only in Nepal but in Bhutan, North Korea and several other Asian countries, and they also worked in Ghana and Ethiopia. Recently their program has enlarged and evolved to become Cure Blindness. In 2007 Ruit was awarded an honorary Order of Australia.

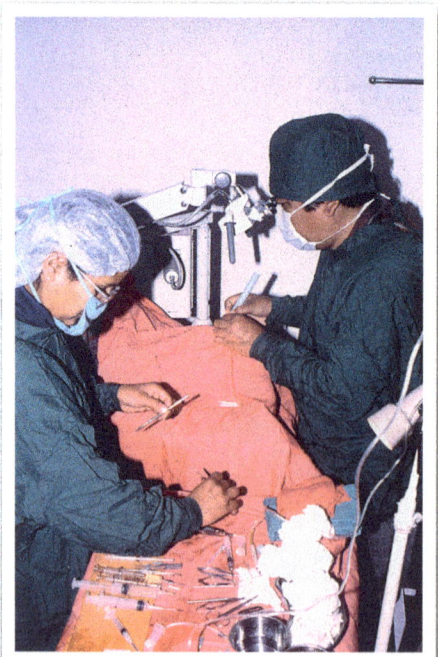

Dr Sanduk Ruit operating in an outreach eye camp

One of Fred's mantras was about making long-term sustainable changes in the provision of eye care 'for all the world to see'. Despite various attempts, the Foundation did not concentrate on achieving long-term sustainable changes in Indigenous eye health within Australia. However, the work overseas, in Asia, Africa and the Pacific grew very well. The Tilganga Eye Institute in Nepal, led by Sanduk Ruit has become a true global leader. A lot of the Pacific work is done through the sister foundation, Fred Hollows New Zealand. I tried hard to encourage the Foundation to concentrate more on Indigenous eye health. Their support was mainly for ophthalmic visits to the Torres Straits, work on otitis media or middle-ear infections, and other work on financial literacy.

I became increasingly frustrated that I could not encourage the Foundation to make some major and ongoing efforts for Indigenous eye health. I had completed an Australian Institute of Company Directors course on how people should work on boards and how boards should practice. In 2004 I retired from the Foundation board, feeling I was not being useful to them and they were not progressing my interest and incidentally, what would have been Fred's preference, in Indigenous eye health. This was a hard decision for me, but it also played into my decision to set up the Indigenous Eye Health Unit (see page 307ff).

Since then, the Fred Hollows Foundation has continued its extensive and useful work overseas, although it still struggles to maintain a consistent approach to improving Indigenous eye health.

WHO and IAPB launched the global initiative called 'VISION2020: The Right to Sight' in 1999. This program aimed to give everyone 'the right to sight' and so eliminate avoidable blindness by 2020. Having worked with many others to develop this program, I was honoured to chair the WHO/PBL Program Advisory Group meeting in Geneva in February 1999 when Vision2020 was officially launched.

I got to know Serge Resnikoff at that time. Serge is a French ophthalmologist trained in Bordeaux with a PhD in public health from Paris. He had worked for years in sub-Saharan Africa,

Allen Foster by the board in an IAPB meeting at WHO, developing the plans for Vision2020, 1998

including time as the head of the African Institute of Tropical Ophthalmology in Bamako, Mali. In the founding year of Vision 2020 Björn Thylefors retired, and Serge moved to Geneva to run the PBL program, then rebranded as the Programme for the Prevention of Blindness and Deafness (PBD). Serge became a dear friend. He is a wine-fanatic and, not surprisingly, spent some time learning about wine as an ophthalmology student in Bordeaux. He has an excellent cellar in his apartment in Geneva and has even more wine stored in Paris. He and his wife, Françoise, are always very generous hosts. Not only is Serge great company and fun to be with, but he is a good leader with wide experience and knowledge, and he worked hard to develop and implement Vision2020. After he left WHO in 2008, he worked for some years as the CEO of Théa, an independent French pharmaceutical company that specialises in research, development and commercialisation of eye-care products. Paul Chibret (1844–1911) was shocked by his work with patients suffering 'Egyptian ophthalmia' (trachoma) and his family has formed an ophthalmic dynasty that continues to drive the Théa global organisation today. Serge continues to work on trachoma and myopia, and consults in global public health, with teaching appointments in Sydney, Paris and London.

Vision2020 had a second launch during the Sixth IAPB General Assembly in Beijing in September 1999. Professor Frank Billson was stepping down as the IAPB Regional Chair for the Western Pacific. Frank taught me paediatric ophthalmology at the Royal Children's Hospital in Melbourne before he moved to Sydney to be the first ophthalmology professor there. He had done a great deal to improve eye care, particularly in Bangladesh, and was the Senior Australian of the Year seven years later. I accepted the role as Frank's successor, and was the IAPB Regional Chair for the Western Pacific for the next eight years.

In Beijing in 1999 I caught up with Brien Holden, Professor of the School of Optometry and Vision Science at the University of New South Wales, who led the Vision Collaborative Research Centre, of which CERA was a participating member.

Brien and I arranged for other Australians to join us for a glass of red wine. We met in a lounge outside the lifts on one floor of the hotel one evening. We said, 'Vision2020 means "the right to sight for all", not everyone except Australians. So, what are we going to do about it in Australia?'

This conversation led us to set up Vision 2020 Australia. With a somewhat unusual professor of optometry and an equally unusual professor of ophthalmology, we came together from two professions that, at that time, usually competed against each other with vigour! We held a series of meeting that brought together people from across the eye-care spectrum. Eventually, we launched Vision 2020 Australia during the 2000 Paralympic Games in Sydney. It was launched officially by Gro Harlem Brundtland, the WHO director general, and Michael Wooldridge, the federal minister for health. Brien and I were co-chairs and

Christian Garms, me, Brien Holden and Dick Porter at the 9th IAPB General Assembly in Beijing for the Vision2020 launch, 1999

we worked harmoniously together. In 2002 Barry Jones, a former minister for science, accepted our invitation to become the chair of Vision 2020 Australia, and Brien and I became the co-deputy chairs.

Vision 2020 Australia continues to do superb work. Over time it has been chaired by Barry Jones, by Amanda Vanstone, a former minister for immigration, and from 2020 by Christopher Pyne, a former minister for defence. I met Christopher when he was the federal minister for education. I had approached him about improving washing facilities and facial cleanliness in outback schools as part of our work on trachoma. He had an interest in eye care that was unusual for a federal minister. His father had been a leading ophthalmologist in Adelaide and president of the Australian College of Ophthalmologists. Vision 2020 Australia brought the eye-care sector together with many initiatives, both nationally and internationally. It has let the sector 'Speak with one voice' and provide a forum for members to meet and talk together and then hopefully work together.

One successful activity has been the Parliamentary Friend's Dinner in Parliament House in Canberra that is held once or twice a year. The non-partisan Parliamentary Friends Group for Eye Health and Vision was an idea I copied from Paul Zimmet, who had set up a similar group for diabetes issues. It brought many parliamentarians and Vision 2020 Australia members together and facilitated many discussions about the needs for eye care. We advocated for changes in government policy and funding. Sometimes these changes actually occurred!

As the IAPB Regional Chair for the Western Pacific I travelled to many countries to hold meetings and workshops.

I was able to recruit the genial Dr Richard Le Mesurier to work as the regional manager to accomplish this. Richard had been a British military ophthalmologist and then worked as an ophthalmologist in Africa and the Pacific. Although he worked hard, he was always ready to have fun. Known as the 'grandfather of ophthalmology in the Pacific' for his work in training and setting up locally-led eye outreach programs throughout the many islands of the Solomons. His replacing the old fly-in/fly-out eye teams, was a high point. His work in Africa too was remarkable, pushing the National Optometry Training Program and setting up regional training in surgical technique at the University of Kumasi in Ghana, another high point. Richard was indispensable, spending a lot of time travelling, networking and meeting with local and national leaders. Working together made a huge difference to what could be achieved. Given my various responsibilities, there was no way that I could have done all that Richard facilitated and accomplished. Later, Richard would become the medical director for the Fred Hollows Foundation. His wife Gillian Cochrane is an optometrist who is equally active

Jill Keeffe and Judy Carrigan waiting for a flight to an IAPB Western Pacific Regional meeting in 2002

in global eye care and works with the Brien Holden Foundation and the Fred Hollows Foundation. Jill Keeffe often came to help with health promotion and low-vision sessions and teaching. My long-serving and long-suffering assistant, Judy Carrigan, organised all the travel and meetings.

Vision 2020 Workshops were held in 20 of the 26 countries in the Western Pacific. I also travelled extensively between 2000 and 2008 as the regional chair. We held subregional meetings in Melbourne, Taipei, Hanoi and Suva. I attended national workshops in China, Japan, Korea, Laos, Mongolia, New Zealand, Thailand and Vietnam.

I also participated in the Korat Course run by Professor Kazuichi Konyama. A gifted leader and teacher, Konyama was then working at the Tokyo WHO Collaborating Centre. We first met when he was a Master of Public Health student at Johns

Dr Konyama, me, Serge Resnikoff and Richard Le Mesurier during a course in Korat, Thailand, 2002

Hopkins. He would come around on Friday afternoons for a smoke. I was still smoking a pipe then and Al liked an occasional cigarette. Konyama was already an ophthalmologist with extensive experience in eye-care delivery in Japan and Thailand. He then worked with WHO in the Western Pacific office in Manilla and later with WHO/PBL in Geneva. He returned to Juntendo University in Tokyo to join Professor Akira Nakajima. The Korat Course, funded by Lions International, was held each year from the late 1990s until 2009, in Nakhon Ratchasima, Korat in its shortform name, in north-east Thailand. It brought together ophthalmologists and mid-level ophthalmic workers from many Southeast Asian countries for a three-to-four-week workshop on public health ophthalmology.

There were almost annual trips to Vietnam, continuing the national workshops I helped organise from 1993. These workshops brought together the various international non-government organisations which worked on eye care in Vietnam. We spent the first day with just the NGOs to talk through issues and

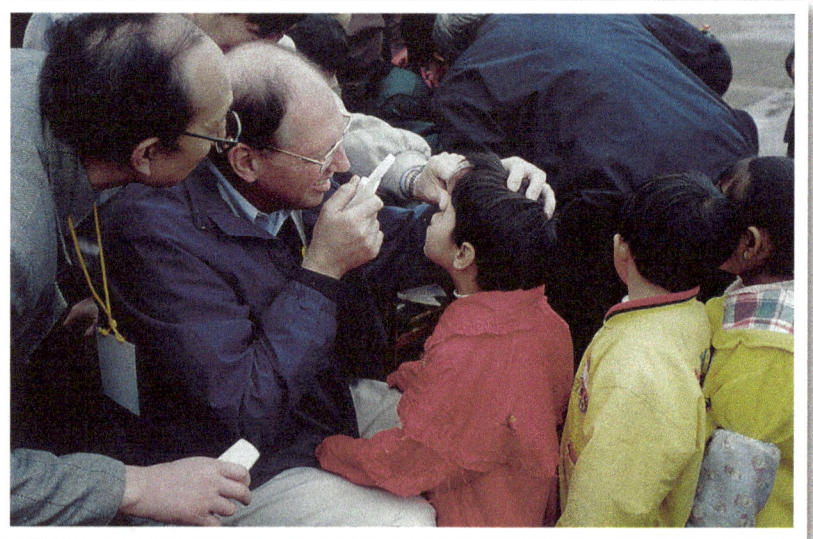

Above: Phoebe, in the middle of a group during the trachoma training in a Vietnamese village

Below: In a village in Yunnan Province, China grading trachoma

sort things out. On following days, we met with the Vietnamese officials and groups. The NGOs, as a group, were able to present a set of coherent ideas for discussion with the Vietnamese and work on planning future activities that met Vietnamese needs.

In 2001 WHO asked me to go to Vietnam to train health workers to grade trachoma. Our daughter Phoebe was 15 and it was during school holidays, so she accompanied me. This was an opportunity to let her see and understand what her dad did when he was away so often. We put her to work in a week-long course in Hanoi and then visited some villages to practice screening and grading. As it happened Liz was also in Hanoi on an HIV mission, staying in a different hotel. Nevertheless, we three caught up and had some excellent Vietnamese street food, which is so good. We also explored each other's accommodation. Liz's was far superior!

The year before I had gone to China for WHO to discuss trachoma and to teach the grading system. We met in Yunnan and worked in the nearby villages. By 2016 China was certified by WHO as having eliminated blinding trachoma. In 2024 Vietnam also achieved that goal.

The Institute for Health Metrics and Evaluation, IHME, was established in 2007 by Chris Murray and Alan Lopez, who'd worked at WHO and in 1990 produced a report for the World Bank on the Global Burden of Disease. The report was updated in 2004. IHME was based in Seattle, Washington and received funding from the Gates Foundation. It aimed to provide an impartial, evidence-based picture of global health trends to inform the work of policymakers, researchers and funders. It ran the Global Burden of Diseases group, GBD.

I was invited to attend the first meeting of the GBD group in Seattle. It ran concurrently with an IAPB meeting in Vancouver. I was able to get to Seattle for a day or so but when asked if I could lead the group to deal with vision, I had to decline. I had met Rupert Bourne when he was studying in the International Centre for Eye Health in London when I was there on sabbatical. Rupert is an ophthalmologist based in Cambridge who has done excellent epidemiologic studies in Bangladesh, the Caribbean and the UK. He agreed to lead the Vision Loss Expert Group, VLEG. The VLEG has gone from success to success. It has a large international group of eye experts and collects and collates all the epidemiologic population-based studies of eye disease and vision loss from the literature reported by VLEG members, and publishes regular updates in the scientific literature. The data it puts together is used by WHO and forms the Vision Atlas of IAPB.

With the GBD the VLEG's periodic reports track the progress being made to eliminate avoidable blindness through Vision 2020 and ongoing efforts of WHO and member countries as well as the social and other improvements being made across the globe. The most recent report, with 2020 data, estimated 43.3 million people world-wide were blind, a 50 percent rise since 1990, but the proportion of people who were blind had fallen by 27 percent. The figures for moderate to severe vision

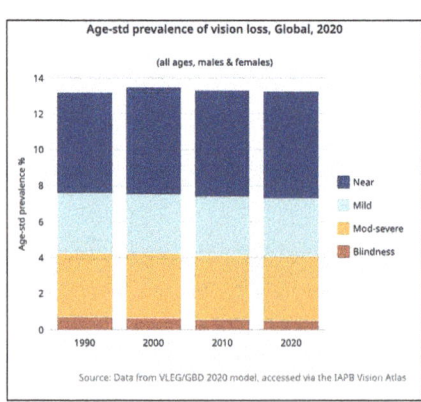
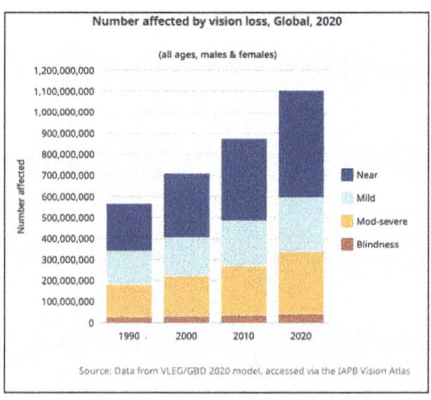

Left: Global age-standardised prevalence of vision loss, 1990 to 2020 (*Source: Vision Loss Expert Group, IAPB Vision Atlas*)

Right: Number of people who have vision loss, 1990 to 2020 (*Source: Vision Loss Expert Group, IAPB Vision Atlas*)

loss were similar, the number affected almost doubling to 295 million, but the prevalence increasing by only 1 percent. The global population is growing and ageing; this leads to more people with vision loss. But services continue to improve so the proportion of people who have vision loss continues to decrease.

WHO also publishes annual reports on trachoma and onchocerciasis with both the numbers affected and the prevalences. Their trachoma report for 2024 showed 114 million people still lived in endemic areas, down from 204 million in 2014. Trachoma remained a public health problem in 31 countries but 19 had eliminated it. (Since that report came out, Pakistan, India, Senegal, Burundi and Papua New Guinea have been certified as having eliminated trachoma.) For oncho, some 250 million people still lived in endemic areas in 28 countries. However, four countries had eliminated oncho, and six more had stopped ivermectin distribution because the transmission of infection has stopped. In the year before, 172 million people received ivermectin. Ivermectin is now also used for lymphatic filariasis or elephantiasis. It is stunning that since 1987 over 5 billion doses of ivermectin have been provided free by Merck. WHO has regional expert advisory groups to monitor the progress being made on the Neglected Tropical Diseases list that includes trachoma and onchocerciasis. Before the COVID pandemic I served for some years on the group run by the WHO Western Pacific Regional Office. We would meet once a year, usually in Manilla but once in Cambodia, to review the progress being made and new developments.

We were making real progress both with vision loss as a whole and with trachoma and onchocerciasis.

However, this sense of progress got a shock in 2019. WHO released its 'World report on vision', stating there were 'at least 2.2 billion people with vision impairment'. This included at least 1 billion people with vision impairment that could be prevented, those we would normally include who were blind or had moderate to severe vision impairment. It also included 826 million people with 'uncorrected presbyopia'. Presbyopia is the difficulty with near vision that affects most people over the age of 40; I would tell my patients it was 'just a sign of growing up'. The figure that really caught us out was the extra 1 billion that they had added; those who would be vision impaired if they were not wearing the glasses they already had. This group is very important to take into consideration when planning and arranging services, because they all will need ongoing eye care and the replacement of their glasses from time to time.

Globally, progress is being made. We know what to do, and know the measures that can be taken, work. The glass is not empty but it is not full yet. There is plenty of work still to do.

In 2007 Brien Holden and I and six others from Vision 2020 Australia's member organisations interested in overseas work, arranged to meet with some Australian government and shadow opposition ministers. We were selling the idea of providing eye care to the Pacific region with a 10-year plan to 'Eliminate avoidable blindness in the Pacific and Southeast Asia'.

One meeting was with Greg Hunt, the parliamentary secretary to Alexander Downer, the foreign minister. Greg was very interested and supportive but in the middle of the discussion, he was called to an emergency meeting held by the prime minister, John Howard. As he left Greg wondered if the PM was about to call an election; instead, the call was about announcing the devastating Northern Territory Intervention. However, an election did follow shortly after that and it brought a change in government.

Another meeting was with shadow minister Bob McMullan. In the new Labor government Bob McMullan became the parliamentary secretary for International Development Assistance. He fully supported the proposal from our 'Global Consortium' and in 2008 he was instrumental in providing $45 million to support its work for three years as a first step. The program was funded again in 2011 as a second phase, but for a lesser amount. Then, in 2013, it was dropped when the government changed again. The new Coalition government of Tony Abbot set different priorities for overseas aid. It was sad to see the great reduction of overseas aid that followed, much of it diverted to commercial or military purposes.

I continued to be a regional chair for the IAPB until the Eighth General Assembly in Buenos Aires in 2008, when I became IAPB's vice president with Christian Garms as the new president. He was the CEO of Christoffel-Blindenmission, CBM. CBM was established by Pastor Ernst J Christoffel, who first set up a home for the blind in Turkey before World War 1 and in World War 2 spent three years in an Iranian prison camp. The CBM was based in Bensheim, Germany, and for many years Christian had worked at CBM and was involved with IAPB and WHO. He also worked with Allan Foster, Björn Thylefors, Serge Resnikoff and others to develop the Vision2020 initiative. Christian was very well organised, and it was a pleasure for me to support him and the work of the IAPB Executive.

The IAPB executive or board met several times a year around the WHO/PBL Program Advisory Group meetings or with other international meetings. Exciting times! Vision2020 was being taken up around the world. We watched and cheered as countries made measurable improvements in eye health and eye care, and reported them through IAPB/WHO/PBL networks. I remained vice president until the Ninth IAPB General Assembly in Hyderabad, India in 2012.

At this time now ex-Senator and ex-MP Bob McMullan had retired from politics, and was elected as IAPB president. Bob had done much to support eye care activities while he had been in parliament, and he continued to do so at IAPB. I remained on the IAPB board as the representative of the International Council of Ophthalmology and as a member of their Guidelines Committee.

The International Council of Ophthalmology, ICO, is the world's oldest international medical society. It started in 1857 with a meeting in Brussels. The main topics at that meeting were trachoma, which was then the major global public health eye problem, and the newly developed direct ophthalmoscope that allowed examination of the retina and the back of the eye for the first time.

Since then, congresses have been held four-yearly, except during the two world wars, until 2008. Then they were renamed the World Ophthalmology Congress, WOC, and scheduled for every two years. A virtual meeting had to be held in 2020 during COVID. These congresses brought together ophthalmologists and eye researchers from around the world to share research and new developments and improvements in eye care. My grandfather had attended the International Congresses in 1950 in London, in Montreal and New York in 1954, a very unusual split meeting, and in Brussels in 1958.

Meeting some of the leaders of the ICO was again fortuitous. While Ed Maumenee was ICO president, he held an ICO board meeting in Baltimore. Ed invited Al Sommer and me to join him and the board members at a dinner held at his home. Through various meetings, including the IAPB and the WHO/PBL meetings, I had met and became friends with two of the future presidents, Akira Nakajima (1990–98) and Gottfried (Fritz) Naumann (1998–2000).

I had been a regular participant in the International Congresses of Ophthalmology starting with San Francisco in 1982, then Rome in 1986, Singapore in 1990, Toronto in 1994, and Amsterdam in 1998. The congress in Rome was memorable as it was just after both the Chernobyl nuclear disaster and TWA flight 840 en route to Athens from Rome being blown up by a terrorist bomb. People were certainly on edge, although the informative and collegial meeting itself went without a hitch. Before the Congress there was a small meeting on ocular immunology held in Padua, my first visit to Italy other than transiting through the Rome airport. It was fascinating to see one of the world's oldest universities and its anatomical theatre that dates from 1595. We were also taken to a wonderful country palazzo for a splendid dinner on the deck overlooking an extensive garden. Not what I was used to at all! Then a group of us drove down to Rome for the Congress.

At the end of 2004 I was at the annual meeting of the American Academy of Ophthalmology, AAO, in New Orleans. The ICO secretary general, Bruce Spivey, invited me to join an informal ICO board meeting they were holding there. Bruce is a real force of nature, insightful, well informed, hardworking, but always keen to share a joke and a laugh, with or without a whisky. He worked tirelessly as an advocate for international ophthalmology. Executive vice-president and the founding CEO of the AAO after it separated from Otolaryngology in 1978, he expanded the number of staff in San Francisco from four to over 100 in a decade and a half. He was the secretary general of the ICO from 1994 to 2006, then became president in 2006.

During this board meeting in 2004 I asked, 'How is the ICO going to let member societies know about the new global initiative, Vision2020?'

'Well, we'll get you to do that,' was Bruce's immediate response. Very foolish of me.

I was appointed the director of the ICO Committee for Advocacy, a committee created on the spot, just then, because of my question.

I enjoyed being a member of the ICO board. It sensibly met at each International Congress: Sydney 2002, São Paulo 2006 and Hong Kong 2008. In between these congresses the board held annual meetings during a regional society's meeting or at the AAO annual meeting. The Advocacy Committee used many approaches to let 'every ophthalmologist in the world' know about the ICO and Vision2020. That was not a straightforward task but it was a worthy goal.

In 2009 Yasuo Tano, a leading vitreoretinal surgeon in Japan, departmental chairman in Osaka and the ICO's treasurer died unexpectedly aged only 60. Bruce Spivey asked me to take over as treasurer. This was a serious challenge for me. Yasuo had only been in that role for a few months. Baldur Gloor, the previous treasurer for 12 years, was prepared to share his experience with me—a tremendous help. Baldur knew the ropes and was very generous with his time and advice. Baldur lived in Zurich, where he had been the professor of ophthalmology.

William (Bill) J Felch Jnr lived in San Francisco, as Bruce Spivey did then. They had worked together at the AAO for many years. Over the years, Bruce had held different roles in many medical organisations and societies. In 1992 he moved to Chicago as the president of the Northwestern Healthcare Network, and in 1997 to New York as president of the Columbia Cornell Care and Network Physicians. He returned to San Francisco in 2002 to establish and run the Pacific Vision Foundation while still secretary general of the ICO. He inveigled Bill Felch to move from the AAO, become the director of the ICO and establish an office in San Francisco. Bill must be one of the kindest and most

Bill Felch, me, Bruce Spivey and Jean Jacques Delaey at the World Ophthalmology Congress, Tokyo, 2014

tolerant people in the world. Always ready to support me in my various ICO roles, he helped me many times, often stepping in to avoid my putting my foot in it. He recruited and ran a great office with superlative staff. It was always fun to work with Bill. Of course we became good friends as did our wives, Liz and Ginny. Bill was always happy to share a Jack on the Rocks after a hard day's work. We have taken 'Jack Daniels photos' around the world to be shared with great amusement.

Bruce was ICO President from 2006 to 2014, at WOC events in Hong Kong in 2008, Berlin 2010 and Abu Dhabi 2012. The 2014 WOC one was held in Tokyo in early April, which coincided with the cherry trees' blossoming, a time of *hanami*, picnics in parks or riverbanks, drinking in the sweet fragrance of the flowers and tea and sake, good cheer, and millions of photographs. Going to and from the congress venues was a delightful, surprising journey. Like French grape growers, Japanese monks have kept records going back many centuries. In the 1850s the date of flowering saw 17 April as a steady average; by the 2010s, it was 12 days earlier, climate change at work. There were nearly 20 000 attendees from 136 countries, the largest WOC ever. At the end of that congress Bruce Spivey retired.

I became the president of the ICO.

Of course, as president, there were many responsibilities and tasks to be accomplished, many emails, conference calls, officers' meetings, board meetings, attendance at various supranational ophthalmic societies' meetings, and so on.

One of the additional things I was to lead was the group that developed the 'ICO Guidelines for Diabetic Eye Care'. A few national guidelines existed in high-income countries, such as the NHMRC guidelines which I had helped develop in Australia. However, there had not been any international guidelines or guidance on the management of diabetic eye disease for low- or medium-income settings. In making recommendations for

As ICO president at the World Ophthalmology Congress, Barcelona 2018

management and treatment we needed to consult widely and take into consideration the potential lack of availability of more specialised services, equipment, including lasers in different countries.

Once the guidelines were endorsed they were translated into Chinese, French, Portuguese, Russian, Serbian, Spanish and Vietnamese. The guidelines were updated in 2017 when new diagnostic and treatment options became available. They continue to provide guidance globally.

A major focus of the ICO was education. The biennial WOC was a major educational opportunity to share information and new findings with ophthalmologists from around the world. The ICO also had some specific education programs that were predominantly funded through the ICO by the ICO Foundation, ICOF. The ICOF had been established by Bruce Spivey and Brad Straatsma as a not-for profit organisation in the US to receive tax-deductable donations from the major ophthalmic pharmaceutical and equipment companies, and other donors. One of the educational programs it funded was the innovative 'Teaching the Teachers'. This was aimed at ophthalmic educators from all countries to help them improve training methods in eye care. It was backed up with the development of curricular and assessment methods. This work was led by Karl Golnik from the US, and the education team he built that included Gabriel Palis and Eduardo Mayorga from Argentina. They developed the on-line Centre for Ophthalmic Educators that has many users. Since the ICO and the ICOF parted ways in 2020 this and the other education programs listed below are now all funded and run by the newly created Ophthalmology Foundation, OF.

Another part of the education program, the ICO Exams, were started in 1995 by Peter Watson from Cambridge, UK, and later run by David Taylor, then Simon Keightley and then Clare Davey. Although the office was based in the UK, the ICO Exams were held each year in many countries around the world. Exams covered different topics and levels of knowledge. Those who passed the earlier exams and the final Advanced Exam were recognised as Fellows of the ICO, FIOC. Later, subspecialty exams were also offered. By 2018 over 30 000 ophthalmologists from 81 countries had sat an ICO Exam.

The ICO also had an ICO Fellowship program started by

Baldur Gloor with the first fellowships awarded in 2003. Later, the Fellowship program was run by Peter Gable and then Berthold Seitz, both from Germany. They set up the International Ophthalmic Fellowship Foundation to receive tax-deductible donations in Germany. The ICOF provided funding to the IOFF initially, but the fellowship program is now funded by the OF. (It is understood that the terminology is all a bit confusing!) ICO offered three-month fellowships so ophthalmologists from developing countries could travel to leading eye centres to learn specific skills. There was also a small number of 12-month fellowships that focused more detailed study of some specific diseases. By 2018 1100 fellowships had been awarded to ophthalmologists from 84 low-income countries.

In 2000 the ICO had developed a global strategy called Advance Eye Health. It pursued this strategy by maintaining strong official relations with WHO and continuing as one of the two founding members of the IAPB. The ICO strongly supported the Vision2020 Program. It promoted the importance of training ophthalmologists and other eye care practitioners to build towards the WHO goal of Universal Eye Care. It had developed and distributed the ICO Guidelines for Diabetic Eye Care, as well as the ICO Guidelines for Glaucoma Eye Care in 2017. The glaucoma guidelines were available in 10 languages. The ICO undertook specific training and support activities in Africa. It supported the creation and development of the African Ophthalmology Society. As part of the ICO Leadership Development program, separate streams were set up for Anglophone and Francophone Africa. It also reached out to Young Ophthalmologists and Emerging Leaders. The ICO supported its member societies as, and when, it was appropriate. There were 118 national societies, eight regional societies and 42 international subspecialty societies.

The ICO was a big organisation. There was a lot going on with many useful programs fully implemented. The president did not have to do everything of course, but I was heavily involved in a range of activities, many meetings of one sort or another, and made a lot of trips. The ICO was held together by Bill Felch, Lindsay Washburn and the ICO staff in San Francisco, together with Nicole Coulter and the ICO Exam Staff in London, and Cordula Obermeyer who managed the ICO Fellowships from Regensburg, Germany.

A major undertaking was organising and running each WOC, conducted in partnership with the national society that was hosting the Congress. WOC2016 was held in Guadalajara, Mexico and was hosted by Enrique Graue from the Mexican Society of Ophthalmology. WOC2018 was held in Barcelona with Rafael Barraquer and the Spanish Society of Ophthalmology. Both these WOCs were highly successful and well attended.

During my presidency, the ICO had achieved a great deal. This was because of the hard work and commitment of so many from across the world with the commitment and concentrated work of the ICO staff. I am personally most proud when I was

Receiving the Champion of Change Award from the Women in Ophthalmology. From left: Lama Al Aswad, me, Lisa Nijm and Erin Shriver during the World Ophthalmology Congress, Barcelona 2018

recognised by the Women in Ophthalmology as a 'Champion of Change'. Over the years I had worked to have women as half the members of all the various ICO groups and committees. One third of the ICO board were women, including Vice President Neeru Gupta, who was the first woman executive officer.

At the end of the WOC2018 I stepped down from the presidency and handed over to Peter Wiedemann, a retinal specialist from Leipzig, Germany. Peter had chaired the Scientific Program Committee for the WOC. It seemed a good hand to hand to.

I remained on the ICO board as the Immediate Past President. The next WOC, WOC2020, was to be held in Cape Town, South Africa and was to be hosted by Eddie Legodi and the South African Society of Ophthalmology.

Things did not go according to plan. WOC2020 was cancelled: COVID pandemic. However, before that, there had been major changes within the ICO. Under duress Bill Felch had resigned and most of staff had been let go. The ICO was completely restructured. Neeru Gupta became acting CEO for quite a while and organised many of the changes. The reasons behind all this were not clear and many did not understand or agree with the changes being made. A great deal of concern was voiced among many board members.

This came to a head at a virtual board meeting in mid-2020 when board membership was drastically revised, and half the board members were not reappointed. Peter Wiedemann stood down as president to take over the constitutional position of Immediate Past President, so I was pushed off the board. Neeru Gupta then became the new president.

Before 2020, the ICO Foundation had been chaired by David Pyott, a longstanding and very successful head of Allergan. Allergan is one of the major global ophthalmic companies. It acquires, develops, makes and sells branded products—drugs and medical devices—in the fields of eye care, central nervous system, medical aesthetics and gastroenterology. It's most well-known product, Botox, was originally developed to be injected into an overly strong eye muscle involved in the rotation of the eye to weaken it, and allow the weaker muscle it interacts with to grow stronger. The injected muscle will, over months, recover, but it and the muscle it works with, will have reached a functional equilibrium, to return to correct eye alignment and regular eye function.

As chair of the ICOF, David also had a seat on the ICO board. However, with the 2020 restructuring, David was removed from the board like Bruce, Brad and many others who questioned the changes in how the ICO was to be run. Following the dramatic changes within the ICO, the ICOF folded up and its assets were transferred to a newly formed organisation, the Ophthalmology Foundation, OF. The OF board was again led by David Pyott and Bruce Spivey and has a similar board composition to the previous ICOF. With industry support, the OF has continued to fund similar educational and fellowship programs to those previously run through the ICO with ICOF funding. With strong industry support these programs continue to develop and expand.

This restructuring of the ICO and the separation of interests and activities was disastrous for the ICO and the WOC. The OF has been able to carry on most of the educational activities, so all was not lost. Nevertheless, one would hope that, given time, the objectives and relationship between the ICO and the OF will once more align in the interests of ophthalmology and the preserving the global leadership in eye care.

One must ponder how such a productive establishment can be brought down.

The Queen Elizabeth Diamond Jubilee Trust was established in 2012 by the Commonwealth Heads of Government to mark the Queen's 60 years of contribution to the Commonwealth. Governments and individual donors funded the Trust's activities. One initiative was the Queen's Young Leaders Awards that over four years enabled 240 young people from 53 Commonwealth countries to spend a year at Cambridge University to learn more about business and social enterprises. Another area was on eye health, including trachoma, diabetic retinopathy, retinopathy of prematurity (retinal changes in premature babies), and eye screening technology. The latter led to the development of a mobile phone device to test vision, PEEK, developed by the International Centre for Eye Health in London.

The trachoma work focussed on the 12 Commonwealth countries with the trust providing funding to NGOs, particularly for trachoma screening, antibiotic treatment and surgery. Similarly with the screening and treatment for diabetic retinopathy, the work focussed on training for screening and treatment and the development of an ongoing consortium called DR-Net.

As with other Commonwealth countries, Australia provided funds to support all this. However, Australia established its own program, led by the former governor general, Major Michael Jeffery, to support work in Australia. I was honoured and pleased to be asked to join the Australian board and the Scientific Advisory Board based in London.

The Australian board met regularly and supported the trachoma work that was in progress.

The Scientific Advisory Board met about once a year. Sometimes this meant a trip to London and sometimes jumping on online when virtual meetings were still rare.

In 2014 the board held a meeting, followed by a reception at Buckingham Palace. What a treat! I was staying close to the Palace in St James, but I hailed a taxi to take me there.

'Where you goin', Guv?'

'To the Palace please.'

'I'll drop you off on the side. Can't get any closer.'

'No. Here is a pass to take us inside the Palace grounds.'

He was quiet for a moment or two. 'I've never done *that* before.'

Meeting Queen Elizabeth in Buckingham Place, 2013

How often can you take a London cabbie somewhere in London he's never been before?

As at the airport, you go through security but in the Palace you must leave your phone behind. No photographs either. At the reception in the State Room, one stood in line to be introduced and shake hands with the Queen and Prince Philip. The rooms are beautifully furnished and the paintings on the wall as good, if not better, than the National Gallery. We were served Mumm champagne: a bit early, but why not? There were many famous people there including John Major who was the chair of the Trust and Sophie, the Countess of Wessex, now Duchess of Edinburgh. I had met her previously at an IAPB meeting held at WHO in Geneva to mark the 10th anniversary of Vision2020. I had been assigned to chaperone her through the meeting and answer any questions she might have had during people's presentations.

The trust was designed to run for five years. To mark its impending closure there was another reception at the Palace in 2019. That was memorable too, but the Queen, warm and welcoming still, moved a little slower. On this last visit I was able to stay with Diane Duke. She now worked in the Palace as the personal assistant to Princess Alexandra. Diane had an apartment in Battersby, just south of the Thames where she lived through the week and returned to her home in Lancaster each weekend. Brian Duke had died some years before but Diane was more than busy and it was always wonderful to see her and to catch up.

Although the trust wound up, the Commonwealth has continued to play a major role in supporting eye care activities in member countries. Its members have been vocal at the World Health Assembly and more recently in the United Nations. For the first time, in 2021, the UN passed a resolution 'Vision is for Everyone: accelerating action to achieve the Sustainable Development Goals', clearly placing eye care on the global agenda.

12

Closing the Gap for Vision

> The attainment of excellence
> needs sustained effort.
>
> Sir Ninian Stephen

A major turning point in my life was seeded in those months of 2006 on sabbatical leave in England, a turn in which chance and preparedness played no part.

Those nearly four months coincided with a lovely but unusual British summer. July was beautiful, warm and dry, but the locals complained. 'This summer's so hot.' In August rain fell almost every day, and the locals said, 'Ah, what a wonderful summer.' Liz and I were left pondering. 'What funny people the Poms are.' That Liz is an erstwhile Pom not withstanding!

Peter Watson, a friend, had recently retired as the professor of ophthalmology at Addenbrooke's Hospital there. He had inherited his father's old two-storey terrace house, which he let out to visiting students. When he heard we were planning a sabbatical in Cambridge, he immediately offered it to us. It was in a quiet street that ran parallel to the Cam River, a block back. The street ended in the park called Jesus Green. Peter was a little surprised when the first thing Liz did was to clean out all the student's rubbish left in the cupboards and asked to have it removed. Judy Carrigan, my personal assistant from CERA, joined us. She stayed a mile or so away and came to our house at 9 am during work days.

We often visited Peter and his wife Ann, shared lovely meals with them and sometimes played tennis on their court. Peter had started an annual meeting, the Cambridge Ophthalmological Symposium. It was a relaxed two-day residential meeting at St John's College and with outstanding speakers and outstanding presentations. The meeting was followed by wonderful Cambridge-college-style dinners and celebrations. Peter died in 2017. I was honoured to be asked to give the first Peter Watson Memorial Lecture in 2020. With COVID the symposium was cancelled. I gave the lecture by Zoom in the next year.

I had a somewhat embarrassing, inapt title—Senior Honorary Visiting Fellow, Department of Clinical Neurosciences, University of Cambridge, Addenbrooke's Hospital, Cambridge—but it was an honour. It gave me access to the university library, allowed me to spend time in the eye clinic at Addenbrooke's, and to meet Keith Martin, the new Professor of Ophthalmology. (Little did I expect that, a dozen years later, Keith would come to Melbourne to be the director of CERA.)

Our time in Cambridge was wonderful, all care and no responsibility. While Judy and I worked on my book on trachoma, Liz was either up in the attic working on papers about HIV testing and laboratory quality assurance or spending time with colleagues in London.

Liz, Judy and I often had lunch in the sun in our back garden or on the lawns of Jesus Green. One day I said to Liz, 'Why aren't I having this much fun at work?'

Me, Judy Carrigan and Liz on our way to lunch in Cambridge

This led me to ponder what I could or should do next. If I gave the appropriate notice, I would have been head of the Department of Ophthalmology for nearly 18 years and of CERA for 12 years. I knew what my father-in-law would have said: 'More than long enough.' Eric Cunningham Dax strongly believed a manger should move every 10 to 15 years. CERA had grown into a splendid organisation. In my musing, I realised that I did not always look at issues with fresh eyes. Sometimes, when a problem came up, I would say, 'Yes, let's do it like this because it worked last time'; at other times a suggestion was made and I would say, 'No, we tried that last time and it didn't work, so we won't do that again.' A fresh perspective from the leadership would have benefits. CERA then had about 100 staff and dozens of students. Each research group was well led and doing productive work: Johnathan Crowston in Basic Science; Tien Wong in Epidemiology; Robyn Guymer in Clinical Research; Jill Keeffe in Population Health; Rasik Vajpayee in Surgical Research; Paul Baird in Ocular Genetics; and Graeme Pollack in the Lions Eye Bank. CERA was excelling on the world stage. It was time for CERA to have a new head. I could have stayed on in some capacity at CERA, but would it not be better for the new head to have a clear run?

So, what should I do next? Stay on as clinician at the Royal Victorian Eye and Ear? Go into private practice? Work in a developing country? Get a job with WHO? What did I really want to do? I thought hard and weighed the options.

My thoughts crystallised on one question: if I could achieve just one more worthwhile thing over the next five to 10 years, what would it be?

I concluded that I should put all my effort into addressing the unmet need for eye care for Aboriginal and Torres Strait people.

At that time no-one was seriously trying to develop and implement the long-term and sustainable changes needed to address the still appalling state of Indigenous eye health. I'd had the previous experience with trachoma, the review of eye health, and the other studies we had been involved with. I felt a bit like the Little Red Hen in the folk tale: if something was to happen to improve Indigenous eye health, then I just had to 'Do it myself.'

Back in Melbourne I spoke with the CERA board and Jim Angus, the Dean of Medicine. They were supportive of my idea—a good start. I told Jim that he should be careful not to let too many department heads take sabbatical leave—it could prove subversive.

I then met with Terry Nolan, then the head of the Melbourne School of Population Health, later renamed the Melbourne School of Population and Global Health. I had first met Terry in the early 1990s when he chaired a sports-injury working group for the Victorian Health Promotion Foundation. I had been invited to join as an ophthalmologist who might contribute something about eye trauma. Terry is a paediatrician with a

Me, Terry Nolan, Head of the School of Population and Global Health, chair of the IEHU Advisory Board, and board member Ian Anderson, 2009

strong interest in vaccine development and use, but he is also a strong and experienced epidemiologist. Earlier, I had been I delighted when he accepted my invitation to serve on the CERA Advisory Board. Terry invited me to move to his school and offered me an office.

A job and an office were all that I needed. From there, I set up the Indigenous Eye Health Unit, IEHU.

Before I left CERA I secured additional funding from the Eye Foundation and the Vision Collaborative Research Centre, the Vision CRC, for a national survey of Indigenous eye health.

The only data on Indigenous eye health available then dated back to the National Trachoma and Eye Health Program, NTEHP, of the 1970s. We undertook an ambitious, Australia-wide, randomly selected sample of Indigenous communities from each of six 'remoteness areas'. To get the appropriate approval for this study in 30 communities we needed to get 72 ethics approvals and agreements. The survey needed community approval from Aboriginal Health Services, from local and regional ethics committees, similar groups at the jurisdictional level, as well as institutional approval. Obtaining all these consents and approvals was laborious and time consuming, but essential.

The field work for the National Indigenous Eye Health Survey, NIEHS, started in late 2007 and finished in 2008. We were honoured by the local Wurundjeri Woi Wurrung Elders to be allowed to use the name *Minum Barreng* for the survey and then the ongoing work of the IEHU. Minum Barreng means to study or use tracking eyes. To reach the selected sample sites across the whole country took considerable time and effort. Sarah Fox, Jill Keeffe, Ross Dunn, Anna-Lena Arnold and Jing Xie played pivotal roles in organising and undertaking the data-gathering work and the analysis. We also had several dozen people who volunteered their time and services to help with community liaison, recruitment and examination.

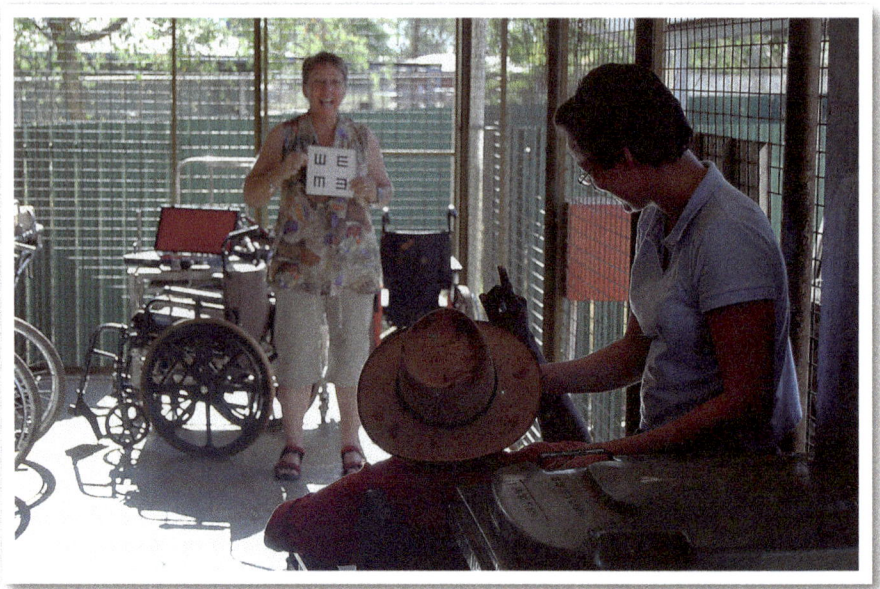

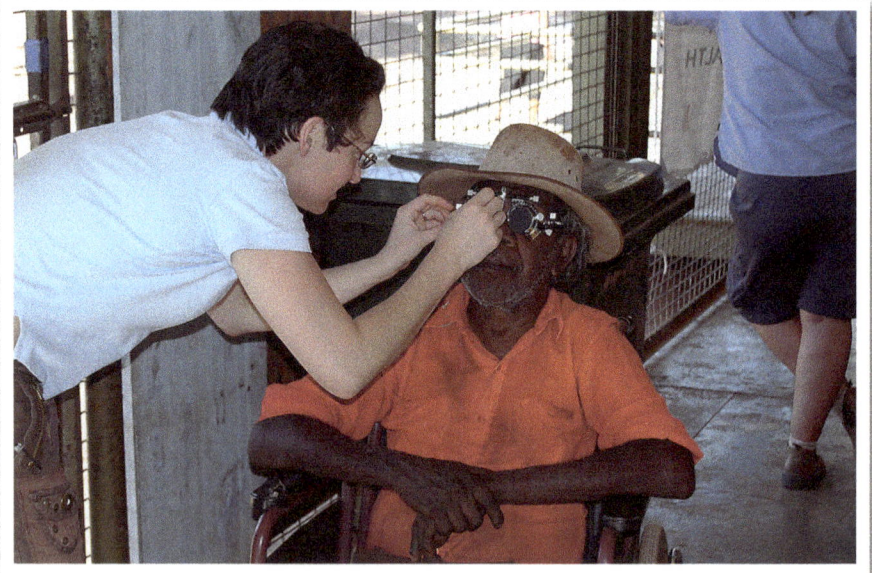

Above: Testing vision during the National Indigenous Eye Health Survey

Below: Sarah Fox adjusting trial frames during the National Indigenous Eye Health Survey

The NIEHS examined nearly 1700 Indigenous children aged from 5 to 15 years. They had five times less poor vision than non-Indigenous Australians, consistent with our earlier findings from the NTEHP. Again, we found low rates of myopia and excellent vision in healthy, Indigenous children—and in adults.

But trachoma was still a problem in children in remote outback communities.

We examined almost 1200 Indigenous adults aged 40 years or older. Blindness rates were six times higher than in the non-Indigenous people examined in the Melbourne Vision Impairment Project and the Blue Mountains Eye Study. The main causes of blindness were cataract, uncorrected refractive error, trachoma and diabetes. Overall, 94 precent of the vision loss was unnecessary; it was either preventable or treatable. What I found most surprising was that the unmet need was the same in the cities as it was in the most remote areas. The rates of vision loss in Fitzroy, where I lived and where the Victorian Aboriginal Health Service was located just a few blocks from the Royal Victorian Eye and Ear Hospital, the largest eye hospital in the Southern Hemisphere, was the same as it was in Fitzroy Crossing, the very remote community in the Kimberly region of Western Australia.

We had to discover why people were not able to access the eye care they needed. What was wrong with the health systems they encountered? Who failed to deliver the services they needed? How come? How to fix this?

The survey work was started while I was still at CERA and the CERA team continued and completed the field work and analysis after I had moved out. In preparation for my move to the School of Population Health, I prepared a document seeking government and philanthropic support for the work I was proposing to do. The request went out over Jim Angus' name and looked at bringing together Ian Anderson and Marcia Langton, both in the school and as part of the CRC for Aboriginal Health, and me, as part of the Vision CRC. The idea was to fund the applied research needed to improve Indigenous eye health over a five-year period and to bring the skills and expertise of the two government-funded CRCs together.

Later, I was the university representative on the CRC for Aboriginal Health. Mick Gooda was closely associated with this CRC and I came to know him well. He later became the Aboriginal and Torres Strait Islander Social Justice Commissioner and continued to provide me with helpful advice and suggestions. Through the CRC I also met Lowitja O'Donoghue, another important leader in Indigenous issues. (The CRC became the Lowitja Institute in 2014.) This was how I met Pat Anderson, who became a good friend and later chaired the IEHU Advisory Board. Pat was one of the leaders of the 'Uluru Statement from the Heart' and the 'Voice' referendum.

This research funding proposal was not successful.

I had undertaken a review of eye health in Aboriginal and Torres Strait communities for Michael Wooldridge, Minister of Health in 1996–97 (see page 234ff). I made recommendations, all of which were adopted in principal but at best only incompletely implemented. In 1998 the Commonwealth Government established a National Aboriginal and Torres Strait Islander Eye Health Program through the Office for Aboriginal and Torres Strait Islander Health, OATSIH, to improve access to eye health care, particularly for people living in remote and rural areas. One partially implemented recommendation was to provide azithromycin for treating trachoma. It was approved for use in the clinics, but only as the adult capsules. A lot more work was needed to have the children's suspension added to the list. There was a call for state-based teams to monitor and treat trachoma and a group to collect their data and make annual reports.

A regional public-private model was recommended for the

provision of specialist eye services—the model was to combine public funding for infrastructure and hospital services, and Medicare bulk-billing for specialist eye services. Of particular concern was access to services for people who live in remote areas. A study in Queensland, for example, reported that only a small proportion of optometrists provided services to rural communities. An overall assessment of eye health in rural Australia found that the number of patients per optometrist was more than 12 700 in remote areas and around 2700 in rural areas compared with the national average of around 1180. There was also an under-supply of ophthalmologists in these areas. To encourage optometrists to visit remote regions of Australia and deliver eye care to Indigenous communities, the Australian Government offered a subsidy in the Visiting Optometrists Scheme (VOS).

The National Aboriginal and Torres Strait Islander Eye Health program (NATSIEHP), based on a regional model of eye health service delivery, comprised three strands: regional eye health services coordination; access to specialised equipment; and training assistance. It was aimed to increase eye health services (particularly specialist support) in Aboriginal and Torres Strait Islander primary health care settings, and included the provision of infrastructure and resources. The program aimed to address eye health problems such as cataract, diabetic retinopathy, trachoma, and refractive error, through increasing access to specialist eye health services within the context of comprehensive primary health care.

The program also sought to promote the WHO SAFE (Surgery, Antibiotic, Facial cleanliness, Environment, (see page 145) strategy for trachoma control. Major components of the program included the establishment of eye health coordinator positions, nationally, within Indigenous primary health care settings, training for coordinators and workers in identified Indigenous community-controlled health services, and provision of ophthalmic equipment.

The Centre for Remote Health in Alice Springs was commissioned by the Office for Aboriginal and Torres Strait Islander Health to undertake a review of the implementation of the National Aboriginal and Torres Strait Islander Eye Health Program. The review was conducted in 2002–03 to determine the then current state of the implementation of the NATSIEHP and make recommendations about further directions for the program.

When I moved to the School at the start of 2008 there were just the two of us, Judy Carrigan, my long-time assistant, and me. In many ways we were jumping off a cliff.

Although as the Ringland Anderson Chair of Ophthalmology I had tenure, the chair needed to stay at MUDO/CERA. So, I gave that up the chair and the tenured position at the University. Then in stepped John Funder, long-standing friend, that excellent judge of butcher shop's lamb cuts and a leading medical endocrinology researcher. He had returned for overseas post-doctoral studies and was at Prince Henry's Hospital at the same time as Liz was doing her PhD in the Department of Medicine. After that he was the director of the Baker Heart and Diabetes Institute, a long-established Melbourne-based independent research body. Our children knew each other well. I was delighted to have Funder as a member of the CERA Board.

He also served on the Harold Mitchell Foundation Board.

Professor John Funder AC, a long-term friend and a great supporter in so many ways

He convinced the philanthropist and ex-advertising company owner, Harold Mitchell, that what I was hoping to do was worth supporting. Out of the blue, and much to my surprise, Harold offered the University a named chair for me with five years of funding if the University would match it. A wonderful offer! The University agreed.

With assistance from Wendy Brooks, the then director of the University's Advancement and Communications Office, we were able to secure a five-year grant from the Ian Potter Foundation. Wendy's help made a huge difference. When we were in the final stages of the grant proposal, I had been invited back to Cambridge for a few days to examine a PhD candidate. I answered key questions about the proposal on the phone with Wendy as I walked on the banks of the Cam.

With the data coming from the NIEHS, we were able to frame the dimensions of the problem and assess the needs for eye care. Next, we had to look at what was causing this large gap between eye care for Indigenous Australians and mainstream Australians. With the funding we now had, I was able to recruit staff in 2009 and 2010, some of whom are still with the Unit. They included Emma Stanford, who had been an advisor to two federal health ministers, Michael Wooldridge and Kay Patterson, then worked at the Baker Institute. Rachael Ferguson joined us. She had the digital, design and photographic skills we needed. It was to our great benefit that Mitchell Anjou joined us in late 2009. Mitchell is a talented and experienced optometrist who had run the clinics and outreach programs for the Victorian, later the Australian, College of Optometry. Mitchell Anjou and I first met when he was setting up the optometry clinic at the Victorian Aboriginal Health Service in 1998, following recommendations I had made in the 1997 Review of Indigenous Eye Health. Fiona Lange joined us at that time; she had experience in community work and health promotion, and became adept in promoting our trachoma messages.

Staff members Mitchell Anjou, Josie Atkinson and Emma Stanford

We established an advisory board for the IEHU, in part to make sure Harold Mitchell's and Ian Potter's donations were spent wisely. To have representatives of the private foundations that helped fund our work on the board as advisors proved invaluable. The advisory board was chaired by Terry Nolan, head of the School. It included Ian Anderson, a Palawa Trowerna man, at that time head of Onemda, the Indigenous research group within the School with the Wurundjeri Woi Wurung name for 'love'; John Funder; Jan Hirst from the Potter Foundation; Wendy Brooks representing the dean and the university; Jilpia Nappaljari Jones, a distinguished Walmadjari woman; and Trevor (Buzza) Buzzacott, an Arabunna man. I had worked with both Jilpia and Buzza on the NTEHP. Also on the board were David Middleton from the Cybec Foundation, a philanthropic

Dr Michael Wooldridge

organisation to foster community self-support and self-help, and Ian Roberts, Amanda Mitchell and Mary Delahunty from the Harold Mitchell Foundation.

Over the next 15 years the membership of the advisory board changed from time to time. We had several former federal ministers from both sides of politics on the board. They included Barry Jones, Michael Wooldridge, Warren Snowdon and Trish Crossin. After an external review the board was restructured at the end of 2022. It was thereafter chaired by Pat Anderson, an Alyawarre woman. Henceforth, the board had a majority of First Nations members on it.

Throughout, the board members were extremely helpful, providing suggestions and advice. They often facilitated meetings and interactions with policy makers and leaders both nationally and within the community. They played a very valuable sounding board for us. Much of what we were able to achieve was owing to their sagacious advice.

Harold Mitchell was keen to see some of our work in the field. Just after the 2008 global financial recession, he offered to

Above: Barry Jones, very long-term supporter and Advisory Board member
Below: Trish Crossin, Milpa, Greg Hunt and me

Closing the Gap for Vision

Above: In the clinic in Amata SA with Christopher Pyne, three staff members, Harold Mitchell and Fiona Lange

Below: Peter Ansstasiou, Rob Bowen and David Middleton after helping at the Melbourne Football Club event at Kalkarindji, NT

take us to some of the communities in his private jet.

'You know Hugh, this is a great time to buy second-hand planes. You can get a plane that costs $50 million new for only $30 million second hand.'

I think I nodded, but not even in my wildest dreams...

We did several trips to remote communities that had runways big enough for us to be able to land. The flights were wonderful, a hostess to tend our every need with food, coffee and drink. Harold had been a teetotaller since his early twenties, but that did not stop him offering wine to others. Among those who joined us were Christopher Pyne, Minister for Education; Jane Halton, Secretary Federal Department of Health; Charles Goode, Chair of the Ian Potter Foundation; other Potter board members including Sir Daryl Dawson, former High Court Justice, and Graeme Ryan; and some of the IEHU Advisory Board members including David Middleton and John Funder. These trips allowed us to develop more personal contacts, showed the visitors the reality of life in these deprived outback communities, and allowed us to show the need for, and impact of, our work.

To build an understanding of the challenges faced in providing eye care for Indigenous Australians, we initiated specific research activities. IEHU started on an ambitious program—'to address the gross disparities in eye health between Indigenous Australians and the mainstream population', or to 'Close the gap for vision'—no less.

In five years we aimed to have:

- assessed Indigenous eye care across the country
- prioritised appropriate and specific intervention strategies
- developed and implemented accessible, appropriate and affordable solutions to have eliminated trachoma in Australia
- reduced the prevalence of vision loss

- and through research, changed health policies to improve the eye health of Indigenous Australians in a long-term, sustainable way

Ambitious aims, but clear goals.

Once again a chance conversation led to long-term changes. Liz and I were keen opera goers. At an opera event, I was sitting next to an elderly woman with whom I struck up a conversation. She asked me what I did and I talked a little about our work on Indigenous eye health.

'That all sounds very interesting. Could I come to you and talk a bit more about it?'

'Yes indeed. Why don't you? We can chat over a cup of tea.'

Shortly later she came to see me in my office where we sat and talked. She said, 'Would $1 million help with the trachoma work?' I was dumbfounded. All I could respond with was, 'Wow! Wow!' I forgot to get the cup of tea I'd offered. Ann Miller is a wonderful and now a long-term supporter of the work we have done on trachoma through her foundation. She is always interested and supportive. She has come with us to Central Australia, often with her foundation board members.

The analysis of the data from the NIEHS was completed in 2009. In addition to papers in the scientific literature, we prepared a formal report, 'National Indigenous Eye Health Survey: Minum Barreng'. This was launched by Governor General Quentin Bryce at an event in the Koori Heritage Trust in Melbourne while the International Agency for the Prevention of Blindness, IAPB, board meeting that was being held in town. Before the official launch, Emma Stanford and I had travelled to each state and territory to brief the appropriate community-controlled health organisations, health ministers, and the heads of the health departments about the survey's findings and how the IEHU was planning to follow these up. These briefings all seemed to

Ann Miller and Milpa

engender interest. Given the awful but unarguable findings, the broad plans we were developing were well received. Also, they paved the way for ongoing communications and meetings as the work progressed.

Our first priority was to identify the barriers to eye-care delivery.

With the support from the Potter Foundation, we were able to provide part-time support to senior researchers within the School of Population Health to work on specific topics.

Margaret Kelaher looked at the Medicare data to prepare a report on 'Access to Eye Health Service among Indigenous Australians'. Margaret was the director of the Centre for Health Policy in the School and had extensive experience with big data. She and Angeline Ferdinand undertook an area-level study of socioeconomic status and remoteness, and the utilisation and

Closing the Gap for Vision

Governor General Quentin Bryce launching the report of the National Indigenous Eye Health Survey

access to ophthalmic and optometric services. They looked at the services in regions across the whole country. The number of eye care providers dropped like stone in remote areas and in those disadvantaged areas with a higher proportion of Indigenous people. Eye examination rates, cataract surgery and diabetes eye care were all much lower there.

Ian Anderson, who headed up the Onemda group at the School and at the Aboriginal CRC, worked with Jilpia Jones, Nerelle Poroch and Graham Henderson from the Australian Institute for Aboriginal and Torres Strait Islander Studies, AIATSIS, on a report called 'A Critical History of Indigenous Eye-health Policy-making: towards effective systems reform'. I was most pleased to work with Jilpia again. Her visits to Melbourne also meant that she and Liz could have occasional shopping expeditions. This report reviewed the peaks and troughs in the policy development for Indigenous eye health over the preceding 30 years. The policies for eye health were reviewed in the context of other Indigenous health policies and the changes over time in general health policies. Their report included a review of the literature and government policies, but it also included interviews with some government policy makers, community-controlled health services, professional service providers and NGOs. The report highlighted many important issues but above all the need for Indigenous leadership and the need for 'A more sophisticated policy framework in Aboriginal health that simultaneously maintains a focus on systems issues and develops targeted strategies'. In a way, this was our 'History Book'.

Russell Gruen and Peter Bragg, with Jason Wasiak and Alex Hewitt, undertook two reviews of the literature, very big reading undertakings. Russell was in the Department of Surgery based at the Royal Melbourne, and a busy surgeon, teacher and researcher.

The first review was on 'Diabetic Retinopathy: accuracy of screening methods for diabetic retinopathy: a systematic review'. This clearly demonstrated the importance of, and the need for, regular screening and the timely treatment eye problems in those with diabetes. They also quantified the role and performance of retinal photography for screening.

The second review was 'Trachoma: antibiotic treatments of trachoma: a systemic review'. This work showed the importance of community-based treatment and the use of azithromycin, together with the need for health education, facial cleanliness and environmental change. It was sophisticated stuff. However, it made plain that no drug, not even azithromycin, could work the magic on its own. It had to be combined with the long term solutions, clean faces and functional washing facilities. This was to be our bottom-line. It had to be easy to communicate when dropping off a copy of the review for a health minister or head of department who was thinking of a quick drug fix.

A further study on the funding of eye services was undertaken by Will Mulholland from McKinsey and Co, who had worked with Angus Turner. They had been friends since university days. Angus had finished his ophthalmology training at the Eye and Ear with us and worked there for a year. He then went back to Western Australia and did an extraordinary job in improving Indigenous Eye Health there and ultimately opened the Lions Outback Vision eye clinic in Broome and organised the $2-million Lions Outback Vision Van which travels 24 000 km a year bringing eye services to remote West Australians on the nearest sealed road. Angus and Will's report, 'Outreach Eye Services in Australia', reviewed the nine existing eye outreach services across the nation. They showed the huge variation in the funding that different outreach services received and the services they provided. The more efficient services had fee-for-service funding, and good integration and coordination between visiting services and the community health services. The report called for a revision in the funding and coordination of these out-reach services.

Emma Stanford and I summarised these reports and the NIEHS data into a short summary report, 'Provision of Indigenous eye health services'. We used this to facilitate discussions and workshops that we then held across the country. When Mitchell Anjou joined us, we had just received funding from Greg Poche and his foundation. Mitchell became a Poche Fellow as did Andrea Boudville and Robyn McNeil. Mitchell brought his experience as an optometrist and his work with Indigenous people. Both Andrea and Robyn had public health backgrounds. Together they formed a dynamic team.

In the meantime, David Dunt and Ya-seng (Arthur) Hsueh prepared another report, 'Projected needs for eye care services for Indigenous Australians'. David and Arthur were both in the Centre for Health Policy at the School. They calculated the needs for eye care in each geographic area across the country using population data from the Australian Bureau of Statistics census and the vision data from the NIEHS. They mapped the areas showing the projected number of Indigenous people who were blind and the annual needs for cataract surgery, diabetic exams, diabetic laser treatment, provision of spectacles, trichiasis surgery, and the number of ophthalmologists and optometrists required to achieve this work. These estimates provided the initial targets for ramping-up eye care in each area to meet their population-based needs. These estimated needs were shown in maps and tables for the service areas within each state and territory. We called this report our 'Geography Book' or 'Atlas'.

At the same time Arthur Hsueh and Alex Brando, with David Dunt and Mitchell Anjou, prepared another report, 'The Cost to Close the Gap for Vision'. Its 40 pages looked at the annual cost to perform all the cataract surgery, provide spectacles, and screen and treat those with diabetic retinopathy. The data were presented both nationally and for each jurisdiction.

They determined that the current annual expenditure on these services was $18 million and an additional $28 million a year was required to meet the identified needs. They recognised the critical importance of the proper co-ordination of the pathway of care and this represented 46 percent of the added costs. We called this report our 'Arithmetic Book'.

We had collected a mountain of information.

Starting in June 2010 we began to collate it and work towards a comprehensive plan. Again, Mitchell Anjou with Andrea Boudville and Robyn McNeil pulled together the 10 published reports and integrated input from both individuals and groups meetings: a mammoth task. They had data from the NIEHS, the eight reviews, the input from extensive community and service-provider consultations to collate, reconcile and fashion into a workable plan.

As we worked on developing what became the Roadmap, we held three more stakeholder workshops.

The first was to establish the broad outlines, the second to seek input and advice on the policy recommendations, and the third sought input into the draft recommendations. Participants in these workshops included representatives from National

Aboriginal Community Controlled Health Organisation, NACCHO, and its more local ACCHOs; federal and state health departments; professional bodies; non-government organisations; and academic and other colleagues. We then wrote a summary draft with recommendations.

We took the draft to 38 separate face-to-face meetings of relevant stakeholders to seek final feedback. In all, over 550 people participated one way or another in these discussion groups and consultations.

Somewhere along the line I learned 'that there are only 25 hours in a day and 8 days in a week. It does not matter how hard you work you cannot fit everything in. You *must* prioritise and delegate.' Fortunately, with Mitchell and the hard-working IEHU team we were able to pretty much achieve all the things we aimed to do.

The final full report contained 148 pages, with a supplement of 160 pages. These documents summarised all the work we had done over the preceding four years and the reports of the various meetings and workshops, including the formidable list

Focus group members at the Victorian Aboriginal Health Service

of the participants. The primary documents were too long and detailed for general readers, so we also launched an accessible 20-page summary we called our 'Roadmap'.

'The Roadmap to Close the Gap for Vision' had clearly set-out pages and displayed the strapline 'Vision loss is 11% of the indigenous health gap. Each additional dollar gives $2.50 of cost benefit,' on the front cover. The Roadmap was launched in February 2012 in Adelaide by Justin Mohamed, the chair of NACCHO, and Warren Snowdon, the federal Minister for

The Roadmap to Close the Gap for Vision

Indigenous Health, who came from one of the two Northern Territory electorates. 'Closing the Gap' had been the name of an essentially bi-partisan political goal, in health and wellbeing, child mortality to life expectancy, education from pre-school to PhD, justice and incarceration rates, land and water, and Australian languages. Within the appalling health area, we had a vision, a contribution to make. We called for a comprehensive approach to give a long-term and sustainable solution and so close the gap for vision. It was launched at the offices of the Aboriginal Health Council of South Australia which was hosting the NACCHO board meeting.

It set out the background, outlined the magnitude and causes of vision loss, framed the population-based needs, and listed 'Nine false reasons for not addressing blindness'. Some echoed a previous publication (see page 361-362), but this one had to counter false objections regarding costs and benefits, and defend an admittedly complex scheme:

The official launch of the Roadmap with Mitchell Anjou, Justin Mohammed as Chair of NACCHO, me, Warren Snowdon as Minister for Health, Andrea Boudville at Aboriginal Health Council of South Australia, March 2012

- Vision loss is not important in Indigenous communities
- Blindness does not kill—… address the life-threatening things
- Eye care is body-part medicine, it is not holistic
- There are many other more pressing priorities than eye care
- It is not worth spending the money on eye care, it is too expensive
- We are already spending too much on Aboriginal health…
- There are not enough specialists to provide the care required
- This… Roadmap is too complex, it is not all necessary
- There is no more money to spend on Indigenous health

The Roadmap detailed the vital 42 recommendations for changes that had to be made under nine subject headings:

1. Primary eye care as part of comprehensive primary health care
2. Indigenous access to eye health services
3. Co-ordination
4. Eye health workforce
5. Elimination of trachoma
6. Monitoring and evaluation
7. Governance
8. Health promotion and awareness
9. Health financing.

We likened the patient journey or the pathway of care, to a leaky pipe. This pipe had 42 leaks or points where people could fall out of the eye-care system. If you only fixed one or two leaks, the pipe would still leak. You had to fix *all* 42 of them. This was clearly going to take considerable time, effort, expertise and much consultation.

Closing the Gap for Vision

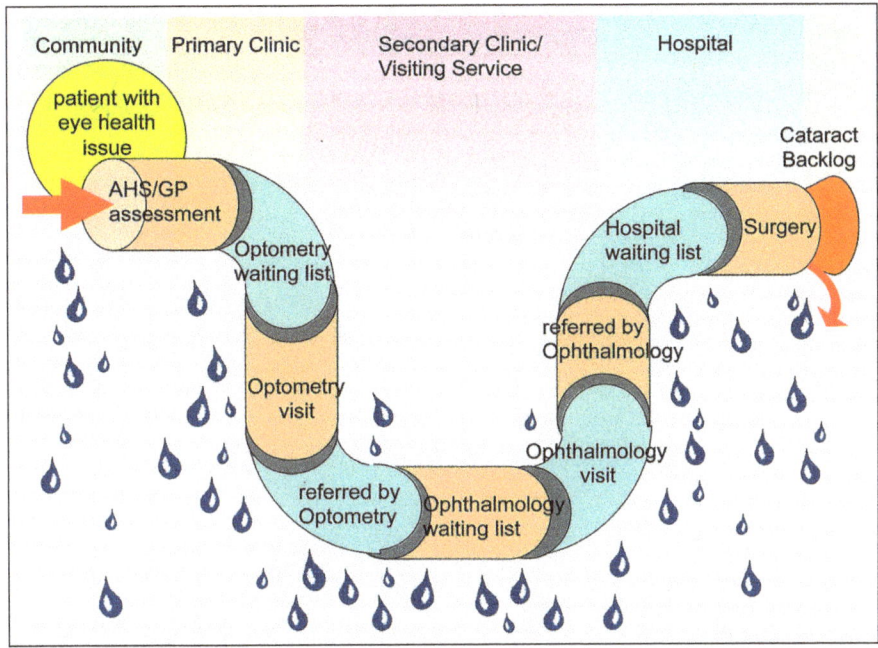

The Leaky Pipe or the patient journey/pathway of care, showing some of the 'leaks' points

Mitchell Anjou working hard, teaching how to measure vision

After the launch of the Roadmap, Mitchell Anjou and his growing team started serious work across the country. We got busy advocating for more funding for Indigenous eye health and outreach services, and sought changes in policies, including for Medicare to cover diabetic retinal screening. We worked hard to get the eye health messages out through webpages and social media. We made personal visits and attended many meetings and community events. Depending on the venue we would include the trachoma, diabetes and Roadmap messages.

Each year from 2013 to 2021 we reported in our 'Annual Update' on the progress that had been made on each of the 42 recommendations. Updates showed which changes were underway, which were fully implemented and which had yet to start. We followed the same format each year and the last of these updates, in 2021, showed that of the 42 recommendations 27 had

Carol Wynne and Nick Wilson manning a stall with our eye health promotion material

been fully implemented. With the commitments already made by the Commonwealth 38, or about 90 percent, would be fully implemented. Each recommendation had several intermediate implementation steps or activities. There were 138 steps in total. By 2021, 121 of these were completed and with the government's commitments they came to 133—over 95 percent.

What were the actual changes in eye health and vision loss in the community?

In 2015–16 Mohamed Dirani, Stuart Keel and Joshua Foreman at CERA undertook the National Eye Health Survey to update the data of the population rates of vision loss. They followed the approach we had used in the earlier NIEHS but also included a non-Indigenous sample. They showed that the rate of Indigenous adult blindness had been halved, from six times higher than in the non-Indigenous folk to three times higher. Low vision was still three times higher. This confirmed

The 2016 Annual Update launched by Pat Turner Chair of NACCHO centre, with Mark Daniell RANZCO President on the left, me on the right during the RANZCO Congress in Melbourne

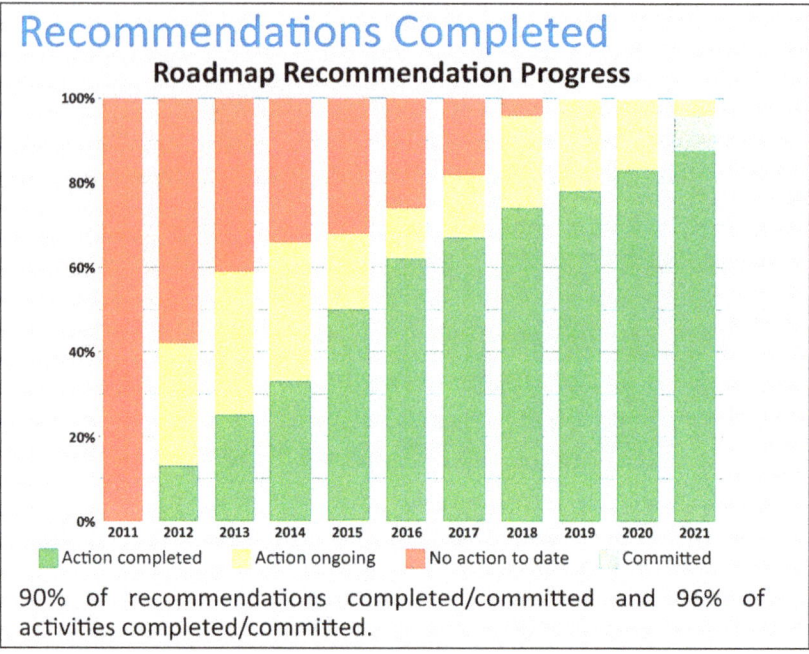

The graph in the 2021 Annual Update showing the progress made in implementing the Roadmap's recommendations

real progress had been made in 'reducing the gap'.

There were hopes that the next follow-up survey would be done in 2019 so results would be available in 2020, a milestone year for vision given Vision2020 and its targets. However, the Health Department kept delaying the funding for the new survey and, when funding was provided, the work was held up by the COVID pandemic. In 2023 this new survey finally got underway. Results are due to be published at the end of 2025.

Unfortunately, with the COVID pandemic and then change in government, these additional commitments are still to be fully implemented. The Commonwealth funded the Australian Institute of Health and Welfare to publish an annual report on 'Eye health measures for Aboriginal and Torres Strait Islander people'. Their 2024 report shows that eye exams had increased over three times, cataract surgery and examination rates for those with diabetes both increased over 2½ times, the waiting times for cataract surgery had fallen and the provision of outreach services by optometrists and ophthalmologists had increased significantly. The proportion of Indigenous people with diabetes who had had an eye exam in the previous 12 months had gone from 20 percent to 50 percent. However, the annual eye exams need to reach 80–85 percent rate to effectively prevent unnecessary blindness and vision loss.

So, as in other areas of my work, the glass is not empty, but it is still only half full. While the progress is encouraging, more still needs to be done.

Apart from the IEHU's Annual Updates, we had other investigations and reports made around the ongoing work on Indigenous eye care.

One was a 2015 review with an economic costing and analysis done by PwC Australia. This showed a significant net *benefit* to government and an even greater net benefit to the Australian community.

Another report, by McKinsey and Co in 2016, reflected on the excellent examples of co-ordination and integration of health care, the widespread collaboration, and the importance of monitoring and evaluation that our work showed.

Late in 2018 Ken Wyatt, the federal Minister of Health, asked Vision 2020 Australia to come up with a new plan for Indigenous eye health. After a year of development, he received the plan 'Strong Eyes, Strong Communities', developed with broad sector engagement including input from NACCHO. The proposal pointed to the remaining areas in our Roadmap that still needed to be addressed, and it stressed the need for continuing funding. It outlined some new initiatives for NACCHO and its affiliates, including investigation of the priority of eye health and the staffing required, as well as the provision of subsidised spectacles. In March 2019 Ken Wyatt took this plan to the Council of Australian Governments, COAG, which endorsed it. In August that year these recommendations were incorporated into 'Australia's Long Term National Health Plan'.

Unfortunately, with the COVID pandemic and subsequent lockdowns, and then the election of the Albanese Labor Government, not much has happened since. These excellent commitments seem to have been shelved, put on ice, gone cold.

For years, IEHU had received support for our implementation work from the Paul Ramsay Foundation. In 2020 the Foundation commissioned two independent reviews of our work. One review was done by ARTD Consultants, who surveyed regional groups and people working in the sector of eye health to assess the effectiveness of the changes in eye care. The other, undertaken by Clear Horizons interviewed stakeholders to assess the role IEHU had played in this process.

IEHU also undertook another literature review and held three co-design workshops. This work was overseen by an Aboriginal and Torres Strait Islander Reference Group. The combined input supported the collaborative regional approach and the need for more resources. Overall, they concurred that IEHU had played an effective role in engagement and facilitation with Indigenous groups and collaborators.. The review stressed the continuing importance of ongoing strong Indigenous leadership and ownership, the need to grow the Indigenous workforce, and to embed eye care in the ACCHOs. It highlighted the importance of collaboration, the need for cultural safety, the importance of collecting data to build on the already strong evidence base, and the importance of intermediary support or, in their word, 'allyship'. Allyship is a term introduced for those non-Indigenous allies who listen to and work with Indigenous peoples and communities.

From this review and from feedback from the annual

The attendees at the 2019 National Indigenous Eye Health Conference in Alice Springs

National Indigenous Eye Health Meetings that IEHU started in 2018, there has grown an exciting and important new group: the First Nations Eye Health Alliance, FNEHA.

FNEHA is Indigenous-led and brings together Indigenous leaders and groups involved in eye care services. FNEHA is taking over the organisation of the annual congress started by IEHU and many of the advocacy roles. It is currently co-chaired by Shaun Tatipata, a Ngarrindjeri and Wuthathi man who lives in Darwin. He was an Aboriginal Health Worker when I first met him in 2000. He then worked with the Fred Hollows Foundation and more recently joined IEHU. He has set up the first Indigenous-run eye care and optometry service, the Deadly Vision Centre, that has its own range of spectacle frames. The other co-chair is Kris Rallah-Baker, a Yuggera, Warrongo and Wiradjuri man who is Australia's first Indigenous ophthalmologist. Kris practices his Profession in Noosa, Queensland and is an honorary associate professor with us in IEHU. The First Nations Eye Health Alliance is now the leading national body in providing and pushing for better eye health for Indigenous men, women and children. At the end of 2022, I handed the leadership of IEHU to Mitchell Anjou and accepted an emeritus professorship at the University of Melbourne. IEHU is in safe hands. Indigenous eye health has improved and will continue to improve.

In 2022 during a break during the COVID pandemic travel restrictions, Vision 2020 Australia arranged for a meeting in Canberra with the prime minister, Scott Morrison. We spoke about the broad range of eye health issues that affected people across the country. As expected, I made a strong push to reinvigorate the Indigenous eye health work that had been stalled significantly by the pandemic. Although there was a lot of talk and smiling, there was not much follow up action and later in the year the government changed.

In 2021, to mark the first 15 years of its work, IEHU commissioned two authors from Croakey Health Media to write an

Meeting with Prime Minister Scott Morrison in his office in Canberra, 2021

external and impartial assessment of our work. They wrote a comprehensive and accessible story of the work, the people and communities we worked with to develop and implement the Roadmap to Close the Gap for Vision. Tess Ryan and Tim Senior's book *Minum Barreng: the story of the Indigenous Eye Health Unit* was published in 2022. Again we used *Minum Barreng*, study or track eyes, as the title. And as Indigenous Australians have the sharpest human eyes for tracking on the planet, preserving those eyes from the harms that can befall them is a privilege I have loved sharing.

Book launch of *Minum Barreng* with Marcia Langton, me, Pat Anderson, Linda Doherty, Tess Ryan and Tim Senior, December 2022

Opening Eyes

13

Diabetes

> I am only one and I cannot do everything, but I
> can do something. Because I cannot do everything,
> I will not refuse to do something I can do.
>
> Helen Keller

Shortly after I'd returned to Melbourne in 1990, I was contacted by Paul Zimmet, the head of the International Diabetes Institute. He had undertaken a survey of diabetes in Fiji and was planning a similar study in Nauru. However, for his next survey, he wanted to include an eye exam and asked for our help to do that. I arranged ophthalmic support. We assisted with his later surveys in Western Samoa and Mauritius, and also the Darwin Regional Urban Indigenous Diabetes study, DRUID.

Paul is a great champion for diabetics and a very persuasive man. Later he was the President of the International Diabetes Federation. Before long Paul had me involved with various working groups, including those developing the various NHMRC guidelines for diabetes, and then those for eye care in diabetes.

The number of adult people worldwide living with diabetes in 1990 was 200 million, and in 2022, 830 million according to the World Health Organisation. Diabetic retinopathy—the damage high blood-sugar levels have done to the blood vessels of the retina—is a disease that blinds people

One way or another I was a member of various government department and ministerial advisory and working groups until

2022. While I was a board member of the International Council of Ophthalmology, I led the development of the first International Guidelines for Eyecare for those with Diabetes. I assembled and worked with a group of world experts on diabetic eye disease, its screening, and its treatment. We set guidelines for care in high-income countries, but also for low- and middle-income settings. These were the first such guidelines for managing diabetic retinopathy in diverse settings.

Diabetes is a potent cause of blindness. With time, changes occur in the small blood vessels of the retina that lead to ischaemia, a shortage of oxygen. This may cause tissues to swell, oedema, or new blood vessels to grow. The new blood vessels are poorly supported and readily bleed which can then lead to the formation of scar tissue. All this damage is harmful to the eye and leads to vision loss and then blindness. Essentially, everyone with diabetes will develop diabetic retinopathy if they live long enough. It develops more quickly in those with poor control of their diabetes. Early changes of diabetic retinopathy can be detected by retinal screening. Vision loss is prevented or halted with laser treatment or injections into the eye. Later changes may be treated in the same way but some will need surgery. Diabetes also increases the chance of the development of cataract and glaucoma.

The Melbourne Vision Impairment Project found about 5 percent of adults over 40 had diabetes, one-third had some retinopathy and one third of these had severe sight-threatening retinopathy. Diabetic retinopathy caused blindness in one in 10 of those who were blind and over 40. This would extrapolate to over 5000 people nationwide.

In the MVIP 40 percent of those with diabetes presented with decreased vision. Of those with diabetes, 29 percent had some diabetic retinopathy. Most of the retinopathy changes were early but 7 percent had sight-threatening disease. The presence of retinopathy was closely linked to the duration of diabetes and poor diabetes control shown by higher glycosylated haemoglobin levels. One third of those with diabetes had never seen an ophthalmologist and one third had never seen an optometrist. Less than half were having two-yearly eye exams from a general practitioner, an optometrist, or an ophthalmologist, as recommended by the National Health and Medical Research Council, NHMRC. Furthermore, two thirds of those who had retinopathy had not seen an ophthalmologist in two years.

Here was confirmation of another clear need for greatly improved eye examination rates for those with diabetes. Non-Indigenous people with diabetes need to have an eye exam once every two years. Indigenous people with diabetes need to have an eye exam every year. This was not arguable: the MVIP was 100 percent in line with diabetes experts and organisations. Here was more work to do, education in the vanguard.

We undertook field studies on ways to screen for eye problems in those with diabetes. In 1994 MUDO started a program with the Rumbalara Medical Service in Shepparton, Victoria using retinal photography to screen for diabetic retinopathy. Joycie Doyle, a local Yorta Yorta woman, was taught how to do the screening by MUDO staff, retinal specialist Alex Harper and health educator Jill Keeffe. This program was well accepted; Joycie was outstanding in performing this work. It showed that local Aboriginal Medical Services, AMS, and their staff could screen effectively for diabetic retinopathy. What was needed was the money for a camera, some space and the ongoing salary, training and support for the health workers.

Rumbalara was where I first met Justin Mohamed, a Gooreng Gooreng man from Queensland, who was managing the Rumbalara AMS. I worked with Justin in a number of his roles. He was the Chair of the National Aboriginal Community Controlled Health Organisation, NACCHO, served on the Vision 2020

Community consultation to develop the appropriate health promotion messages for promoting eye examinations for those with diabetes

Australia Board, was CEO of Reconciliation Australia, was Deputy Secretary of Aboriginal Justice in the Victorian Government and is now Australia's inaugural Ambassador for First Nations People. He made enormous contributions to Indigenous health in these roles.

After the 1997 release of the Review of Indigenous Eye Health I did for the Commonwealth government, the Victorian government gave one year's funding to train Aboriginal Health Workers in Victoria to carry out retinal screening. Working with Lisa Briggs and Jimmy Peters from the Victorian Aboriginal Community Controlled Health Organisation we trained 34 health workers from across Victoria. Lisa and Jimmy had one camera and they would travel with it to each AMS. However, people drifted off and this approach was not sustainable. To be successful and provide continuity a camera and a trained person needed to be funded and based in each AMS.

While working with Michael Wooldridge on the Review of Indigenous Eye Health, it occurred to me that to make retinal screening photography for diabetic retinopathy sustainable, we had to have a Medicare Item for it.

Medicare is the national health program that pays for the provision of health-care examinations and services. With a Medicare item number there would be government reimbursement each time someone with diabetes had retinal photos taken. As I understand it, Michael put the suggestion to the federal cabinet but it was rejected. This was my first attempt at trying to get this Medicare item number approved.

I tried again with Medicare in 2000. This time I understand that the Australian Medical Association did not think it was needed and Optometry Australia said optometrists could easily do all the screening that might be needed. Again, I failed.

I tried a third time in 2010 and prepared another lengthy submission. Then the complex format required for submissions was changed, so a new lengthy submission had to be prepared in the new format.

During this time colleagues at CERA had completed an NHMRC-funded trial of screening photography for diabetic retinopathy in pathology services. Patients would come in for this screening at the same time they came for their other pathology tests. The trial was successful and well received. It showed how effective diabetic retinopathy screening could be in a pathology sense. The pathology services were interested in adding this capability.

Finally, in 2017 a Medicare Item was approved for screening of Indigenous people with diabetes and another item for screening of non-Indigenous people. It had taken 20 years to achieve this important goal.

The Commonwealth provided 160 retinal cameras and

training for staff in each of the AMSs across the country. However, the Medicare administration decided not to approve these items for pathologists. Consequently, the uptake of screening within non-Indigenous practices was very slow. How many general practices could afford $10,000 or more to buy their own retinal cameras?

So far, this work had as much to do with diabetic eye care for non-Indigenous people as it did for Indigenous Australians. In 2008, when I started the Indigenous Eye Health Unit, IEHU, my focus was particularly on the needs of Indigenous people.

Our efforts to address diabetic eye disease in Indigenous Australians focussed on health promotion. We started a program 'Check Today, See Tomorrow'. Carol Wynne on our team worked closely with community groups in Ballarat, in regional Victoria; Morton Bay, an urban area in Queensland; and Looma, a remote community in Western Australia to develop the graphics, messages and videos for a comprehensive campaign promoting annual eye exams for those with diabetes. We also developed matching materials for clinical staff emphasising the need for the annual exams and the simple steps on how to do them. The educational materials all involve and include Indigenous people. We have also had the Melbourne Football players involved in the diabetes health promotion as well as in trachoma work.

The health promotion and educational materials, together with the provision of the retinal cameras and training have made a huge difference. The eye examination rates of Indigenous people with diabetes almost trebled, from less than 20 percent in 2012 to over 50 percent in 2023. However, we need to get 85 percent or more of those with diabetes screened regularly so treatment could be started and vision loss prevented. More recently some of the Aboriginal Medical Services have obtained newer OCT machines to detect the more subtle early changes of diabetic retinopathy.

Diabetes

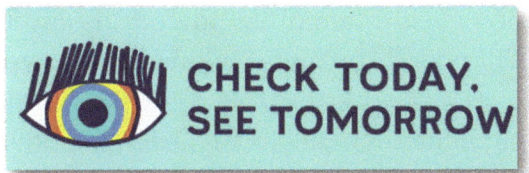

The Check Today, See Tomorrow logo

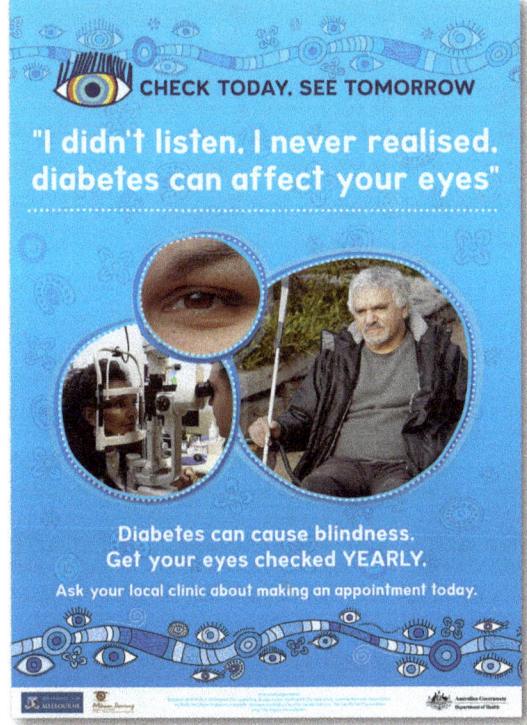

A community-designed diabetes health promotion poster

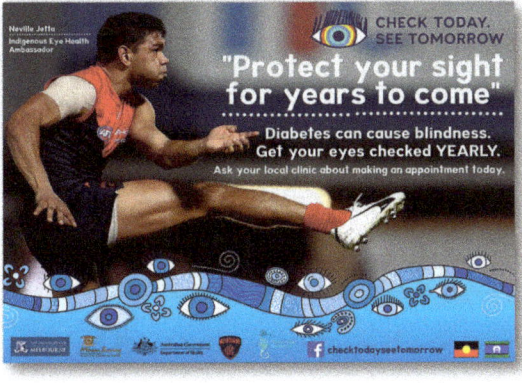

Nevill Jetta, Melbourne Football Club player promotion of eye exams for those with diabetes

Workers in Indigenous health are often powerfully motivated. Faye Clarke, a Muandik, Ngarrindjei, Gunditjmara and Wotjobaluk diabetes nurse and educator, told a 'Check Today, See Tomorrow' gathering in Parliament House, Canberra, how her 'dad got diabetes at about the age of 35. By the time he was 40, he had gangrene in his fingers and toes—and he was a plumber in Ballarat; it's cold here. I remember the pain he was in trying to do his work with fingers that couldn't move.' Her father died at 41. 'It was a big driver for me when I would see patients' results… and try and get them into the clinic and do as much as I could and as often as I could.' For her and many of her patients, the grief and loss and mental health problems stemming from the Stolen Generations complicates care.

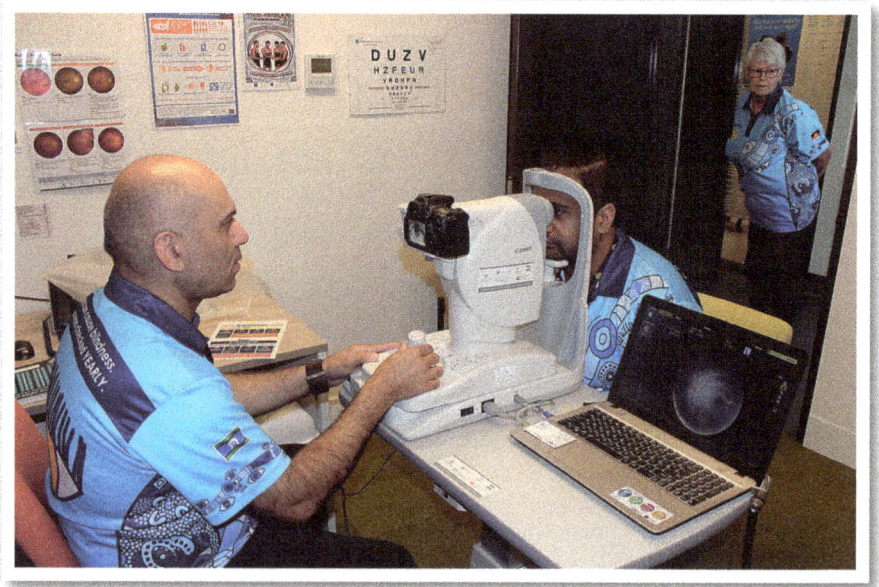

Aboriginal Health Worker with retinal camera to screen for diabetic retinopathy

Screening and detecting diabetic retinopathy is one thing, but those found to have retinopathy need to be referred and treated. This is where the regional coordinating groups play a key role. The groups need to establish their regional referral pathways

Diabetes

and processes, and to monitor their coverage rates. A coverage rate is measured as the proportion of those with diabetes who have had their eyes examined in the past year. People with mild retinopathy may need more regular eye exams by an optometrist or ophthalmologist, but those with more severe disease need ongoing ophthalmic care, usually with regular retinal injections or laser treatment.

People with diabetes form about three quarters of the Indigenous adults who need an eye exam each year. In addition to screening for diabetic retinopathy, they also may need new glasses or cataract surgery, and so referral pathways for glasses or surgery also need to be developed. These pathways would be the same for those with diabetes as for those who don't but who need glasses or surgery. So, the focus on diabetic eye care has wider ramifications for improving eye-care pathways for all Indigenous people.

Warren Snowdon, a Northern Territory MP, federal Minister for Indigenous Health from 2009 to 2013, was tremendously helpful and supportive of this work. Greg Hunt, federal Minister for Health and Aged Care from 2017 to 2022 was also a firm supporter. Both recognised the need to improve eye care for those with diabetes.

I had met Greg Hunt soon after he entered the Australian Parliament. He had worked for a while at McKinsey's, where he had met our daughter Kate. In 2015 Kate started up an IT company with CERA called Oculo. It grew as a cloud-based, patient-centred, internet platform and connected optometrists, ophthalmologists and general practitioners. They could seamlessly share not only notes and clinical information—a fax machine can do that—but also the optical imaging and other test data. This proved easy to use, effective and was widely taken up. In 2024 Oculo was bought out by the Finnish company Revenio that markets iCare products. Kate is now a vice-president of Revenio.

Opening Eyes

 CHECK TODAY. SEE TOMORROW

Diabetic Retinopathy Screening Card

Check for Red and White Signs*. Look at where they are located and how much of the retina is affected – does the retina look normal, abnormal or sight-threatening? *See other side

Normal

Vision
Presenting vision 6/12 or better in each eye

Retina
No signs of Diabetic Retinopathy

Routine eye examination
(Indigenous within 12 months,
Non-Indigenous within 2 years)

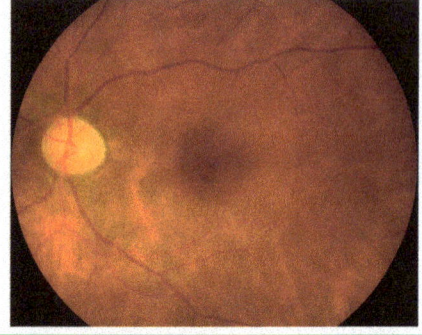

Abnormal

Vision
Presenting vision worse than 6/12 in either eye or

Retina
Unable to View Retina or
Diabetic Retinopathy showing any:

Red Signs
- Haemorrhages (h) in less than 4 quadrants
- Venous beading (v) in 1 quadrant*

White Signs
- Cotton wool spots (w)
- Hard exudates (e) more than 1 optic disc diameter from macula (as outlined with dots)

Refer to optometrist or ophthalmologist
(to be seen within 90 days)

Sight-threatening

Retina
Severe Diabetic Retinopathy or
Macular Oedema showing any:

Red Signs
- New blood vessels (n) on optic disc or elsewhere
- Venous beading (v) in 2 or more quadrants
- Haemorrhages (h) in all 4 quadrants
- Intra retinal microvascular abnormalities*
- Vitreous haemorrhage*

White Signs
- Hard exudates (e) within 1 optic disc diameter of macula

Refer urgently to the ophthalmologist
(to be seen within 30 days)

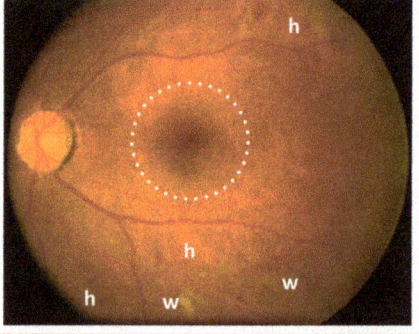

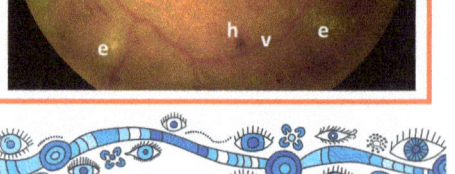

The diabetes retinopathy screen card we developed

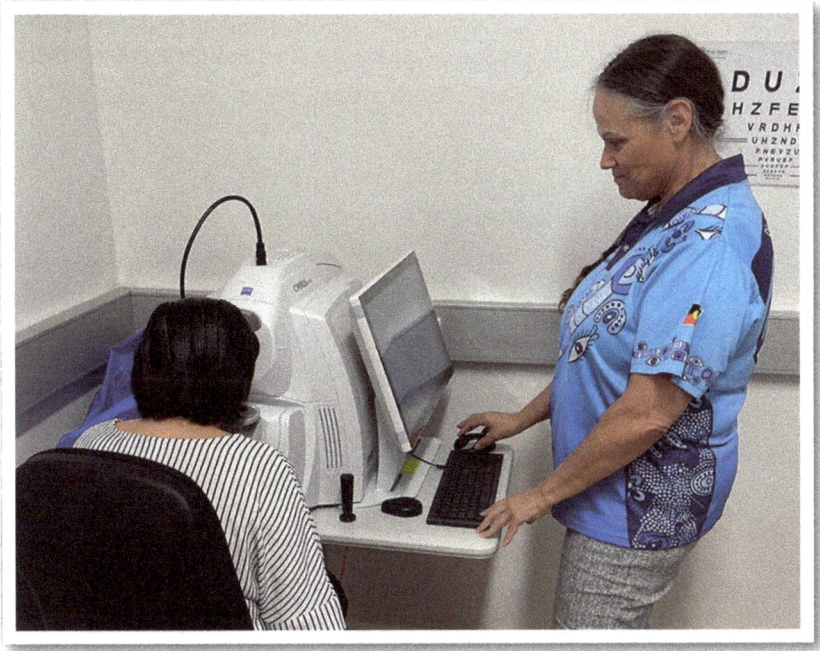

Aboriginal health worker Kerry Woods, with new OCT retinal screening laser to detect more subtle change in diabetic retinopathy

Oculo worked so well that in 2018 a joint initiative led by Diabetes Australia launched a new program, 'KeepSight'. All people with diabetes were actively encouraged to sign up to KeepSight. Those with diabetes and their primary doctors receive reminders when the next eye exam was due. The optometrist and ophthalmologist were linked together and all the relevant data are shared.

This reminder and the information and results from their exams were all linked so that each person and their optometrist and ophthalmologist was kept in the information loop. Now, about two thirds of the 1.3 million Australians with diabetes are signed into KeepSight as are most optometrists and ophthalmologists.

In 2023 the number of Indigenous people with diabetes who had an eye examination had increased nearly three times to 52 percent. Although this is very encouraging, more work is still needed to bring this up to a satisfactory level of above 85 percent, as it is for non-Indigenous Australians.

One way or another with the collection of data, the design of programs and health promotion, along with co-ordinated and persistent advocacy there have been many advances. There are improvements in the awareness of the need for eye screening in those with diabetes, new and better ways to perform this screening, government funding to enable this, and development of new and improved treatments to manage the damage diabetes causes in the eyes. This work has transformed the impact of diabetes as a cause of blindness.

KeepSight logo

14

Attacking Australia's Sandy Blight

Drugs? I'd prescribe water. If governments were to put water on, nobody would have trachoma!

Ida Mann, 1966

Following the NTEHP and the continuing work of Fred Hollows, funding was provided by the Commonwealth for the Australian states and territories to perform trachoma screening and treatment. However, these activities had not been reviewed for a long time. In 1996 I was asked by the federal Minister for Health, Michael Wooldridge, to undertake a review of eye health in Aboriginal and Torres Strait Islander people. I looked at all aspects of eye care for Indigenous people, including trachoma.

Overall, the rates of trachoma had fallen. However, in one community in the Pilbara region in Western Australia I was astonished and distressed to see that the high rate of trachoma I had found in 1977 in that community had not changed in 20 years. It was still over 70 percent!

I made recommendations. Although all were strongly endorsed, at best most were only implemented incompletely. One recommendation was for the provision of azithromycin for the treatment of people with trachoma. Initially, it was approved for adults, but the provision of the suspension for children was overlooked. It took a good deal of further work with the Therapeutic Goods Administration to get the children's suspension made available.

In early 1995 we had started an open study of azithromycin treatment with Andrew Lamming in Central Australia. Andrew was a medical graduate from Queensland who was doing a master's degree at the University of Sydney but asked to work with me on a study on trachoma. He went on to train in ophthalmology. (Later, he worked in some different positions including for a while at the World Bank. In 2004 he became a member of the Australian parliament, winning the seat of Bowman—by 64 votes!) For his master's degree Andrew studied trachoma in Aboriginal children aged from 6 months to 15 years in one community. The baseline trachoma prevalence rate was 44 percent and fell to 22 percent six to eight months after azithromycin treatment. Without any other interventions, at 12 months the prevalence for trachoma had bounced back, to 31 percent. We had not included any emphasis on facial cleanliness in this study, but it showed that even this exciting new one-off oral antibiotic on its own was not sufficient to achieve the ultimate goal: the elimination of trachoma. Andrew Lamming's work needed to be extended to include the full implementation of the SAFE Strategy (see pages 363-367).

Van Lansingh undertook a study in the Anangu Pitjantjatjara Yankunytjatjara area, or APY Lands in far north-west South Australia. Van was a young Mexican ophthalmologist who had worked for a year or two as a missionary ophthalmologist in the highlands of Papua New Guinea. He was doing a PhD with me. (Van later provided great leadership for IAPB and Vision2020 in Latin America.)

With support from Christoffel-Blindenmission and working with the Health Habitat organisation, Van started a controlled trial in two remote communities in the APY Lands. In both we screened and provided surgery for trichiasis, distributed mass administration of azithromycin, and promoted facial cleanliness.

To help promote facial cleanliness we had a song, a video and posters made that used a beautiful painting we had specifically commissioned from Jennifer Summerfield, an outstanding local artist. The original painting hangs in the office of the Nganampa Health Council. Later and with permission, I used it for the cover of my book on trachoma.

In the first community. Van implemented the first three components of the SAFE Strategy, Surgery, Antibiotic and Facial Cleanliness. In the other community he implemented them all

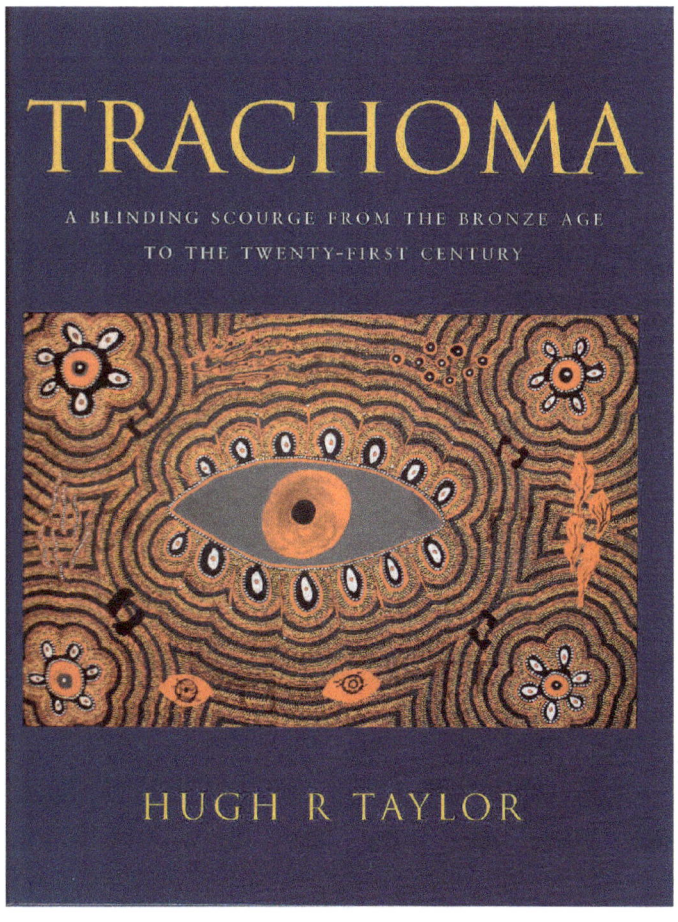

The cover of my book, *Trachoma*, with the work by Jennifer Summerfield painted to support Van Lansingh's project in the APY Lands

including E, Environmental improvement. We went all out with E. A bit over $1.5 million was spent on repairs and maintenance in all the houses, improvements to water supply and sewerage, road repairs and dust control. However, after one year, the decrease in trachoma was the same in each community. All that extra effort on the Environment, although of unquestionable benefit to the community, had not further reduced an illness that makes people blind. This showed we do not need to spend millions of dollars in each community to get rid of trachoma. We need clean faces.

Heathcote Wright, a young medical graduate doing a PhD with us, undertook a study to look at the impact that installing a swimming pool has on trachoma. At that time, Fiona Stanley and her group from the Telethon Institute in Perth had reported the decrease in the middle-ear infection 'otitis media', and other childhood infections in a community in the Kimberley after a swimming pool had been built. Heathcote identified three communities he could study where swimming pools were to be built. Could a swimming pool knock out trachoma?

Before he could start his study, one community had built their pool after receiving a private donation. The second community was devastated by a cyclone: repairs and reconstruction meant that a pool was out of the question at that time. That left one community Heathcote could study, Yuendumu. He did all the baseline trachoma grading, prepared health promotion material with the community. Then, sat and waited years for the promised pool. Community members trained as lifeguards, but still no pool. In the end, his PhD thesis was essentially about the barriers to trachoma interventions. Eventually a pool was built, but Heathcote had moved on. (Later, Heathcote provided eye care to Aboriginal people and others in outer Melbourne.)

With another ophthalmology registrar, Anu Mathew, Heathcote looked at the impact of installing swimming pools in two communities in south-western South Australia. The rates of

Attacking Australia's Sandy Blight

Above: Children in front of the poster Heathcote developed for when the pool would come to Yuendumu

Below: Heathcote Wright examining children in Yuendumu, NT

trachoma in young children were low at 7 to 8 percent and did not change over 12 months after the pools were installed. The 'No school, no pool' policy may have affected pool usage, although the communities reported very positively about the other benefits the pool brought, such as exercise and recreation—as well as improved school attendance!

Despite my 1997 review of Indigenous eye health for the Commonwealth, little seemed to be happening with work on trachoma. Michael Wooldridge had retired, and Tony Abbott was the new health minister. With further advocacy, I was finally able to convince him to do something concrete about trachoma. In 1995 he committed funds to the jurisdictions to do trachoma screening and treatment distribution, and funds to set up the National Trachoma Reporting and Surveillance Unit, NTSRU.

I ran the NTSRU at the Centre for Eye Research Australia and the Melbourne School of Population Health until 2009, when the contract went to the Kirby Institute in the University of New

Book launch of Trachoma book with Jilpia Jones

South Wales. The NTRSU has been, and is, an important part of the process. It provides the annual data on the trachoma rates in the endemic areas, the screening and treatment coverage rates, and the numbers of trichiasis surgeries. The NTSRU provides the essential data so we know where trachoma is endemic and can track the progress to elimination.

I felt pleased with myself in September 2006 when I returned to Melbourne after my sabbatical in England. I had been away for four months and had finished writing my book, *Trachoma: a blinding scourge from the Bronze Age to the Twenty-First century*. I caught up with what was happening in CERA and at the Eye and Ear. But what to do about trachoma in Australia?

Of course, trachoma had been a significant problem in Australia since white settlement, as it had been in most developed and developing countries. In Australia it was often called 'Sandy Blight'. It had disappeared from mainstream Australia by the 1930s but was still an unresolved problem in the outback Indigenous communities.

In England I'd meet Helen Lee and Claude Michel from the Department of Haematology at Cambridge University, and we'd talked about trachoma. They had developed a rapid test suitable for point-of-care testing for chlamydia. A point-of-care test means one could test whether chlamydia was present or not on the spot, without having to send a swab to the laboratory and wait for the result to come back. This could be a great advantage—if it worked well.

We set up a study led by Katrina Roper in the Katherine region in the Northern Territory. Katrina was working as a field epidemiologist at the Centre for Disease Control in Darwin. (Subsequently, she worked with WHO, the Commonwealth Health Department, and at the Australian National University.) We assessed the new point-of-care test, and compared it with the standard Polymerase Chain Reaction, PCR, the laboratory test

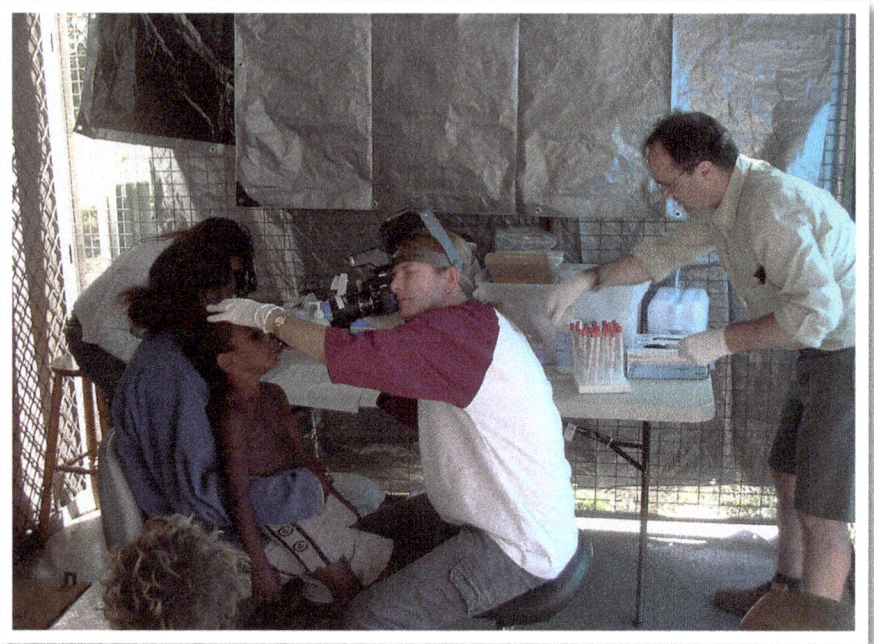

Katrina Roper and Claude Michel working in the Katherine study

for chlamydia and the clinical grading of trachoma. We studied people of all ages in five Aboriginal communities, examined 1316 or 85 percent of the residents. We did not assess facial cleanliness.

We found 20 percent of the children under 10 years had trachoma. As defined by the WHO grading, they had TF, or active trachoma. We used a finer grading system for trachoma that also included the WHO definitions, and we took photos for later grading. The highest rates of trachoma were seen in children aged 2 to 4. However, slightly more children under 10 years, 124 of them, had definite trachoma that was less severe than the WHO grade of TF. An additional 108 children had more advanced trachoma and met the WHO definition of TF.

Those with milder trachoma would have been missed using the standard WHO trachoma-grading protocol. The Australian trachoma guidelines called for the screening of school-aged children, aged 5 to 9 years, although WHO specified the age range as 1 to 9 years. Based on experience from the Kimberly, it was decided it was easier and more expedient just to screen the children at school. This meant, by following the Australian guidelines, many of the younger children with trachoma and those with milder trachoma would have been missed.

Unfortunately, the point-of-care test did not detect chlamydial infection as well as we hoped and expected. The PCR test turned up interesting results. It showed that 18 percent of those with active trachoma, TF, were PCR positive for chlamydia, but 52 percent of the positive PCR tests were from people with mild trachoma, not advanced enough to be graded as TF.

This showed that the threshold set by the WHO grade of TF missed many milder cases, some of which would be PCR positive with demonstrable infection. To be graded TF the person infected needed at least five follicles that were 0.5 mm in diameter. Those with four large follicles or many small follicles are not graded TF. The threshold was set to identify communities at risk of blinding trachoma, not for the diagnosis of individuals.

These outcomes showed the simplicity of using TF rates, or PCR positive rates, as indicators of the presence and distribution of trachoma in a community. TF from the Simplified Grading is a good simple tool for public-health work and for the effort to eliminate trachoma as a public health problem, but it is too simple for more detailed studies of the disease. WHO set one of the thresholds for 'the elimination of blinding trachoma as a public health problem' as having a rate for TF of less than 5 percent of children. At that lesser level of active trachoma, it is believed that very few—if any—will have severe enough infection and inflammation for long enough to develop blindness. The limitations of the Simplified Grading are particularly relevant for studies that use hypersensitive laboratory tests like PCR or antibody testing.

In the review of Eye Health in Aboriginal and Torres Strait

communities I made in 1996–97, I recommended state-based teams monitor and treat trachoma using the WHO SAFE Strategy and a body to collect their data and make annual reports.

The follow-up review of Indigenous eye health was conducted in 2002–03 to assess the implementation and make recommendations about further directions for the program. Not a lot had improved, despite the improved funding for the state-based teams and setting up the NTSRU. The rates were not coming down. There were some screening and limited antibiotic distribution, but the concentrated efforts that were required to reduce trachoma, including the promotion of facial cleanliness, were not being followed.

Barry Jones was a member of the Advisory Board for the Indigenous Eye Health Unit, IEHU, and Chair of Vision 2020 Australia. I had heard of Barry from childhood, listening to him on the radio winning quiz show after quiz show. Barry is a most amazing Australian, a former federal minister for science and a polymath; writer, teacher, politician, talkback-radio pioneer, arts advocate, social activist, and former member of the Executive Board of the United Nations Education, Scientific and Cultural Organization, UNESCO. He is a man with enormous social conscience. I met him when he came to see me about his eye problem. What a chance that encounter was!

In late 2007, I talked with Barry about the lack of progress we were making on trachoma in Australia, the need for it to be taken seriously and to properly resource fighting it. Australia had a new Labor government with Kevin Rudd as prime minister. Barry said he would arrange for us to meet him to talk about the lack of progress and the need to address trachoma actively. Barry was also the Chair of the Port Arthur Historic Site Management Committee. In August 2008 Prime Minister Rudd was to open a renovated convict prison cell block at Port Arthur, Tasmania. Barry thought the opening would be a fine time to talk about trachoma with the prime minister. I flew down with Barry and

Meeting at Port Arthur with Kevin Rudd and Barry Jones

went with him to Port Arthur. After the official proceedings, we walked around Port Arthur in wild weather. Barry pulled the prime minister aside. Under an umbrella sheltering us from the wind and the cold rain on an exposed promontory in south-eastern Tasmania, I explained in three or four freezing minutes why trachoma—'sandy blight'—was still a problem in the hot, dry communities in the Outback, and what we had to do about it. I felt Sandy Blight Junction on the Gunbarrel Highway 500 km west of Alice would have been a better red-dirt venue. Warmer too. Nevertheless, Kevin Rudd was trapped and listened.

For this meeting I had prepared a 20-page booklet, 'Eliminating Blinding Trachoma' that set out our arguments and our requests. I gave this to Kevin Rudd. The page of which I am particularly proud listed the Eight False Excuses for Not Controlling Trachoma:

> Trachoma is not a problem
> Trachoma does not blind Indigenous Australians
> We do not know enough about the severity and distribution of trachoma (Or: We need more information before we can act)
> Trachoma is not a priority because it does not kill people
> Trachoma control measures will not work
> Trachoma control is not cost-effective
> Trachoma will not be eliminated until Aboriginal housing is improved
> Trachoma control is not possible in Aboriginal communities because people move too much

These misconceptions were each given a short rebuff to head off policy makers who did not want to pursue this. For example, the rebuff for 'Trachoma does not kill people':

> The assumption that trachoma and vision loss do not affect mortality is not true. The presence of trichiasis alone increases mortality sevenfold and increases the risk of blindness 19-fold. The presence of blindness increases mortality between two and four times and in trachoma-endemic areas is associated with an 18 year decrease in life expectancy for people over the age of 40... trachoma can clearly be eliminated, it is a discrete, achievable goal.

This approach designed to combat ministerial pushback—first, block the easy exits—arose from when I worked with WHO in Pakistan and presented my report on eye-health services to the minister for health (see page 1-3), and dumbfounded me with 'Thank you, but I am really more concerned with maternal and child health.' Next time, I swore, I would be better prepared. Since then, at other times when presenting to policy makers, I have followed this approach, used a variety of solid defences and worked out how to be ahead of the game. So, when a put-down came, one could say, 'Yes, some may think that, but look at the second point on page 7.' This approach has been useful in advocating for the broader work on improving eye health for Indigenous Australians. Predictable points like 'Blindness doesn't kill you,' or 'You can't do anything about it anyway' will get raised. Prepared responses can refocus people's attention and move people to act.

That Australia was the only developed nation on Earth still with a trachoma problem was a good goad; that eliminating trachoma was, relatively, shovel-ready, low-hanging fruit, a do-able thing et cetera made it a goal attractive to politicians and others.

Six months later, Kevin Rudd made the commitment in parliament for Australia to Eliminate Trachoma by 2020. This was in line with the long-standing WHO goal Australia had already signed up to. He provided $16 million to start the elimination program.

At CERA we continued the work on trachoma health promotion. In 2005 I had received the Mectizan Award from Merck & Co. for the studies I had done on ivermectin for the treatment of onchocerciasis. This was a great honour, particularly as so many others worked on the provision and distribution of ivermectin.

When MSD, as Merck is known in Australia, heard about this award, they invited me to Sydney to talk about the work we were doing. After I covered the work on oncho and ivermectin, I talked about trachoma and Indigenous eye health in Australia. Without my making a request or even expecting anything, they offered funds to develop health-promotion material to encourage Indigenous children to look after their eyes and keep their faces clean. Recognition for the work on river blindness in rainforests had led to funding for work on sandy blight in an arid land.

At CERA Jill Keeffe and I talked with graphic artist Lilly McDonnell. Using MSD funding she developed a poster that listed six things we defined that children need to do to protect their eyes and ensure good vision. These were the need for clean faces, sun protection, safety when playing and to get their eyes checked regularly. We developed this poster when we were working in the Katherine region on the trachoma project that was looking at the correlation of infection and clinical disease. As we were working with the Katherine West Health Board, KWHB, they arranged for their community groups to help us develop the poster. Their suggestion was to use a big goanna as a logo. The posters promoted good general eye health for children and were widely distributed.

In 2009 we went back to the KWHB to develop some more specific health-promotion materials that focused on trachoma and promoted the importance of clean faces. WHO had a good graphic which outlined the SAFE strategy for trachoma control:

But the WHO graphics were very Africa-orientated. We needed strong, sustained community support to make eyes healthy, to make the campaign work. We needed to rework the WHO message to put it in an Australian context. We needed to be sure the materials were culturally acceptable and clearly understood in the communities. We needed *input* from the communities, and we needed their ownership, from the start line in Katherine West, and then onwards. By then, the Melbourne partner in this national cooperative push was the Indigenous Eye Health Unit, the IEHU.

Attacking Australia's Sandy Blight

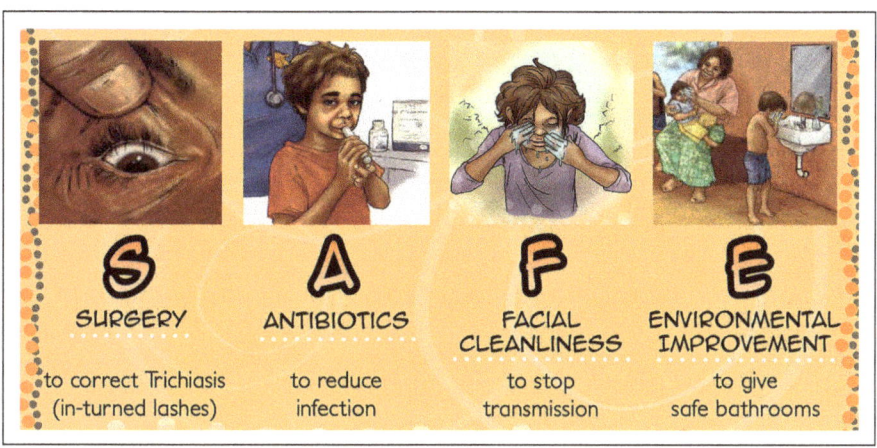

Above: The Australian version of the SAFE Strategy for trachoma control

Left: A poster with Milpa promoting Clean faces, Strong Eyes

At the end of 2010 Fiona Lange had joined us. The trachoma health promotion work progressed rapidly. She worked with community elders in several KWHB communities to develop educational materials. Also, Joobin Houshmand, a recent medical graduate, and Meg Torpey, a Dharug/Dharawal woman and member of the IEHU, spent a lot of time 'sitting in the dirt' working on draft materials and talking about health promotion with members of the KWHB and community members. They discussed in detail the right way to give culturally safe and appropriate messages and how best to present and illustrate these. They then gave feedback to Lilly McDonnell who reworked the graphics. Joobin and Meg then returned to the community members to fine tune the materials. The community came up with 'Clean faces, strong eyes', the slogan that has appeared on all the trachoma materials we have developed in the 15 years since and counting!

Throughout this development work in Katherine, Andrew Bell and David Lines at KWHB gave tremendous support. There were also visits to communities in Central Australia with support from Cate Coffey, the head of the Northern Territory Trachoma program based in Alice Springs. When the elders in Yuendumu saw this material, they gave us the name 'Milpa' ('eyes' in Walpiri) for the trachoma goanna, and the goanna has been called Milpa ever since.

Emma Stanford, Fiona Lange and Josie Atkins, a Gumbaynggirr woman, put together a 'Trachoma Resource Book'. This gave the background information on trachoma and described with appropriate language and illustrations its screening and grading, and the SAFE strategy. This was to give the jurisdictional and regional trachoma teams more information to help with their work. An online grading course and a more detailed online trachoma course were also developed.

With all the community feedback, a broad set of health promotion material was developed, all with the Milpa logo on them.

They included posters, stickers, flip charts, wrist bands, stick-on tattoos, T-shirts and mirrors, and were distributed at school and sports events. Artists from Melbourne would travel to communities and work with local artists and community members to paint murals with Milpa promoting clean faces. Radio and TV community service announcements

Right: Fiona Lange working with young children

Below: A mural in Mutitjulu painted with the engagement of community members with Milpa and its message

Opening Eyes

about 'Clean faces, strong eyes' appeared regularly. There are nowadays 15 Milpa mascot suits distributed across the country for actors to don at events. The Milpa mascot appears at a range of community events and on TV. Some of this health promotion work received government funding, but much of it has been supported by private donors and foundations.

Milpa does not speak, but we had others who could do that very well. Milpa started appearing on TV and in community health-promotion events. Milpa also became a guest on *Yamba's Playtime*, a children's program a bit like an Indigenous *Sesame Street*. It was run by Impaja Television, the Indigenous TV station based in Alice Springs. 'Yamaba' was a honey ant who was supported by 'Jacinta', a local First Nations flesh-and-blood woman, Jacinta Nampijinpa Price. Milpa would join Yamaba, and Yamaba would sing, 'I have a friend called Milpa the goanna and Milpa has a message for you—"Clean faces, strong eyes".' We

Yamaba, Milpa and Jacinta working in a community school

organised regular road trips to communities to hold health-promotion days with Jacinta, Yamba and Milpa.

Later, Impaja stopped producing *Yamba's Playtime*, but Jacinta continued to help us via media with community events. Later, Jacinta Nampijinpa Price was elected to the local government of Alice Springs Council, and she left as ex-deputy mayor. She's a noted country-and-western singer-songwriter with an Australian twist; the launch of her album *Dry River* on the banks of the River Todd in Alice was an achingly beautiful performance. Her voice kisses the words and touches the sky.

Jacinta became a federal senator for the Northen Territory. She became the shadow minister for Indigenous Australians. She was of great help to us, and I am in her debt. But Jacinta played a prominent role in the 'Vote No' campaign in opposition to the referendum to change the constitution to guarantee Indigenous Australians a Voice to parliament. Most Indigenous people did not support her or her viewpoint. This was a side to her I had not recognised when we worked together. I find it hugely disappointing to us and our history. However, having read her autobiography I truly respect her concerns about having real changes made on the ground, at the community level, to address appalling issues such as domestic violence and to provide meaningful employment.

When I was working in various medical service clinics up North and in Central Australia there were health posters everywhere. Public health messages covering smoking, diet, diabetes, vaccination and so forth were always prominent. The best posters always seemed to showcase an Indigenous football player such as Nicky Winmar or Adam Goodes.

What we needed, I thought, was a poster about trachoma with a football player. Of course, I thought that had to be a Melbourne player as I had l been a supporter of the Melbourne Football Club, the Mighty Demons, since I was a small child. As

I grew up, Melbourne was an exciting team to support. They played in each grand final between 1954 and 1964, and they won six of them. Then, the long drought until they won the grand final in 2021.

I wrote to the club asking if they would be interested in helping promote the work on trachoma but got no answer. I spoke to a friend, a strong Melbourne club supporter, who suggested giving it another try, so I wrote again. This time I received an invitation to meet and discuss the idea, then another one, to explain the idea to the board. The board supported the idea and agreed to have players made available to make community-service announcements for radio and TV and help us with posters. They chose their two leading Indigenous players for this: Aaron Davey and Liam Jurrah.

However, a greater surprise was in store. Melbourne was to start playing one or two matches a year in the Northern

Melbourne football players Liam Jarrah and Aaron Jetta, and me

Territory, one in Alice Springs and usually another in Darwin. A day or two before the Alice game, the board was happy for some players and staff to travel to a community to hold an event, a football clinic to teach children how to kick and mark the ball, and to engage with them about how to wash their faces. That first clinic, in 2010, was particularly exciting because it was held at Yuendumu, Liam Jurrah's home community. His parents and family were excited to welcome us. The whole community came out to watch the children and players work together. This visit was a very big deal as it was led by the club president and former player, Jimmy Steins, with the players, coaching staff

Milpa and the Melbourne football mascot before a match in Alice Springs

and supporter group members. Then when they played their match in Alice Springs three days later, Milpa did the rounds of the football oval.

Since then, except during the COVID lockdowns, clinics have

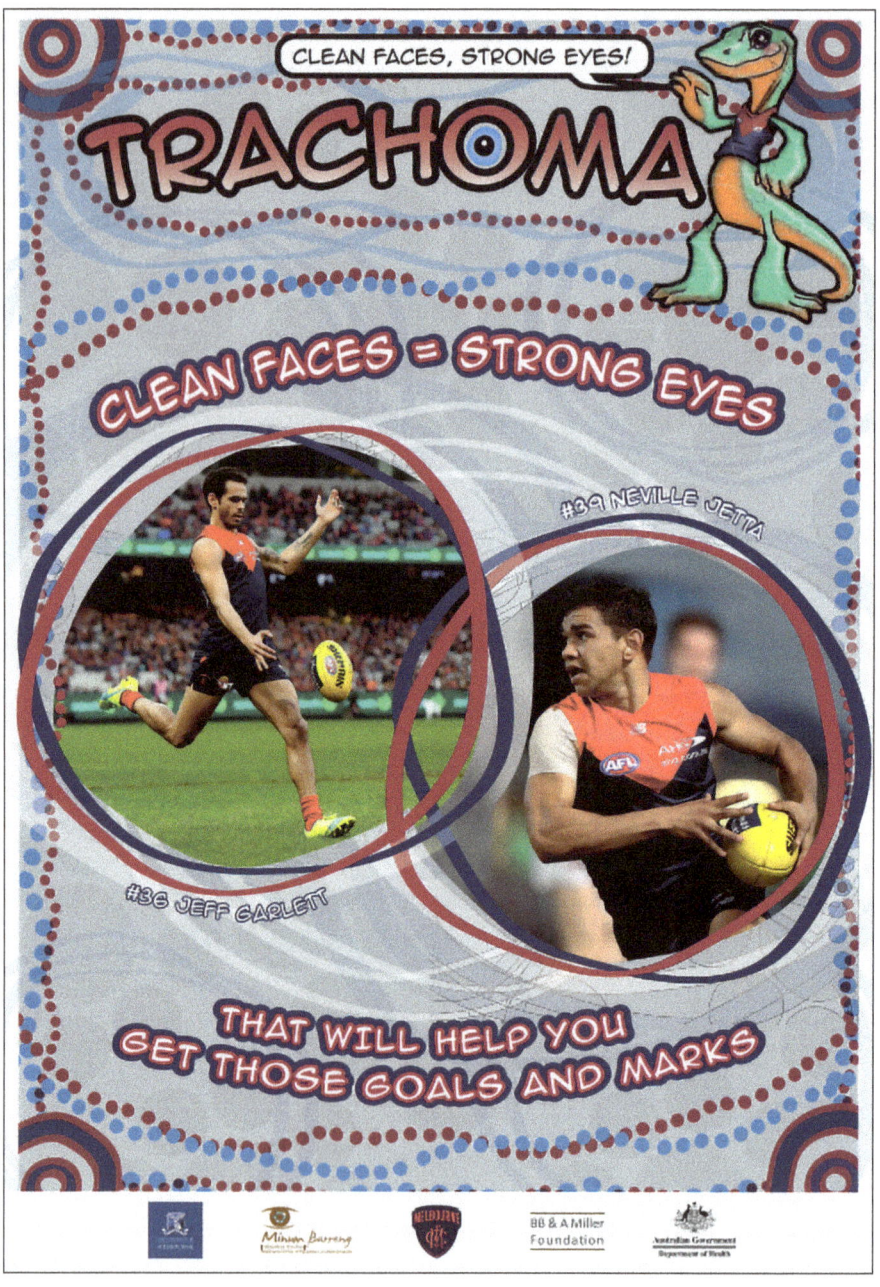

Melbourne Football Club trachoma poster

been held every year in various communities. Each year some of the Indigenous players make new health promotional videos and posters for us as well.

In Santa Teresa, an Aboriginal community in the MacDonnell Ranges, 85 km south-east of Darwin, the Ltyentye Apurte Football Club had a red-dirt football field, one that teachers were reluctant to let children play on because of the high dust levels. Suzie Lowe, community leader there in communication with the Melbourne club, added a cheeky after-thought to an email, 'Well, you could grass our oval', and got 'Leave it with us' in reply. Now the community has become 'The MCG of the

Some of the trachoma team, Fiona Lange, me, Georgina Phillips and Emma Stanford with one of our vehicles

Nick Wilson, Walter Bathern and Lesley Martin promoting trachoma and diabetes messages and materials

Desert'. Turf covers the whole playing area. Goalposts, once used in a MCG grand final, stand tall. And the message 'Clean faces, strong eyes' is hard to miss.

The IEHU trachoma team has been led by Emma Stanford and Fiona Lange. Over 15 years we have had a diligent and successful team of people working with us. Currently, Lesley Martin, an Arrernte woman, is based in Alice Springs. Until recently Walter Bathern, an Arrernte/Luritja man, was also in Alice Springs and Nick Wilson, a Ngarrindjeri man, worked with us from Darwin. Our work has placed a major focus on promoting facial cleanliness.

Milpa's messages have been broadened to include nose blowing, hand and face washing, showering, brushing teeth, and not sharing towels. I kept saying, 'You can wash your hands without washing your face, but you cannot wash your face without washing your hands.' The line caught on, and was repeated over and over again. The 'Six Steps to Stop Germs' will not only impact trachoma, but other childhood infections. As these include middle-ear, respiratory, gastrointestinal and skin infections, infections that can and have led to rheumatic fever and chronic kidney failure, the spin-off health advantages of our trachoma suppression measures have become obvious.

We have worked with education departments to make curriculum changes to include facial cleanliness and activities. However, during our fieldwork, we noted the children did not realise when their faces were dirty and they lacked soap to help wash them.

We approached Wesfarmers, then the owners of Coles supermarkets and Bunnings hardware stores, and asked for supplies to make hygiene packs, soap from Coles and mirrors from Bunnings. We were delighted when Coles donated thousands of hygiene bags and packs that contained soap, shampoo, detergent, toilet cleaner and other cleaning products. Bunnings' donated

The Six Steps to Stop Germs poster

mirrors, with Milpa and 'Clean faces, strong eyes' etched on them. These were distributed during health promotion clinics, and placed in schools, stores, clinics and houses.

I was invited to give a talk on our work on trachoma to one of the Rotary Club of Melbourne's regular meetings. Following that, they showed great interest: what could Rotary do to help?

First, they put us in touch with a charity called Soap Aid. Rotarians collect unused soap from hotels and motels. We have all used a new small bar of soap for the shower in the morning after the one night we stayed. Instead throwing these out, proprietors and staff would save them for Soap Aid. It collected them and took bulk lots to a soap factory to be reprocessed into new, large bars of soap. Initially, the soap was sent to charities in India, but Soap Aid was happy to send some to Aboriginal communities as part of the trachoma work. After discussion, we had Milpa's shape pressed into the reprocessed bars. At the time of writing, something like a million bars of soap have been distributed to remote communities, particularly in Western Australia.

Melbourne Rotary, led by Peter Rogers, wanted to do more. Peter was someone I had met from time to time since my childhood. His father, Hugh Rogers, was a close life-long friend of my

Recycled Soap Aid soap with Milpa imprinted for free distribution to Indigenous communities

One of the Melbourne Rotary interactive trailers in use in the Katherine region

father, and it has been speculated that I was named 'Hugh' after him. Peter and Rotary raised funds to build three interactive water trailers and worked with engineering students at Monash University to design then.

Often, there is no access to running water at football ovals or rodeos or other outside community recreation areas where trachoma and hygiene education takes place. Many communities don't have public amenities such as toilets, shower blocks, laundries or wash troughs.

These large bright trailers display the well known and loved Milpa, 'the Trachoma Goanna', have interactive water and sound games that provide fun and encourage play while face washing. At the same time the sound system plays trachoma songs, many in language from remote communities. They also provide water for drinking and washing at community events. Children enthusiastically play games with the various buttons on the trailers and use watery showers to wash their face and hands. These trailers are incorporated into health promotion events in remote communities and are a big hit.

Australian Rotary was coming up to its Centennial Year in 2021 and they made 'End Trachoma' a centenary project. Led by Robert McGuirk and initially with help from Lien Trinh, they have supported multiple trachoma programs across the country that have included water tanks, mirrors, soap and community events.

More work needs to be done to improve facial cleanliness, particularly in younger children. In the regions where trachoma has been eliminated some 90 percent of children in the age-ranges of 1 to 4, 5 to 9 and 10 to 15, have clean faces.

However, in regions where trachoma can still be found, only 30 percent of the 1-to 4-year-olds, 60 percent of those 5 to 9, and 90 percent of those 10 to 15 have a clean face. Here, all these children live in the same community and in the same houses, and share the same bedrooms, bathrooms and washing facilities but there is a wide variation in how the children use them as they grow up.

The difference in the frequency of clean faces is behavioural. A study we did with Ninti One, an Indigenous research group based in Alice Springs, looked at cultural factors that influenced children's hygiene. It showed the importance of factors that particularly affect younger mothers with young children and their approach to keeping their children's faces clean.

Although our emphasis had been on the 'software', one has to have the appropriate 'hardware' in place too. There is an imperative to have safe and functional bathrooms and washing facilities. Most Aboriginal people in the outback communities live in rental housing. They are forbidden to do any repairs or maintenance. If they make the repairs themselves, they are likely to be evicted!

When something stops working, they are supposed to report the fact and wait, sometimes for three to six months, for a registered tradesperson to come and do the repair. Usually, the tradespeople come from outside the community, sometimes from out-of-state. A lot of occupants do not bother to report faults because 'Nothing ever gets done about them'. When enough things stop working, people move out of one defective house and into another. This causes and exacerbates overcrowding with two families now squeezing into the next poorly maintained house. Overcrowding only makes the demand on facilities worse and the facilities more likely to fail. We were told that almost 90 percent of the problems only need a handyman to fix them. Only 10 to 15 percent need a tradesperson.

Australian governments make statements about Aboriginal housing but have not addressed these issues successfully. They have done little to address the issues around the required 'prompt repair and planned maintenance'.

The Western Australia government has made changes. After some further training, environmental health officers can go into houses to make repairs. We have been pushing for some time for the other jurisdictions to start similar programs with local, community-based house maintenance officers who could do these simple, handyman repairs in a timely manner.

Each year 'The Australian Surveillance Trachoma Report' is released to monitor the progress being made with the elimination of trachoma. The 2023 report shows that trachoma has been eliminated from nine of the 13 regions where trachoma had been a problem. South Australia has had no children with trachoma for the last two years. When reporting started in 2007 there were 252 communities thought to be at risk; by 2023 there were only 67. Only 62 communities had any children with TF. There were nine communities considered 'hot spot' communities, with over 20 percent of children having trachoma. Some of these statistics can be misleading as some communities are quite small, with say two children out of eight or 10 having TF. This gives a rate of trachoma of 20 percent or more, even when only a couple of children are affected. Again in 2023, only 74 children aged between 5 and 9 years still had trachoma, or an overall trachoma prevalence of 1.8 percent. Overall, the jurisdictional trachoma teams have done a wonderful job. A mere 9 adults (over 15 years old for survey purpose) had trichiasis, a rate of 0.11 percent. To maintain these improvements continuing support for local health work must continue.

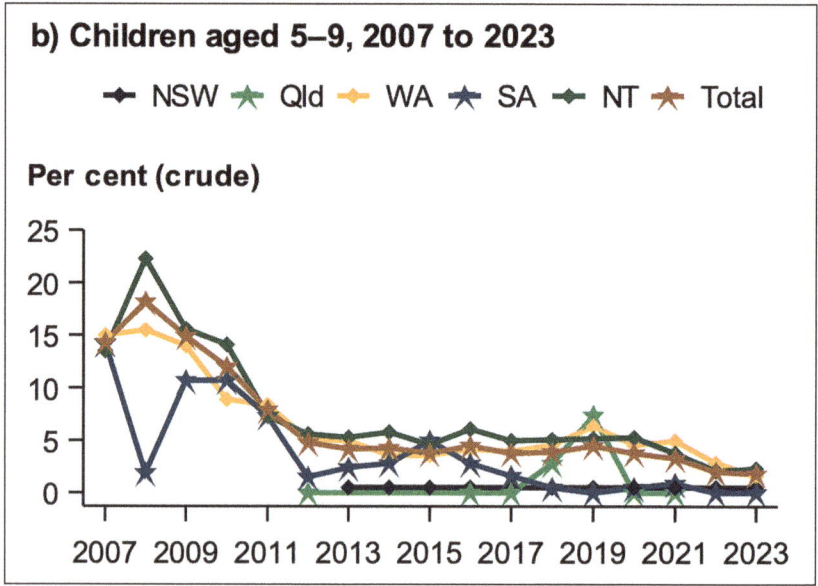

A graph showing the marked decrease in prevalence of trachoma in Aboriginal children (5 to 9 years) in each jurisdiction over time

The WHO criteria for the 'Elimination of trachoma as a public health problem' are to have active trachoma (TF) rates of less than 5 percent in children 1 to 9 years and trichiasis rates of less than 0.2 percent in those 15 years and older. They also require a plan for ongoing surveillance.

The government has made the commitment for Australia to

meet the WHO target of the elimination of trachoma as a public health problem. For Australia, as a high-income country, it was decided early on that we should try to 'eliminate' trachoma from 'all communities', later changed to the 'elimination' in 'all regions'.

I am always embarrassed at the various international trachoma meetings that Australia is the only developed nation to still have the problem. People working on trachoma in Africa and elsewhere cannot believe this is the case.

Although Australia has clearly missed the initial target of 2020, in part because of COVID-19, progress is looking promising. In 2025 Australia is preparing a dossier to send to WHO for approval and confirmation that—at last—Australia has eliminated blinding trachoma as a public health problem.

Me, Geoff Ford, Dave James and John Pilkington at Sandy Blight Junction with the sign showing the way to Docker River

Progress and promise gave time for a personal odyssey of sorts. In May 2017 John and Cara Pilkington, Geoff and Marg Ford, Dave and Glenda James, and Liz and I retraced some of the steps the four 'boys' had made as university students in 1967, the adventure that saw us bogged in the Petermann Ranges for over a week. Instead of starting from Broome as we had then, we met in Alice Springs. Pilks and Geoff were well set up with their own vehicles. Dave and I rented 4-wheel drive vehicles in Alice. Our wives had not seen much of the country so we drove slowly down to Docker River. A community, Kaltukatjara, had been built there. We camped as close to where we had been bogged as we could for two days.

Next, we drove up the Sandy Blight Junction Road to the actual junction, a real trachoma landmark. Then we drove slowly back to Alice enjoying the country, slow time and reviving shared memories.

We revisited Lasseter's Cave, where the prospector Lewis Lasseter rested in 1931 before he died as he tried to walk back having run out of food. He reported he had found a rich gold deposit on a previous exploration, gold he was trying to relocate at the time of his death. Lasseter's Reef has never been found and has assumed mythical proportions. It is territory that inspires big dreams.

15

Today

> An emeritus professor just keeps working.
> They just don't get paid any more.
> Old saying among senior academics

At the end of 2022 I retired from the Indigenous Eye Health Unit. Mitchell Anjou took over as director. I had fewer responsibilities but ends to tie up, a book to write and plenty to do.

After our mother's death my sister Janet and I took over the old family property in Olinda in the Dandenongs. In 2016 Liz and I bought out Janet. The house is an old single-storey weatherboard, built in the 1920s with an Arts-and-Crafts style interior. We undertook a typical urban rebuild and repair but retained the original style and feeling. The lovely verandas present one of the best views. The property has a magnificent old garden laid out by my grandparents in the 1940s with the guidance of the landscape and garden designer, Edna Walling. Her associates Eric Hammond and Ellis Stones worked to establish the garden structure including the rock steps and walls. In Balwyn our garden and pool were built by Gordon Ford, who had trained under Ellis Stones and was the third generation of this lineage.

When we took over the garden at Olinda it needed a lot of work, a complete renovation. We were advised, 'You can't do it all at once. You need to have a 10-year plan.' We listened and we are now on our third '10-year plan'! We spent a weekend or so a month there, depending on travel and other commitments. We were in Olinda when the COVID lockdowns started. Like many people, we started to 'work from home'. With an upgrade to the internet and a new printer, Liz and I settled in to living in Olinda. Now we only use the apartment in town when we need to after late-night events, more convenient than driving back and forth on consecutive days; each trip an hour on the road. One compelling and frequent reason to go to town is the opera. We love most types of music but are dedicated to opera.

At Olinda we have lots of gardening to do to keep us well and truly busy between email obligations and zoom meetings. Like some other Dandenong properties, we have several dozen mature chestnut trees, trees we planted when Bart was 6 months old. Each winter parents and children from the local kindergarten and primary school arrive and collect the fallen nuts to sell at their annual Chestnut Festival to raise money for the school. The nuts are cracked and the kernel denuded, sold raw, roasted, toasted, ground to flour for baking cakes and pastries, made into paste or candied for desserts, and packaged for gluten-free addition to soups and stews by our community's skills, nous, energy and commitment.

The Olinda house in the Dandenongs, east of Melbourne

Today

View from our veranda

Having all four of our children living in Melbourne—well, most of the time—is a blessing for a father in his seventies, especially so for one who had so often not been there when they were young. People often comment that there is a 14-year gap between Kate and Phoebe. My response is, 'Whenever we had a pay rise, we had another child.'

Our first born, Kathryn, always called Kate, left Baltimore for her last year of school and stayed with her grandmother. She finished her medical training in Melbourne, earned a Master of Public Health degree at Johns Hopkins as a Fulbright Scholar, and started her ophthalmology training with us in Melbourne.

A career in ophthalmology was not to be. She had to terminate her training and career because a severe allergy to latex ruled out practicing clinical medicine. She then worked with McKinsey & Co. Having achieved expertise in three areas—medicine, public health and business—she was appointed a director of global health at the World Economic Forum in Geneva. She was headhunted by the International AIDS Vaccine Initiative in New York, adding another area of experience. GSK in Brussels recruited her, but after several years the vaccination program she worked on ended and she returned to Australia. She married Rod Scott, an international banker. They have two children, Julia and Will. Kate then started an IT company, Oculo (see page 343) that is now part of Finnish company Revenio. This means she, a vice president of Revenio, has frequent trips to Helsinki. (She reflects the travel patterns of her parents!)

Kate and Rod and their children Julia and Will

Bartholomew, Bart, started school in Baltimore and finished the last two years of school at Scotch College in Melbourne. He studied mechanical engineering, then focused on fire safety of large buildings. Bart is now the managing director of a very successful national building services company. He married Claire in 2000. She is a maternal and childcare nurse. They have four children: Isabel, Jimmy, Emeline and Joe. They spent three years in New Zealand while Bart worked there. When they left they had two children and returned to Melbourne with three. Joe was born not long after the homecoming. Liz and I were thinking of downsizing as all our children had left home. We found a convenient apartment to rent, and Bart and Claire moved into our family house for a while before buying their own.

Bart and Claire with their children, Jimmy, Joe, Isabel and Emy, with me and Liz

Edward, Ned, was 10 when we returned to Melbourne. After completing his schooling at Scotch he started an arts degree, originally intending to do arts and law. During his second year of university, having read some of Carl Sagan's books, his ideas changed; he completed a science degree as well as the arts degree. Then he went to Leiden, The Netherlands, to complete a PhD in astrophysics.

After we moved for Bart and his family we lived in the rented apartment. We started to look for an apartment to buy near the university and the city. Ned had returned to write up his thesis. Liz went out for coffee with him one morning. When she returned, I asked, 'How was Ned and the coffee?' Liz replied, 'Ned is good, the coffee was good. Oh, and I bought an apartment. No, actually, I bought two. Off the plan.' I cannot repeat my reply! However, with time the two apartments were reconfigured into one where we lived very happily from 2011 until we moved to Olinda.

Ned is now an associate professor in astrophysics at Swinburne University in Melbourne, running a massive international grant to map the Southern Universe. He is also working with CERA on the mathematical analysis and the software for their hyperspectral retinal imaging. His partner, Pia, also has a PhD and works on the ways to channel global donor funds to women affected by climate change. They have a son, Hugh.

Ned and Pia with their son, Hugh

Today

Phoebe (*Photo courtesy of Incognita Enterprises,* Shakespeare Republic, *season 2, director Sally McLean, cinematographer Shaun Herbertson*)

Our youngest, Phoebe, was five when we came back to Melbourne. She is our thespian. After completing an arts degree, she has done a range of studies and has carved out a creative career, acting, writing plays and poetry, directing and managing events, and recording talking books. She has won multiple international awards including the CIME Golden Eagle Award as a member of the Shakespeare Republic and several other WebFest awards, including the 'Best Performer Award' from the Baltimore WebFest, her old hometown! Based in Melbourne, she has also studied and worked in Europe.

When we first returned to Melbourne we took the children on trips around Victoria. To indulge my interest in wine we would stop at the occasional winery. Although Kate and Bart could legally taste wine with us, Phoebe certainly could not. For peace and quiet she could have a very tiny taste of port which was sweet. Later I bought a large barrel of tawny port. We would decant some bottles for us and the older children once a year. As Phoebe had been our 'port-taster', the decanting was usually done on or around her birthday. Every year or two we bought more port to top up the barrel to replace what we had decanted and the 'angels' share'.

Liz

Liz continues to look after me extraordinarily well. She supports our love of life in the hills. She retired from the National Serology Reference Labatory in 2008. Since then, she has kept more than busy, serving on not-for-profit boards concerned with the arts, mental health, women's health, political integrity, opera and cultural heritage, and with cultural events, as well as serving as chair of the Fitzroy apartment owners' corporation. She has also served as chair of other boards. Liz has been of tremendous help to me in writing and preparing this book, helping me remember things correctly, editing various drafts, and proof reading.

Over the years some of my international work was recognised, often with a bit of embarrassment because most of the work was accomplished with teams of people working cohesively, not just by me, certainly not on my own. I cannot draw attention to this without acknowledging the sacrifices and support of my family. Their high degree of tolerance and encouragement made it all possible.

I was honoured to receive the Hellen Keller Prize for Vision Research in 2009. This is awarded annually for research excellence as demonstrated by significant contributions to vision science. Given my grandfather's links with the extraordinary Miss Keller (see pages 8-9), this was a sweet reward as well as a high honour. I was subsequently asked to serve on the prize selection committee and to meet and work with members of the Helen Keller Foundation that supports the prize.

Among other awards I received are: the Gold Medal, International Organization Against Trachoma and The League Against Trachoma; Senior Achievement Award, International Blindness Prevention Award, and LXIII Edward Jackson Memorial Lecturer Award, American Academy of Ophthalmology; Outstanding Services Award for Prevention of Blindness, and Jose Rizal Medal, Asia Pacific Academy of Ophthalmology; Mildred Weisenfeld Award, Association for Research in Vision and Ophthalmology; HRH Prince Abdulaziz Ahmed Abdulaziz Al Saud Shield for Prevention of Blindness, Saudi Arabia; Chanchlani Global Vision Research Award, Canadian National Institute for the Blind; Lucian Howe Medal, American Ophthalmological Society; International Gold Award, Chinese Ophthalmological Society; Vision Excellence Award, International Agency for the Prevention of Blindness; Samuel P Asper Award for Achievement in Advancing International Medical Education, Johns Hopkins Medicine; and the College Medal, Distinguished Aboriginal and Torres Strait Islander Peoples Award Royal Australian and New Zealand College of Ophthalmologists. I was also a finalist in Victoria as the Australian of the Year Victoria, and later as the Senior Australian of the Year Victoria in the Australian of the Year Awards.

Named lectures include: E A Baker Memorial Lecture, The Canadian Ophthalmic Society; Lang Lecture, Royal Society of Medicine, London; Doyne Memorial Lecture, Oxford Ophthalmological Congress; Peter Watson Memorial Lecture, Cambridge Ophthalmological Symposium (see page 303ff); De Ocampo Lecture and Holmes Lecture, Asia Pacific Academy of Ophthalmology; and the The Award Lecture, Academia Ophthalmologica Internationalis. In Australia I have also given the Council Lecture, Fred Hollows Lecture and Sir Norman Gregg Lecture at Royal Australian and New Zealand College of Ophthalmologists congresses.

In 2024 the Asia Pacific Journal of Ophthalmology in their 'World EyeCon21' ranked me the world's fifth most influential ophthalmologist of the 21st century. In 2013 the University of Melbourne awarded me it's highest award, an honorary Doctor of Laws. I had never thought I would have law degree, even an honorary law degree.

In 2021 the Indigenous Eye Health Unit, the team, all of us, received the University of Melbourne's Award for Excellence in Engagement. Such a credit and recognition more well deserved and exhilarating would be hard to find.

These accolades have been reassuring and are pleasing. They are just milestones along the life journey of an ordinary boy for whom a variety of opportunities presented themselves and led him to develop into someone who was able to help save the sight of many and prevent the loss of vision in wide communities.

My thanks go to all who have contributed to this story.

Epilogue

*There is no limit to what a man can achieve
if he does not mind who gets the credit.*

Robert Woodruff

When I left that eye care report on the minster of health's desk in Islamabad and left Pakistan in 1980, I was deeply disappointed. Personally disappointed. I was young, had worked hard, and come up with some clear and sensible recommendations. I was disappointed for the World Health Organisation and for its country representative who had supported my information gathering in so many ways, all the way to that minister's desk. I was disappointed for the ophthalmologists and provincial health officials who had given me their time, records, experience, opinions, arguments and hopes, ophthalmologists like Mohammad Daud Khan of Peshawar in the Khyber province and particularly for Pakistan's 72 million people, nearly 1.5 million, about 2 percent of them, blind.

By the time I landed in Baltimore, I'd turned my thoughts to my family, particularly infant Ned, then 6 months old and about to have his first Christmas.

I presumed the report would gather dust somewhere. For several years I heard little to suggest otherwise from Pakistani ophthalmologists who attended international conferences.

After a while though, it seemed every Pakistani attendee I met had read or heard about 'The Hugh Taylor Report' or 'The

1980 Report' or 'The WHO Report', and that my 'wake-up call' was deemed responsible for a lot of the good things happening there.

In 2011 Daud Khan delivered the Duke Elder Lecture at the World Ophthalmology Congress in Berlin:

'The WHO document was used for political and professional advocacy. The then President of Pakistan, General Muhammad Zia ul Haq, who already had a soft corner for disabled people, was sensitised about the issue through strong advocacy. He created a national eye camp committee through a presidential order as a short-term measure for this purpose. This committee soon evolved into a national committee for prevention of blindness. The Ministry of Health notified the maiden committee in 1985 and appointed the first group of national and provincial coordinators. Professor Saleh Memon was appointed as the first national coordinator for prevention of blindness.'

Professor Daud Khan receiving the Duke Elder Award from Bill Felch and Bruce Spivey at the World Ophthalmology Congress, Professor N H Butt standing behind, Berlin 2010

Epilogue

Daud listed the events that followed: the first national blindness survey in 1987, linking up with SightSavers International, training a young ophthalmologist in community eye health at the International Centre for Eye Health in London each year, setting up laboratory testing and comprehensive eye care services in all 166 districts, concentration on cataract surgery, mobile operation theatres, an increased uptake of services especially by females in rural Pakistan; a five-year national plan for prevention of blindness in 1994 (supported by the Fred Hollows Foundation of Australia among others), a second in 1999, under Vision2020 guidelines, taskforces directed at priority diseases such as cataract and trachoma…

In 2011 the population of Pakistan was 198.6 million. Despite devastating earthquakes and floods, civil disorder, martial law, involvement in war, and accommodating millions of Afghani refugees, the rate of blindness had more than halved.

Receiving the M Lateef Chaudhry Award in Lahore, December 2024 with, from left, Professors Tayyaba Afghani, Khalil Rana, Saleem Akhtar and Muhammad Moin

Opening Eyes

5 December 2024: I took a 5.30 am cab to Melbourne International. At 7 am, a flight to Sydney, then Bangkok, and finally Lahore's Allamba Iqbal International, 10.40 pm local time. I arrived at Lahore's Pearl Continental Hotel at midnight, my home and conference space for the next four days of the 42nd Lahore Ophthalmo, a guest of the Ophthalmological Society of Pakistan. I was scheduled to talk in four sessions including delivering the M Lateef Chaudhry Award Lecture. I had looked forward to seeing Daud again, but that was not to be. His back problem kept him in Peshawar.

When I was invited to the conference, I knew that Pakistan had made application to WHO for trachoma-free status. This status is won when WHO is satisfied that less than 5 percent of children under 10 years old have trachoma three years after stopping antibiotic treatment, and less than 1 in 500 over 15 years have trichiasis. In October, WHO had announced that Pakistan had eliminated blinding trachoma. With joy I updated my power-point presentations to reflect this truly magnificent achievement.

In my fourth presentation, 'Australian Indigenous Eye Health', I, of course, added a congratulation to Pakistan. But earlier images like 'Aboriginal People had 10 times more blindness…' took on a new personal perspective. I wondered what my audience, predominately from now trachoma-free Pakistan would make of this oddity: in Australia, a rich country, trachoma exists. Much poorer countries, are now trachoma-free. My decision in 2008 to fix this in Australia will not add much to my scientific or medical reputation in the annals of eye care. Though it will go down as preventing blindness.

Epilogue

Beswick Falls, Northern Territory, 2011. *Courtesy David Middleton.*

Opening Eyes

Acknowledgements

Most of this story is about how opportunities have arisen by chance and led me into new areas, how chance favours the prepared mind. The following name people and organisations that presented those opportunities, opened new pathways.

Peter Morris, who offered me a research year that allowed me to find how exciting research could be. Gerry Crock offering me a summer position in the Department of Ophthalmology. When I naively asked Fred Hollows if I could join him for a weekend in Bourke, the work with Fred opened my eyes to a whole new world, not only to trachoma and Indigenous health but to epidemiology and public health. Walter Stark, whose interest in the work on transplantation immunology I had done with Peter Morris resulted in my studying at Johns Hopkins. Art Silverstein asking me what I had done before coming to Baltimore and discussing trachoma, leading to the animal and then field projects that in many ways helped to redefine trachoma activities. Asking Maurice Langham why he did not have a control group in his onchocerciasis study: look where that led me and led the treatment of onchocerciasis. Working with Al Sommer and the host of new things we were able to do, including the work on UV-B rays and smoking, and how these led to major health-promotion messages. The broad support I received in setting up CERA. The wholehearted support from Jim Angus, Terry Nolan and then Harold Mitchell that let me set up the IEHU and all the work we have been able to do to try to close the gap for vision. And the support I have received from so many in the teams I have had the pleasure to have worked with. I must make special mention of the wonderful support and work done by Mitchell Anjou and Emma Stanford and of course, Judy Carrigan, who worked tirelessly for me for over two decades.

I stress the help and support I received without question from Liz and the family. Through all my active career Liz was working fulltime, studying and often travelling, carving out her own influential career while she looked after me and our four children, and achieved three doctorates. She took on a heavy load of responsibility. Against all odds, all our children now live in Melbourne. They well could have been scattered all over the world. We are blessed.

Thanks to Barry Jones for foreword, John Kerr for reading, editorial advice and copy editing, and Paul Taylder of Xigrafix Media for book design.

Index

9–11 attacks, 240

AAO, 291, 292
Abbey, Helen, 215
Abbott, Tony, 236, 288, 356
ABC, 215
Abidjan, 185–6
Aboriginal Health Council SA, 327
'Access to Eye Health among Indigenous Australians', 321
ACCHOs, 325, 334
'Achieving Community Support for Trachoma Control', 145
Addenbrooke's Hospital, 303, 304
Advance Eye Health, 296
Afghani, Tayyaba, 395
Afghanistan, 1
AFIP, 164
African Institute of Tropical Ophthalmology, 278
African Ophthalmology Society, 296
African Program for Onchocerciasis Control, 197
Afwerki, Isias, 274, 275
Age, 13
Age-Related Eye Diseases Study, 259, 260ff
Age-related Macular Degeneration, 215–216, 256ff
Agra, 96
AIATSIS, 321
AIDS, 91
Akhtar, Saleem, 395
Akron, 190
Alaska, 103–104
Albiez, Eberhard, 184
Alexandra, Princess, 302
Alice Springs, 56, 62, 63, 70, 72, 75, 335, 366, 369, 370
Allergan, 298
Alyawerre, 315
Alzheimer's Disease, 242
Amata, 60, 61, 70, 317
Amazon, 47, 103
AMD, 215–216, 256ff
American Academy of Ophthalmology, 291

American Academy of Ophthalmology Award, 391
Amethi, 272
AMSA, 37
Anangu Pitjantjatjara Yankunytjatjara lands, 52,55, 58, 60, 352ff
Anderson, Elisabeth (Lib), 6
Anderson, Ian, 309, 313, 321
Anderson, Joseph Ringland, 5–9, 39, 46, 290, 391
Anderson, Mary (Nairne), 6–9, 39–40, 265
Anderson, Pat, 310, 315, 337
Angus, Jim, 306, 309
Anjou, Mitchell, 313, 325, 329, 330, 383
Ansell Foundation, 229, 231
Ansell, Kathleen, 231
Ansell, Lloyd, 231
Ansett Australia, 240
Ansstasiou, Peter, 317
Antarctica, 42ff
ANU, 55, 357
Aphakic glasses, 84, 96
APOC, 197
Apollo 11 conjunctivitis, 102
APY lands, 52,55, 58, 60, 352ff
Arabunna, 315
AREDS, 259, 260ff
Armadale, 7
Armed Forces Institute of Pathology, 164
Armstong, Louis, 22
Army Medical Services, 61
Arnold, Anna-Lena, 307
Arrente, 374
ARTD Consultants, 334
ARVO, 74
Asia Pacific Academy of Ophthalmologists, 56
Asia Pacific Academy of Ophthalmology Award, 391
Asia Pacific Academy of Ophthalmology Lecture, 392
Asia Pacific Journal of Ophthalmology, 392
Asian Medical Students Congress, 37
Asilomar, 97, 270
ASIO, 37, 40, 48
Asmara, 274

Association for Research in Vision and Ophthalmology, 74
Association for Research in Vision and Ophthalmology Award, 391
Association for the Blind, 232
Aswad, Lama Al, 297
Atkins, Joyce, 366
Atkinson, Josie, 313
Austin Hospital, 30 ff, 37, 40ff
'Australia's Long Term National Health Plan', 333
Australian Army Field Hospital, 60, 61
Australian Broadcasting Corporation, 215
Australian College of Ophthalmologists, 40, 44, 46, 56, 280
Australian Institute for Aboriginal and Torres Strait Islander Studies, 321
Australian Medical Association, 343
Australian Medical Student's Association, 37
Australian National University, 55, 357
Australian of the Year, 200, 273, 279, 391
Australian Open, 264
Australian Security and Intelligence Organisation, 37, 40, 48
'Australian Surveillance Trachoma Report', 379
Australian War Museum, 15
Awadzi, Kwablah, 168, 169, 173, 199
Award Lecture, Academia Ophthalmologica Internationalis, 392
Azithromycin, 138, 144–146, 310, 322, 351–352
Aziz, Mohammed, 171–173, 177, 181

Bailey, Jan, 211
Bailey, Robin, 135, 144, 211
Baird, Paul, 229ff, 305
Bakalain, Alexander, 209
Baker Heart & Diabetes Institute, 313
Baker Institute, 313
Baldwin, Marjorie, 51
Baldwin, William (Bill) 195
Balfour, Beverley, 6
Balfour, Tom, 6
Ballarat, 344–345
Baltimore, 206
Baltimore Colts, 83
Baltimore Longitudinal Study of Aging, 259
Baltimore Orioles, 83, 218

Baltimore Sun, 171, 215
Baltimore Symphony Orchestra, 94
Balwyn, 219, 383
Bangladeshi War of Independence, 100
Barchua, John, 188
Barraquer, Rafael, 297
Barton, Ian, 86, 205
Bathern, Walter, 373, 374
Beaver Dam Study, 265
Bebedouro, 124
Bedouin, 142ff
Beijing, 280
Bell, Andrew, 366
Bendigo, 5, 10
Bensheim, 289
Beresford, Bruce, 28
Berlin, 394
Bernhard-Nocht Institute, 184
Beswick Falls, 397
Bethesda, 82
Bhutan, 276
Biafran Civil War, 61
'Big Five, The', 101
Billson, Frank, 279
Binse, Margie, 220
Bionic Ear Institute, 231
Bionic Eye, 242, 243
Bird, Alan, 164
Birendra, King, 275
Biscoe, Gordon, 51
Bjelke-Petersen, Joh, 74
Black flies, 148ff, 179
Blind Boys from Alabama, 107
Blomberg, Michael, 109
'Blue Berry', 56, 57
Blue Mountains Study, 250, 265
BMC Software, 195
Bolivia, 102–103
Bond, Colin (Chesty), 19
Bong Mine, 160
Botox, 299
Boudville, Andrea, 323, 327
Bourke, 46, 47
Bourne, Robert, 286
Bowman, 352
Boy Scouts, 16, 19
Boyd, Robin, 16
Bragg, Peter, 322
Brando, Alex, 324
Brazil, 124
Breitner, Wendy, 82

Index

Bressler, Neil, 211
Bressler, Susan, 211
Bridgestone, 191
Brien Holden Foundation, 238, 282
Brien Holden Vision Institute, 238
Briggs, Lisa, 342
Briscoe, Fred, 51
Briscoe, Gordon (Biggo), 55, 60
British Empire Society for the Blind, 269
Broken Hill, 64
Brooks, Anne, 230
Brooks, Wendy, 313, 315
Broome, 26 ff, 73, 323
Brotman, Betsy, 160, 179
Brown, Brian, 65
Brumby, John, 237
Brundtland, Gro Harlem, 279
Brussels, 290
Buchanan, 174, 177
Buchanan, Rob, 15
Buckingham Palace, 300ff
Buffalo Bills, 83
Bullimore, Mark, 211
Bunnings, 374
Bureau of Statistics, 324
Burkina Faso, 98, 151, 153, 168, 173
Burma, 121
Burnet, Frank Macfarlane, 35
Butt, N H, 394
Buzzacott, Trevor (Buzza) 48–49, 55, 57, 315
Byrce, Quentin, 319, 320

Cairo, 99
Caldwell, Harlan, 91
Calgary, 120
Cam River, 303, 313
Cambridge, 303ff, 313
Cambridge Ophthalmological Symposium, 304
Cambridge Ophthalmological Symposium Lecture, 392
Cambridge University, 300, 357
Cameroon, 162
Campbell, William (Bill), 171, 172
Canadian National Institute for the Blind Award, 391
Canadian Ophthalmic Society Lecture, 392
Canberra, 15, 241
Cancer Council, 263

Carlton, 33–35
Carnarvon, 72
Carrigan, Judy, 282, 302, 304, 312
Carrol, Nan, 222, 223
Carter Center, 194
Carter, Jimmy, 194, 196
Carthage, 99
Case Western Reserve, 164
Cataract, 203, 210, 340
Catherine the Great, 104
CBM, 126, 289
CDK, 86, 205, 215
CEIS, 164ff
Centre for Disease Control, 357
Centre for Eye Research Australia, 231ff, 304–307, 309, 312ff, 331, 343, 347, 363, 388
Centre for Health Policy, 323
Centre for Ophthalmic Educators, 295
Centro de Investigaciones Ecologicas del Sureste, 164 ff
CERA, 231ff, 304–307, 309, 312ff, 331, 343, 347, 363, 388
Champion of Change Award, 297ff
Chanchlani Global Vision Research Award, 391
Charquini Glacier, 103
Charters Towers, 75
'Check today…', 345, 346
Chernobyl, 290
Chesapeake Bay, 206ff
Chesapeake Bay Waterman Study, 254ff
Chestnut Festival, 384
Chew, Emily, 85, 94, 167, 259, 260ff
Chiapas, 111ff, 164
Chibret, Paul, 278–279
Chichon, El, 114
China, 255
Chinese Ophthalmological Society Award, 391
Christie, Norwell, 99
Christoffel, Ernst J, 289
Christoffel-Blindenmission, 126, 289, 352
Chylack, Leo, 211
CIME Golden Eagle Award, 389
Clark Foundation, 118ff, 126, 139, 145–146, 181
Clark, Graeme, 231
Clarke, Faye, 346
'Clean faces…', 365–373
Clear Horizons, 334

403

Clemenger, Peter, 265
Climatic Droplet Keratopathy, 86, 205, 215
Closing the Gap, 327
COAG, 334
Cochrane Collaboration, 59
Cochrane, Archie, 48, 59, 86
Cochrane, Gillian, 281
Coffey, Cate, 366
Cogan, David, 39
Coles, 374
Collarenebri, 72
College Medal, 391
College of Ophthalmology, 73
Colombia, 200
Columbia Cornell and Network Physicians, 292
Columbia University, 101
Comedians, The, 102
Comissiona, Sergiu, 94
Commonwealth Scientific & Industry Organisation, 86, 205
Commonwealth Serum Laboratory, 218
Communist Party (NZ), 48
Congo, 199
Cook, Joesph (Joe), 118, 119, 146, 181
Coolfront, 118
Coombs, Nugget, 70
Cooperative Research Centre, 239
Copemna, Bruce, 173
Cornell University, 178
Cortical cataract, 203
Coulter, Nicole, 297
Council Lecture, 392
Council of Australian Governments, 334
Couper, Tery, 226
COVID, 200–201, 298, 333ff, 336, 371, 381, 384
Cowan, Claude, 83, 84
Craw-craw, 150
Crisfield, 213
'Critical History of Indigenous Eye-health Policy-making', 321
Croakey Health Media, 337
CRC, 239
Crock, Gerrard (Gerry), 39, 43ff, 60, 108, 222ff, 231
Crock, Harry, 222
Crossin, Trish, 315, 316
Crowston, Jonathon, 242, 305
CSIRO, 86, 205

Cunderin, 65–69
Cupp, Ed, 178, 179
Cybec Foundation, 315

D'Anna, Sam, 174, 177, 182
Daghfous, M T, 121
Dana Center, 124, 128, 134, 138, 141, 161
Dana Center for Preventative Ophthalmology, 109
Dana Foundation, 109
Dandenongs, 383ff
Daniell, Mark, 230
Darwin, 370
Darwin Regional Urban Indigenous Diabetes, 339
Davenport, 54
Davey, Aaron, 370
Dawson, Chan, 88, 121, 144
Dawson, Daryl, 318
Dax, Elizabeth (Liz), 15, 24ff, 32, 58, 81ff, 154–6, 201, 217ff, 227, 239, 259, 265, 270, 293, 303ff, 312, 381, 390
Dax, Eric Cunningham, 24, 305
Dax, Judith, 25
Dax, Kathleen (Katie), 24, 265
Dax, Richard, 24–25
Dax, Susannah (Sue), 24
De Jong, Paulus, 265
De Ocampo Lecture, 392
Deakin University, 11
DEC, 148ff, 166, 174–178, 181
Dejong, Laurie, 88
Delaey, Jacques, 292
Delahunty, Mary, 315
DelMonte, Monte, 84, 161
Denholm, Rosie, 51
Derby, 73
Dexamethasone, 166
DFA, 117, 129, 134
Dhaka, 100
Diabetes, 258, 261
Diabetes Australia, 349
Diabetic retinopathy screening card, 348
'Diabetic Retinopathy: ... a systemic review', 322
Diallo, Samba, 173
Diamox, 148
Diethylcarbamazine, 148ff, 166, 174–178, 181
Diploma of Ophthalmology, 41
Dirani, Mohamed, 331

Index

Direct micro-immunofluoresence cytology, 117
Disneyland LA, 81
Distinguished Aboriginal & Torres Strait Islander Peoples Award RANZCO, 391
Docker River, 27–28, 58, 69, 381–382
Doctor of Laws, 392
Doctor of Medicine, 86
Doe, Samuel, 164, 174, 190
Doherty, Linda, 337
Dominguez-Vazquez, Alfredo, 165
'Don't Fry Your Eyes', 264
Donnelly, John, 181
Douglas, Les, 275
Downer, Alexander, 288
Doxycycline, 185, 186
Doyle, Joysie, 341
Doyne Memorial Lecture, 392
DRC, 199
DR-Net, 300
Drugs for Neglected Diseases, 199
DRUID, 339
Dry River, 369
Duke Elder Lecture, 394
Duke, Brian, 162ff, 174, 181, 184, 193 ff, 195, 196, 198, 271, 302
Duke, Diane, 163, 198, 302
Duke, Lotti, 163
Duke, Molly, 163
Duke-Elder, Stuart, 10
Dundee, 227
Dunedin, 17, 48
Dunn, Ross, 307
Dunt, David, 323–324
Durmont d'Urville, 42–43

E A Baker Memorial Lecture, 392
Early Treatment of Diabetic Retinopathy Study, 85
East Baltimore Eye Study, 265
EB, 135
Echuca, 38
Ecuador, 200
Edna McConnell Clark Foundation, 118ff, 126, 139, 145–146, 181
Edward Jackson Memorial Lecturer Award, 391
Egypt, 99, 144
Egyptian ophthalmia, 279
Eighty Mile Beach, 26

El Salvador, 100
Elementary Body, 135
Elephantiasis, 152
'Eliminating Blinding Trachoma', 361–362
Elixir of Youth, 260
Elizabeth 2, Queen, 13, 14, 184
Emment, Edward (Ted) 211
'End Trachoma', 378
Enlighten Imaging, 242
ERDRS, 85
ESPEN, 197
Ethiopia, 276
Evans, Gareth, 274, 275
Everest, Mt, 276
Expanded Special Project for the Elimination of Neglected Tropical Diseases, 197
Expert Advisory Committee, Onchocerciasis Control Program, 192
Extracapsular surgery, 84
Eye and Ear, 39ff, 309
'Eye Care for the Community', 236
Eye Foundation, 307
'Eye health measures for Aboriginal & Torres Strait people', 333v
Eye worm, 199

Fairfield Infectious Disease Hospital, 13, 218
Falls Creek, 18
FAO, 153
Farnham House, 45–46, 273
Felch, Ginny, 293
Felch, William (Bill) J Jnr, 292ff, 297, 298, 394
Ferdinand, Angeline, 321
Ferguson, Donald, 61
Ferguson, Rachel, 313
Ferris, Frederich (Rick), 85, 94, 259, 260ff
Fiji, 81, 339
Filatov Institute of Eye Diseases, 104, 105
Fine, Stuart, 171, 208, 211
Fink SA, 63
Firestone Rubber Plantation, 157, 164, 190
First Nations Eye Health Alliance, 335
Fitzroy Crossing WA, 73, 307
Fitzroy Vic, 307
Flinders Ranges, 54, 55
Flubendazole, 167
Flynn, Frank, 46

FNEHA, 335
Food and Agriculture Organisation, 153
Food and Drug Administration, 199–200
Ford, Geoff, 381
Ford, Gordon, 383
Ford, Mary, 381
Foreman, Joshua, 331
Fort Douglas, 87
Foster, Allen, 126–127, 131
Fox, Charity, 84
Fox, Sarah, 307, 308
Francis, Victoria, 145
Frankston, 10, 22
Fred Hollow Foundation, 223, 273, 277, 281, 282, 395
Fred Hollows Lecture, 392
Freire, Paulo, 47
Fringe Dwellers, The, 28
Fulbright Scholar, 385
Funder, John, 95, 312. 313, 314, 318

GABA agonist, 178
Gable, Peter, 296
Galbraith, Dick, 44, 47, 60, 60, 62, 73
Galbraith, Penny, 61
Gallin, Michaela, 183
Gambia, 135, 144
Gang Show, 17
Garland, Suzanne, 118, 245
Garms, Christian, 280, 289
Gates Foundation, 285
GBD, 285ff
Geelong, 29
Geneva, 192, 272
George, Terry, 166–169
GET2020 145–146
Ghan, The, 63–64
Ghana, 168, 181, 199, 276
Ghandi, Rajiv, 272
Gibson Desert, 28
Giesma dye, 117
Giles, Ernest, 72
Glaucoma, 43, 205, 258, 261, 340
Glaxo, 96
GlaxoSmithKline, 112, 113, 194
Global Burden of Diseases, 285ff
Global Fund, 194
Global Health Investment Fund, 199
Gloor, Baldur, 292, 296
Golnik, Karl, 295
Gooda, Mick, 310

Goode, Charles, 318
Goodenough, Miss, 12
Goodes, Adam, 369
Gooreng, 341
Gorbachev, Mikhail, 105
Gower, Emily, 139
Graham, Billy, 10
Grant, John, 38–39
Graue, Enrique, 297
Gray, Nigel, 263, 266
Greene, Bruce, 81, 119, 153ff, 159, 161–164, 73, 175, 177ff, 181ff
Greene, Graham, 102
Greene, Jim, 184
Greene, Theo, 81
Gruen, Rusell, 322
Guatemala, 154ff, 200
Guest, Charles, 246
'Guidelines for Diabetic Eye Care', 296
'Guidelines for Glaucoma Eye Care', 296
'Guidelines for Programmes for the Prevention of Blindness Programs', 97
'Guidelines for the Rapid Assessment for Blinding Trachoma', 146
Guiness Book of Records, 68
Gumbaynggirr, 366
Gunditjmara, 345
Gupta, Neeru, 298ff
Gurindji, 48
Gurung, Reeta, 274
Gust, Ian, 218
Guymer, Robyn, 230, 305

Haiti, 102
Halton, Janet, 318
Hammond, Eric, 383
Hanoi, 273
Hardy, Frank, 48
Harold Mitchell Foundation, 313–314
Harper, Alex, 230
Havard University, 101, 211
Hawaii, 81
Head of the River, 15
Health Habitat, 352
Healthy Eyes, 237
HeLa cells, 84
Helen Keller Foundation, 391
Helen Keller International, 145
Helen Kellher Award, 391
Helsinki, 386
Henderson, Graham, 321

Index

Henty, 25
Hepatitis B, 218
Hepatitis C, 160
Hermitage Museum, 223
Hewitt, Alex, 322
Hill, David, 263, 266
Himalayan Cataract Program, 276
Hirst, John, 314
Hirst, Lawrence, 79, 8
HIV, 218
HIV/AIDS, 106ff, 191, 194
HLA, 33, 44, 84
Hobart, 43
Hohoe, 199
Holden, Brien, 236, 238ff, 279–280, 288
Hollows, Gabi, 98, 275
Hollows, Cam, 274
Hollows, Fred, 44ff, 79, 98,119, 204, 223, 250, 270, 273–274
Holmes Lecture, 392
Holmes, King K, 90, 91
Home Vision Test Kit, 234
Hong Kong, 37
Hotel Oloffson, 102
Houshmand, Joobin, 366
Howard Florey Institute, 223
Howard University, 83
Howard, John, 288
HRH Prince Abdulaziz Ahmed Abdulaziz Al Saud Shield for Prevention of Blindness, 391
HSP60, 91
Hsueh, Ya-seng (Arthur), 323–324
HT, 4, 7
HTLV, 201
HTLVIII, 91
Hudson, Alan, 135
Hudson, Judy Whittam, 89–90
Human Leukocyte Antigens, 33, 44, 84
Human T-cell Lymphotropic Virus, 201
Hunt, Greg, 288, 315, 316, 347
Hurler syndrome, 55
Hyderabad, 289

Ian Potter Foundation, 313, 314, 315, 318, 320
IAPB, 75, 76, 96ff, 142, 269ff, 319, 352
IAPB Vision Atlas, 286
IBM, 195
iCare, 347
ICEPO, 271
ICO, 100, 109, 126, 271, 290, 291, 292
ICO Fellowship program, 295
ICO Foundation, 295
'ICO Guidelines for Diabetic Eye Care', 293
'ICO Guidelines Glaucoma Eye Care', 296
ICOF, 295, 299
IEHU, 307, 320, 360, 364, 383, 392
IgE, 181
IHME, 285
Impaja Television, 368, 369
IMPACT, 270
Indigenous Eye Health Unit, 307, 320, 360, 364, 383, 392
Indira Ghandi Eye Hospital and Research Centre, 272
Indulkana, 52
Institute for Health & Evaluation, 283
International Agency for Research on Cancer, 263
International Agency for the Prevention of Blindness, 75, 76, 96, 269
International Agency for the Prevention of Blindness Award, 391
International Blindness Prevention Award, 391
International Center for Epidemiologic Prevention of Blindness, 100
International Center for Preventative Ophthalmology, 271
International Centre for Eye Health, 126, 286, 300, 395
International Council of Ophthalmology, 76, 290, 291, 292, 340
International Diabetes Federation, 339
International Diabetes Institute, 339
International Gold Award, 391
International Organization Against Trachoma Gold Medal, 391
International Trachoma Initiative, 119
Intracapsular surgery, 84
Intra-ocular lens, 84
Inuit, 103
IOL, 84
IRAC, 263
Iranian Revolution, 95
Ischemia, 340
Islamabad, 393
ITI, 119, 146
Ivermectin, 171ff, 287ff

407

Ivory Coast, 185–6

Jagger, Mick, 102
James Cook University, 173
James, Dave, 381
James, Glenda, 381
James, Willian (Digger), 61
Jeffery, Michael, 300
Jesus Green, 303, 304
Jetta, Aaron, 370
Jetta, Neville, 345
Jigalong, 72
Johns Hopkins University, 44, 74, 385
Johns Hopkins Bloomberg School of Public Health, 109
Johns Hopkins Hospital, 79ff
Johns Hopkins Medicine Award, 391
Johns Hopkins School of Hygiene and Public Health, 109
Johnston, Colin, 40
Johnson, Lyndon, 24
Johnson, Shirley, 88, 127
Jones, Barrie, 73, 97, 98, 121, 73, 164, 280
Jones, Barry, 315, 316, 360ff
Jones, Jilpia Nappaljari, 51, 55, 315, 321, 356
Jones, Pauline, 98
Jose Rizal Medal, 391
Juntendo University, 283
Jurrah, Liam, 370, 371

Kalgoorlie, 64, 69
Kalkarindji, 317
Kalorkerinos, Archivides (Archie) 72
Katala, Sydney, 127
Katherine, 357, 358, 377
Katherine West Health Board, 364, 366
Kathmandu, 274, 275
Kattukatjara, 382
Katz, Joanne, 141
Kaufman, David, 62, 73
Keeffe, Jill, 230, 234ff, 282, 305, 307, 341, 363
Keel, Stuart, 331
KeepSight program, 349–350
Keightley, Simon, 295
Kelaher, Margaret, 321
Keller, Helen, 9–10, 224
Kenya, 96–97, 184
Khan, Daud, 393–396
Khodadoust Line, 95

Khodadoust, Ali, 95
Khyber, 393
Kimberley, 73
King, Martin Luther, 83
Kirkby Institute, 356
Kitching, Frances, 213
Kline, Barbara, 265
Kline, Ron, 265
Kline, Tony, 21,
Koirala, G P, 275
Komernang Ski Club
Kongwa, 127
Konyama, Kazuichi, 282ff
Koori Heritage Trust, 319
Korat course, 282ff
Kuesel, Annette, 199
KWHB, 364, 366

La Paz, 102–103
LAC, 174, 182ff, 186ff, 190
Lacks, Henrietta, 84
Lae, 18
Lahore Ophthalmo, 396
Lamming, Andrew, 144, 352
Lance Dixon, 56
Lancet, The, 171, 273–274
Lang Lecture, 392
Lange, Fiona, 313, 317, 366, 367, 373ff
Langham, Maurice, 147–148, 153ff
Langton, Marcia, 309, 337
Lansingh, Van, 352–353
Lasker Award, 93, 101
Lasseter, Lewis, 382
Lasseter's Cave, 382
Lasseter's Reef, 382
Laviviere, Michel, 173
Lawson, Wayne (Hon), 207, 210, 213
Le Mesurier, Richard, 281, 283
League Against Trachoma Gold Medal, 391
Leaky pipe, 329–330
Lee, Helen, 357
Legodi, Eddie, 298
LEHP, 235
Leiden, 387
Lens Opacity grading, 211
Levamisole, 166
Liberia, 157ff, 106, 164, 184, 186ff, 90–191, 199
Liberian Agricultural Co, 174, 182ff, 186ff, 190

Index

Liberian Institute of Biomedical Research, 160, 178
LIBR, 160, 178
Lima, 106
Lines, David, 366
Lions Club, 232
Lions Eye Bank, 224–225
Lions Eye Health Promotion, 235
Lions Outback Vision, 323
Lions Tissue Donation Service, 226
Lions Vision Initiative, 234, 235ff
Little St Margaret School, 11
Livingstone, Trish, 248, 262
Loa Loa, 199
Lobos, Edgar, 182
LOCS, 211
LogMAR charts, 85
Loiasis, 199
Long Bay Gaol, 45
Low Vision Clinic, 222
Lowe, Ronald, 56
Lowe, Suzie, 373
Lowitja Institute, 310
Ltyente Apurte Football Club, 373
Lucas, Ade, 194
Lucian Howe Medal, 391
Lucknow, 95–96
Luritja, 373
Lwin, S, 121
Lynch, Matt, 127, 135
Lynskey, Mike, 273, 274

M Lateef Chaudhry Award, 395, 396
Macquarie Island, 42
Madurai, 96
Magrabi, Akel al, 142, 143
Maguire, Maureen, 208
Major, John, 301
Malatt, Anne, 245
Malawi, 119–120
Mali, 278
Mann, Ida, 10, 46
Martin, Keith, 242, 304
Martin, Lesley, 373, 374
Martin, Ray, 273, 274
Marx, Karl, 47
Maryland Eye Bank, 225
Mathew, Anu, 354
Maumenee, Ed (Dr), 75–76, 92, 97, 270, 290
Maumenee, Irene, 270

Mauritis, 339
Mayorga, Eduardo, 295
Mazzotti Reaction, 152, 153, 156, 160, 166, 167
Mazzotti, L, 152
McCarty, Cathy, 246, 249
McCarty, Dan, 246
McCaughey, Davis, 33, 106
McCaughey, Jean, 106
McComas Family Laboratory, 229
McComas Fellowship, 82
McComas, John Wesley, 229
McComas, Robert, 6
McDonalds, 180
McDonnell, Lilly, 363, 366
McGhee, Charles, 227
McGhee, Jane, 227
McGuirk, Robert, 378
McKenzie, Charles, 166
McKinsey & Co, 323, 333, 347, 386
McLean, Hector, 221, 223, 230
McLennan, Roger, 28
McMullan, Bob, 288, 289ff
McNeil, John, 259
McNeil, Robyn, 323
MD, 86
Measles, 125, 126
Mebendazole, 164ff, 166
Mectizan, 194
Mectizan Award, 198, 363
Mectizan Donation Program, 194
Medawar, Peter, 35
Medicare, 311, 321, 330, 343
Medicines Development for Global Health, 199
Medina, Norma, 124, 125
Medline, 265
Melatonin, 272
Melbourne Department of Ophthalmology, 39ff
Melbourne Excimer Laser Group, 226ff
Melbourne Film Festival, 11
Melbourne Football Club, 31, 219, 317, 344, 345, 369ff
Melbourne Grammar, 17
Melbourne School of Population and Global Health, 306,, 309, 320
Melbourne School of Population and Health, 306, 309, 320
Melbourne University Medical School, 19, 21ff,

Melbourne University Medical Students Society, 37
Melbourne Vision Impairment Project, 245ff, 340, 341, 245ff
Melvin Jones Award, 235k
Memon, Saleh, 394
Menindee, 64
Merbs, Shanna, 139
Merck & Co, 171, 181, 193ff, 98, 200, 287, 363
Merck Sharp & Dome, 171
Methodist Ladies College, 24, 219
Mexico, 111ff, 200
Meyerhoff, 94
Michel, Claude, 357, 358
Middleton, David, 315, 317, 318
Mildred Weisenfeld Award, 391
Miller, Ann, 319, 320
Miller, Neil, 81
Milpa, 316, 320, 365, 366, 368, 371
Minum Barreng (book), 307, 319, 337
Minum Barreng (word), 307
Mirinda boards, 128–130
Mirugen, 242
Mitchell, Amanda, 315
Mitchell, Harold, 313, 314, 317ff
Mitchell, Paul, 249, 265
Mkocha, Henry, 134, 135
Mmbaga, B B O, 126, 135
Mohamed, Justin, 327, 341ff
Moin, Muhammed, 395
Mombasa, 184
Monash University, 259, 376
Monash University Department of Medicine, 40
Monk, Thelonius, 22
Monterey Peninsula, 97
Moores, Barry, 195
Moores, John, 195
Moores, Rebecca (Becky), 195
Moorfields Eye Hospital, 48, 265
Moran, David, 51
Morris Winery, 30
Morris, Peter, 31, 34–35
Morrison, Scott, 336
Morson, Lib, 8, 10, 14, 39, 64
Morson, Stuart, 8, 10, 14, 39, 64
Moscow, 105
Moxidectin, 199ff
Mrs Kitching's Guest House, 213
MSD, 171, 363

Mt Hotham, 29
Mt Washington, 80, 81, 93
Muandik, 345
MUDO, 39, 217ff, 312
Mulholland, Will, 323
Muñoz, Beatriz, 128, 135, 215
Murphy, Bob, 94–95, 167, 174, 176, 182, 206
Murray, Reg, 51, 53, 54, 65
Murray, Rose, 51
Mutitjulu, 367
MVIP, 245ff, 340, 341
Mvumi, 125ff
Myer, Sidney, 5
Myopia, 255

NACCHO, 325, 327, 331, 334, 341
Nakajima, Akira, 283
Nakajima, Akira, 290
National Aboriginal & Torres Strait Islander Eye Health Program, 311
National Aboriginal Community Controlled Health Organisation, 325, 327, 331, 334, 341
National Eye Institute, 85, 95, 208, 216, 259, 260
National Health & Medical Research Council, 246, 259, 341
National HIV Reference Laboratory, 217
National Indigenous Eye Health Survey, 307ff, 313, 323
National Institute of Health, 82, 89, 182
National Institute on Aging, 82, 106, 259
National Institute on Drug Abuse, 106, 259
National Optometry Training Program, 281
National Serology Reference Laboratory, 217ff, 390
National Trachoma and Eye Health Program, 47ff, 204, 307, 309, 312, 315, 391ff
National Trachoma Reporting & Surveillance Unit, 356ff, 360
NATSIEHP, 311
Naumann, Gottfried (Fritz), 290
Nauru, 339
Neglected Tropical Diseases, 287
Negrel, Dominique, 145
NEI, 95, 208, 216, 259, 260
Nellie, 21ff

Index

Nepal, 141, 225
Netherlands, 387
Neurophysins, 40
New Delhi, 95, 272
New Drug with a Priority Review Voucher, 200
New England Journal of Medicine, 182, 215, 265
New York Blood Center, 160
New York Times, 171
New Zealand, 17, 48, 387
New Zealand Security and Intelligence Service, 48
Newland, Henry, 161, 182, 187, 213
Nganampa Health Council, 353
Ngannyatjarra Country, 28
Ngarrindei, 345, 374
NHMRC, 246, 259, 339, 341, 343
NIA, 82,106, 259
NIDA, 106, 259
NIEHS, 307ff, 313 323, 319ff
Niger, 200
Nigeria, 61
NIH, 82, 89, 182
Nijm, Lisa, 297
Ninety Mile Beach, 33
Ninti One, 378
Nobel Prize, 172
Nolan, Terry, 258, 306–307, 313
Noosa, 336
North Korea, 276
Northern Territory Intervention, 288
Northern Territory trachoma program, 366
Northwestern Healthcare Network, 292
NRL, 217ff, 390
NTEHP, 47ff, 204, 307, 309, 312, 315, 391ff
NTSRU, 356ff, 360
Nuclear cataract, 203
Nui Dat, 61
Nullarbor, 26
Nutman, Tom, 182

O'Connor, G Richard (Dick), 98
O'Donoghue, Lowitja, 310
O'Neil, John, 150
O'Shaunessy, Patricia (Trish), 53
O'Sullivan, Gabi, 48
OATISH, 310. 311
Obermeyer, Cordula, 297
OCP, 153, 162, 164, 170, 344, 345, 349

Oculo, 242, 347, 349
OCT, 344, 345, 349
Odessa, 104
OEPA, 196
OF, 295, 299
Office for Aboriginal & Torres Strait Islander Health, 310, 311, 312
Okinawa, 88
Olinda, 9, 10, 22, 25, 383ff
Olympic Games, 13ff
Oman, 138–139
Omura, Satoshi, 172
Oncho, 148ff
Onchocerca gibsoni, 173
Onchocerca lienalis, 181
Onchocerca volvulus, 148, 178
Onchocerciasis, 92, 147ff
Onchocerciasis Chemo-therapy Research Centre, 168
Onchocerciasis Control Program, 153, 170, 271
Onchocerciasis Elimination for the Americas, 196
Onchocerciasis Elimination Program, 165
One Disease at a Time, 201
Onemda, 313, 321
Oodnadatta, 63–64
Ophthalmia neonatorum, 118
Ophthalmia Range, 72
Ophthalmic Research Institute, 246
Ophthalmology Foundation, 295
OPSM, 54
Optical Coherence Tomography, 344, 345, 349, 344, 345, 349
Optometry Australia, 343
Order of Australia, 239ff
Ormond College, 86, 22ff, 28ff, 106
Ormond Ski Club, 29–30
Ouagadougou, 98, 151, 153, 168, 170, 173, 185, 192
Outback Café, 57
'Outback Eye Services in…', 323
Outstanding Services Award for Prevention of Blindness, 391
OV-16 183
Oxchuc, 116
Oxford MD, 139
Oxford Ophthalmological Congress, 392
Oxytocin, 40

Pacific Vision Foundation, 292

411

Pacque, Michele, 187
Padua, 290ff
PAHO, 106
Pakistan, 1–3, 99, 362, 393–396
Palawa Trowerna, 313
Palis, Gabriel, 295
Palme d'Or, 265
Pan American Health Organisation, 106, 196
Papua New Guinea, 18, 352
Paralympic Games, 279
Pararajasegaram (Para), 64, 98, 121
Paris, 172, 180
Parliament House ACT, 345
Parliamentary Friends Dinner, 281
Patterson, Kay, 313
Patton, Dolly, 91–92
Patuxent River, 206
Patz, Arnall, 92, 270
Paul Ramsay Foundation, 334
PBL, 97, 99, 120, 162, 271
PCR, 124, 135
PCR test, 357ff
Pearce, Nate, 90
Pearl Continental Hotel, 396
Pedagogy of the Oppressed, 47
Pedrique, Belen, 199
PEEK, 300
Peoplescape, 241
Perkins, Charlie, 55
Perocic, Lubjo, 222, 223
Perth, 26
Peshawar, 393
Peter Watson Memorial Lecture, 304, 392
Petermann Ranges, 27–28, 58, 69, 381–382
Peters, Jimmy, 342
Pfizer, 119, 146
Phacoemulsification, 84
Phillips, Georgina, 373
Pilbara, 351
Pilkerton, Cara, 381
Pilkerton, John, 381
Pine Gap, 63
Pitt, Alison, 234
Poche, Greg, 323
Polaires Françaises, 42
Pollack, Graeme, 225, 305
Polymerase Chain Reaction, 135
Polymerase Chain Reaction test, 357ff
Poroch, Nerelle, 321
Port Arthur Historic Site, 360–361

Port au Prince, 102
Port Augusta, 47, 48, 54, 63–4
Port Hedland, 72
Port Lonsdale, 22
Port Moseby, 18
Porter, Dick, 280
Posterior sub-capsular cataract, 203
Potemkin Steps, 104
Prendergast, Bob, 87, 89
Presbyopia, 288
Prevention of Blindness Program, 97, 120, 271
Price of Wales Hospital, 45
Price, Jacinta Nampijinpa, 368ff
Prince Henry's Hospital, 40, 41, 312
Prince Phillip, 25, 301
Prince, Alfred, 160
Prince, Sam, 201
Princeton University, 106
Proctor Institute, 88, 98
'Projected needs for eye care services for…', 323
'Provision of Indigenous Eye health…', 323
Psuedoexfoliation, 205
Pterygium, 86, 205, 215
PwC, 333
PXF, 205
Pyne, Christopher, 280, 317, 318
Pyott, David, 298ff
Pyrethrum, 96

Queen Elizabeth 2, 25, 301
Queen Elizabeth Diamond Jubilee Trust, 299ff
Queen's Young Leaders Awards, 299–300
Quinn, Tom, 90–91, 118
QUIT campaign, 266

Rabaul, 18
Rado, Erwin, 11
Rahmatullah's, 127
Rahway, 181
Rait, Julian, 230
Rallah-Baker, Kris, 336
Rana, Khalil, 395
RANZCO, 46, 331
Rapoza, Peter, 118, 127, 133
Reacher, Mark, 138–139
Reagan, Ronald, 105
Recife, 125

412

Index

Reconciliation Australia, 342
'Red Cherry' 56, 57, 63
Red Crescent, 2
Redfern Aboriginal Health Service, 51, 55
Resnikoff, Françoise, 278
Resnikoff, Serge, 239
Resnikoff, Serge, 277–279, 283
Returned Services League, 61
Revenio, 347
Review of Indigenous Eye Health, 313
Rhondda Fach, 59
Ringland Anderson Chair, 217, 229, 312
Rivas-Alcals, Roberto, 165
River blindness, 147ff
River Blindness Foundation, 195, 196, 200
'Roadmap to Close the Gap for Vision', 326–327, 332ff
Robert, Ian, 315
Robertsfield Airport, 157, 158
Robin, Todd, 249
Rockefeller Foundation, 160
Rocky Mountains Laboratory, 91
Roebuck Bay Hotel, 27
Rogers, Hugh, 6, 376
Rogers, Peter, 376
Roll Back Malaria, 194
Roper, Katrina, 357, 358
Rosenthal, Frank, 208, 209
Rotary Club, 376, 377ff
Rotterdam Eye Study, 265
Roxon, Nicola, 266–267
Royal Australasian College of Surgeons, 40, 44
Royal Australasian College of Surgeons, 60
Royal Australian & New Zealand College of Ophthalmologists, 46, 331
Royal Australian College of Ophthalmologists, 231
Royal Blind Society of NSW, 232
Royal Commonwealth Society for the Blind, 75, 97, 269
Royal Life Saving Society, 17
Royal Melbourne Hospital, 60
Royal Society of Medicine Lecture, 392
Royal Victorian Eye and Ear Hospital, 39, 40, 43 309
Royal Victorian Institute for the Blind, 232
Royal Women's Hospital, 36, 40
Rudd, Kevin, 360–363

Ruit, Sanduk, 274–277
Rumbalara AMS, 341
Rumbalara Medical Service, 341
Ryan, Graeme, 318
Ryan, Tess, 337

SAFE strategy, 145, 311–312, 352, 353, 364–366
Sagan, Carl, 387
Samuel P Asper Award for Achievement in Advancing International Medical Education, 391
San Cristobal, 111, 64
San Diego, 195–196
San Francisco, 105
Sandy blight, 357
Sandy Blight Junction, 381–382
Santa Teresa, 373
Saud, Abdulaziz Ahmed Abdulazia Al –, 142, 143
Saudi Arabia, 141
Scabies, 201
Schachter, Julie, 88, 144
Schein, Oliver, 208
Schiavone, Joan, 31
Schistosomiasis, 153
School of Tropical Medicine and Hygiene, 126
Schroeder, Jack R, 207
Schulz-Key, Hartwig, 160ff, 173
Scientific Working Group, 272
Scientific Working Group on Filiaris, 191
Scientific Working Group on Onchocerciasis Chemotherapy, 192
Scotch College, 11ff, 13, 218
Scott, Julia, 386
Scott, Rod, 386
Scott, Will, 386
Scrimgeour, John, 222, 223
Seaspray, 33
'Seek some shade', 263
Seekers, The, 22
Seitz, Berthold, 296
Semba, Richard, 181ff
Senegal, 172
Senile cataract, 204
Senior Australian of the Year Victoria, 391
Shakespeare Republic, 389
Shark Bay, 72
Shepparton, 341
Shiraz, 95

Shriver, Erin, 297
Sierra Leone, 182
SightSavers, 97, 269, 395
Siler, Jon, 134
Silverstein, Arthur (Art), 86–89, 95
Simpson, O J, 83
Simpsons, The, 218
Simulium damnosum, 148
Sinclair, Peter (Porky), 30–31
Singapore, 255
Sir Norman Gregg Lecture, 392
Sitapur, 95, 96
'Six Steps to Stop Germs', 374, 375
Ski Rescue Service, 18
Sklovsky, Grecia, 41–42
Slave trade, 152
Sleeping sickness, 152
'Slide on some sunnies', 263
'Slip, Slop Slap', 263
Smith Island, 213, 214
'Smoking cause Blindness' 266
Snail fever, 153
Snibson, Grant, 230
Snowden, Warren, 315, 327, 347
Soap Aid, 376
Soboslay, Bob, 178
Solomon Islands, 44, 47, 60
Sommer, Alfred (Al), 93, 100 ff, 115–116, 119, 125, 141, 265, 271, 290
Sommer, Charles, 100, 101, 108
Sommer, Jill, 100
Sommer, Marni, 101
Sophie, Duchess, 301
South Africa, 48
South African Society of Ophthalmology, 298
South Korea, 255
Spanish Civil War, 59
Spence, John, 31
Spivey, Bruce, 291–293, 295, 299, 394
Sports Safety Committee, 258
Spry, Charles, 36–37
Squamous Cell Cancer, 216
St Hilda's College, 24
St John's Ambulance, 61
St Petersburg, 223
Stanford, Emma, 313, 314, 320, 323, 366, 373ff
Stanley, Fiona, 354
Stark, Walter, 43, 79, 82–84
Steins, Jimmy, 371

Stokes, Tommy, 12
Stolen Generation, 345
Stones, Ellis, 383
Straatsma, Brad, 295
Strang, Robert, 14
'Strong Eyes, Strong Communities', 333
Student Christian Movement, 6
Sullivan, Mark, 199, 200
Summerfield, Jennifer, 353
Suramin, 152
Swan, Norman, 215
Swinburne University, 388
Swiss Air, 272

Tabin, Geoffrey, 276
Taiwan, 255
Tamale, 168
Tano, Yasuo, 292
Tanzania, 125ff
Tarizzo, Mario, 97–98, 162, 271
Task Force for Global Health, 194
Taxila, 99
Taylor, Bart, 218
Taylor, Batholomew (Bart), 39ff, 80, 81, 82, 83, 108, 184ff, 218, 386ff
Taylor, Charles, 190
Taylor, Claire, 386
Taylor, Cyril, 5
Taylor, David, 295
Taylor, Edward (Ned), 106, 218, 387ff
Taylor, Elizabeth (Libby), 6
Taylor, Elva, 5–6
Taylor, Emeline (Emy), 386
Taylor, Ian McComas, 6, 15
Taylor, Isabel, 386
Taylor, James, 6, 15
Taylor, Janet, 6, 8, 24, 383
Taylor, Jimmy, 386
Taylor, Joe, 386
Taylor, Joe, 125, 386
Taylor, Kathryn (Kate), 36–39, 40, 71, 80, 82, 83, 107, 116, 191, 194, 218, 242, 347, 384ff
Taylor, May, 5
Taylor, Neil, 5–8, 10 ff, 14, 32, 64–65, 95
Taylor, Norma, 5
Taylor, Phillis, 5
Taylor, Phoebe Anne, 95, 106, 219, 241, 284, 389
TB, 194
TDR, 191ff, 194

Index

TDR, 194
TDR, 272
'Teaching the Teachers', 295
Telethon Institute, 354
Terai, 141
Tern, 10
Tetracycline, 138
Thala Dan, MV, 42–43
Thea, 278
Therapeutic Goods Administration, 352
Thompson, John, 51
Thwaites, John, 236, 247ff
Thylefors, Bente, 162
Thylefors, Björn, 87, 120ff, 162, 164, 271, 278
Tielsch, Jim, 119, 265
Tilganga Eye Institute, 274–277
Tjungurrayi, (Shorty) Lungkata, 70
'To eliminate blinding trachoma as a public health problem by, 2020', 145
Tobacco Plain Packaging Act, 266
Todd River, 369
Tolbert, William, 164
Toorak, 8
Torpey, Meg, 366
Torquay, 22
Torres Strait, 277
Trachoma (book), 353, 357
Trachoma Grading card, 122ff
'Trachoma House', 56
'Trachoma Resource Book', 366
'Trachoma: antibiotic… a systemic review', 322
Traeculectomy, 43–44
Treetops, 184
Triechel, Hugh, 388
Triechel, Pia, 388
Trinh, Lien, 378
Tripis, Milan, 112, 179, 190
Tropical Disease Research program, 191ff, 194
Tropical Diseases Research, 272
Trump, Donald, 200
Trypanosomiasis, 152
Tunis, 121
Tunisia, 99
Turkey, 11
Turner, Angus, 323
Turner, Ginny, 129, 145
Turner, Pat, 331
TWA flight, 480 290

Tzeltal, 114

Uluru Statement, 310
UN Education, Scientific & Cultural Organisation, 360
UN Environment Programme, 272
UN High Commission for Refugees, 1–2, 99
UN International Children's Emergency Fund, 1
UNESCO, 360
UNHCR, 1–2, 99
UNICEF, 1, 100
United Nations, 302
Uniting Church, 106
University of California, 97
University of Kumasi, 281
University of Melbourne Award for Excellence & Engagement, 392
University of Otago, 48
University of Queensland, 81
US Army, 190
US Biological Research Center, 87
USAID, 103
Useless Loop, 72
UV-B radiation, 86, 205ff

Vagelos, Roy, 181, 193
Vajpayee, Rasik, 305
Vanstone, Amanda, 280
Vasopressin, 40
Vaudrey, Bev, 222
Velasco, Francisco Milan, 111ff
VECAT, 260
Velez, Vivian, 88
Victorian Aboriginal Health Service, 309, 313
Victorian Health Promotion Foundation, 246
Victorian Health Promotion Foundation, 306
Vietnam, 38, 62,105, 225, 283, 284
Vietnam War, 24, 29
Vietnamese Institute of Ophthalmology, 273
Vision, 2020 Australia, 232, 236, 333, 341
Vision Collaborative Research Council, 239, 307
Vision Excellence Award, 391
Vision Loss Expert Group, 286
'Vision of Australian Aborigines' 86

Vision2020 236, 271, 277ff, 279ff, 289, 291, 296, 360, 395
Visiting Optometrists Scheme, 311
Vitale, Susan, 259
Vitamin A, 1–2, 93, 100–102, 125, 141
Vitamin C, 72
Vitamin D, 205
Vitamin E, 260
Vitamin E & Cataract Studies, 260
Vitamins, 259
VLEG, 286
Voice referendum, 310, 369
VOS, 311

Wales, 48
Walling, Edna, 8, 383
Walmadjari, 315
Walter and Eliza Hall Institute, 35, 223, 231
Warburton Mission, 28
Washburn, Lindsay, 297
Wasiak, Jason, 322
Watermen, 206ff
Watson, Ann, 304
Watson, Peter, 43, 295, 303–304
Wave Hill Strike, 48
Webfest Award, 389
Webster, Ross, 17, 21ff, 32ff
Weigall, Celia, 42
Weigall, Janey, 42
Wesfarmers, 374
West, Keith, 119, 141
West, Shelia, 121, 126, 131, 135, 141, 145, 210, 212, 214, 216, 259
Western District Victoria, 5
Western Samoa, 339
White, Albert, 174, 175, 182ff
White, Patrick, 45
Whitlam, Gough, 239
WHO, 1–3, 46, 76, 97, 99, 100, 109, 119, 124, 145, 153, 162, 192, 199, 357ff, 363, 380ff, 393–396
WHO Collaborating Centre, 99, 109, 218, 228–229, 242ff, 271, 273, 282
WHO Expert Advisory Panel, 272
WHO Expert Committee on Onchocerciasis, 192
WHO Filariasis Program, 271
WHO Global Scientific Meetings, 146
WHO World Report on Vision, 287ff
Wiedemann, Peter, 298
Wilmer Eye Institute, 43, 74, 79ff, 100, 127, 147, 148, 181ff, 270
Wilson, John, 75–76, 97, 148, 269
Wilson, Martha, 117
Wilson, Nick, 330, 373, 374
Winmar, Nicky, 369
Wire, The, 107
Wittenoom, 26
WOC, 290, 292
Wolf, Seth, 84
'Women's Dreaming (Two Women)', 70
Wong, Tien, 242, 305
Wooldridge, Michael, 234ff, 236, 279, 310, 313, 315, 344, 351, 356
World Bank, 153, 196, 352
World Economic Forum, 192, 386
World EyeCon21 392
World Health Assembly, 302
World Health Organisation, 1–3, 46, 76, 97, 99, 100, 109, 119, 124, 145, 153, 162, 192, 199, 357ff, 363, 393–396
World Ophthalmic Congress, 290, 292, 293–295
Wotjobaluk, 345
Wright, Heathcote, 354, 355
Wucheria bancrofti, 152
Wurundjeri Woi Wurrung, 307, 314
Wyatt, Ken, 333ff
Wyeth, 199
Wynne, Carol, 330, 344

Xerophalmia, 1, 93, 100–102, 126
Xie, Jing, 307

Yamba, 368
Yamba's Playtime, 368–369
Yarralumla, 240
Yemen, 200
Yo Yo Ma, 94
Yorta lands, 51, Yorta Yorta, 341
Yosemite, 98
Young Ophthalmologists and Emerging Leaders, 296
Young, Elaine, 84, 89
Yuendumu, 354, 355, Yuendumu, 371
Yuggera Warrongo Wiradjuri, 336
Yunnan, 284

Zambrero, 201
Zia ul Haq, Muhammed, 394
Ziman, David, 94
Zimmet, Paul, 246, 281, 339

www.ingramcontent.com/pod-product-compliance
Lightning Source LLC
Chambersburg PA
CBHW040744020526
44114CB00048B/2901